HMH Tennessee Science

This Interactive Student Edition belongs to

_____

Teacher/Room

_____

Houghton Mifflin Harcourt

Consulting Authors

Michael A. DiSpezio

Global Educator
North Falmouth, Massachusetts

Michael DiSpezio has authored many HMH instructional programs for science and mathematics. He has also authored numerous trade books and multimedia programs on various topics and hosted dozens of studio and location broadcasts for various organizations in the U.S. and worldwide. Most recently, he has been working with educators to provide strategies for implementing science and engineering practices, including engineering design challenges. To all his projects, he brings his extensive background in science, his expertise in classroom teaching at the elementary, middle, and high school levels, and his deep experience in producing interactive and engaging instructional materials.

Marjorie Frank

Science Writer and Content-Area Reading Specialist
Brooklyn, New York

An educator and linguist by training, a writer and poet by nature, Marjorie Frank has authored and designed a generation of instructional materials in all subject areas, including past HMH Science programs. Her other credits include authoring science issues of an award-winning children's magazine, writing game-based digital assessments, developing blended learning materials for young children, and serving as instructional designer and co-author of pioneering school-to-work software. In addition, she has served on the adjunct faculty of Hunter, Manhattan, and Brooklyn Colleges, teaching courses in science methods, literacy, and writing.

Acknowledgments for Cover

Front cover: *DNA model* ©Carl Goodman/Science Source

Copyright © 2019 by Houghton Mifflin Harcourt Publishing Company

Tennessee Academic Standards courtesy of the Tennessee Department of Education.

Printed in the U.S.A.

ISBN 978-1-328-82861-3

9 10   0868   26 25 24 23 22 21 20

4500790208   B C D E F G

Michael R. Heithaus

Dean, College Of Arts, Sciences & Education
Professor, Department Of Biological Sciences
Florida International University
Miami, Florida

Mike Heithaus joined the FIU Biology Department in 2003, has served as Director of the Marine Sciences Program, and as Executive Director of the School of Environment, Arts, and Society, which brings together the natural and social sciences and humanities to develop solutions to today's environmental challenges. He now serves as Dean of the College of Arts, Sciences & Education. His research focuses on predator-prey interactions and the ecological importance of large marine species. He has helped to guide the development of Life Science content in this science program, with a focus on strategies for teaching challenging content as well as the science and engineering practices of analyzing data and using computational thinking.

Tennessee Reviewers

Emily C. Grayer
Richview Middle School
Clarksville, TN

Dale Land
Kenwood Middle School
Clarksville-Montgomery County
School System
Clarksville, TN

Patrece Morrow
Science, NBCT
Sherwood Middle School
Memphis, TN

Shari Myers
Academic Coach
Rossview Elementary School
Clarksville-Montgomery County
School System
Clarksville, TN

Sarah Becky Spain
Kenrose Elementary School
Brentwood, TN

Christy Walker, Ed.D., NBCT
Manley Elementary School
Morristown, TN

Content Reviewers

Paul D. Asimow, PhD
*Professor of Geology
and Geochemistry*
Division of Geological and Planetary Sciences
California Institute of Technology
Pasadena, CA

Laura K. Baumgartner, PhD
Postdoctoral Researcher
Molecular, Cellular, and Developmental
Biology
University of Colorado
Boulder, CO

Eileen Cashman, PhD
Professor
Department of Environmental Resources
Engineering
Humboldt State University
Arcata, CA

Hilary Clement Olson, PhD
Research Scientist Associate V
Institute for Geophysics, Jackson School of
Geosciences
The University of Texas at Austin
Austin, TX

Joe W. Crim, PhD
Professor Emeritus
Department of Cellular Biology
The University of Georgia
Athens, GA

Elizabeth A. De Stasio, PhD
*Raymond H. Herzog Professor
of Science*
Professor of Biology
Department of Biology
Lawrence University
Appleton, WI

Dan Franck, PhD
Botany Education Consultant
Chatham, NY

Julia R. Greer, PhD
*Assistant Professor of Materials Science and
Mechanics*
Division of Engineering and Applied Science
California Institute of Technology
Pasadena, CA

John E. Hoover, PhD
Professor
Department of Biology
Millersville University
Millersville, PA

William H. Ingham, PhD
Professor (Emeritus)
Department of Physics and Astronomy
James Madison University
Harrisonburg, VA

Charles W. Johnson, PhD
*Chairman, Division of Natural Sciences,
Mathematics, and Physical Education*
Associate Professor of Physics
South Georgia College
Douglas, GA

Tatiana A. Krivosheev, PhD
Associate Professor of Physics
Department of Natural Sciences
Clayton State University
Morrow, GA

Joseph A. McClure, PhD
Associate Professor Emeritus
Department of Physics
Georgetown University
Washington, DC

Mark Moldwin, PhD
Professor of Space Sciences
Atmospheric, Oceanic, and Space Sciences
University of Michigan
Ann Arbor, MI

Russell Patrick, PhD
Professor of Physics
Department of Biology, Chemistry, and Physics
Southern Polytechnic State University
Marietta, GA

Patricia M. Pauley, PhD
Meteorologist, Data Assimilation Group
Naval Research Laboratory
Monterey, CA

Stephen F. Pavkovic, PhD
Professor Emeritus
Department of Chemistry
Loyola University of Chicago
Chicago, IL

L. Jeanne Perry, PhD
Director (Retired)
Protein Expression Technology Center
Institute for Genomics and Proteomics
University of California,
Los Angeles
Los Angeles, CA

Kenneth H. Rubin, PhD
Professor
Department of Geology and Geophysics
University of Hawaii
Honolulu, HI

Brandon E. Schwab, PhD
Associate Professor
Department of Geology
Humboldt State University
Arcata, CA

Marllin L. Simon, PhD
Associate Professor
Department of Physics
Auburn University
Auburn, AL

Larry Stookey, PE
Upper Iowa University
Wausau, WI

Kim Withers, PhD
Associate Research Scientist
Center for Coastal Studies
Texas A&M University-Corpus Christi
Corpus Christi, TX

Matthew A. Wood, PhD
Professor
Department of Physics & Space Sciences
Florida Institute of Technology
Melbourne, FL

Adam D. Woods, PhD
Associate Professor
Department of Geological Sciences
California State University, Fullerton
Fullerton, CA

Natalie Zayas, MS, EdD
Lecturer
Division of Science and Environmental Policy
California State University, Monterey Bay
Seaside, CA

Contents
in Brief

Tennessee Academic Standards for Science

Dear Students and Families,

This book and this class are structured around the Tennessee Academic Standards for Science for Grade 7. As you read, experiment, and study, you will learn the concepts listed on these pages. You will also continue to build your science literacy, which will enrich your life both in and out of school.

Best wishes for a good school year,

The HMH Tennessee Science Team

PHYSICAL SCIENCES

7.PS1: Matter and Its Interactions

1) Develop and use models to illustrate the structure of atoms, including the subatomic particles with their relative positions and charge.
2) Compare and contrast elemental molecules and compound molecules.
3) Classify matter as pure substances or mixtures based on composition.
4) Analyze and interpret chemical reactions to determine if the total number of atoms in the reactants and products support the Law of Conservation of Mass.
5) Use the periodic table as a model to analyze and interpret evidence relating to physical and chemical properties to identify a sample of matter.
6) Create and interpret models of substances whose atoms represent the states of matter with respect to temperature and pressure.

LIFE SCIENCES

7.LS1: From Molecules to Organisms: Structures and Processes

1) Develop and construct models that identify and explain the structure and function of major cell organelles as they contribute to the life activities of the cell and organism.
2) Conduct an investigation to demonstrate how the cell membrane maintains homeostasis through the process of passive transport.
3) Evaluate evidence that cells have structural similarities and differences in organisms across kingdoms.
4) Diagram the hierarchical organization of multicellular organisms from cells to organism.
5) Explain that the body is a system comprised of subsystems that maintain equilibrium and support life through digestion, respiration, excretion, circulation, sensation (nervous and integumentary), and locomotion (musculoskeletal).
6) Develop an argument based on empirical evidence and scientific reasoning to explain how behavioral and structural adaptations in animals and plants affect the probability of survival and reproductive success.
7) Evaluate and communicate evidence that compares and contrasts the advantages and disadvantages of sexual and asexual reproduction.

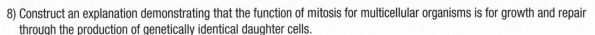

8) Construct an explanation demonstrating that the function of mitosis for multicellular organisms is for growth and repair through the production of genetically identical daughter cells.

9) Construct a scientific explanation based on compiled evidence for the processes of photosynthesis, cellular respiration, and anaerobic respiration in the cycling of matter and flow of energy into and out of organisms.

7.LS2: Ecosystems: Interactions, Energy, and Dynamics

1) Develop a model to depict the cycling of matter, including carbon and oxygen, including the flow of energy among biotic and abiotic parts of an ecosystem.

7.LS3: Heredity: Inheritance and Variation of Traits

1) Hypothesize that the impact of structural changes to genes (i.e., mutations) located on chromosomes may result in harmful, beneficial, or neutral effects to the structure and function of the organism.

2) Distinguish between mitosis and meiosis and compare the resulting daughter cells.

3) Predict the probability of individual dominant and recessive alleles to be transmitted from each parent to offspring during sexual reproduction and represent the phenotypic and genotypic patterns using ratios.

EARTH AND SPACE SCIENCES

7.ESS3: Earth and Human Activity

1) Graphically represent the composition of the atmosphere as a mixture of gases and discuss the potential for atmospheric change.

2) Engage in a scientific argument through graphing and translating data regarding human activity and climate.

ENGINEERING, TECHNOLOGY, AND APPLICATIONS OF SCIENCE

7.ETS2: Links Among Engineering, Technology, and Applications of Science

1) Examine a problem from the medical field pertaining to biomaterials and design a solution taking into consideration the criteria, constraints, and relevant scientific principles of the problem that may limit possible solutions.

Contents

The same particles of matter in our bodies today may once have been a part of a dinosaur or a star!

© Houghton Mifflin Harcourt Publishing Company • Image Credits: © moodboard/Corbis

Matter is made up of elements that interact with each other in predictable ways. Sometimes you can see those reactions!

Assignments:

Contents (continued)

Butterfly wings are covered in tiny, colorful scales, which protect the membranes of the wings.

© Houghton Mifflin Harcourt Publishing Company • Image Credits: (l) ©Danita Delimont/Alamy; (inset) ©Edward Kinsman/Photo Researchers, Inc.

Assignments:

_____

_____

_____

_____

_____

Matter and energy cycle through ecosystems using processes that draw on the resources and organisms of those environments. How are matter and energy cycled?

Contents (continued)

Assignments:

_____

_____

_____

_____

Organisms reproduce, making it possible for their species to survive, as well as to pass their traits on to their offspring.

The 206 bones in our skeletal system not only protect our organs, but they also help us move, store minerals, and make blood cells for us.

Contents (continued)

Earth's atmosphere is affected by factors that are natural, like eruptions, and factors that are not. Humans have the power to help improve the quality of Earth's atmosphere. That means you can make a difference!

Assignments:

_____

_____

_____

_____

UNIT 1
Matter

7.PS1.2, 7.PS1.3, 7.PS1.6

What do you think?

A large iceberg floats in water, but an anchor sinks. What is different about these two objects that causes them to behave differently in water?

Unit 1
Matter

Deep Freeze

When outdoor temperatures reach 0 °C (32 °F), liquid water can freeze to form a solid. Snow, ice, sleet, and hail are examples of the solid form of water. Understanding the properties of water in its different states helps people to stay safe during icy weather.

1 Think About It

How is liquid water different from solid ice?

_____

_____

_____

_____

This truck is applying salt to an icy road. Do you know what effect this will have on the ice?

② Ask A Question

What precautions should be taken during freezing weather?

Would you believe that the ice on these fruit trees is actually protecting them? The trees are being sprayed with water, which turns to ice in freezing weather. The formation of ice helps to keep the plants warmer. With a partner, research some of the ways in which people protect other areas and living things during icy weather.

Think about the impact that ice could have on

✔ plants

✔ people

✔ bodies of water

✔ pets and other animals

③ Apply Your Knowledge

A List some areas in your community that could be affected by the formation of ice.

_____

_____

_____

B What precautions could your community take before freezing weather arrives to keep these areas safe?

_____

_____

_____

_____

C What could your community do after freezing weather arrives to keep these areas safe?

_____

_____

_____

Take It Home

How do you prepare a home for icy weather? Draw a map of a home and the surrounding area. Identify areas on your map that could become hazardous in freezing conditions. Then, create a plan for protecting these areas. See *ScienceSaurus*® for more information about weather.

Introduction to Matter

ESSENTIAL QUESTION

What properties define matter?

By the end of this lesson, you should be able to relate mass, weight, volume, and density to one another.

Hot air takes balloons aloft because hot air is less dense than the cooler air around it.

✋ Lesson Labs

Quick Labs
- Mass and Weight
- Finding Volume by Displacement
- How Much Mass?

Exploration Lab
- Comparing Buoyancy

🧠 Engage Your Brain

1 Describe Fill in the blank with the word or phrase that you think correctly completes the following sentences.

A(n) _____ can hold a greater volume of water than a mug.

A hamster weighs less than a(n)

_____ .

A bowling ball is harder to lift than a basketball because _____

_____ .

2 Explain List some similarities and differences between the golf ball on the left and the table-tennis ball on the right in the photo below.

_____

_____

_____

_____

_____

_____

✏️ Active Reading

3 Apply Many scientific words, such as *matter*, also have everyday meanings. Use context clues to write your own definition for each meaning of the word *matter*.

Example sentence
What is this gooey <u>matter</u> on the table?

matter:

_____

_____

_____

Example sentence
Please vote! Your opinions <u>matter</u>.

matter:

_____

_____

_____

Vocabulary Terms

- matter
- mass
- weight
- volume
- density

4 Identify This list contains the vocabulary terms you'll learn in this lesson. As you read, circle the definition of each term.

What's the MATTER?

What is matter?

Suppose your class takes a field trip to a museum. During the course of the day you see mammoth bones, sparkling crystals, hot-air balloons, and an astronaut's space suit. All of these things are matter.

As you will see, **matter** is anything that has mass and takes up space. Your body is matter. The air that you breathe and the water that you drink are also matter. Matter makes up the materials around you.

However, not everything is matter. Light and sound, for example, are not matter. Light does not take up space or have mass in the same way that a table does. Although air is matter, a sound traveling through air is not.

Active Reading **5 Explain** How can you tell if something is matter?

_____

_____

_____

Visualize It!

6 Identify Name three examples of matter found in this photo.

_____

_____

_____

What is mass?

You cannot always tell how much matter is in an object simply by observing the object's size. But you *can* measure the object's mass. **Mass** describes the amount of matter in an object.

Compare the two balloons at the right. The digital scales show that the balloon filled with compressed air has a greater mass than the other balloon. This is because the compressed air adds mass to the balloon. Air may seem to be made of nothing, but it has mass. The readings on the scale are in grams (g). A gram is the unit of mass you will use most often in science class.

Objects that are the same size can be made up of different amounts of matter. For example, a large sponge is about the same size as a brick. But the brick contains more matter. Therefore, the brick has a greater mass than the sponge.

The readings on these digital scales show that all matter, even air, has mass.

0.010 g

0.005 g

How does mass differ from weight?

The words *weight* and *mass* are often used as though they mean the same thing, but they do not. **Weight** is a measure of the gravitational force (grav•ih•TAY•shuhn•uhl FAWRS) on an object. Gravitational force keeps objects on Earth from floating into space. The gravitational force between an object and Earth depends partly on the object's mass. The greater that the mass of an object is, the greater the gravitational force on the object will be and the greater the object's weight will be.

An object's weight can change depending on the object's location. For example, you would weigh less on the moon than you do on Earth because the moon has less mass—and therefore exerts less gravitational force—than Earth does. However, you would have the same mass in both places. An object's mass does not change unless the amount of matter in an object changes.

The weight of this dachshund on the moon is about one-sixth of its weight on Earth.

![Active Reading] **7 Explain** Why do astronauts weigh less on the moon than they do on Earth?

_____

_____

The balance below works by moving the masses on the right along the beams until they "balance" the pan on the left. Moving the masses changes the amount of force the levers exert on the pan. The more massive the object on the pan, the more force will be needed on the levers to balance the two sides.

8 Infer Would this balance give the same value for mass if used on the moon? Explain.

_____

_____

_____

_____

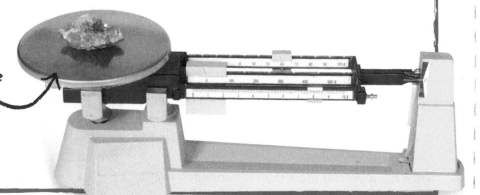

A triple-beam balance can be used to measure the mass of small objects such as this geode fragment.

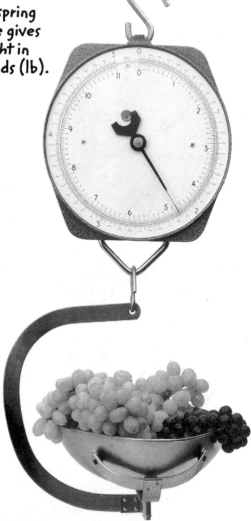

The spring scale gives weight in pounds (lb).

How are mass and weight measured?

Mass is often measured by using a triple-beam balance such as the one shown above. The balance compares an object's mass to known standards of mass called *countermasses*. The countermasses slide across each of three beams. When the countermasses balance the mass of the object in the balance pan, the pointer will rest at 0. Then, the mass can be read from the position of the countermasses on the beams.

Weight is measured with devices such as the spring scale shown at the left. The spring measures the force between the mass in the pan and Earth. The more massive the object placed in the pan, the more forceful is the attraction between it and Earth, and the more the spring will stretch. Greater stretch means greater weight.

Because weight is a measure of gravitational force, it is given in units of force. You probably are most familiar with weight given in pounds (lb), like the units shown on the scale. The standard scientific unit for weight, however, is the newton (N). A 100-g mass weighs approximately 1 N on Earth. One newton is about one-fourth of a pound.

Measuring Space

How is the amount of space occupied by matter measured?

All matter takes up space. The amount of space that an object takes up, or occupies, is known as the object's **volume.**

Objects with similar volumes do not always have the same mass. In the photos, the bowling ball and the balloon have about the same volume, but the bowling ball contains a lot more mass than the balloon. You know this because the bowling ball weighs much more than the balloon. The different masses take up about the same amount of space, so both objects have about the same volume.

Active Reading **9 Define** What does volume measure?

_____

_____

The bowling ball has a lot more mass than the balloon.

The balloon is similar in volume but has much less mass than the bowling ball.

Think Outside the Book **Inquiry**

10 Infer Big things can look very small when seen from far away. Describe how you know big things far away aren't really small.

How can volume be determined?

There are different ways to find the volume of an object. For objects that have well-defined shapes, you can take a few measurements and calculate the volume using a formula. For objects that are irregularly shaped, such as a rock, you can use water displacement to measure volume. For liquids, you can use a graduated cylinder.

Using a Formula

Some objects have well-defined shapes. For these objects, the easiest way to find their volume is to measure the dimensions of the object and use a formula. Different shapes use different volume formulas. For example, to find the volume of a rectangular box, you would use a different formula than if you were to find the volume of a spherical ball.

The volume of a solid is measured in units of length cubed. For example, if you measure the length, width, and height of a box in centimeters (cm), the volume of the box has units of centimeters multiplied by centimeters multiplied by centimeters, or cubic centimeters (cm^3). In order to calculate volume, make sure that all the measurements are in the same units.

> To find the volume of a rectangular box, use the following formula:
> $$Volume = (length)(width)(height)$$
> $$V = lwh$$

 **Do the Math** **Sample Problem**

Find the volume of the lunch box.

Identify

A. What do you know?

length = 25 cm, width = 18 cm, height = 10 cm

B. What do you want to find? Volume

Plan

C. Draw and label a sketch: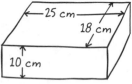

D. Write the formula: $V = lwh$

E. Substitute into the formula: $V = (25\ cm)(18\ cm)(10\ cm)$

Solve

F. Multiply: $(25\ cm)(18\ cm)(10\ cm) = 4{,}500\ cm^3$

G. Check that your units agree: The given units are centimeters, and the measure found is volume. Therefore, the units should be cm^3. The units agree.

Answer: $4{,}500\ cm^3$

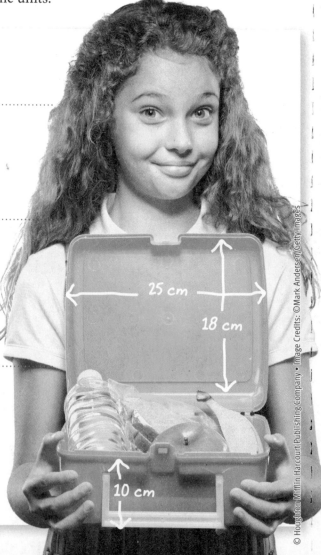

The volume of your locker will tell you how much stuff will fit inside.

30 cm

200 cm

40 cm

 Do the Math You Try It

11 Calculate Find the volume of a locker that is 30 cm long, 40 cm wide, and 200 cm high.

Identify

A. What do you know?

B. What do you want to find?

Plan

C. Draw and label a sketch:

D. Write the formula:

E. Substitute the given values into the formula:

Solve

F. Multiply:

G. Check that your units agree:

Answer:

Using Water Displacement

In the lab, you can use a beaker or graduated cylinder to measure the volume of liquids. Graduated cylinders are used to measure liquid volume when accuracy is important. The volume of liquids is often expressed in liters (L) or milliliters (mL). Milliliters and cubic centimeters are equivalent; in other words, 1 mL = 1 cm³. The volume of any amount of liquid, from one raindrop to an entire ocean, can be expressed in these units.

Two objects cannot occupy the same space at the same time. For example, as a builder stacks bricks to build a wall, she adds each brick on top of the other. No brick can occupy the same place that another brick occupies. Similarly, when an object is placed in water, the object pushes some of the water out of the way. This process, called *displacement*, can be used to measure the volume of an irregularly shaped solid object.

In the photos at the right, you can see that the level of the water in the graduated cylinder has risen after the chess piece is placed inside. The volume of water displaced is found by subtracting the original volume in the graduated cylinder from the new volume. This is equal to the volume of the chess piece.

When deciding the units of the volume found using water displacement, it is helpful to remember that 1 mL of water is equal to 1 cm³. Therefore, you can report the volume of the object in cubic centimeters.

Do the Math

You Try It

12 Calculate The two images below show a graduated cylinder filled with water before and after a chess piece is placed inside. Use the images to calculate the volume of the chess piece.

Volume without chess piece = _____

Volume with chess piece = _____

Volume of chess piece = _____

Don't forget to check the units of volume of the chess piece!

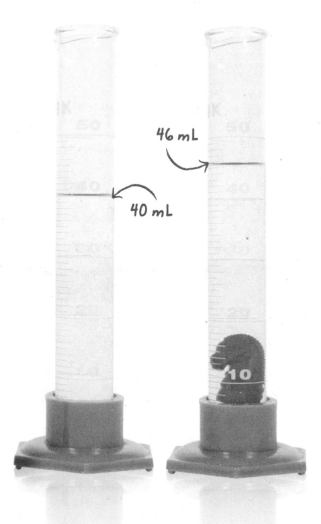

46 mL

40 mL

Packing It In!

What is density?

Mass and volume are properties of all substances. These two properties are related to another property called density (DEN•sih•tee). **Density** is a measure of the amount of mass in a given volume. Objects containing the same amount of mass can take up different amounts of space. For example, the pile of feathers above takes up more space than the tomato. But they have the same mass. This is because the tomato is more dense. The tomato has more mass in a smaller space.

The density of a given substance remains the same no matter how much of the substance you have. For example, if you divide a piece of clay in half, both halves will have the same density as the original piece.

The tomato and the pile of feathers have similar masses, but the tomato has less volume. This means that the tomato is more dense.

Active Reading

13 Explain What is density?

_____

_____

_____

14 Predict Circle the item in each pair that is more dense.

Golf ball	Empty milk carton	Foam ball
Table-tennis ball	Milk carton full of milk	Baseball

How is density determined?

Units for density consist of a mass unit divided by a volume unit. Units that are often used for density are grams per cubic centimeter (g/cm³) for solids, and grams per milliliter (g/mL) for liquids. In other words, density is the mass in grams divided by the volume in cubic centimeters or milliliters.

To find an object's density (D), find its mass (m) and its volume (V). Then, use the given formula to calculate the density of the object.

$$D = \frac{m}{V}$$

The density of water is 1 g/mL (g/cm³). Any object with a density greater than 1 g/mL will sink in water and with a density less than 1 g/mL will float. Density, therefore, can be a useful thing to know. The sample problem below shows how to calculate the density of a volcanic rock called pumice.

Pumice and obsidian are two igneous volcanic rocks with very different densities.

Do the Math

Sample Problem

Pumice is an igneous volcanic rock, formed by the rapid cooling of lava. What is the density of a 49.8 g piece of pumice that has a volume of 83 cm³?

Identify

A. What do you know?

   mass = 49.8 g, volume = 83 cm³

B. What do you want to find? Density

Plan

C. Write the formula: $D = \frac{m}{V}$

D. Substitute the given values into the formula:

   $D = \frac{49.8\text{ g}}{83\text{ cm}^3}$

Solve

E. Divide: $\frac{49.8\text{ g}}{83\text{ cm}^3} = 0.6$ g/cm³

F. Check that your units agree: The given units are grams and cubic centimeters, and the measure found is density. Therefore, the units should be g/cm³. The units agree.

Answer: 0.6 g/cm³

You Try It

15 Calculate Obsidian is another type of igneous rock. What is the density of a piece of obsidian that has a mass of 239.2 g and a volume of 92 cm³?

Identify

A. What do you know?

B. What do you want to find?

Plan

C. Write the formula:

D. Substitute the given values into the formula:

Solve

E. Divide:

F. Check that your units agree:

Answer:

Do the Math

Sample Problem

A basalt rock displaces 16 mL of water. The density of the rock is 3.0 g/cm³. What is the mass of the rock?

Identify

A. What do you know?

volume = 16 mL, density = 3.0 g/cm³

B. What do you want to find? Mass

Plan

C. Rearrange the formula $D = \dfrac{m}{V}$ to solve for mass. You can do this by multiplying each side by V.

$$D = \frac{m}{V}$$
$$m = D \cdot V$$

D. Substitute the given values into the formula. Recall that 1 mL = 1 cm³, so 16 mL = 16 cm³.

$$m = \frac{3.0\ \text{g}}{\text{cm}^3} \cdot 16\ \text{cm}^3$$

Solve

E. Multiply: $\dfrac{3.0\ \text{g}}{\text{cm}^3} \cdot 16\ \text{cm}^3 = 48\ \text{g}$

F. Check that your units agree: The given units are g/cm³ and mL, and the measure found is mass. Therefore, the units should be g. The units agree.

Answer: 48 g

You Try It

16 Calculate A rhyolite rock has a volume of 9.5 mL. The density of the rock is 2.6 g/cm³. What is the mass of the rock?

Identify

A. What do you know?

B. What do you want to find?

Plan

C. Write the formula:

D. Substitute the given values into the formula:

Solve

E. Multiply:

F. Check that your units agree:

Answer:

Kilauea is the youngest volcano on the Big Island of Hawaii. "Kilauea" means "spewing" or "much spreading," apparently in reference to the lava flows that it erupts.

Visual Summary

To complete this summary, check the box that indicates true or false. Then, use the key below to check your answers. You can use this page to review the main concepts of the lesson.

Relating Mass, Weight, Volume, and Density

Mass is the amount of matter in an object. Weight is a measure of the gravitational force on an object.

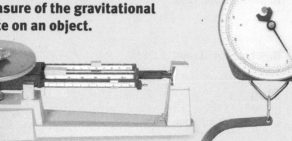

Mass

Weight

	T	F	
17	☐	☐	An object's weight is the amount of space it occupies.
18	☐	☐	The mass of an object is equal to its weight.

Volume is the amount of space that matter in an object occupies.
To find the volume of a rectangular box, use the formula:

$$V = lwh$$

	T	F	
19	☐	☐	The volume of a solid can be expressed in units of cm³.

Density describes the mass of a substance in a given volume.
To find the density of a substance, use the formula:

$$D = \frac{m}{V}$$

	T	F	
20	☐	☐	An object that floats in water is less dense than water.

21 Describe Write a set of instructions that describe how to find the density of an object. Write the instructions so that they work for a regularly shaped object and for an irregularly shaped object.

Lesson Review

Vocabulary

Fill in the blank with the term that best completes the following sentence.

1 _____ is the amount of space that matter in an object occupies.

2 _____ is anything that has mass and takes up space.

3 _____ is the amount of matter in an object.

4 _____ is a measure of the amount of matter in a given amount of space.

5 _____ is a measure of the gravitational force on an object.

Key Concepts

6 Classify Is air matter? How can you tell?

_____

_____

_____

7 Describe Is it possible for an object's weight to change while its mass remains constant? Explain.

_____

_____

_____

8 Compare Explain why a golf ball is heavier than a table-tennis ball, even though the balls are the same size.

_____

_____

_____

9 Calculate A block of wood has a mass of 120 g and a volume of 200 cm³. What is the density of the wood?

Critical Thinking

Use this table to answer the following questions.

Substance	Density (g/cm³)
Zinc (solid)	7.13
Silver (solid)	10.50
Lead (solid)	11.35

10 Identify Suppose that 273 g of one of the substances listed above displaces 26 mL of water. What is the substance?

_____

_____

_____

11 Evaluate How many mL of water would be displaced by 408 g of lead?

_____

_____

_____

12 Predict How can you determine that a coin is not pure silver if you know the mass and volume of the coin?

_____

_____

_____

_____

13 Calculate A truck whose bed is 2.5 m long, 1.5 m wide, and 1.0 m high is delivering sand for a sand-sculpture competition. About how many trips must the truck make to deliver 7 m³ of sand?

My Notes

Evaluating Scientific Evidence

Many people and companies claim to use scientific evidence to support their ideas, arguments, or products. Some of this evidence may be strong and well-supported by scientific investigation. But some evidence may be biased, or may not be supported by valid scientific investigation. How can you recognize the difference?

Tutorial

The advertisement below highlights some things that you should consider as you try to evaluate scientific evidence.

Grow your best Indian blanket wildflowers using new Fertilizer Formulation!

Fertilizer Formulation

We tested 20 patches of Indian blanket wildflowers in the <u>Valdosta, Georgia, area</u>. Plants that received the recommended amount of fertilizer grew an average of 30% taller. This fertilizer is made of <u>all-natural ingredients</u> and provides the best mixture of nutrients for <u>any garden</u>.

Everyone should use this fertilizer!

Weakness This sample is biased. The advertisement says that everyone should use the fertilizer, but the sample plants were all from the Valdosta, Georgia, area. An unbiased test would include samples from other parts of the country.

Weakness "All-natural ingredients" is a vague statement that advertisers use because people tend to believe that "natural" is better. However, in many cases that statement doesn't really mean anything. The minerals found in all fertilizers are "natural".

Weakness This generalization is not supported by the evidence. The fertilizer was only tested on Indian blanket wildflowers. It is impossible to say, based on that evidence, whether the fertilizer would be good for gardens with other types of plants.

You Try It!

Read the following advertisement, and answer the questions below to evaluate whether the evidence supports the claims being made.

GroBig
Soil Additive

GroBig will work on all types of wildflowers!

Buy GroBig today, and watch your flowers grow!
$19.95 per liter

"I've found the secret to the best wildflower garden—using GroBig Soil Additive. Now, you can have your best garden, too."
— A. Gardener

Botanists at a private nursery near Tampa, Florida, selected two tall samples of a common wildflower, the narrow-leaved sunflower. One plant received the recommended amount of GroBig Soil Additive. The other did not. After 2 weeks, the plant given GroBig Soil Additive had grown 4 cm. The other plant had grown just 2 cm. What a difference!

1 Identifying Conclusions Identify the claim that the advertisers are making.

_____

_____

_____

_____

2 Evaluating Evidence Identify two weaknesses in the evidence presented in this advertisement.

_____

_____

_____

_____

_____

3 Applying Concepts List three questions you would need to answer in order to support the claims being made about GroBig.

_____

_____

_____

_____

_____

_____

_____

Take It Home

Find an article or advertisement in a newspaper or magazine that contains a scientific claim and supporting information. Identify the evidence that is being used to support the claims in the article or advertisement. Write a paragraph that summarizes the article or advertisement and its scientific evidence.

Properties of Matter

ESSENTIAL QUESTION

What are physical and chemical properties of matter?

By the end of this lesson, you should be able to classify and compare substances based on their physical and chemical properties.

To harvest cranberries, the dry beds are flooded with water. Next, water reels loosen the berries from the vines. Since cranberries are less dense than water, they float. Harvesters take advantage of this property to gather and easily float them toward collection sites.

Lesson Labs

Quick Labs
• Comparing Two Elements
• Observe Physical Properties

Exploration Lab
• Identifying an Unknown Substance

Engage Your Brain

1 Predict Check T or F to show whether you think each statement is true or false.

T	F	
☐	☐	Liquid water freezes at the same temperature at which ice melts: 0 °C.
☐	☐	A bowling ball weighs less than a foam ball of the same size.
☐	☐	An object with a density greater than the density of water will float in water.
☐	☐	Solubility is the ability of one substance to dissolve in another.

2 Describe If you were asked to describe an orange to someone who had never seen an orange, what would you tell the person?

_____
_____
_____
_____
_____

Active Reading

3 Synthesize Many English words have their roots in other languages. The root of the word *solubility* is the Latin word *solvere,* which means "to loosen." Make an educated guess about the meaning of the word *solubility.*

_____
_____
_____
_____

Vocabulary Terms

• **physical property**
• **chemical property**

4 Apply As you learn the definition of each vocabulary term in this lesson, create your own definition or sketch to help you remember the meaning of the term.

Physical Education

What are physical properties of matter?

What words would you use to describe a table? A chair? A piece of cloth? You would probably say something about the shape, color, and size of each object. Next, you might consider whether the object is hard or soft, smooth or rough. Normally, when describing an object, you identify what it is about that object that you can observe without changing its identity.

They Are Used to Describe a Substance

A characteristic of a substance that can be observed and measured without changing the identity of the substance is called a **physical property**. Gold is one metal prized for its physical properties. Gold can be bent and shaped easily and has a lasting shine. Both properties make it an excellent metal for making coins and jewelry.

All of your senses can be used to detect physical properties. Color, shape, size, and texture are a few of the physical properties you encounter. Think of how you would describe an object to a friend. Most likely, your description would be a list of the object's physical properties.

Active Reading **5 Describe** Does observing a physical property of a substance change the identity of the substance? Explain.

_____
_____
_____
_____
_____

Gold is a highly sought-after metal for making jewelry. Gold is dense, soft, and shiny, and it is resistant to tarnishing. Gold is often mixed with other metals to make it stronger.

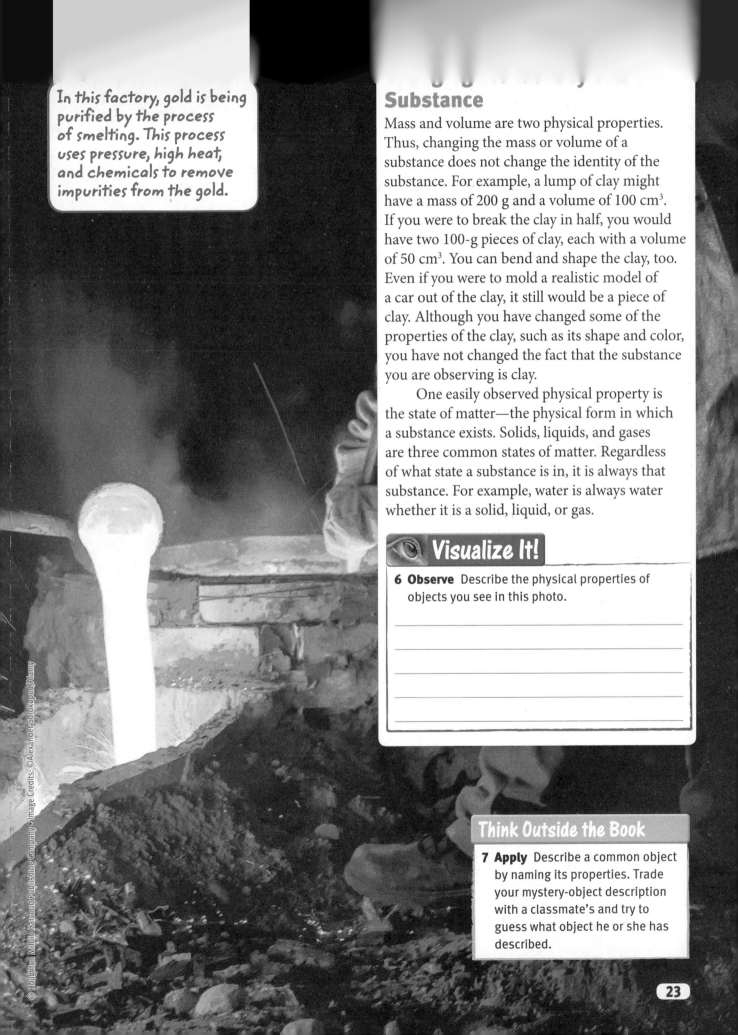

In this factory, gold is being purified by the process of smelting. This process uses pressure, high heat, and chemicals to remove impurities from the gold.

Substance

Mass and volume are two physical properties. Thus, changing the mass or volume of a substance does not change the identity of the substance. For example, a lump of clay might have a mass of 200 g and a volume of 100 cm³. If you were to break the clay in half, you would have two 100-g pieces of clay, each with a volume of 50 cm³. You can bend and shape the clay, too. Even if you were to mold a realistic model of a car out of the clay, it still would be a piece of clay. Although you have changed some of the properties of the clay, such as its shape and color, you have not changed the fact that the substance you are observing is clay.

One easily observed physical property is the state of matter—the physical form in which a substance exists. Solids, liquids, and gases are three common states of matter. Regardless of what state a substance is in, it is always that substance. For example, water is always water whether it is a solid, liquid, or gas.

Visualize It!

6 **Observe** Describe the physical properties of objects you see in this photo.

_____

_____

_____

_____

_____

Think Outside the Book

7 **Apply** Describe a common object by naming its properties. Trade your mystery-object description with a classmate's and try to guess what object he or she has described.

Common Physical Properties

On these two pages, you can read about some common physical properties. The physical properties of a substance often describe how the substance can be useful.

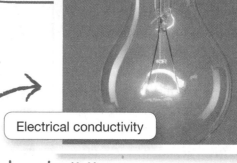

Electrical conductivity

Electrical conductivity is a measure of how well an electric current can move through a substance.

Density

Density is a measure of the amount of mass in a given amount of volume.

8 Explain The photo above shows oil and vinegar in a pitcher. The top layer is the oil. Describe the density of the vinegar compared to the density of the oil.

_____

_____

_____

Thermal conductivity

Thermal conductivity is the rate at which a substance transfers heat.

Solubility

Solubility is the ability of a substance to dissolve in another substance. This powdered drink mix is dissolving in water. When fully dissolved, the particles of the drink mix will be spread throughout the water.

9 Predict If you let all of the liquid evaporate out of the pitcher, would you be able to see the solid particles of the drink mix? Explain.

_____

_____

_____

_____

Malleability

Malleability (MAL·ee·uh·bil·i·tee) is the ability of a substance to be rolled or pounded into various shapes. Aluminum has the property of malleability.

10 Identify Name something made of aluminum and explain why malleability is a useful property.

_____

_____

_____

Luster

Many metals often have a shine, or luster, that make them prized by decorators.

Some metals exert a magnetic attraction. Magnetic attraction can act at a distance.

Magnetic attraction

Melting point

The melting point of a substance is the temperature at which it changes from a solid to a liquid.

Boiling water beneath the surface of Earth powers this geyser.

Boiling point

Inquiry

11 Infer Compare what happens when a geyser erupts to what happens when a tea kettle whistles.

_____

_____

_____

_____

_____

Identity Theft

What are chemical properties of matter?

Active Reading **12 Identify** As you read, underline the definition of a chemical property.

Physical properties are not the only properties that describe matter. A **chemical property** describes a substance's ability to change into a new substance with different properties. Common chemical properties include flammability and reactivity with substances such as oxygen, water, and acids.

They Describe How a Substance Changes

Can you think of a chemical property for the metal iron? When left outdoors in wet weather, iron rusts. The ability to rust is a chemical property of iron. The metal silver does not rust, but eventually a darker substance, called tarnish, forms on its surface. You may have noticed a layer of tarnish on some silver spoons or jewelry. Rusting and tarnishing are chemical properties because the metal changes. After rusting or tarnishing, a portion of the metal is no longer the metal but a different substance.

The ability to ripen is a chemical property.

13 Predict Why do automobiles rust more easily in wet climates than drier climates?

_____

_____

_____

Iron can form rust, turning a once shiny car into a crumbling relic.

They Can Be Observed Only as the Identity of a Substance Changes

Chemical properties can be identified by the changes they produce. A marshmallow and wood for a campfire both have the chemical property of flammability. Flammability is the ability of a substance to burn. When wood burns, new substances are formed: water, carbon dioxide, and ash. These new substances have different properties than the wood had. Some materials do not burn as readily.

Reactivity is another chemical property. Reactivity is the ability of a substance to interact with another substance and form one or more new substances. If you add baking soda to vinegar, bubbles will form. This is because vinegar and baking soda react to make new substances: carbon dioxide gas and water. Vinegar has the property of reactivity with baking soda.

Reactivity is a chemical property. Vinegar and baking soda react to make carbon dioxide gas and water.

Flammability, or the ability of a substance to burn, is a chemical property. For example, the wood building in the photo is flammable and the suits that help keep the firefighters safe are flame resistant.

Property [Boundaries]

What is the difference between physical and chemical properties?

How do you tell a physical property from a chemical property? A physical property can be observed without changing the identity of a substance. For example, determining the mass of a substance does not change its identity. Therefore, mass is a physical property.

A chemical property can be observed only by changing the identity of a substance. For example, to witness a log's flammability, you must set the log on fire. Afterward, the log is no longer a log. It is a pile of ashes. So, flammability is a chemical property.

Active Reading **14 Describe** In your own words, describe the difference between a physical property and a chemical property.

_____

_____

Visualize It!

Bending an iron nail will change its shape but not its identity.

An iron nail can react with oxygen in the air to form iron oxide, or rust.

15 Distinguish What type of property is being shown by each nail? How do you know what property it is?

_____

_____

16 Predict Check the correct box to show whether each property of an iron nail is a physical or a chemical property.

Malleable	☐ Physical ☐ Chemical
Reacts with oxygen	☐ Physical ☐ Chemical
Magnetic	☐ Physical ☐ Chemical
Luster	☐ Physical ☐ Chemical
Nonflammable	☐ Physical ☐ Chemical

Why It Matters

At the Scene

The collection and study of physical evidence in a criminal investigation is known as *forensic science*. **Forensic scientists are experts in observing the physical and chemical properties of evidence at crime scenes.**

Arson Investigation

A forensic scientist can gently heat ashes from an arson scene to help determine what chemicals were used to start the fire. If detectives know how the fire began, then they might be able to determine who is responsible for the crime.

Studying Paint

Flecks of paint left on a tree where a car hit it can be examined with a special microscope. How the paint absorbs light can reveal what chemicals were used in the paint. This information could help authorities determine what kind of vehicle a criminal suspect drove.

Fiber Analysis

Magnified fibers, like those shown above, can provide clues, too. An acrylic fiber might be material from a boat cover or a rug. Or, polyester could have come from a suspect's shirt.

Extend

Inquiry

17 Identify List physical and chemical properties used to identify evidence at a crime scene.

18 Predict When examining evidence, why might investigators want to be more careful examining chemical properties than physical properties?

19 Evaluate By examining the physical and chemical properties of evidence at a crime scene, investigators can often be more certain about what a suspicious substance is not than about what it is. Why do you think this is the case?

29

FORENSIC SCIENCE

Identify Yourself

How can physical and chemical properties identify a substance?

Properties unique to a substance are its *characteristic properties*. Characteristic properties can be physical properties, such as density, or chemical properties, such as flammability. Characteristic properties stay the same regardless of the amount of a sample. They can help identify a substance.

Iron pyrite is one of several minerals having a color similar to that of gold. Miners can find iron pyrite near deposits of gold, and sometimes mistake it for gold. Color and location, however, are about the only properties iron pyrite shares with gold. The two substances have quite different characteristic properties.

For example, gold flattens when hit with a hammer, but iron pyrite shatters. When rubbed on a ceramic plate, gold leaves a yellow streak, but iron pyrite leaves a greenish black one. Gold keeps its shine even if beneath the sea for years, but iron pyrite turns green if exposed to water.

An easy way for miners to tell iron pyrite and gold apart is by using the property of density. Miners collect gold by sifting through dirt in pans. Because of its high density, gold stays in the pan while dirt and most other substances wash over the side as the miner swirls the contents in the pan. Since gold has a density almost four times that of iron pyrite, distinguishing gold from iron pyrite should be an easy task for the experienced miner.

> To find the density of a substance, use the following formula, where D is density, m is mass, and V is volume:
>
> $$D = \frac{m}{V}$$

---

20 Infer Check the box to show which would tell you for sure if you had a sample of real gold.

	Yes	No
Color of your sample.	☐	☐
What happens when you strike your sample with a hammer.	☐	☐
The location where your sample was found.	☐	☐

In pan mining, as the contents in the pan are swirled, less dense substances are washed away.

© Houghton Mifflin Harcourt Publishing Company • Image Credits: ©Neil Overy//Getty Images

 **Do the Math**

Sample Problem

A sample of gold has a mass of 579 g. The volume of the sample is 30 cm³. What is the density of the gold sample?

Identify

A. What do you know?

mass = 579 g, volume = 30 cm³

B. What do you want to find? Density

Plan

C. Write the formula: $D = \dfrac{m}{V}$

D. Substitute the given values into the formula:

$D = \dfrac{579 \text{ g}}{30 \text{ cm}^3}$

Solve

E. Divide: $\dfrac{579 \text{ g}}{30 \text{ cm}^3} = 19.3 \text{ g/cm}^3$

F. Check that your units agree:

The given units are grams and cubic centimeters, and the measure found is density. Therefore, the units should be g/cm³. The units agree.

Answer: 19.3 g/cm³

You Try It

21 Calculate A student finds an object with a mass of 64.54 g and a volume of 14 cm³. Find the density of the object. Could the object be gold?

Identify

A. What do you know?

B. What do you want to find?

Plan

C. Write the formula:

D. Substitute the given values into the formula:

Solve

E. Divide:

F. Check that your units agree:

Answer:

Gold

Iron pyrite

	Yes	No
Could the object be gold?	☐	☐

Visual Summary

To complete this summary, circle the correct word. Then use the key below to check your answers. You can use this page to review the main concepts of the lesson.

Physical and Chemical Properties

A physical property is a property that can be observed or measured without changing the identity of the substance.

22 Solubility / Flammability is a physical property.

23 The melting point of a substance is the temperature at which the substance changes from a solid to a gas / liquid.

A chemical property is a property that describes a substance's ability to form new substances.

24 Reactivity with water / Magnetism is a chemical property.

25 Flammability is the ability of a substance to transfer heat / burn.

The properties that are most useful in identifying a substance are its characteristic properties. Characteristic properties can be physical properties or chemical properties.

26 The characteristic properties of a substance do / do not depend on the size of the sample.

Answers: 22 Solubility; 23 liquid; 24 Reactivity with water; 25 burn; 26 do not

27 Synthesize You have two solid substances that look the same. What measurements would you take and which tests would you perform to determine whether they actually are the same?

Lesson Review

Vocabulary

Fill in the blanks with the term that best completes the following sentences.

1 Flammability is an example of a
_____ property.

2 Electrical conductivity is an example of a
_____ property.

Key Concepts

3 Identify What are three physical properties of aluminum foil?

_____

_____

_____

4 Describe What effect does observing a substance's physical properties have on the substance?

_____

_____

_____

_____

5 Explain Describe how a physical property, such as mass or texture, can change without causing a change in the substance.

_____

_____

_____

_____

6 Justify Must new substances be formed when you observe a chemical property? Explain.

_____

_____

_____

_____

_____

_____

Critical Thinking

Use this table to answer the following question.

Element	Melting Point (°C)	Boiling Point (°C)
Bromine	−7.2	59
Chlorine	−100	−35
Iodine	110	180

7 Infer You are given samples of the substances shown in the table. The samples are labeled A, B, and C. At room temperature, sample A is a solid, sample B is a liquid, and sample C is a gas. What are the identities of samples A, B, and C? (Hint: Room temperature is about 20 °C.)

_____

_____

_____

8 Conclude The density of gold is 19.3 g/cm³. The density of iron pyrite is 5.0 g/cm³. If a nugget of iron pyrite and a nugget of gold each have a mass of 50 g, what can you conclude about the volume of each nugget?

_____

_____

_____

9 Predict Suppose you need to build a raft to cross a fast-moving river. Describe the physical and chemical properties of the raft that would be important to ensure your safety.

_____

_____

_____

_____

_____

My Notes

Physical and Chemical Changes

ESSENTIAL QUESTION

What are physical and chemical changes of matter?

By the end of this lesson, you should be able to distinguish between physical and chemical changes of matter.

Rusty beams are all that remain of these large boats. The rust is the result of an interaction of the iron beams with water and air.

© Houghton Mifflin Harcourt Publishing Company • Image Credits: ©Markus Renner//Getty Images

Engage Your Brain

1 Predict Check T or F to show whether you think each statement is true or false.

T F

☐ ☐ When an ice cube melts, it is still water.

☐ ☐ Matter is lost when a candle is burned.

☐ ☐ When your body digests food, the food is changed into new substances.

2 Describe Write a word or phrase beginning with each letter of the word CHANGE that describes changes you have observed in everyday objects.

C _____

H _____

A _____

N _____

G _____

E _____

Active Reading

3 Apply Use context clues to write your own definitions for the words *interact* and *indicate*.

Example sentence
As the two substances <u>interact</u>, gas bubbles are given off.

interact:

_____

_____

_____

Example sentence
A color change may <u>indicate</u> that a chemical change has taken place.

indicate:

_____

_____

_____

Vocabulary Terms

- physical change
- chemical change
- law of conservation of mass

4 Apply As you learn the definition of each vocabulary term in this lesson, create your own definition or sketch to help you remember the meaning of the term.

Change of Appearance

What are physical changes of matter?

A physical property of matter is any property that can be observed or measured without changing the chemical identity of the substance. A **physical change** is a change that affects one or more physical properties of a substance. Physical changes occur when a substance changes from one form to another. However, the chemical identity of the substance remains the same.

Changes in Observable Properties

The appearance, shape, or size of a substance may be altered during a physical change. For example, the process of turning wool into a sweater requires that the wool undergoes physical changes. Wool is sheared from the sheep. The wool is then cleaned, and the wool fibers are separated from one another. Shearing and separating the fibers are physical changes that change the shape, volume, and texture of the wool.

Active Reading

5 Explain What happens to a substance during a physical change?

_____

_____

_____

Physical Changes Turn Wool into a Sweater

A Wool is sheared from the sheep. The raw wool is then cleaned and placed into a machine that separates the wool fibers from one another.

B The wool fibers are spun into yarn. Again, the shape and volume of the wool change. The fibers are twisted so that they are packed more closely together and are intertwined with one another.

C The yarn is dyed. The dye changes the color of the wool, but it does not change the wool into another substance. This type of color change is a physical change.

Changes That Do Not Alter the Chemical Identity of the Substance

During the process of turning wool into a sweater, many physical changes occur in the wool. However, the wool does not change into some other substance as a result of these changes. Therefore, physical changes do not change the chemical identity of a substance.

Another example of a physical change happens when you fill an ice cube tray with water and place it inside a freezer. If the water gets cold enough, it will freeze to form ice cubes. Freezing water does not change its chemical makeup. In fact, you could melt the ice cube and have liquid water again! Changes of state, and all physical changes, do not change the chemical makeup of the substance.

---

6 Identify The list below gives several examples of physical changes. Write your own examples of physical changes on the blank lines.

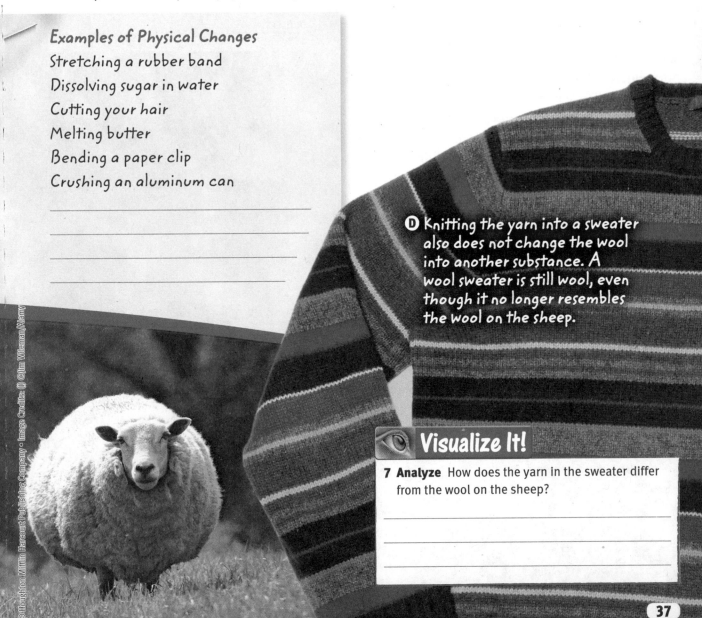

Examples of Physical Changes
Stretching a rubber band
Dissolving sugar in water
Cutting your hair
Melting butter
Bending a paper clip
Crushing an aluminum can

_____

_____

_____

D Knitting the yarn into a sweater also does not change the wool into another substance. A wool sweater is still wool, even though it no longer resembles the wool on the sheep.

Visualize It!

7 Analyze How does the yarn in the sweater differ from the wool on the sheep?

_____

_____

_____

Change from

What are chemical changes of matter?

Think about what happens to the burning logs in a campfire. They start out dry, rough, and dense. After flames surround them, the logs emerge as black and powdery ashes. The campfire releases a lot of heat and smoke in the process. Something has obviously happened, something more than simply a change of appearance. The wood has stopped being wood. It has undergone a chemical change.

Changes in Substance Identity

A **chemical change** occurs when one or more substances change into entirely new substances with different properties. For example, in the campfire, the dry, dense wood became the powdery ashes—new substances with different properties. When a cake is baked, the liquid cake batter becomes the solid, spongy treat. Whenever a new substance is formed, a chemical change has occurred.

Be aware that chemical *changes* are not exactly the same as chemical *properties*. Burning is a chemical change; flammability is a chemical property. The chemical properties of a substance describe which chemical changes can or cannot happen to that substance. Chemical changes are the *processes* by which substances actually change into new substances. You can learn about a substance's chemical properties by watching the chemical changes that substance undergoes.

Visualize It!

8 Identify Use the boxes provided to identify the wood, ashes, and flames involved in the chemical change. Then write a caption describing the chemical changes you see in the photo.

_____

_____

_____

_____

the Inside

A _____

B _____

C _____

Changes to the Chemical Makeup of a Substance

In a chemical change, a substance's identity changes because its chemical makeup changes. This happens as the particles and chemical bonds that make up the substance get rearranged. For example, when iron rusts, molecules of oxygen from the air combine with iron atoms to form a new compound. Rust is not iron or oxygen. It is a new substance made up of oxygen and iron joined together.

Because chemical changes involve changes in the arrangements of particles, they are often influenced by temperature. At higher temperatures, the particles in a substance have more average kinetic energy. They move around a lot more freely and so rearrange more easily. Therefore, at higher temperatures, chemical reactions often happen more quickly. Think of baking a cake. The higher the temperature of the oven, the less time the cake will need to bake because the faster the chemical reactions occur.

Active Reading 9 **Explain** How do higher temperatures influence a chemical change?

_____

_____

_____

Think Outside the Book Inquiry

10 **Infer** Think of ways you control temperature to influence chemical changes during a typical day. (Hint: Cooking, Art class)

Look for the Signs

How can you tell a chemical change has happened?

Physical changes and chemical changes are different. Chemical changes result in new substances, while physical changes do not. However, it may not be obvious that any new substances have formed during a chemical change. Here are some signs that a chemical change may have occurred. If you observe two or more of these signs during a change, you likely are observing a chemical change.

Active Reading **11 Compare** How are physical and chemical changes different?

_____

_____

_____

_____

Production of an Odor

Some chemical changes produce odors. The chemical change that occurs when an egg is rotting, for example, produces the smell of sulfur. Milk that has soured also has an unpleasant smell—because bacteria have formed new substances in the milk. And if you've gone outdoors after a thunderstorm, you've probably noticed a distinct smell. This odor is an indication that lightning has caused a chemical change in the air.

Production of a Gas

Chemical changes often cause fizzing or foaming. For example, a chemical change is involved when an antacid tablet is dropped into a glass of water. As the tablet makes contact with the water and begins to react with it, bubbles of gas appear. One of the new substances that is formed is carbon dioxide gas, which forms the bubbles that you see.

It is important to note that some physical changes, such as boiling, can also produce gas bubbles. Therefore, the only way to know for sure whether a chemical change has taken place is to identify new substances.

Bubbles form when an antacid tablet reacts with water. The bubbles contain a new, gaseous substance, which signals that a chemical change has happened.

40 Unit 1 Matter

Formation of a Precipitate

Chemical changes may result in products in different physical states. Liquids sometimes combine to form a solid called a *precipitate*. For example, colorless potassium iodide and lead nitrate combine to form the bright yellow precipitate lead iodide, as shown below.

Bright yellow lead iodide precipitates from the clear solution.

Change in Color

A change in color is often an indication of a chemical change. For example, when gray iron rusts, the product that forms is brown.

Change in Energy

Chemical changes can cause *energy*, which is the ability to do work, to change from one form into another. For example, in a burning candle, the chemical energy stored in the candle converts to heat and light energy.

A change in temperature is often a sign of a chemical change. The change need not always be as dramatic as the one in the photo, however.

The reaction of heated aluminum with oxygen produces so much heat that welders use it in thermite welding.

12 Infer List the observations you might make as you witness each of the changes below. Then classify each change as a physical change or a chemical change.

Change	Signs/observations	Type of change
Boiling water		
Baking a cake		
Burning wood		
Painting a door		

Conservation is the Law

What is the law of conservation of mass?

If you freeze 5 mL of water and then let the ice melt, you have 5 mL of water again. You can freeze and melt the water as much as you like. The mass of water will not change.

This does not always seem true for chemical changes. The ashes remaining after a fire contain much less mass than the logs that produced them. Mass seems to vanish. In other chemical changes, such as those that cause the growth of plants, mass seems to appear out of nowhere. This puzzled scientists for years. Where did the mass go? Where did it come from?

In the 1770s, the French chemist Antoine Lavoisier (an•TWAHN luh•VWAH•zee•ay) studied chemical changes in which substances seemed to lose or gain mass. He showed that the mass was most often lost to or gained from gases in the air. Lavoisier demonstrated this transformation of mass by observing chemical changes in sealed glass bulbs. This was the first demonstration of the *law of conservation of mass*. The **law of conservation of mass** states that in ordinary chemical and physical changes, mass is not created or destroyed but is only transformed into different substances.

The examples at the right will help you understand how the law works in both physical and chemical changes. In the top example, the second robot may have a different shape than the first, but it clearly has the same parts. In the second example, vinegar and baking soda undergo a chemical change. Mix the baking soda with the vinegar in the flask, and mass seems to vanish. Yet the balloon shows that what really happens is the production of a gas—carbon dioxide gas.

Active Reading **13 Identify** What is the law of conservation of mass?

_____

_____

_____

The water may freeze or the ice may melt, but the amount of matter in this glass will stay the same.

Conservation of Mass in Physical Changes

When the long gray piece is moved from its arms to its waist, the toy robot gets a new look. It's still a toy robot—its parts are just rearranged. Most physical changes are reversible. All physical changes follow the law of conservation of mass.

👁 **Visualize It!**

14 Describe How is the physical change in the robot reversible, and how can you tell that the change follows the law of conservation of mass?

_____

_____

_____

_____

_____

Before

After

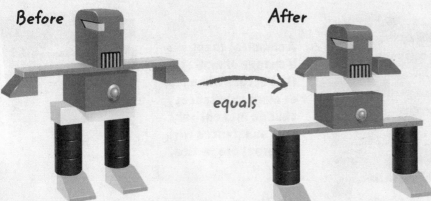

equals

Conservation of Mass in Chemical Changes

When vinegar and baking soda are combined, they undergo a chemical change. The balloon at the right is inflated with carbon dioxide gas that was produced as a result of the change. The mass of the starting materials is the same as the mass of the products. Without the balloon to catch it, however, the gas would seem to disappear.

Before

After

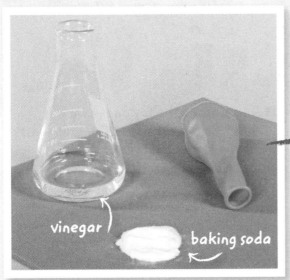

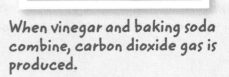

equals

When vinegar and baking soda combine, carbon dioxide gas is produced.

👁 **Visualize It!**

15 Infer What would you observe about the mass in the flask if you did not put the balloon on top? Why?

_____

_____

Visual Summary

To complete this summary, circle the correct word or phrase. Then use the key below to check your answers. You can use this page to review the main concepts of the lesson.

How Matter Changes

A physical change is a change of matter from one form to another without a change in the identity of the substance.

16 Burning / Dyeing wool is an example of a physical change.

A chemical change is a change of matter that occurs when one or more substances change into entirely new substances with different properties.

17 The formation of a precipitate signals a physical / chemical change.

Chemical changes often cause the production of an odor, fizzing or foaming, the formation of a precipitate, or changes in color or temperature.

18 This physical / chemical change results in the formation of new substances.

The law of conservation of mass states that mass cannot be created or destroyed in ordinary chemical and physical changes.

19 The mass of the toy on the right is the same as / different from the mass of the toy on the left.

Answers: 16 Dyeing; 17 chemical; 18 chemical; 19 the same as

20 Explain Do changes that cannot be easily reversed, such as burning, observe the law of conservation of mass? Explain.

Lesson Review

Vocabulary

In your own words, define the following terms.

1 physical change

_____

_____

_____

2 chemical change

_____

_____

_____

3 law of conservation of mass

_____

_____

_____

Key Concepts

4 Identify Give an example of a physical change and an example of a chemical change.

_____

_____

_____

_____

5 Compare How is a chemical change different from a physical change?

_____

_____

_____

_____

6 Apply Suppose a log's mass is 5 kg. After burning, the mass of the ash is 1 kg. Explain what may have happened to the other 4 kg.

_____

_____

_____

_____

_____

Critical Thinking

Use this photo to answer the following question.

7 Analyze As the bright sun shines upon the water, the water slowly disappears. The same sunlight gives energy to the surrounding plants to convert water and carbon dioxide into sugar and oxygen gas. Which change is physical and which is chemical?

_____

_____

_____

8 Compare Relate the statement "You can't get something for nothing" to the law of conservation of mass.

_____

_____

_____

_____

9 Infer Sharpening a pencil leaves behind pencil shavings. Is sharpening a pencil a physical change or a chemical change? Explain.

_____

_____

_____

_____

_____

My Notes

Engineering Design Process

Skills

Identify a need

Conduct research

✔ Brainstorm solutions

✔ Select a solution

✔ Design a prototype

✔ Build a prototype

✔ Test and evaluate

Redesign to improve

✔ Communicate results

Objectives

• List and rank insulation materials according to effectiveness.

• Design a technological solution to keep an ice cube frozen.

• Test a prototype insulated ice cooler and communicate whether it achieved the desired results.

Building an Insulated Cooler

What do freezers, ovens, and polar bears have in common? They are all insulated! *Insulation* is a type of material that slows the transfer of energy such as heat. Refrigerators and freezers use insulation to keep the food inside cold. Insulation around ovens keeps energy inside the oven. And some animals have hair, fur, and fat layers that provide them with insulation, too.

1 Apply Which items in this picture provide insulation?

_____

_____

_____

_____

_____

2 List Name other everyday objects not shown here where insulation is used to keep objects warm or cool.

_____

_____

_____

_____

_____

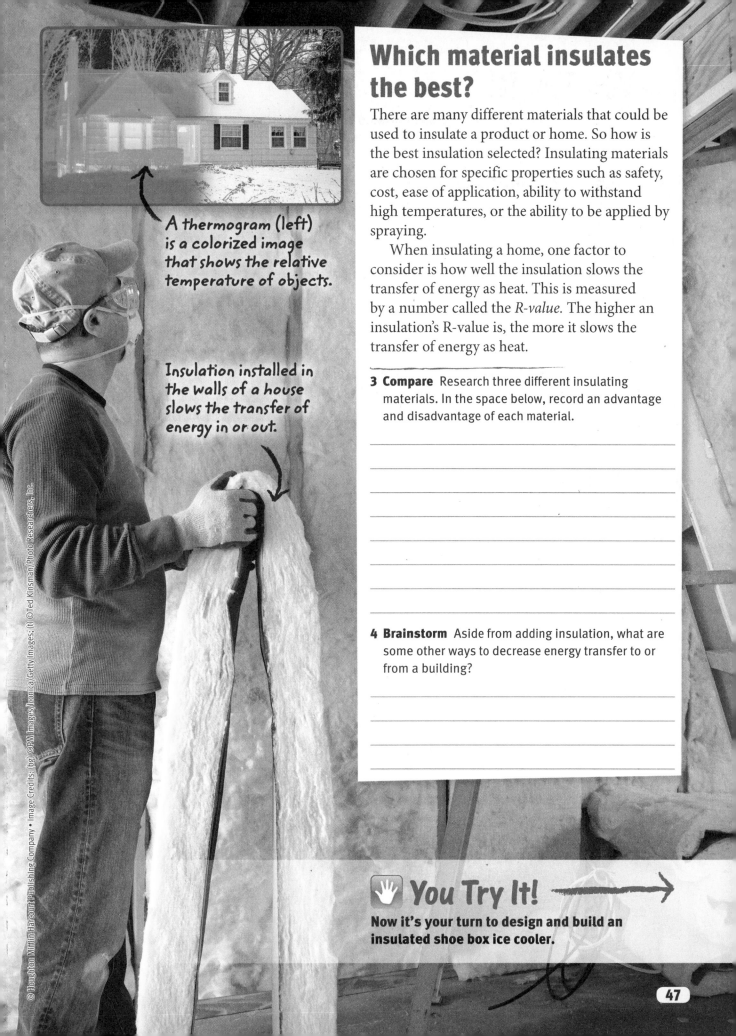

A thermogram (left) is a colorized image that shows the relative temperature of objects.

Insulation installed in the walls of a house slows the transfer of energy in or out.

Which material insulates the best?

There are many different materials that could be used to insulate a product or home. So how is the best insulation selected? Insulating materials are chosen for specific properties such as safety, cost, ease of application, ability to withstand high temperatures, or the ability to be applied by spraying.

When insulating a home, one factor to consider is how well the insulation slows the transfer of energy as heat. This is measured by a number called the *R-value.* The higher an insulation's R-value is, the more it slows the transfer of energy as heat.

---

3 Compare Research three different insulating materials. In the space below, record an advantage and disadvantage of each material.

_____

_____

_____

_____

_____

_____

_____

_____

_____

4 Brainstorm Aside from adding insulation, what are some other ways to decrease energy transfer to or from a building?

_____

_____

_____

_____

✋ You Try It! ⟶

Now it's your turn to design and build an insulated shoe box ice cooler.

 # You Try It!

Now it's your turn to design and build an insulated cooler that will keep an ice cube frozen for an entire class period.

(1) Brainstorm Solutions

Brainstorm ideas to construct an insulated shoe box cooler that will keep an ice cube frozen for a class period.

A What insulation materials could you put into the empty shoe box to prevent the transfer of energy as heat?

_____

_____

B What waterproof container will you place under or around the ice cube so water doesn't affect the insulation as the ice cube melts?

_____

_____

(2) Select a Solution

Which materials and design offer the best promise for success? Why?

_____

_____

_____

_____

(3) Design a Prototype

In the space below, draw a prototype of your insulated cooler. Be sure to include all the parts you will need and show how they will be connected.

You Will Need

✔ balance

✔ duct tape or packing tape

✔ ice cube

✔ insulation materials

✔ plastic bag or waterproof container

✔ shoe box, empty

✔ paper towels or cloths

(4) Build a Prototype

Now build your insulated cooler. What parts, if any, did you have to revise as you were building the prototype?

_____

_____

_____

_____

(5) Test and Evaluate

A At the beginning of a class period, find the mass of an ice cube. Record your result below.

_____

B Place the ice cube in your cooler and close it. At the end of the class period, open the cooler and observe the ice cube. Find the ice cube's mass and record your result below.

_____

C Was part of the ice still frozen? Calculate the fraction of the ice cube that remained frozen.

_____

_____

(6) Communicate Results

A Did your cooler provide effective insulation? Explain.

_____

_____

_____

_____

B Is there anything you could have done to increase the amount of ice remaining?

_____

_____

_____

_____

_____

_____

Pure Substances
and Mixtures

ESSENTIAL QUESTION

How do pure substances and mixtures compare?

By the end of this lesson, you should be able to distinguish between pure substances and mixtures.

7.PS1.2, 7.PS1.3

Seawater is a unique mixture that contains many dissolved substances. One such substance, called calcium carbonate, is used by these stony corals to build their hard skeletons.

Lesson Labs

Quick Labs
• Observing Mixtures
• Identifying Elements and Compounds

Exploration Lab
• Investigating Separating Mixtures

Engage Your Brain

1 Predict Check T or F to show whether you think each statement is true or false.

T   F

☐ ☐ Atoms combine in different ways to make up all of the substances you encounter every day.

☐ ☐ Saltwater can be separated into salt and water.

☐ ☐ A mixture of soil has the same chemical composition throughout.

2 Apply Think of a substance that does not dissolve in water. Draw a sketch below that shows what happens when this substance is added to water.

Active Reading

3 Synthesize Many English words have their roots in other languages. Use the Greek words below to make an educated guess about the meanings of the words *homogeneous* and *heterogeneous*.

Greek word	Meaning
genus	type
homos	same
heteros	different

Example sentence
Saltwater is <u>homogeneous</u> throughout.

homogeneous:

_____

_____

Example sentence
A <u>heterogeneous</u> mixture of rocks varies from handful to handful.

heterogeneous:

_____

_____

Vocabulary Terms

• atom
• element
• compound
• mixture
• pure substance
• heterogeneous
• homogeneous

4 Identify This list contains the key terms you'll learn in this lesson. As you read, circle the definition of each term.

A Great Combination

How can matter be classified?

What kinds of food could you make with the ingredients shown below? You could eat slices of tomato as a snack. Or, you could combine tomato slices with lettuce to make a salad. Combine more ingredients, such as bread and cheese, and you have a sandwich. Just as these meals are made up of simpler foods, matter is made up of basic "ingredients" known as *atoms*. **Atoms** are the smallest unit of an element that maintains the properties of that element. Atoms, like the foods shown here, can be combined in different ways to produce different substances.

The substances you encounter every day can be classified into one of the three major classes of matter: *elements, compounds,* and *mixtures*. Atoms are the basic building blocks for all three types of matter. Elements, compounds, and mixtures differ in the way that atoms are combined.

Active Reading 5 **Compare** What do elements, compounds, and mixtures have in common?

_____

_____

Think Outside the Book Inquiry

6 **Predict** If you have ever baked a cake or bread, you know that the ingredients that combine to make it taste different from the baked food. Why do you think that is?

Just as these ingredients combine to make a tasty sandwich, atoms are the basic "ingredients" that make up matter.

© Houghton Mifflin Harcourt Publishing Company

Matter Can Be Classified into Elements, Compounds, and Mixtures

You can think of atoms as the building blocks of matter. Like these toy blocks, atoms can be connected in different ways. The models below show how atoms make up elements and compounds. Elements and compounds, in turn, make up mixtures.

 An atom is like a building block of matter.

 An **element** is made up of one or more of the same kind of atom chemically combined into a molecule.

Oxygen

 A **compound** is made up of different kinds of atoms chemically combined into a molecule. Compounds have different properties from the elements that make them up.

Water

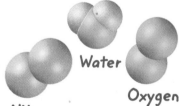 A **mixture** contains a variety of elements and compounds that are not chemically combined with each other into a molecule.

Water

Nitrogen   Oxygen

Visualize It!

7 Contrast How are the oxygen and nitrogen molecules different from the water molecule?

_____

_____

_____

_____

Pure Genius

What are pure substances?

Elements and compounds are **pure substances**. A pure substance is a substance that has definite physical and chemical properties such as appearance, melting point, and reactivity. The amount of a pure substance you have does not matter; it will always have the same properties. This is because pure substances are made up of one type of particle.

Pure Substances Are Made Up of One Type of Particle

Copper, like all elements, is a pure substance. The atoms that make up copper are all the same. No matter where in the world you find pure copper, it will always have the same properties.

Compounds are also pure substances. Consider water, shown on the next page. Two different kinds of atoms make up each chemically combined particle, or *molecule.* There are elemental and compound molecules. Elemental molecules have atoms that are all the same. Compound molecules have a combination of different types of atoms. Every water molecule is identical. Each molecule is made up of exactly two hydrogen atoms and one oxygen atom. Because water is a pure substance, we can define certain properties of water. For example, at standard pressure, water always freezes at 0 °C and boils at 100 °C.

---

8 Compare For the chart below, compare what happens when you mix various elements together. What type of molecule do you get (elemental or compound)? What common household product results when they are all mixed together?

_____

_____

Elements	Type of Molecule
Sodium (Na) ✚ Sodium (Na)	_____
Chlorine (Cl) ✚ Chlorine (Cl)	_____
Sodium (Na) ✚ Chlorine (Cl)	_____

© Houghton Mifflin Harcourt Publishing Company • Image Credits: (bkgd) ©imagewerks//Getty Images

Pure Substances Cannot Be Formed or Broken Down by Physical Changes

Physical changes such as melting, freezing, cutting, or smashing do not change the identity of pure substances. For example, if you cut copper pipe into short pieces, the material is still copper. And if you freeze liquid water, the particles that make up the ice remain the same: two hydrogen atoms combined with one oxygen atom.

The chemical bonds that hold atoms together cannot be broken easily. To break or form chemical bonds, a chemical change is required. For example, when an electric current is passed through water, a chemical change takes place. The atoms that make up the compound break apart into two elements: hydrogen and oxygen. When a pure substance undergoes a chemical change, it is no longer that same substance. A chemical change affects the identity of the substance. Individual atoms cannot be broken down into smaller parts by normal physical or chemical changes.

 **9 Identify** What happens when a pure substance undergoes a chemical change?

_____

_____

_____

Visualize It!

10 Identify Fill in the blanks to label the two particle models.

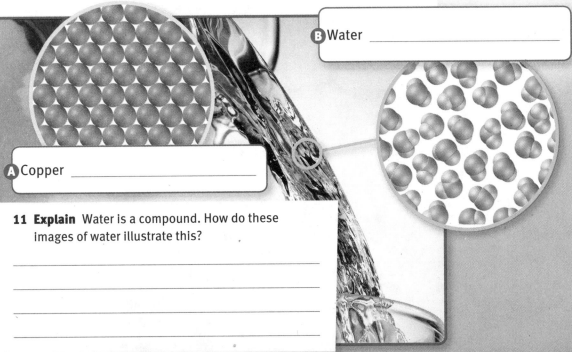

B Water _____

A Copper _____

11 Explain Water is a compound. How do these images of water illustrate this?

_____

_____

_____

Classified Information

How can elements be classified?

Differences in physical and chemical properties allow us to classify elements. By knowing the category to which an element belongs, you can predict some of its properties. Elements are broadly classified as metals, nonmetals, or metalloids. Most metals are shiny, conduct heat and electricity well, and can be shaped into thin sheets and wires. Nonmetals are not shiny and do not conduct heat or electricity well. Metalloids have some properties of both metals and nonmetals.

There are over 100 elements known to exist. Each element has a place in an arrangement called the periodic table of the elements. The periodic table is a useful tool that can help you to identify elements that have similar properties. Metals, nonmetals, and metalloids occupy different regions in the periodic table. Metals start at the left and make up most of the elements in the periodic table. Nonmetals are at the right and are often shaded with a color different from that of the metals. Not surprisingly, the metalloids lie between the metals and nonmetals. In many instances, you can even predict which elements combine with others to form compounds based on their positions in the periodic table.

Active Reading

12 Identify As you read, underline the ways in which elements are organized on the periodic table.

Aluminum, like many metals, can be formed into a thin foil.

Charcoal, made mostly of carbon atoms, is brittle and dull like many other nonmetals.

How can compounds be classified?

You are surrounded by compounds. Compounds make up the food you eat, the school supplies you use, and the clothes you wear—even you! There are so many compounds that it would be very difficult to list or describe them all. Fortunately, these compounds can be grouped into a few basic categories by their properties.

By Their pH

Compounds can be classified as acidic, basic, or neutral by measuring a special value known as *pH*. Acids have a pH value below 7. Vinegar contains acetic acid, which gives a sharp, sour taste to salad dressings. Bases, on the other hand, have pH values greater than 7. Baking soda is an example of a basic compound. Bases have a slippery feel and a bitter taste. Neutral compounds, such as pure water and table salt, have a pH value of 7. Water and salt are formed when an acid and a base react. A type of paper called litmus paper can be used to test whether a compound is an acid or a base. Blue litmus paper turns red in the presence of an acid. Red litmus paper turns blue in the presence of a base. Although some foods are acidic or basic, you should NEVER taste, smell, or touch a chemical to classify it. Many acids and bases can damage your body or clothing.

13 Classify Read about some of the ways in which compounds can be classified. Then fill in the blanks to complete the photo captions.

Baking soda is an example of a(n) _____.

As Organic or Inorganic

You may have heard of organically grown foods. But in chemistry, the word *organic* refers to compounds that contain carbon and hydrogen. Organic compounds are found in most foods. They can also be found in synthetic goods. For example, gasoline contains a number of organic compounds, such as octane and heptane.

The compounds that make up plastic are _____ because they contain carbon.

By Their Role in the Body

Organic compounds that are made by living things are called biochemicals. Biochemicals are divided into four categories: carbohydrates, lipids, proteins, and nucleic acids. *Carbohydrates* are used as a source of energy and include sugars, starches, and fiber. *Lipids* are biochemicals that store excess energy in the body and make up cell membranes. Lipids include fats, oils, and waxes. *Proteins* are one of the most abundant types of compounds in your body. They regulate the chemical activities of the body and build and repair body structures. *Nucleic acids* such as DNA and RNA contain genetic information and help the body build proteins.

Your body gets _____ such as sugars, starches, and fiber, from many of the foods you eat.

What are mixtures?

Imagine that you roll out some dough, add tomato sauce, and sprinkle some cheese on top. Then you add green peppers, mushrooms, and pepperoni. What have you just made? A pizza, of course! But that's not all. You have also created a mixture.

A mixture is a combination of two or more substances that are combined physically but not chemically. When two or more materials are put together, they form a mixture if they do not change chemically to form a new substance. For example, cheese and tomato sauce do not react when they are combined to make a pizza. They keep their original identities and properties. So, a pizza is a mixture.

Mixtures Are Made Up of More Than One Type of Particle

Unlike elements and compounds, mixtures are not pure substances. Mixtures contain more than one type of substance. Each substance in a mixture has the same chemical makeup it had before the mixture formed.

Unlike pure substances, mixtures do not have definite properties. Granite from different parts of the world could contain different minerals in different ratios. Pizzas made by different people could have different toppings. Mixtures do not have defined properties because they do not have a defined chemical makeup.

Visualize It!

14 Describe This student is going to make and separate a mixture of sand and salt. Complete these captions to describe what is taking place in each photo.

Ⓐ Sand and salt are poured into a single beaker. The result is a mixture because

_____

_____

_____

_____ .

Mixtures Can Be Separated by Physical Changes

You don't like mushrooms on your pizza? Just pick them off. This change is a physical change of the mixture because the identities of the substances do not change. But not all mixtures are as easy to separate as a pizza. You cannot just pick salt out of a saltwater mixture. One way to separate the salt from the water is to heat the mixture until the water evaporates. The salt is left behind. Other ways to separate mixtures are shown at the right and below.

Active Reading **15 Devise** How could you separate a mixture of rocks and sand?

_____

_____

_____

A magnet can separate a mixture of aluminum nails and iron nails.

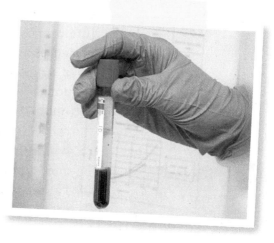

A machine called a centrifuge separates mixtures by the densities of the components. It can be used to separate the different parts of blood.

B When water is added to the sand-salt mixture,

_____

_____

_____

_____

_____.

C When the liquid is poured through a filter,

_____

_____

_____

_____

_____.

D The remaining saltwater is heated until

_____

_____

_____

_____

_____.

A Simple Solution

Active Reading

16 Identify As you read, underline the everyday examples of mixtures on this page.

How can mixtures be classified?

A snow globe contains a suspension.

It is clear that something is a mixture when you can see the different substances in it. For example, if you scoop up a handful of soil, it might contain dirt, rocks, leaves, and even insects. Exactly what you see depends on what part of the soil is scooped. Such a mixture is called a heterogeneous (het•uhr•uh•JEE•nee•uhs) mixture. A **heterogeneous** mixture is one that does not have a uniform composition. In other types of mixtures, the substances are evenly spread throughout. If you add sugar to a cup of water, the sugar dissolves. Each part of the sugar-water mixture has the same sweet taste. This is called a **homogeneous** (hoh•muh•JEE•nee•uhs) mixture.

As Suspensions

The snow globe (above) contains a type of heterogeneous mixture called a *suspension*. Suspensions are mixtures in which the particles of a material are spread throughout a liquid or gas but are too large to stay mixed without being stirred or shaken. If a suspension is allowed to sit, the particles will settle out.

As Solutions

Tea is a solution.

Tea is an example of a type of homogeneous mixture known as a *solution*. In a solution, one substance is dissolved in another substance. When you make tea, some of the compounds inside the tea leaves dissolve in the hot water. These compounds give your tea its unique color and taste. Many familiar solutions are liquids. However, solutions may also be gases or solids. Air is an example of a gaseous solution. Alloys, such as brass and steel, are solid solutions in which substances are dissolved in metals.

As Colloids

Gelatin is a colloid.

Colloids are a third type of mixture that falls somewhere between suspensions and solutions. As in a suspension, the particles in a colloid are spread throughout a liquid or gas. Unlike the particles in a suspension, colloid particles are small and do not settle out quickly. Milk and gelatin are colloids. Colloids look homogeneous, but we consider them to be heterogeneous.

17 Classify Complete the graphic organizer below by filling in the blanks with terms from this lesson. Then add definitions or sketches of each term inside the appropriate box.

Classifying Matter

Matter
Definition:

Matter is anything that has mass and takes up space. Matter is made up of building blocks called atoms.

Pure Substances
Definition:

_____
_____
_____
_____
_____

Sketch:

Elements
Sketch:

Definition:

_____
_____
_____
_____

Sketch:

Homogeneous
Definition:

_____
_____
_____
_____

Suspensions
Sketch:

Colloids
Definition:

_____
_____
_____
_____

Sketch:

_____
_____
_____
_____

Visual Summary

To complete this summary, circle the correct word or phrase. Then use the key below to check your answers. You can use this page to review the main concepts of the lesson.

Pure substances are made up of a single type of particle and cannot be formed or broken down by physical changes.

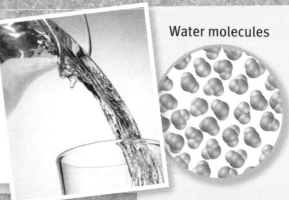

Water molecules

18 Water is a pure substance / mixture.

19 Water is a(n) element / compound.

Pure Substances and Mixtures

Mixtures are made up of more than one type of particle and can be separated into their component parts by physical changes.

20 Saltwater and sand can be separated with a magnet / filter.

21 Saltwater is a homogeneous / heterogeneous mixture.

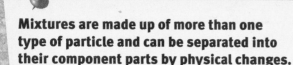

Answers: 18 pure substance; 19 compound; 20 filter; 21 homogeneous

22 Predict Why do you think that the particles of a suspension settle out but the particles of a colloid do not?

Lesson Review

Vocabulary

Fill in the blanks with the term that best completes the following sentences.

1 The basic building blocks of matter are called

_____.

2 A(n) _____ is a substance that is made up of a single kind of atom.

3 Elements and compounds are two types of

_____.

4 A(n) _____ is a combination of substances that are combined physically but not chemically.

Key Concepts

5 Identify What kind of mixture is a solution? A suspension? A colloid?

_____

_____

_____

_____

6 Apply Fish give off the compound ammonia, which has a pH above 7. To which class of compounds does ammonia belong?

_____

7 Compare Fill in the following table with properties of elements and compounds.

How are elements and compounds similar?	How are elements and compounds different?

Use this drawing to answer the following question.

8 Identify What type of mixture is this salad dressing?

_____

Critical Thinking

9 Explain Could a mixture be made up of only elements and no compounds? Explain.

_____

_____

_____

_____

_____

10 Synthesize Describe a procedure to separate a mixture of sugar, black pepper, and pebbles.

_____

_____

_____

_____

_____

_____

_____

_____

_____

_____

_____

My Notes

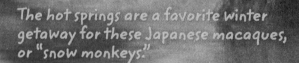

States of Matter

ESSENTIAL QUESTION

How do particles in solids, liquids, and gases move?

By the end of this lesson, you should be able to model the motion of particles in solids, liquids, and gases.

7.PS1.6

At these hot springs in Japan, you can find water in the form of a solid, a liquid, and a gas.

The hot springs are a favorite winter getaway for these Japanese macaques, or "snow monkeys."

Engage Your Brain

1 Describe Fill in the blank with a word or phrase that you think correctly completes the following sentences.

_____ is an example of a solid.

_____ is an example of a gas.

Unlike solids, gases can _____

_____ .

2 Identify Unscramble the letters below to find substances that are liquids. Write your words on the blank lines.

TWRAE _____

EICJU _____

RIVAENG _____

LIKM _____

PSAOMOH _____

Active Reading

3 Apply Use context clues to write your own definitions for the words *definite* and *occupy*.

Example sentence
Solid is the state of matter that has a <u>definite</u> shape and volume.

definite:

_____

_____

Example sentence
A larger container will allow a gas to <u>occupy</u> more space.

occupy:

_____

_____

Vocabulary Terms
- **solid**
- **liquid**
- **gas**

4 Identify As you read, place a question mark next to any words that you don't understand. When you finish reading the lesson, go back and review the text that you marked. If the information is still confusing, consult a classmate or a teacher.

Particles in Motion

How do particles move in solids, liquids, and gases?

All matter is made of atoms or groups of atoms that are in constant motion. This idea is the basis for the *kinetic theory of matter*. How much the particles move and how often they bump into each other determine the state of matter of the substance. This view of a movie theater helps to illustrate the differences between the particle motion in each of the three common states of matter.

In Solids, Particles Vibrate in Place

A **solid** substance has a definite volume and shape. The particles in a solid are close together and do not move freely. The particles vibrate but are fixed in place. Often, the particles in a solid are packed together to form a regular pattern like the one shown at the right.

For most substances, the particles in a solid are closer together than the particles in a liquid. For example, the atoms in solid steel are closer together than the atoms in liquid steel. Water is an important exception to this rule. The molecules that make up ice actually have more space between them than the molecules in liquid water do.

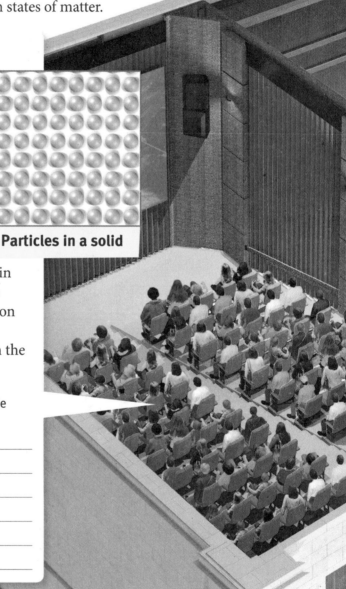

Particles in a solid

5 Describe How are particles in a solid like people sitting in a crowded movie theater?

_____

_____

_____

_____

_____

_____

In Liquids, Particles Slide Past One Another

A **liquid** substance has a definite volume but not a definite shape. Particles in a liquid, shown at the right, have more kinetic energy than particles in a solid do. The particles are attracted to one another and are close together. However, particles in a liquid are not fixed in place and can move from one place to another.

Particles in a liquid

6 Describe How are particles in a liquid like people in a movie theater lobby?

_____

_____

_____

_____

_____

_____

In Gases, Particles Move Freely

A **gas** does not have a definite volume or shape. A substance in the gaseous state has particles with the most kinetic energy of the three states. As you can see in the model at the right, gas particles are not close to one another and can move easily in any direction. There is much more space between gas particles than there is between particles in a liquid or a solid. The space between gas particles can increase or decrease with changes in temperature or pressure.

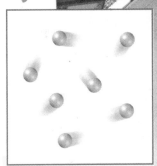

Particles in a gas

7 Describe How are particles in a gas like people outside of a movie theater?

_____

_____

_____

_____

_____

Shape Up!

How does particle motion affect the properties of solids, liquids, and gases?

Imagine what you would see if you put a few ice cubes into a pan on a hot stove. The hard blocks of ice would melt to form liquid water. If the pan is hot enough, the water would boil, giving off steam. Ice, liquid water, and the gaseous water in steam are all made up of the same water molecules. Yet ice looks and behaves differently than water or steam does. The kinetic theory of matter helps to explain the different properties of solids, liquids, and gases.

Active Reading **8 Identify** Underline words or phrases that describe the properties of solids, liquids, and gases.

Solids Have a Definite Volume and Shape

The fishbowl at the right contains a small toy castle. When the castle was added to the glass container, the castle kept its original size and shape. The castle, like all solid substances, has a definite shape and volume. The container does not change these properties of the toy. The particles in a solid are in fixed positions and are close together. Although the particles vibrate, they cannot move from one part of the solid to another part. As a result, a solid cannot easily change its shape or volume. If you force the particles apart, you can change the shape of a solid by breaking it into pieces. However, each of those pieces will still be a solid and have its own definite shape.

Think Outside the Book **Inquiry**

9 Model Think about the general shape and behavior of particles in solids, liquids, and gases within a container. What objects could be used as a model of particles? How could you model a container for your particles? Gather the materials and make your model. If you heat up your container, predict how your substances change their states of matter with respect to their temperature. What would happen if you put your container in a freezer? What would happen if you put your model in a container half its size? Gather the materials and make your model.

© Houghton Mifflin Harcourt Publishing Company • Image Credits: ©GK Hart/Vikki Hart/Taxi/Getty Images

Liquids Have a Definite Volume but Can Change Shape

Unlike the solid toy castle, the water in this fishbowl does not have a definite shape. The water has taken the shape of the round fishbowl. If you poured this same water into a rectangular fish tank, the water would take the shape of that container. However, the water would have the same volume as it did before. It would still take up the same amount of space. Like water, all liquids have a definite volume but no definite shape. The particles in a liquid are close together, but they are not tightly attached to one another as the particles in a solid are. Instead, particles in liquids can slide past one another. As a result, liquids can flow. Instead of having a rigid form, the particles in a liquid move and fill the bottom of the container they are in.

Gases Can Change in Volume and Shape

The small bubbles in this fishbowl are filled with gas. Gases do not have a definite volume or shape. The particles in a gas are very far apart compared to the particles in a solid or a liquid. The amount of space between the particles in a gas can change easily. If a rigid container has a certain amount of air inside and more air is pumped in, the volume of the gas does not change. The gas will still fill the entire container. Instead, the particles will be closer together. If the container is opened, the particles will spread out and mix with the air in the atmosphere.

Visualize It!

10 Apply Identify substances A, B, and C as a solid, a liquid, or a gas by placing a letter in each of the small circles below. In the larger circles, draw models of the particles of each substance.

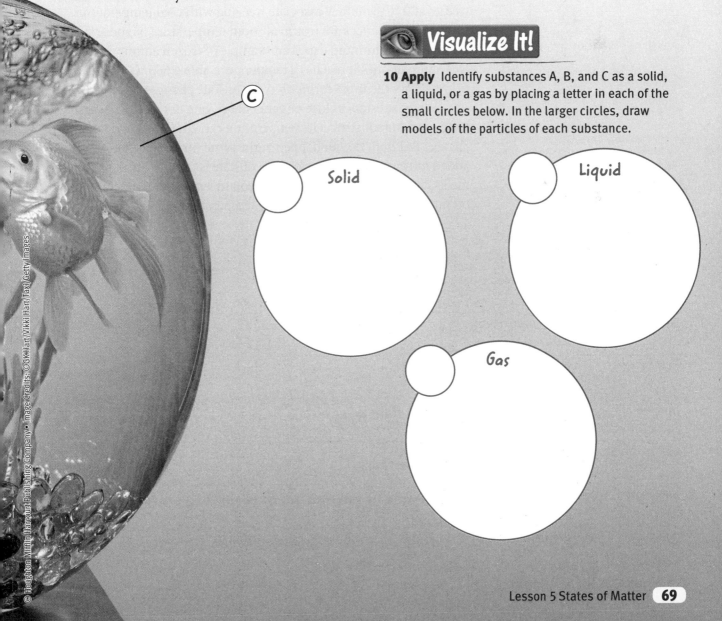

C

Solid

Liquid

Gas

Icicles grow as water drips down them and then freezes, sticking to the ice that is already there. Freezing is an example of a change of state.

What happens when substances change state?

Ice, liquid water, and water vapor are different states of the same substance. As liquid water turns into ice or water vapor, the water molecules themselves do not change. What changes are the motion of the molecules and the amount of space between them.

The Motion of the Particles Changes

The particles of a substance, even a solid, are always in motion. As a solid is heated, its particles gain energy and vibrate faster. Increased heat creates an increase in pressure, too. If the vibrations are fast enough, the particles break loose and slide past one another. The process in which a solid becomes a liquid is known as *melting*. As the temperature of a liquid is lowered, its particles lose energy, and therefore have a decrease in pressure. Eventually, the particles move slowly enough for the attractions between them to cause the liquid to become a solid. This process is called *freezing*. Because water freezes at 0 °C, you may associate freezing with cold temperatures. But some substances are frozen at room temperature or above. For example, an aluminum can is an example of frozen aluminum. It will not melt until it reaches a temperature above 660 °C! The table below shows the most common types of state changes.

When substances lose or gain energy, one of two things can happen to the substance: its temperature can change, or its state can change. But both do not happen at the same time. The energy that is added or removed during a change of state is used to break or form the attractions between particles. If you measure the temperature of boiling water, you will find that the temperature stays at 100 °C until all of the liquid has become a gas.

11 Apply Complete the table below with examples of state changes.

State change	Result	Example
Melting	A solid becomes a liquid.	
Freezing	A liquid becomes a solid.	
Boiling	A liquid becomes a gas (throughout).	
Evaporation	A liquid becomes a gas (at the liquid's surface).	A puddle dries out.
Condensation	A gas becomes a liquid.	
Sublimation	A solid becomes a gas.	Dry ice becomes a gas at room temperature.
Deposition	A gas becomes a solid.	Frost forms on a cold windowpane.

Making Glass

You can see through it, drink water from it, and create objects of art with it. It's glass, a substance that has been crafted by humans for about 5,000 years! Read on to see how a few simple ingredients can become a beautiful work of art.

Glassblowing

Glassblowing is the technique of shaping glass by blowing air into a blob of molten glass at the end of a tube. The *blowpipe* is the long, hollow tube that the glass blower uses to shape the molten glass. By blowing air through the blowpipe, a glass blower expands the open space inside the glass. This process is similar to inflating a balloon.

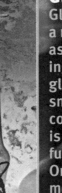

Glass from Sand?

Glass is made by heating a mixture of sand, soda ash, limestone, and other ingredients. Colored glass is made by adding small amounts of metal compounds. The mixture is melted in a roaring hot furnace at about 1,600 °C. Once the mixture melts, the molten glass can be shaped and allowed to cool into the solid state.

© Houghton Mifflin Harcourt Publishing Company • Image Credits: (bkgd) ©Niklas Bernstone/Johner Images Royalty-Free/Getty Images; (inset) ©James L. Amos/Photo Researchers, Inc.

Extend

Inquiry

12 Describe In your own words, describe the glass-blowing process.

13 Investigate People once thought that old glass windows are thicker at the bottom because the solid glass had flowed to the bottom over time. Research this theory and report your findings.

14 Investigate Research the various methods of making glass objects. Present your findings by doing one of the following:
- make a poster
- write a short essay
- draw a graphic novel

Visual Summary

To complete this summary, check the box that indicates true or false. Then use the key below to check your answers. You can use this page to review the main concepts of the lesson.

The particles in solids vibrate in place.

T F
15 ☐ ☐ Solids can easily change in volume.

States of Matter

The particles in liquids slide past each other.

T F
16 ☐ ☐ Liquids take the shape of their container.

The particles in gases move freely.

T F
17 ☐ ☐ When the distance between gas particles increases, the volume of the gas increases.

Answers: 15 F; 16 T; 17 T

---

18 Describe What happens to the kinetic energy of the particles of a substance as the substance changes from a liquid to a gas?

Lesson Review

Vocabulary

Draw a line to connect the following terms to the description of their particle motion.

1 solid

2 liquid

3 gas

A Particles are close together and locked in place.

B Particles are far apart and can move freely.

C Particles are close together and can slide past each other.

Key Concepts

4 Define What is the kinetic theory of matter?

_____

_____

_____

_____

_____

5 Analyze What happens to the temperature of a substance while it is changing state? Explain.

_____

_____

_____

_____

_____

6 Analyze What could you do to change the volume of a gas?

_____

_____

_____

Critical Thinking

7 Apply Can a tank of oxygen gas ever be half empty? Explain.

_____

_____

_____

_____

Use this drawing to answer the following questions.

8 Predict This jar contains helium gas. What would happen if the lid of this jar were removed?

_____

_____

_____

9 Explain How are the helium gas atoms in the jar different than particles in a liquid?

_____

_____

_____

_____

_____

10 Infer The particles that make up a rock are constantly in motion; however, a rock does not visibly vibrate. Why do you think this is?

_____

_____

_____

_____

_____

_____

_____

My Notes

Lesson 6

Changes of State

ESSENTIAL QUESTION

What happens when matter changes state?

By the end of this lesson, you should be able to describe changes of state in terms of the attraction and motion of particles.

7.PS1.6

Two changes of state happen at the hot springs in Yellowstone National Park. Very hot liquid water changes to invisible water vapor, or gas, above the surface of the spring. Then the water vapor changes back into a liquid as it cools in the air. This liquid water can be seen as fog.

Lesson Labs

Quick Labs
- Investigating Conservation of Mass
- Modeling Particle Motion
- Boiling Water Without Heating It

Exploration Lab
- Changes of State

Engage Your Brain

1 Identify Unscramble the letters of each word below to find objects in your classroom that are solids. Write the words on the blank lines.

PCLINE

_____

SKED

_____

OSBOK

_____

ODRO

_____

2 Describe Write your own caption for this photo.

_____

_____

_____

 ## Active Reading

3 Apply Use context clues to write your own definitions for the words *converted* and *constantly*.

Example sentence
When an ice cube melts, a solid is <u>converted</u> to a liquid.

converted:

_____

_____

Example sentence
The particles that make up matter are <u>constantly</u> in motion.

constantly:

_____

_____

Vocabulary Terms
- freezing
- melting
- evaporation
- boiling
- condensation
- sublimation
- deposition

4 Identify This list contains the vocabulary terms you'll learn in this lesson. As you read, circle the definition of each term.

The Fact of the Matter

Active Reading

5 Identify As you read, underline the three most familiar states of matter.

What happens when matter changes state?

Eating ice cream on a hot summer day can be a messy business. Faster than you can lick it, the ice cream melts and drips down your hand. As ice cream melts, it goes through a change of state. The three most familiar states of matter are solid, liquid, and gas. A change of state is the change of a substance from one physical form of matter to another. When a substance undergoes a physical change, it changes its appearance, not its identity.

Energy Is Gained and Lost

Energy must be added or removed to change a substance from one state to another. When a substance gains or loses energy, its temperature changes or its state changes. These two changes do not happen at the same time; the temperature remains constant until the change of state is complete. In the graph below, notice that the temperature of a solid remains the same until all of the solid has melted into a liquid. Also, the temperature of a substance remains the same until all of the liquid changes to a gas.

Solid wax becomes liquid when the warmth of the flame causes a change of state.

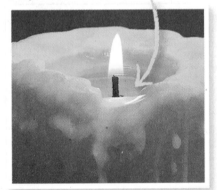

Visualize It!

6 Apply Use the graph to determine which point—A, B, or C—represents a candle melting. Circle the correct letter.

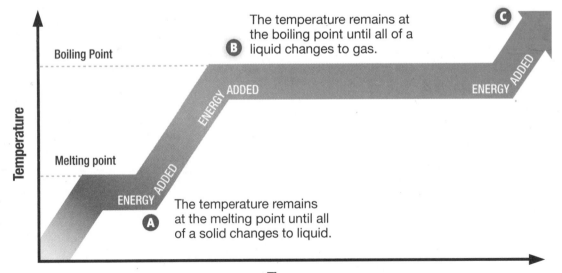

The temperature remains at the boiling point until all of a liquid changes to gas. **B**

The temperature remains at the melting point until all of a solid changes to liquid. **A**

Boiling Point

Melting point

Temperature

ENERGY ADDED

Time

Particle Motion Changes

All matter is made of tiny particles that are in constant motion. During a change of state, the motion of the particles changes. Particles can break away from each other and gain more freedom to move. This happens when a solid changes to a liquid or a liquid changes to a gas. Particles can also attract each other more strongly and have less freedom to move. This happens when gas changes to a liquid or a liquid changes to a solid.

Energy Is Conserved

During a change of state, a substance must gain energy from the environment or lose energy to the environment, but the total amount of energy is conserved. Look at the diagram of the water cycle below. Water is converted from liquid water to water vapor, to solid snow, and back to liquid. Each change of state represents a transfer of energy either into or out of the water cycle from the surrounding environment, but energy is never created or destroyed.

 **Visualize It!**

7 Analyze Determine whether water particles will have more or less freedom to move at each stage, A, B, and C. Write *more freedom* or *less freedom* in each box.

Loss of Energy

Loss of Energy

B

Gain of Energy

C

A

Gain of Energy

8 Categorize Identify whether each picture below shows a (1) gain of energy or a (2) loss of energy for the substance. Write the appropriate number in the box at the bottom of each picture.

An ice cube melts.

A puddle dries up.

A lake freezes.

Solid Facts

How do solids and liquids change states?

Temperature and pressure affect the changing states of solids and liquids. Particles in a liquid can slide past each other, but particles in a solid can only move enough to vibrate. Removing energy from a liquid can cause it to change to a solid as the particles stop sliding past each other. Adding energy to a solid can cause it to change to a liquid as particles begin sliding past each other.

By Freezing

The change in state in which a liquid becomes a solid is called **freezing**. When a liquid is cooled, its particles have less energy than they did before. This means it also has less pressure. The particles slow down, and the attractions between particles increase. Eventually, the particles lock into the fixed arrangement of a typical solid. The temperature at which a liquid substance changes into a solid is the liquid's *freezing point*. Different substances have different freezing points. For example, the freezing point of water is 0 °C. When energy is removed at 0 °C, water converts to its frozen state—ice. The freezing point of the element mercury is –38.8 °C. At 0 °C, mercury is still a liquid.

9 Predict In which sample of water do the water particles have more energy: 5 grams (g) of ice cubes at –10 °C, or 5 g of liquid water at 20 °C? How do you know?

_____
_____
_____
_____

Visualize It!

10 Identify In the box below each picture, write the state of the substance shown.

Solids can change to liquids.
Liquids can change to solids.

A _____   B _____

The freezing point of water is 0 °C (32 °F). Liquid water changes to solid ice at this temperature. You can see this change taking place in the waterfall.

By Melting

Particles in a solid have an ordered arrangement. When a solid is warmed, its particles have more energy than they did before. This also means the particles have higher pressure. The particles speed up, and the attraction between the particles decreases. Eventually, the particles are able to slide past one another. This change of state from a solid to a liquid is called **melting**. The temperature at which the substance changes from a solid to a liquid is called the *melting point*. Melting is the reverse of freezing. Water freezes and melts at 0 °C. Mercury freezes and melts at −38.8 °C.

Think about a melting snowman. Energy from the sun is added to the solid snow. The particles in the snow begin to move faster. When the temperature of the snow reaches 0° C, the added energy of the particles will overcome some of the attractions that hold the particles in place. The snow starts to melt. As the sun continues to shine on the snowman, even more attractions are broken. Eventually, all of the snow turns to liquid water.

Active Reading **11 Apply** Describe what happens to water particles when ice melts.

_____

_____

_____

_____

_____

_____

© Houghton Mifflin Harcourt Publishing Company • Image Credits: (bg) ©ION/amanaimagesRF/Getty Images

Think Outside the Book

12 Model Draw the model of a substance that changes from one state of matter to another when exposed to certain temperatures or pressures. Then create a second model that shows the effects of the temperature or pressure on the substance. Your model should represent the changes to the atoms of that substance. Interpret your model by writing a summary that describes how the atoms change from the first state to the second.

Inquiry

13 Infer Both the freezing temperature and the melting temperature of water are the same (0 °C). Explain why a substance like water freezes and melts at the same temperature.

_____

_____

_____

_____

Bubbling Over

How do liquids and gases change state?

Particles in a gas have a great deal of energy. Removing enough energy from a gas causes a gas to change into a liquid or a solid. Adding enough energy to a liquid or a solid causes it to change into a gas. The process by which a liquid or a solid changes to a gas is *vaporization*.

By Evaporation or Boiling

As a liquid is warmed, its particles gain energy. Some particles gain enough energy that they escape from the surface of the liquid and become a gas. This process is called **evaporation**. Evaporation occurs slowly at a range of temperatures, but it happens more quickly at higher temperatures.

A rapid change from a liquid to a gas, or vapor, is called **boiling**. This change takes place throughout a liquid, not just at the surface. As a liquid is warmed to a high enough temperature, bubbles form. The specific temperature at which this occurs in a liquid is called the *boiling point*. As air pressure changes at different elevations above sea level, so does the boiling point of liquids. The greater the air pressure, the higher the boiling point of a liquid.

14 Predict What would happen to the boiling point of water at 8,000 m above sea level, where air pressure is lower?

_____

_____

_____

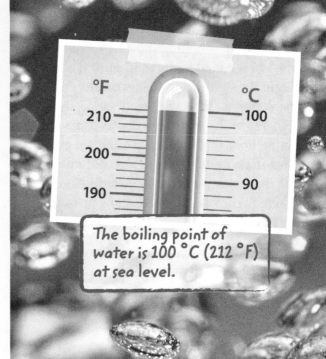

The boiling point of water is 100 °C (212 °F) at sea level.

Visualize It!

15 Identify In the box below each picture, write the state of the substance shown.

Liquids change to gases.
Gases change to liquids.

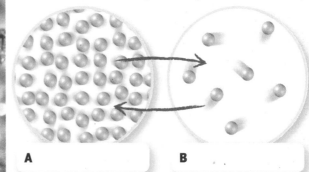

A   B

By Condensation

Particles in a gas have very little attraction to one another. As a gas is cooled, its particles lose energy. The attraction between particles overcomes the speed of their motion, and a liquid forms. This change of state from a gas to a liquid is called **condensation**. Condensation is the reverse of evaporation.

Grass is often wet in early morning because gaseous water vapor in the air condenses on the cool grass. Water droplets form on the outside of a cold glass of lemonade when water vapor in the warm air condenses on the cool glass.

Look at the photo below of contrail lines left by jet planes. Water vapor and soot form when fuel burns in jet engines. The gaseous water vapor condenses as tiny liquid water droplets. The water droplets then freeze into ice crystals on the soot particles to form a contrail. The word *contrail* is short for condensation trail.

16 Apply Indicate whether the change of state in each process causes particles to (A) have more freedom or (B) have less freedom. Write the appropriate letter next to each process.

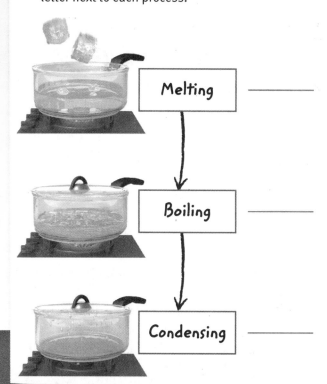

Melting _____

Boiling _____

Condensing _____

Visualize It!

17 Compare How are the planes' contrail lines similar to clouds?

_____

_____

_____

_____

_____

The dramatic effect of contrails is the result of condensation and freezing.

Into Thin Air

How do solids and gases change state?

Under the right conditions, some solids and gases can change state without ever becoming a liquid. The substance must gain or lose a great deal of energy for this to occur.

By Sublimation

Have you ever received a package of food shipped in dry ice to keep it frozen? If so, you may have noticed that the ice disappears without leaving a puddle of liquid. Dry ice is frozen carbon dioxide (CO_2). It changes from its solid state directly into a gas. The change from a solid state directly into a gas is called **sublimation**. As the particles of solid dry ice gain energy, their motion completely overcomes the attraction between the particles, and the particles escape into the air as gas.

Dry ice is extremely cold, about $-80\ °C$, and at room temperature, $25\ °C$, the air provides the energy for the dry ice to sublimate. A fog is observed as water vapor condenses when it comes in contact with cold CO_2 gas.

Snow and ice formed by water sublimate at below-freezing temperatures. To see sublimation in action, hang wet clothes outside on a day when temperatures are below freezing. First, the water in the clothes freezes, and then the solid ice sublimates into the air.

No liquid is visible in the bowl as the solid CO_2 disappears. It sublimates from a solid directly to an invisible gas.

> ### Think Outside the Book
>
> **18 Research** With a partner, find another substance that can sublimate. Describe the conditions under which sublimation occurs.

By Deposition

In physical science, **deposition** is the change in state from a gas directly to a solid. Deposition is the process by which ice crystals form in clouds. The photo on this page shows deposition of invisible water vapor into ice crystals on a cold window.

When conditions are right, deposition occurs when the particles of a gas lose energy. Attraction between particles locks the particles into the rigid structure of a solid. No liquid is formed in the process.

Active Reading **19 Compare** Explain how sublimation and deposition are alike and how they are different.

_____

_____

_____

_____

> Ice crystals form on a cold window when water vapor in the air is converted to ice by the process of deposition.

20 Relate Complete Column 1 and Column 2 to identify opposite processes. In the third column, indicate whether the process in Column 1 or Column 2 is the result of a gain of energy.

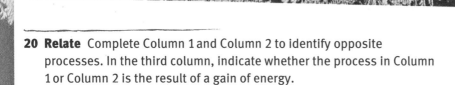

Column 1	Column 2	
The opposite of...	is	Gain in Energy
deposition		
	condensation	Column 1
melting		

Conserve

What happens to matter when a change of state occurs?

When matter changes from one state to another, it remains the same kind of matter. Its physical state changes, but its chemical identity does not. For example, an ice cube and the puddle it forms when it melts are both made up of water.

Energy and Motion of Particles Change

You might ask, "What *does* change as a result of a change of state?" The answer is that the energy of the particles, the movement of the particles, and the distance between them change. You can see these changes in the diagram below.

Active Reading

21 Identify As you read, underline the ways particles of matter are affected by a change of state.

Visualize It!

22 Apply Label the state changes that are taking place in both directions of the arrows at stage A, B, and C. Draw the missing model for the gas state.

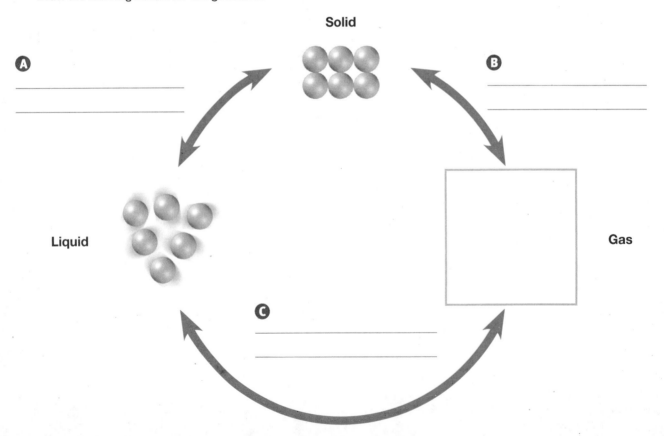

Solid

A _____

B _____

Liquid

Gas

C _____

Mass Is Conserved

What happens to the *amount* of matter in a change of state? Suppose you do an experiment. You put ice cubes in a sealed container so that the container plus the ice has a total mass of 100 g. You warm the ice to the melting point. It becomes liquid water. Then you continue to warm the water to the boiling point so that it becomes a gas. After each step, you measure the mass of the water. You find no difference in the mass. The sealed container at each state has a mass of 100 g. You know that the mass of the container itself cannot change. So you can conclude that the gaseous water vapor has the same mass as the liquid water and the solid ice. The mass of a substance does not change when its state changes. Each state contains the same amount of matter.

Think about the particles of water in the closed container. They do not disappear. Even the particles that escape from the liquid state stay in the container as gas. Because the number of particles in the container stays the same, the amount of matter is conserved.

water   ice

Mass is conserved when a change of state occurs.

Visualize It!

23 Apply A flask of water is sealed with a balloon and heated to various temperatures on a hot plate. Fill in the missing information below.

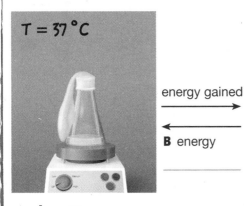 T = 37 °C

energy gained →

← **B** energy
_____

  T = 100 °C

C energy
_____
←

energy lost →

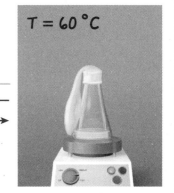 T = 60 °C

A m = _____   m = 52 g   **D** m = _____

24 Evaluate Explain how the system of the flask and the balloon illustrates the conservation of mass.

_____

_____

_____

_____

Visual Summary

To complete this summary, fill in the blanks with the correct word or phrase. Then use the key below to check your answers. You can use this page to review the main concepts of the lesson.

Changes of State

A solid can change to a liquid or gas.

25 The change from a solid to a liquid is called _____.

26 The change of a solid directly to a gas is called _____.

A gas can change to a solid or a liquid.

27 Water vapor changes directly to ice by _____.

28 _____ is the process in which water vapor changes to a liquid.

A liquid can change to a gas or a solid.

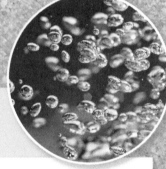

29 Ice is formed from liquid water during the process of _____.

30 Two ways that liquid water can become a gas are by _____.

Mass is conserved when a change of state occurs.

31 The amount of mass _____ _____ during a change of state.

Answers: 25 melting; 26 sublimation; 27 deposition; 28 Condensation; 29 freezing; 30 boiling and evaporation; 31 stays the same

32 Predict What would happen to the amount of matter on Earth if mass were not conserved during changes of state?

Lesson Review

Vocabulary

Draw a line to connect the following terms to their definitions.

1 freezing

2 evaporation

3 sublimation

4 melting

A change of state from solid to liquid

B change of state from liquid to gas

C change of state from solid to gas

D change of state from liquid to solid

Key Concepts

5 Describe What happens to particles when a substance gains energy and changes state?

_____

_____

_____

6 Explain What happens to the energy that is lost when water freezes?

_____

_____

_____

7 Compare How does the movement of particles in a stick of butter differ from the movement of particles in a dish of melted butter?

_____

_____

_____

_____

8 Identify As water is cooled, at what temperature do its particles become fixed in place?

_____

_____

Critical Thinking

Use this drawing to answer the following questions.

9 Relate The drawing represents the movement of particles in a substance. What changes of state can this substance undergo?

_____

_____

_____

10 Describe What processes will the substance in the drawing undergo when those changes of state occur? Explain.

_____

_____

_____

_____

_____

_____

11 Compare How do evaporation and boiling differ?

_____

_____

_____

12 Apply The boiling point of a substance in City A is found to be 145 °C. The boiling point of the same substance in City B is 141 °C. Which city, A or B, is at a higher elevation? How do you know?

_____

_____

My Notes

Unit 1

Lesson 1
ESSENTIAL QUESTION
What properties define matter?

Relate mass, weight, volume, and density to one another.

Lesson 4
ESSENTIAL QUESTION
How do pure substances and mixtures compare?

Distinguish between pure substances and mixtures.

Lesson 2
ESSENTIAL QUESTION
What are physical and chemical properties of matter?

Classify and compare substances based on their physical and chemical properties.

Lesson 5
ESSENTIAL QUESTION
How do particles in solids, liquids, and gases move?

Model the motion of particles in solids, liquids, and gases.

Lesson 3
ESSENTIAL QUESTION
What are physical and chemical changes of matter?

Distinguish between physical and chemical changes of matter.

Lesson 6
ESSENTIAL QUESTION
What happens when matter changes state?

Describe changes of state in terms of the attraction and motion of particles.

Think Outside the Book

2 Synthesize Choose one of these activities to help synthesize what you have learned in this unit.

☐ Using what you learned in lessons 1, 2, 3, and 4, explain how matter can be classified by its physical and chemical properties by creating an informative brochure. Include examples of both pure substances and mixtures.

☐ Using what you learned in lessons 5 and 6, create a presentation that describes the particle movement in a substance as it changes from a solid, to a liquid, to a gas, and then back to a solid.

Connect ESSENTIAL QUESTIONS
Lessons 4, 5, and 6

1 Synthesize How can understanding changes of state help you to separate a saltwater solution?

_____

_____

_____

_____

_____

Unit 1 Review

Vocabulary

Check the box to show whether each statement is true or false.

T	F	
☐	☐	**1** <u>Matter</u> is anything that has mass and takes up space.
☐	☐	**2** The difference between an elemental molecule and a <u>compound</u> molecule is the type of atoms with which it is made.
☐	☐	**3** <u>Evaporation</u> is the change of state from a gas to a liquid.
☐	☐	**4** A <u>solid</u> has a definite volume and shape.
☐	☐	**5** A <u>physical property</u> can be measured without changing the identity of the substance.

Key Concepts

Read each question below, and circle the best answer.

6 One chemical property that can be measured in a substance is its reactivity with water. What is another chemical property that can be measured in a substance?

A density

B flammability

C malleability

D solubility

7 Matter is made up of particles. Which of the following statements is true about these particles?

A The particles that make up solids do not move.

B The particles that make up liquids do not move.

C The particles that make up all matter are constantly in motion.

D Only the particles that make up gases are constantly in motion.

8 Two balloons are inflated to an equal volume. Balloon 2 is placed in the freezer for 20 minutes.

Balloon 1   Balloon 2

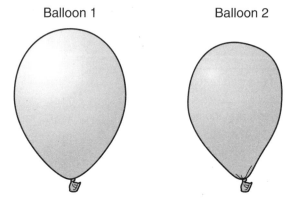

Why would freezing a balloon produce the results shown in Balloon 2?

A Increased kinetic energy decreases the attraction between particles inside the balloon.

B Increased kinetic energy increases the attraction between particles inside the balloon.

C Decreased kinetic energy decreases the attraction between particles inside the balloon.

D Decreased kinetic energy increases the attraction between particles inside the balloon.

9 Which of the following statements describes a liquid?

A A liquid has both a definite shape and a definite volume.

B A liquid has neither a definite shape nor a definite volume.

C A liquid has a definite shape but not a definite volume.

D A liquid has a definite volume but not a definite shape.

10 A water molecule is made up of one oxygen atom and two hydrogen atoms. Why is water considered a pure substance?

A Water can be broken down by physical means.

B Water can be combined with other substances by physical means.

C Each water molecule is identical.

D Water molecules are made up of different types of atoms.

11 A beaker containing a certain substance has heat applied to it. The particles that make up the substance begin to move farther apart from each other.

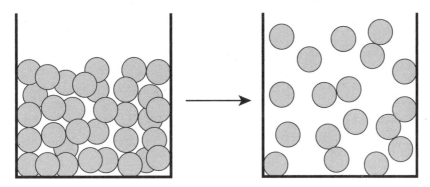

What change of state could be occurring to the substance in the beaker?

A The substance is changing from a gas to a liquid.

B The substance is changing from a gas to a solid.

C The substance is changing from a liquid to a solid.

D The substance is changing from a liquid to a gas.

12 The law of conservation of mass states that mass cannot be created or destroyed. To what type of change does this law apply?

A physical changes only

B chemical changes only

C both physical and chemical changes

D only mass that is not undergoing change

13 A beaker containing ice and water is placed on a warm hot plate. Will the ice in the beaker undergo a physical or chemical change?

A a physical change because it will change state

B a chemical change because it will change state

C a physical change because it will form a new substance

D a chemical change because it will form a new substance

14 What is the boiling point of water?

A 0 °C   **C** 100 °C

B 32 °C   **D** 212 °C

15 A rock is dropped into a graduated cylinder filled with 35 mL of water.

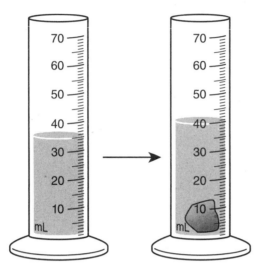

What is the volume of the rock? (Hint: 1 mL water = 1 cm³)

A 40 cm³

B 14 cm³

C 5 cm³

D 35 cm³

16 The instrument below is used to measure an object.

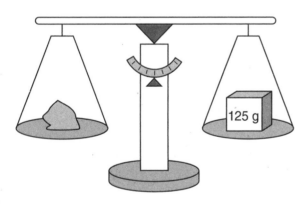

What is the instrument measuring?

A gravity

B weight

C density

D mass

17 The diagram below shows a chemical reaction.

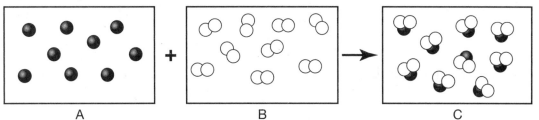

What is being formed in the box labeled C?

A a compound   **C** a mixture

B an element   **D** an atom

Critical Thinking

Answer the following questions in the space provided.

18 In the space below, sketch the particles in a solution, a suspension, and a colloid.

Give an example of a solution, a suspension, and a colloid.

Solution: _____

Suspension: _____

Colloid: _____

19 A sample liquid is heated in a closed container until it changes to a gas. What happens to the size of the particles in the sample?

_____

What happens to the number of particles in the sample?

_____

What happens to the average speed of the particles?

_____

20 Describe the difference between a chemical change and a physical change.

_____

_____

What are three examples of physical changes?

_____

_____

_____

What are three signs that a chemical change has taken place?

_____

_____

_____

How does temperature affect chemical changes?

_____

_____

Connect ESSENTIAL QUESTIONS
Lessons 1 and 2

Answer the following question in the space provided.

21 An unknown substance has a volume of 2 cm³ and a mass of 38.6 grams. What is the density of the sample? _____

Material	Density (g/cm³)
water	1.0
aluminum	2.7
iron	7.9
silver	10.5
gold	19.3

Use the chart above to find the identity of the unknown sample: _____

List three other physical properties that could be used to identify this sample.

_____

_____

_____

Atoms and Interactions of Matter

Big Idea

The atomic structure of an element determines the properties of the element and determines how the element interacts with other elements.

▭ 7.PS1.1, 7.PS1.4, 7.PS1.5

At room temperature, gold is a solid. At very high temperatures, however, solid gold becomes a liquid that flows.

What do you think?

Gold and water have different properties, but they are both made of matter. Matter can also be changed through chemical reactions. Can you think of any matter that might change its properties through a chemical reaction?

Unit 2
Atoms and Interactions of Matter

Matter Up Close

Matter is anything that has mass and takes up space. All things on Earth, large and small, are made up of matter. Atoms are the smallest parts of the matter you see. You can't see atoms with your eyes alone.

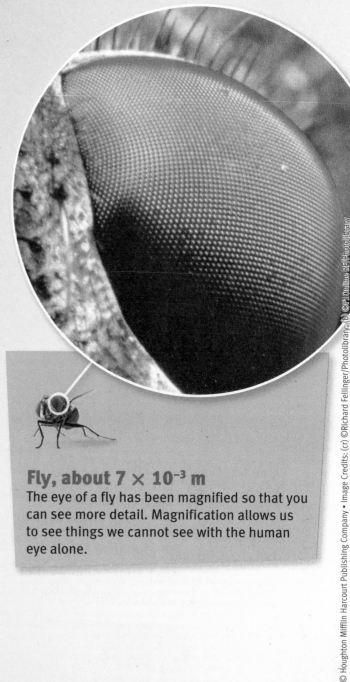

Fly, about 7×10^{-3} m
The eye of a fly has been magnified so that you can see more detail. Magnification allows us to see things we cannot see with the human eye alone.

Grain of salt, about 5×10^{-4} m

This seasoning and preservative can be harvested from seawater.

Table salt

Rhinovirus, about 3×10^{-8} m

Watch out for this virus—it causes the common cold.

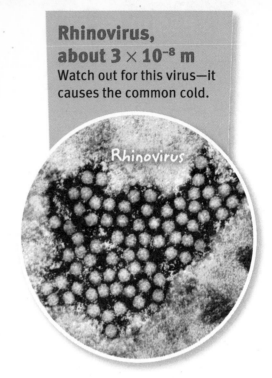

Rhinovirus

Helium atom, about 3×10^{-11} m

Atoms are so small that they cannot be viewed with traditional microscopes. Often, they are represented by models such as this one.

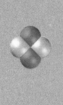

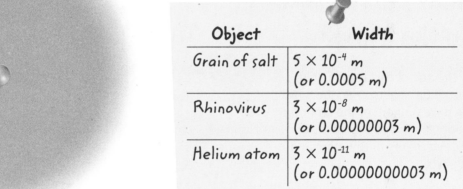

Object	Width
Grain of salt	5×10^{-4} m (or 0.0005 m)
Rhinovirus	3×10^{-8} m (or 0.00000003 m)
Helium atom	3×10^{-11} m (or 0.00000000003 m)

Take It Home   Size Is Relative

By looking at ratios of sizes, you can compare the relative sizes of objects. How many times greater is the size of a grain of salt than a rhinovirus particle? You can write a ratio to find the answer:

$$\frac{\text{grain of salt}}{\text{rhinovirus}} = \frac{0.0005 \text{ m}}{0.00000003 \text{ m}} \approx 17,000$$

A grain of salt is about 17,000 times the size of a rhinovirus.

A Determine how many times greater a rhinovirus is than a helium atom.

B Measure the width of one of your textbooks to the nearest millimeter. How many helium atoms could you line up across the book?

See **ScienceSaurus**® for more information about atoms.

The Atom

ESSENTIAL QUESTION

How do we know what parts make up the atom?

By the end of this lesson, you should be able to describe how the development of the atomic theory has led to the modern understanding of the atom and its parts.

7.PS1.1

This sand castle is made up of tiny grains of sand. Each grain of sand is made up of particles called atoms, which are too small to see.

Engage Your Brain

1 Identify Read over the following vocabulary terms. In the spaces provided, place a + if you know the term well, a ~ if you have heard the term but are not sure what it means, and a ? if you are unfamiliar with the term. Then write a sentence that includes the word you are most familiar with.

_____ atom

_____ electron

_____ neutron

_____ proton

_____ nucleus

Sentence using known word:

_____

_____

2 Compare Use the figure below to answer the questions. Check T or F to show whether you think each statement is true or false.

T	F	
☐	☐	Electrons move in orbits in the same way planets orbit the sun.
☐	☐	If this were a model of the atom, the nucleus would be in the same place as the sun.

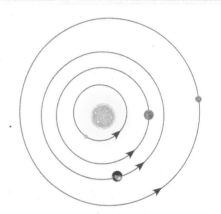

Active Reading

3 Apply Use context clues to write your own definition for the words *theory* and *revise*.

Example sentence
The scientist developed a <u>theory</u> to explain the structure of the atom.

theory:

_____

_____

Example sentence
As scientists learned new information about atoms, they had to <u>revise</u> the model of the atom.

revise:

_____

_____

Vocabulary Terms

- atom
- electron
- nucleus
- proton
- neutron
- electron cloud
- atomic number
- mass number

4 Apply As you learn the definition of each vocabulary term in this lesson, create your own definition or sketch to help you remember the meaning of the term.

© Houghton Mifflin Harcourt Publishing Company • Image Credits: (bg) ©Stuart Dee/Photographer's Choice/Getty Images

As a Matter of Fact

What makes up matter?

Imagine that you are cutting fabric to make a quilt. You cut a piece of fabric in half. Then you cut each half in half again. Could you keep cutting the pieces in half forever? Around 400 BCE, a Greek philosopher named Democritus (dih·MAHK·rih·tuhs) thought that you would eventually end up with a particle that could not be cut. He called this particle *atomos,* a Greek word meaning "not able to be divided." Aristotle (AIR·ih·staht'l), another Greek philosopher, disagreed. He did not believe that such a particle could make up all substances found in nature.

Neither Democritus nor Aristotle did experiments to test their ideas. It would be centuries before scientists tested these hypotheses. Within the past 200 years, scientists have come to agree that matter is made up of small particles. Democritus's term *atom* is used to describe these particles.

There is a limit to how small you can cut a piece of fabric. Even the smallest piece of fabric you can cut is made up of a huge number of particles of many different elements.

Atoms

An **atom** is the smallest particle into which an element can be divided and still be the same element. People used to think that atoms could not be divided into anything simpler. Scientists now know that atoms are made of even smaller particles. But the atom is still considered to be the basic unit of matter because it is the smallest unit that has the chemical properties of an element.

You cannot see individual atoms. But they make up everything you do see. The food you eat and the water you drink are made of atoms. Plants, such as moss, are made of atoms. Even things you cannot see are made of atoms. The air you breathe is made of atoms. There are many types of atoms that combine in different ways to make all substances.

You can use a light microscope to see the cells that make up a tiny moss leaf. But you cannot see the atoms that make up the substances in the cells. Atoms are so small that you cannot see them with an ordinary microscope. Only powerful instruments can make images of atoms. How small are atoms? Think about a penny. A penny contains about 2×10^{22}, or 20,000,000,000,000,000,000,000 atoms of copper and zinc. That's almost 3,000 billion times more atoms than there are people living on Earth!

Moss

Atoms are much smaller than the cells in living things.

Visualize It! (Inquiry)

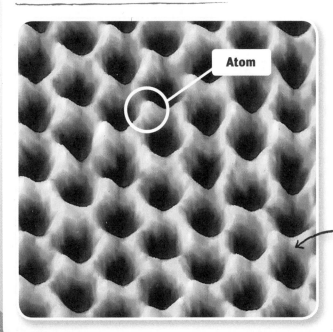

Atom

This image shows how carbon atoms are connected in a substance. The photo was taken with a special type of electron microscope.

6 Analyze What can you infer about atoms from this image? What can't you infer from the image?

_____

_____

_____

_____

_____

Something Old, Something New

Who developed the atomic theory?

In 1808, a British chemist named John Dalton published an atomic theory. This was the start of the modern theory of the atom. Dalton's theory could explain most observations of matter at that time. Over time, scientists learned more about atoms. The atomic theory was revised as scientists discovered new information.

John Dalton

Active Reading **7 Identify** As you read, underline the four main ideas of Dalton's theory of the atom.

Unlike the ideas of Democritus and Aristotle, John Dalton's theory was based on evidence from experiments. Dalton's theory stated that all matter is made up of atoms. He also thought that atoms cannot be created, divided, or destroyed.

Dalton's theory also stated that all atoms of a certain element are identical. But they are different from atoms of all other elements. For example, every atom of carbon is the same as every other atom of carbon. However, every atom of carbon is different from any atom of oxygen. Dalton also thought that atoms join with other atoms to make new substances. For example, an oxygen atom combines with two hydrogen atoms to form water. Every substance is made up of atoms combined in certain ways.

J. J. Thomson

In 1897, J. J. Thomson's experiments provided evidence that atoms are made up of even smaller particles. He found particles within the atom that have a negative charge. These negatively charged particles later became known as **electrons**. Thomson thought that an atom was a positive sphere with the electrons mixed through it, as shown below.

1897

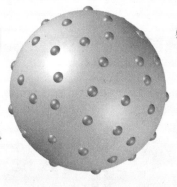

8 Model Describe how you would illustrate J. J. Thomson's model of the atom using small beads and clay.

_____

_____

_____

_____

1808

Ernest Rutherford

In 1909, Ernest Rutherford conducted an experiment to study the parts of the atom. His experiment suggested that atoms have a **nucleus**—a small, dense center that has a positive charge and is surrounded by moving electrons. Rutherford later found that the nucleus is made up of smaller particles. He called the positively charged particles in the nucleus **protons**.

Niels Bohr

Four years later, Niels Bohr made observations that led to a new theory of how the electrons in the atom behaved. Bohr agreed that an atom has a positive nucleus surrounded by electrons. In his model, electrons move around the nucleus in circular paths. Each path is a certain distance from the nucleus. Bohr's model helped scientists predict the chemical properties of elements. However, scientists have since made observations that could not be explained by Bohr's model. The model of the atom has been revised to explain these observations.

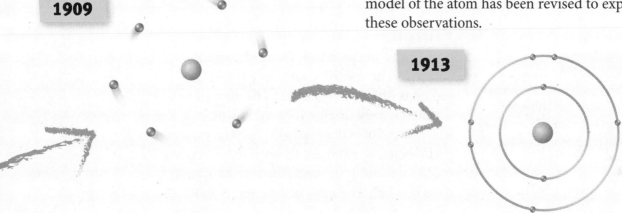

1909

1913

What is the current atomic theory?

Modern atomic theory is based on the work of many scientists. It keeps Dalton's ideas that atoms are the basic unit of matter and that the atoms of each element are unique. The experiments of Thomson and Rutherford showed that atoms are made up of electrons and protons. James Chadwick was Rutherford's student. In 1932, Chadwick discovered that the nucleus contains uncharged particles called **neutrons**. Protons, electrons, and neutrons are called subatomic particles because they are smaller than the atom. In the current atomic theory, electrons do not move in circular paths around the nucleus as Bohr thought. Instead, the current theory suggests that electrons move within an area around the nucleus called the **electron cloud**.

9 Analyze Today's model of the atom looks different from the models that came before it. Why has the model of the atom changed?

_____

_____

_____

_____

Up and Atom!

What are the parts of an atom?

This model of an atom shows where protons, neutrons, and electrons are found within the atom. Protons and neutrons are found in the center of the electron cloud. The particles in this model are not shown in their correct proportions. If they were, the protons and neutrons would be too small to see.

Active Reading

10 Identify As you read this page and the next, underline the sentences that define the three types of particles that make up an atom.

Protons

Protons are the positively charged particles of atoms. The relative charge of a single proton is often written as 1+. The mass of a proton is very small—1.7×10^{-24} g, or 0.0000000000000000000000017 g. The masses of particles in the atom are so small that scientists made a new unit for them: the unified atomic mass unit (u). The mass of a proton is about 1 u.

Neutrons

Neutrons are particles that have no electric charge. They are a little more massive than protons are. But the mass of a neutron is still very close to 1 u. Atoms usually have at least as many neutrons as they have protons.

Together, protons and neutrons form the nucleus of the atom. The nucleus is located at the center of an atom. This model of a beryllium atom shows that the nucleus of this atom is made up of four protons and five neutrons. Because each proton has a 1+ charge, the overall charge of this nucleus is 4+. (Remember: Neutrons have no electric charge.) The volume of the nucleus is very small compared to the rest of the atom. But protons and neutrons are the most massive particles in an atom. So, the nucleus is very dense. If it were possible to have a nucleus the volume of a grape, that nucleus would have a mass greater than 9 million metric tons!

Proton

Neutron

Nucleus

The Electron Cloud

The negatively charged particles of the atom are called electrons. Electrons move around the nucleus very quickly. Scientists have found that it is not possible to determine both their exact positions and speed at the same time. This is why we picture the electrons as being in an electron cloud around the nucleus.

Compared with protons and neutrons, electrons have very little mass. It takes more than 1,800 electrons to equal the mass of 1 proton. The mass of an electron is so small that it is usually thought of as almost 0 u.

The charge of a single electron is represented as 1–. The charges of protons and electrons are opposite but equal. The number of protons in an atom equals the number of electrons. So the atom has a net, or overall, charge of 0. For example, this beryllium atom contains four electrons. The combined charge of the electrons is 4–. But remember that the charge of the nucleus is 4+.

$$(4+) + (4-) = 0$$

The net charge of the atom is 0.

An atom can lose or gain electrons. When this happens, we refer to the atom as an *ion*. Ions have a net charge that is not 0.

11 Summarize Complete the following table with information about the parts of the atom.

Part of the atom	Location in the atom	Electric charge	Relative mass
Proton			Slightly less massive than a neutron
	Nucleus		
		1–	

Take a Number!

How can we describe atoms?

Think of all the substances you see and touch every day. Are all of these substances the same? No. The substances that make up this book are quite different from the substances in the air you are breathing. If all atoms are composed of the same particles, how can there be so many different types of substances? Different combinations of protons, neutrons, and electrons produce atoms with different properties. The number of each kind of particle within an atom determines that atom's unique properties. In turn, these different atoms combine to form the different substances all around us.

By Atomic Number

The number of protons distinguishes the atoms of one element from the atoms of another. For example, every hydrogen atom contains one proton. And every carbon atom has exactly six protons in its nucleus.

The number of protons in the nucleus of an atom is the **atomic number** of that atom. Hydrogen has an atomic number of 1 because each of its atoms contains just one proton. Carbon has an atomic number of 6 because each of its atoms contains six protons.

Active Reading 12 **Compare** How are two atoms of the same element alike?

_____

_____

_____

_____

_____

Think Outside the Book (Inquiry)

13 **Apply** Research how scientists make new types of atoms using particle accelerators. Choose one element that has been made by scientists. Create a brochure that describes its properties and how it was made.

14 **Model** Choose an element, and develop a two-dimensional model of an atom of this element.

Be sure to illustrate its structure by including the correct number of protons, neutrons, and electrons and their relative positions to one another. Calculate and illustrate the charges for each. Now draw a model of a different element, including its protons, neutrons, and electrons. How do they differ? Are their properties the same?

By Mass Number

The atoms of a certain element always have the same number of protons. But they may not always have the same number of neutrons. For example, all chlorine atoms have 17 protons. But some chlorine atoms have 18 neutrons. Other chlorine atoms have 20 neutrons. These two types of chlorine atoms are called isotopes. *Isotopes* are atoms of the same element that have different numbers of neutrons. Some elements have many isotopes, and other elements have just a few.

The total number of protons and neutrons in an atom's nucleus is its **mass number**. Different isotopes of chlorine have different mass numbers. What is the mass number of a chlorine atom that contains 18 neutrons?

$$17 + 18 = 35$$

The mass number of this atom is 35.

The helium in these balloons is less massive than an equal volume of the nitrogen in the air, so the balloons float.

---

15 Calculate Use this model of a helium atom to find its atomic number and mass number.

Proton

Neutron

Atomic number:

Mass number:

Visual Summary

To complete this summary, check the box that indicates true or false. Then use the key below to check your answers. You can use this page to review the main concepts of the lesson.

The Atom

An atom is the smallest particle of an element. All substances are made up of atoms.

T F
16 ☐ ☐ You can use a light microscope to see the atoms in fabric.

Atomic theory has changed over time as scientists learned more about the particles that make up matter.

T F
17 ☐ ☐ According to current atomic theory, electrons are in fixed locations.

Atoms contain a positively charged nucleus surrounded by a negatively charged electron cloud.

T F
18 ☐ ☐ The nucleus contains neutrons and electrons.

Atomic number and mass number are used to describe atoms.

T F
19 ☐ ☐ Every atom of the same element has the same atomic number.

Answers: 16 False; 17 False; 18 False; 19 True

20 Predict Explain why you think the current model of the atom will or will not change over time.

Lesson Review

Vocabulary

Draw a line to connect the following terms to their definitions.

1 atom

2 proton

3 neutron

A a positively charged atomic particle

B an uncharged atomic particle

C the smallest particle of an element that has the chemical properties of that element

Key Concepts

4 Compare Compare the charges and masses of protons, neutrons, and electrons.

_____

_____

_____

_____

_____

5 Explain How can atoms make up all of the substances around you?

_____

_____

_____

6 Compare How does the current model of the atom differ from J. J. Thomson's model?

_____

_____

_____

_____

7 Calculate What is the atomic number of a sodium atom that has 11 protons and 12 neutrons?

_____

Critical Thinking

Use this model to answer the following questions.

8 Analyze The red sphere represents a proton. What is the atomic number of this atom? Explain how you found the atomic number.

_____

_____

_____

9 Apply What is the mass number of an isotope of this atom that has 2 neutrons?

_____

10 Analyze Where are the nucleus and the electrons located in this atom?

_____

_____

_____

_____

_____

11 Infer If atoms are made of smaller parts such as electrons, why are atoms considered the basic unit of matter?

_____

_____

_____

_____

My Notes

The Periodic Table

ESSENTIAL QUESTION

How are elements arranged on the periodic table?

By the end of this lesson, you should be able to describe the relationship between the arrangement of elements on the periodic table and the properties of those elements.

◢◢ **7.PS1.5**

In this market, similar foods are arranged in groups. Can you identify some of the properties each group shares?

Engage Your Brain

1 Describe Write a word or phrase beginning with each letter of the word GOLD that describes the properties of these gold coins.

G _____

O _____

L _____

D _____

2 Describe As you will learn in this lesson, elements are arranged by their properties on the periodic table. What other objects are often arranged by their properties?

_____

_____

_____

_____

_____

_____

 ## Active Reading

3 Apply Many scientific words, such as *table*, also have everyday meanings. Use context clues to write your own definition for each meaning of the word *table*.

Example sentence
The books are on the <u>table</u>.

table:

_____

_____

Example sentence
A data <u>table</u> is a useful way to organize information.

table:

_____

_____

Vocabulary Terms
- periodic table
- chemical symbol
- average atomic mass
- metal
- nonmetal
- metalloid
- group
- period

4 Apply As you learn the definition of each vocabulary term in this lesson, create your own definition or sketch to help you remember the meaning of the term.

Get Organized!

What are elements?

People have long sought to find the basic substances of matter. It was once believed that fire, wind, earth, and water, in various combinations, made up all objects. By the 1860s, however, scientists believed that there were at least 60 different basic substances, or elements. They saw that many of these elements shared certain physical and chemical properties and began classifying them. Knowing what you know about the properties of matter, try classifying the elements below.

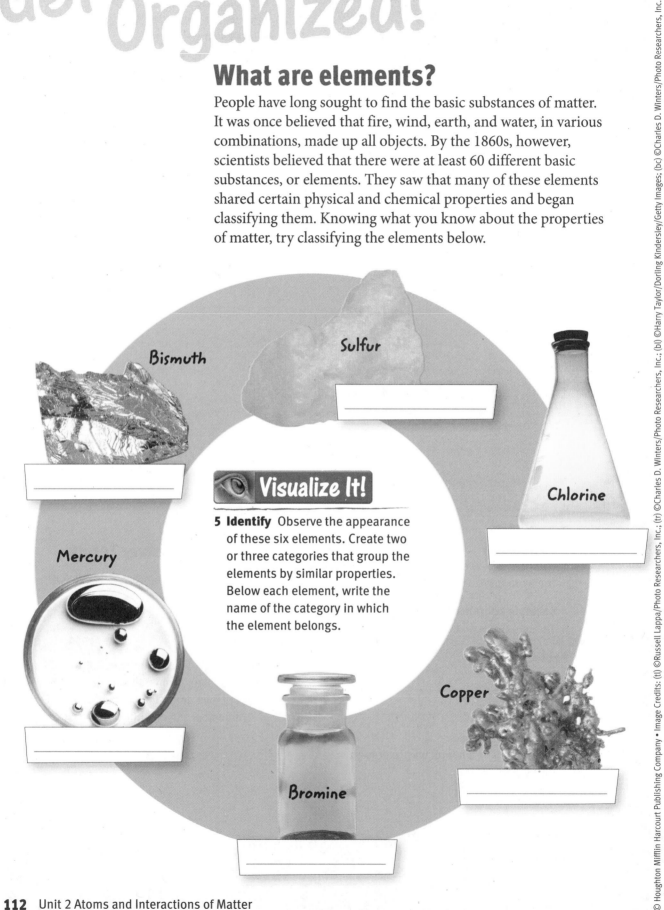

Bismuth

Sulfur

Chlorine

Mercury

Visualize It!

5 Identify Observe the appearance of these six elements. Create two or three categories that group the elements by similar properties. Below each element, write the name of the category in which the element belongs.

Copper

Bromine

How are the elements organized?

In the late 1860s, a Russian chemist named Dmitri Mendeleev (dih•MEE•tree men•duh•LAY•uhf) began thinking about how he could organize the elements based on their properties. To help him decide how to arrange the elements, Mendeleev made a set of element cards. Each card listed the mass of an atom of each element as well as some of the element's properties. Mendeleev arranged the cards in various ways, looking for a pattern to emerge. When he arranged the element cards in order of increasing atomic mass, the properties of those elements occurred in a *periodic,* or regularly repeating, pattern. For this reason, Mendeleev's arrangement of the elements became known as the **periodic table**. Mendeleev used the periodic pattern in his table to predict elements that had not yet been discovered.

In the early 1900s, British scientist Henry Moseley showed how Mendeleev's periodic table could be rearranged. After determining the numbers of protons in the atoms of the elements, he arranged the elements on the table in order of increasing number of protons, or *atomic number.* Moseley's new arrangement of the elements corrected some of the flaws in Mendeleev's table.

The periodic table is a useful tool to scientists because it makes clear many patterns among the elements' properties. The periodic table is like a map or a calendar of the elements.

7 Apply What are you doing this week? Fill in the calendar with activities or plans you have for this week and next. Do any events occur periodically? Explain.

_____

_____

_____

6 Explain How did Henry Moseley revise Mendeleev's periodic table?

_____

_____

_____

_____

_____

What does the periodic table have in common with a calendar? They both show a periodic pattern. On a calendar, the days of the week repeat in the same order every 7 days.

Sunday	Monday	Tuesday	Wednesday	Thursday	Friday	Saturday

© Houghton Mifflin Harcourt Publishing Company

The Periodic Table of Elements

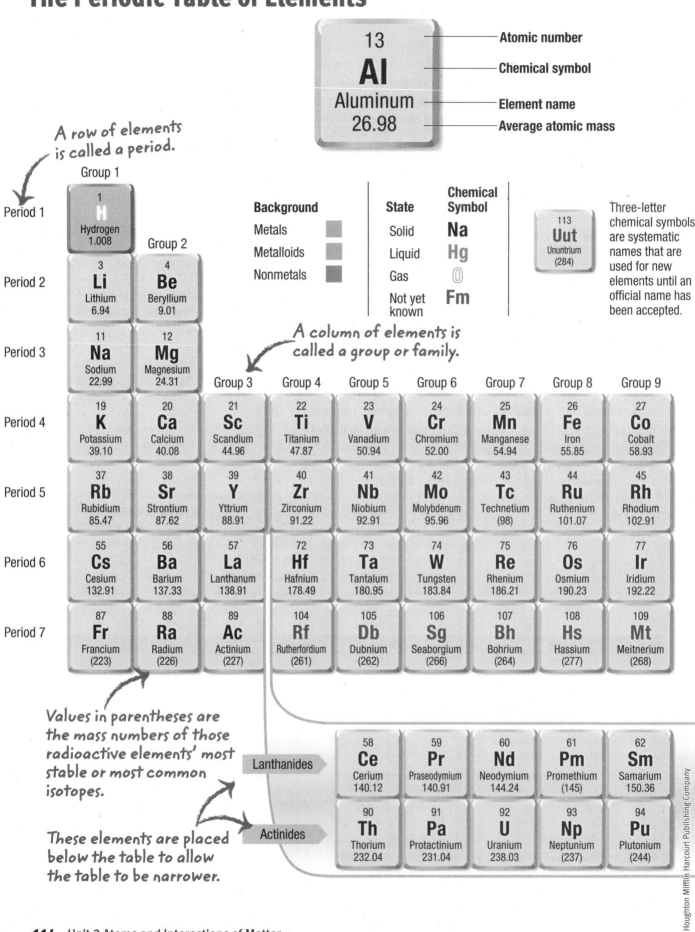

				Atomic number
	13			
	Al			Chemical symbol
	Aluminum			Element name
	26.98			Average atomic mass

A row of elements is called a period.

Background
- Metals
- Metalloids
- Nonmetals

State	Chemical Symbol
Solid	**Na**
Liquid	**Hg**
Gas	ⓞ
Not yet known	**Fm**

113
Uut
Ununtrium
(284)

Three-letter chemical symbols are systematic names that are used for new elements until an official name has been accepted.

A column of elements is called a group or family.

Group 1

Period 1 — 1 **H** Hydrogen 1.008

Group 2

Period 2 — 3 **Li** Lithium 6.94 | 4 **Be** Beryllium 9.01

Period 3 — 11 **Na** Sodium 22.99 | 12 **Mg** Magnesium 24.31

	Group 3	Group 4	Group 5	Group 6	Group 7	Group 8	Group 9
Period 4	21 **Sc** Scandium 44.96	22 **Ti** Titanium 47.87	23 **V** Vanadium 50.94	24 **Cr** Chromium 52.00	25 **Mn** Manganese 54.94	26 **Fe** Iron 55.85	27 **Co** Cobalt 58.93
Period 5	39 **Y** Yttrium 88.91	40 **Zr** Zirconium 91.22	41 **Nb** Niobium 92.91	42 **Mo** Molybdenum 95.96	43 **Tc** Technetium (98)	44 **Ru** Ruthenium 101.07	45 **Rh** Rhodium 102.91
Period 6	57 **La** Lanthanum 138.91	72 **Hf** Hafnium 178.49	73 **Ta** Tantalum 180.95	74 **W** Tungsten 183.84	75 **Re** Rhenium 186.21	76 **Os** Osmium 190.23	77 **Ir** Iridium 192.22
Period 7	89 **Ac** Actinium (227)	104 **Rf** Rutherfordium (261)	105 **Db** Dubnium (262)	106 **Sg** Seaborgium (266)	107 **Bh** Bohrium (264)	108 **Hs** Hassium (277)	109 **Mt** Meitnerium (268)

Period 4 — 19 **K** Potassium 39.10 | 20 **Ca** Calcium 40.08

Period 5 — 37 **Rb** Rubidium 85.47 | 38 **Sr** Strontium 87.62

Period 6 — 55 **Cs** Cesium 132.91 | 56 **Ba** Barium 137.33

Period 7 — 87 **Fr** Francium (223) | 88 **Ra** Radium (226)

Values in parentheses are the mass numbers of those radioactive elements' most stable or most common isotopes.

These elements are placed below the table to allow the table to be narrower.

Lanthanides

58 **Ce** Cerium 140.12	59 **Pr** Praseodymium 140.91	60 **Nd** Neodymium 144.24	61 **Pm** Promethium (145)	62 **Sm** Samarium 150.36

Actinides

90 **Th** Thorium 232.04	91 **Pa** Protactinium 231.04	92 **U** Uranium 238.03	93 **Np** Neptunium (237)	94 **Pu** Plutonium (244)

8 Analyze According to the periodic table, how many elements are a liquid at room temperature?

_____

9 Analyze According to the periodic table, how many elements are metalloids?

_____

The zigzag line separates metals from nonmetals.

			Group 13	Group 14	Group 15	Group 16	Group 17	Group 18
								2 **He** Helium 4.003
			5 **B** Boron 10.81	6 **C** Carbon 12.01	7 **N** Nitrogen 14.01	8 **O** Oxygen 16.00	9 **F** Fluorine 19.00	10 **Ne** Neon 20.18
Group 10	Group 11	Group 12	13 **Al** Aluminum 26.98	14 **Si** Silicon 28.09	15 **P** Phosphorus 30.97	16 **S** Sulfur 32.06	17 **Cl** Chlorine 35.45	18 **Ar** Argon 39.95
28 **Ni** Nickel 58.69	29 **Cu** Copper 63.55	30 **Zn** Zinc 65.38	31 **Ga** Gallium 69.72	32 **Ge** Germanium 72.63	33 **As** Arsenic 74.92	34 **Se** Selenium 78.96	35 **Br** Bromine 79.90	36 **Kr** Krypton 83.80
46 **Pd** Palladium 106.42	47 **Ag** Silver 107.87	48 **Cd** Cadmium 112.41	49 **In** Indium 114.82	50 **Sn** Tin 118.71	51 **Sb** Antimony 121.76	52 **Te** Tellurium 127.60	53 **I** Iodine 126.90	54 **Xe** Xenon 131.29
78 **Pt** Platinum 195.08	79 **Au** Gold 196.97	80 **Hg** Mercury 200.59	81 **Tl** Thallium 204.38	82 **Pb** Lead 207.2	83 **Bi** Bismuth 208.98	84 **Po** Polonium (209)	85 **At** Astatine (210)	86 **Rn** Radon (222)
110 **Ds** Darmstadtium (271)	111 **Rg** Roentgenium (272)	112 **Cn** Copernicium (285)	113 **Nh** Nihonium (284)	114 **Fl** Flerovium (289)	115 **Mc** Moscovium (288)	116 **Lv** Livermorium (293)	117 **Ts** Tennessine (294)	118 **Og** Oganesson (294)

63 **Eu** Europium 151.96	64 **Gd** Gadolinium 157.25	65 **Tb** Terbium 158.93	66 **Dy** Dysprosium 162.50	67 **Ho** Holmium 164.93	68 **Er** Erbium 167.26	69 **Tm** Thulium 168.93	70 **Yb** Ytterbium 173.05	71 **Lu** Lutetium 174.97
95 **Am** Americium (243)	96 **Cm** Curium (247)	97 **Bk** Berkelium (247)	98 **Cf** Californium (251)	99 **Es** Einsteinium (252)	100 **Fm** Fermium (257)	101 **Md** Mendelevium (258)	102 **No** Nobelium (259)	103 **Lr** Lawrencium (262)

MaKing Arrangements

10 Analyze Imagine you are working on a team of scientists, and you just discovered a sample of matter that came from a different planet. After studying the sample, you discover that the matter has an atomic number of 47 and an atomic mass of 107.8682. The matter looks shiny and you decide it is a type of metal. It also seems to not react to gases, like oxygen. Use the periodic table to identify this sample of matter.

What information is contained in each square on the periodic table?

The periodic table is not simply a list of element names. The table contains useful information about each of the elements. The periodic table is usually shown as a grid of squares. Each square contains an element's chemical name, atomic number, chemical symbol, and average atomic mass.

Atomic Number

The number at the top of the square is the atomic number. The atomic number is the number of protons in the nucleus of an atom of that element. All atoms of an element have the same atomic number. For example, every aluminum atom has 13 protons in its nucleus. So the atomic number of aluminum is 13.

Chemical Symbol

The **chemical symbol** is an abbreviation for the element's name. The first letter is always capitalized. Any other letter is always lowercase. For most elements, the chemical symbol is a one- or two-letter symbol. However, some elements have temporary three-letter symbols. These elements will receive a permanent one- or two-letter symbol once each element has been reviewed by an international committee of scientists.

```
    13
    Al
  Aluminum
   26.98
```

Chemical Name

The names of the elements come from many sources. Some elements, such as mendelevium, are named after scientists. Others, such as californium, are named after places.

Average Atomic Mass

All atoms of a given element contain the same number of protons. But the number of neutrons in those atoms can vary. So different atoms of an element can have different masses. The **average atomic mass** of an atom is the weighted average of the masses of all of the naturally occurring isotopes of that element. A weighted average accounts for the percentages of each isotope. The unit for atomic mass is u.

Active Reading

11 Apply What is the average atomic mass of aluminum?

How are the elements arranged on the periodic table?

Have you ever noticed how items in a grocery store are arranged? Each aisle contains a different kind of product. Within an aisle, similar products are grouped together on shelves. Because the items are arranged in categories, it is easy to find your favorite brand of cereal. Similarly, the elements are arranged in a certain order on the periodic table. If you understand how the periodic table is organized, you can easily find and compare elements.

Metals, Nonmetals, and Metalloids Are Found in Three Distinct Regions

Elements on the periodic table can be classified into three major categories: metals, nonmetals, and metalloids. The zigzag line on the periodic table can help you identify where these three classes of elements are located. Except for hydrogen, the elements to the left of the zigzag line are metals. **Metals** are elements that are shiny and conduct heat and electricity well. Most metals are solid at room temperature. Many metals are *malleable,* or able to be formed into different shapes. Some metals are *ductile,* meaning that they can be made into wires. The elements to the right of the zigzag line are nonmetals. **Nonmetals** are poor conductors of heat and electricity. Nonmetals are often dull and brittle. Metalloids border the zigzag line on the periodic table. **Metalloids** are elements that have some properties of metals and some properties of nonmetals. Some metalloids are used to make semiconductor chips in computers.

12 Identify Fill in the blanks below with the word *metal, nonmetal,* or *metalloid*.

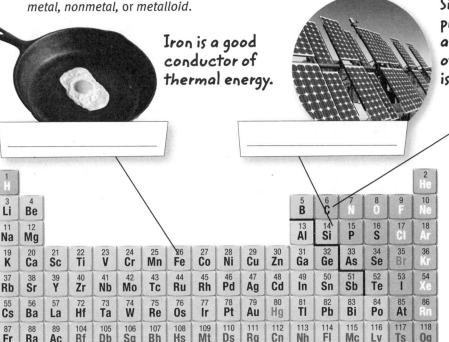

Iron is a good conductor of thermal energy.

Silicon has some properties of metals and some properties of nonmetals. Silicon is used in solar panels.

Graphite is brittle, meaning that it breaks easily. Graphite is made of carbon.

Elements in Each Column Have Similar Properties

The periodic table groups elements with similar properties together. Each vertical column of elements (from top to bottom) on the periodic table is called a **group**. Elements in the same group often have similar physical and chemical properties. For this reason, a group is sometimes called a *family*.

The properties of elements in a group are similar because the atoms of these elements have the same number of *valence electrons*. Valence electrons are found in the outermost portion of the electron cloud of an atom. Because they are far from the the attractive force of the nucleus, valence electrons are able to participate in chemical bonding. The number of valence electrons helps determine what kind of chemical reactions the atom can undergo. For example, all of the atoms of elements in Group 1 have a single valence electron. These elements are very reactive. The atoms of elements in Group 18 have a full set of valence electrons. The elements in Group 18 are all unreactive gases.

Active Reading 13 **Explain** Why do elements within a group have similar chemical properties?

_____

_____

_____

Just as this family is made up of members that have similar characteristics, families in the periodic table are made up of elements that have similar properties.

Groups of Elements Have Similar Properties

Observe the similarities of elements found in Group 1 and in Group 18.

Alkali metals, found in Group 1, share the property of reactivity with water.

Sodium has 1 valence electron.

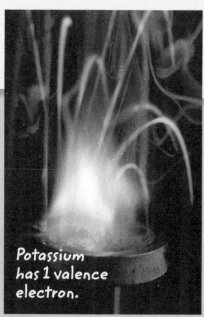

Potassium has 1 valence electron.

© Houghton Mifflin Harcourt Publishing Company • Image Credits: (t) ©Hill Street Studios/Getty Images; (bl) ©Charles D. Winters/Photo Researchers, Inc.; (br) ©Charles D. Winters/Photo Researchers, Inc.

Elements in Each Row Follow Periodic Trends

Each horizontal row of elements (from left to right) on the periodic table is called a **period**. The physical and chemical properties of elements change in predictable ways from one end of the period to the other. For example, within any given period on the periodic table, atomic size decreases as you move from left to right. The densities of elements also follow a pattern. Within a period, elements at the left and right sides of the table are the least dense, and the elements in the middle are the most dense. The element osmium has the highest known density, and it is located at the center of the table. Chemists cannot predict the exact size or density of an atom of an element based on that of another. However, these trends are a valuable tool in predicting the properties of different substances.

Elements Are Arranged in Order of Increasing Atomic Number

As you move from left to right within a period, the atomic number of each element increases by one. Once you've reached the end of the period, the pattern resumes on the next period. You might have noticed that two rows of elements are set apart from the rest of the periodic table. These rows, the lanthanides and actinides, are placed below the table to allow it to be narrower. These elements are also arranged in order of increasing atomic number.

Think Outside the Book Inquiry

14 **Apply** Imagine that you have just discovered a new element. Explain where this element would appear on the periodic table and why. Describe the element's properties, and propose a chemical symbol and name for the element.

Noble gases, found in Group 18, glow brightly when an electric current is passed through them.

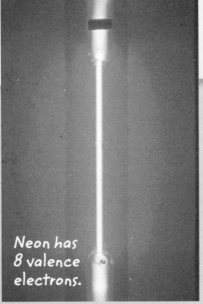

Neon has 8 valence electrons.

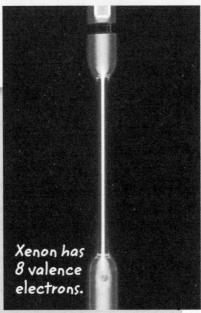

Xenon has 8 valence electrons.

15 **Analyze** List three other elements that have 1 valence electron. (Hint: Refer to the periodic table.)

_____

_____

16 **Analyze** List three other elements that have 8 valence electrons. (Hint: Refer to the periodic table.)

_____

_____

Visual Summary

To complete this summary, fill in the blanks with the correct word or phrase. Then use the key below to check your answers. You can use this page to review the main concepts of the lesson.

The periodic table arranges elements in columns and rows.

17 Elements in the same _____ have similar properties.

18 Rows on the periodic table are known as _____ .

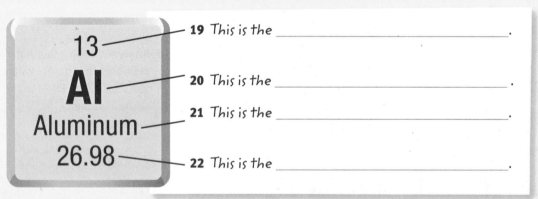

The Periodic Table

The periodic table contains information about each element.

13

Al

Aluminum

26.98

19 This is the _____ .

20 This is the _____ .

21 This is the _____ .

22 This is the _____ .

Answers: 17 group; 18 periods; 19 atomic number; 20 chemical symbol; 21 chemical name; 22 average atomic mass

23 Describe Some elements are highly unstable and break apart within seconds, making them difficult to study. How can the periodic table help scientists infer the properties of these elements?

Lesson Review

Vocabulary

Draw a line to connect the following terms to their definitions.

1 metal

2 nonmetal

3 metalloid

A an element that has properties of both metals and nonmetals

B an element that is shiny and that conducts heat and electricity well

C an element that conducts heat and electricity poorly

Key Concepts

4 Identify Elements in the same _____ on the periodic table have the same number of valence electrons.

5 Identify Properties of elements within a _____ on the periodic table change in a predictable way from one side of the table to the other.

6 Describe What is the purpose of the zigzag line on the periodic table?

_____

_____

7 Apply Thorium (Th) has an average atomic mass of 232.04 u and an atomic number of 90. In the space below, draw a square from the periodic table to represent thorium.

Critical Thinking

Use this graphic to answer the following questions.

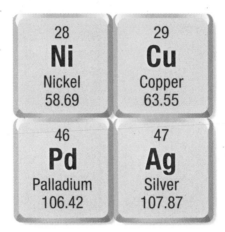

8 Infer What can you infer about copper and silver based on their position relative to each other?

_____

_____

_____

9 Apply How does the nucleus of a copper atom compare to the nucleus of a nickel atom?

_____

_____

_____

10 Explain Explain how chemists can state with certainty that no one will discover an element that would appear on the periodic table between sulfur (S) and chlorine (Cl).

_____

_____

_____

_____

_____

_____

My Notes

Chemical Reactions

ESSENTIAL QUESTION

How are chemical reactions modeled?

By the end of this lesson, you should be able to use balanced chemical equations to model chemical reactions.

7.PS1.4

A chemical reaction that releases light energy occurs inside lightning bugs.

 **Lesson Labs**

Quick Labs
- Breaking Bonds in a Chemical Reaction
- Catalysts and Chemical Reactions

Exploration Lab
- Change of Pace

Engage Your Brain

1 Identify Unscramble the letters below to find two types of energy that can be released when chemical reactions occur. Write your words on the blank lines.

GLITH _____

DSNUO _____

2 Describe Write your own caption to the photo below. Describe what kind of changes have happened to the ship and anchor.

_____

_____

_____

_____

Active Reading

3 Synthesize You can often define an unknown word if you know the meaning of its word parts. Use the word parts and sentence below to make an educated guess about the meaning of the word *exothermic*.

Word part	Meaning
exo-	go out, exit
therm-	heat

Example sentence
Exothermic reactions can sometimes quickly release so much heat that they can melt iron.

exothermic:

_____

_____

_____

Vocabulary Terms
- chemical reaction
- chemical formula
- chemical equation
- reactant
- product
- law of conservation of mass
- endothermic reaction
- exothermic reaction
- law of conservation of energy

4 Identify This list contains the vocabulary terms you'll learn in this lesson. As you read, circle the definition of each term.

Change It Up!

What are the signs of a chemical reaction?

Have you seen leaves change color in the fall or smelled sour milk? The changes in leaves and milk are caused by chemical reactions. A **chemical reaction** is the process in which atoms are rearranged to produce new substances. During a chemical reaction, the bonds that hold atoms together may be formed or broken. The properties of the substances produced in a chemical reaction are different than the properties of the original substances. So, a change in properties is a sign that a chemical reaction may have happened. For example, a solid substance called a *precipitate* may form in a solution. A color change, a change in odor, precipitate formation, and the appearance of gas bubbles are all evidence of a chemical reaction.

Visualize It!

5 Identify In each blank box, identify the evidence that a chemical reaction has taken place.

B _____

A black column forms when sugar reacts with sulfuric acid.

A yellow liquid and a colorless liquid react to form a red precipitate.

C _____

New substances that smell bad are produced when milk turns sour.

Gas bubbles form when baking soda and vinegar react.

A _____

D _____

How are chemical reactions modeled?

You can describe the substances before and after a reaction by their properties. You can also use symbols to identify the substances. Each element has its own chemical symbol. For example, H is the symbol for hydrogen, and O is the symbol for oxygen. You can use the periodic table to find the chemical symbol for any element. A **chemical formula** uses chemical symbols and numbers to represent a given substance. The chemical symbols in a chemical formula tell you what elements make up a substance. The numbers written below and to the right of chemical symbols are called *subscripts*. Subscripts tell you how many of each type of atom are in a molecule. For example, the chemical formula for water is H_2O. The subscript 2 tells you that there are two atoms of hydrogen in each water molecule. There is no subscript on O, so each molecule of water contains only one oxygen atom.

With Chemical Equations

To model reactions, chemical formulas can be joined together in an equation. A **chemical equation** is an expression that uses symbols to show the relationship between the starting substances and the substances that are produced by a chemical reaction. The chemical equation below shows that carbon and oxygen react to form carbon dioxide. The chemical formulas of carbon and oxygen are written to the left of the arrow. The chemical formula of carbon dioxide is written to the right of the arrow. Plus signs separate the chemical formulas of multiple products or reactants.

6 Identify Circle the subscript in the chemical formula below.

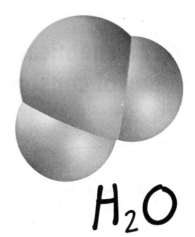

H_2O

A water molecule has two hydrogen (H) atoms and one oxygen (O) atom.

Visualize It!

Reactants are the substances that participate in a chemical reaction. Their chemical formulas are written on the left.

Products are the substances formed in a reaction. Their chemical formulas are written on the right.

$$C + O_2 \longrightarrow CO_2$$

An arrow known as a *yields sign* points from reactants to products.

7 Analyze Atoms of which elements are involved in this reaction?

8 Apply How many atoms of each element are in one molecule of the product?

A Balancing Act

How do chemical equations show the law of conservation of mass?

The **law of conservation of mass** states that matter is neither created nor destroyed in ordinary physical and chemical changes. This law means that a chemical equation must show the same numbers and kinds of atoms on both sides of the arrow. When writing a chemical equation, you must be sure that the reactants and products contain the same number of atoms of each element. This is called *balancing the equation*.

You use coefficients to balance an equation. A *coefficient* is a number that is placed in front of a chemical formula. For example, $3H_2O$ represents three water molecules. The number 3 is the coefficient. For an equation to be balanced, all atoms must be counted. So, you must multiply the subscript of each element in a formula by the formula's coefficient. There are a total of six hydrogen atoms and three oxygen atoms in $3H_2O$. Only coefficients—not subscripts—can be changed when balancing equations. Changing the subscripts in the chemical formula of a compound would change the identity of that compound. For example, H_2O_2 represents the compound hydrogen peroxide, not water.

Active Reading **9 Compare** What is the difference between a coefficient and a subscript?

_____

_____

_____

_____

_____

_____

Do the Math **Sample Problem**

Follow these steps to write a balanced chemical equation.

Identify

A Count the atoms of each element in the reactants and in the product. You can see that there are more oxygen atoms in the reactants than in the product.

$$C \quad + \quad O_2 \quad \longrightarrow \quad CO$$

$$C = 1 \qquad O = 2 \qquad C = 1 \quad O = 1$$

Solve

B To balance the number of oxygen atoms, place the coefficient 2 in front of CO. Now the number of oxygen atoms in the reactants is the same as in the product. Next, the number of carbon atoms needs to be balanced. Place the coefficient 2 in front of C. Finally, be sure to double-check your work!

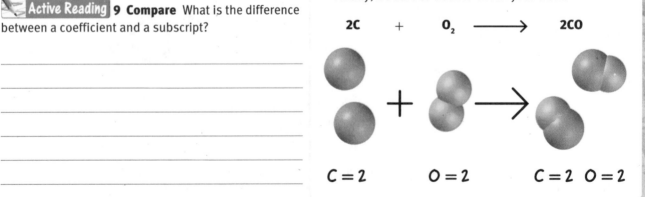

$$2C \quad + \quad O_2 \quad \longrightarrow \quad 2CO$$

$$C = 2 \qquad O = 2 \qquad C = 2 \quad O = 2$$

© Houghton Mifflin Harcourt Publishing Company • Image Credits: (bg) ©NASA

Do the Math You Try It

10 Calculate Fill in the blanks below to balance this chemical equation. Sketch the products and reactants to show that the number of each type of atom is the same.

Identify

A Count the atoms of each element in the reactants and product in the unbalanced equation.

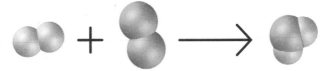

H_2 $+$ O_2 $\longrightarrow$ H_2O

$H =$ _____ $O =$ _____ $H =$ _____ $O =$ _____

Solve

B To balance the number of each type of atom, place coefficients in front of the appropriate chemical formulas. Sketch the products and reactants, showing the correct number of molecules of each.

_____ H_2 $+$ _____ O_2 $\longrightarrow$ _____ H_2O

$+$ $\rightarrow$

$H =$ _____ $O =$ _____ $H =$ _____ $O =$ _____

Hydrogen and oxygen release energy when they react to form water, which forms the cloud shown. The released energy helped to propel this space shuttle.

Think Outside the Book Inquiry

11 Apply Research hydrogen-powered vehicles. Create a poster that describes the advantages and disadvantages of vehicles that use hydrogen as a fuel. Be sure to include a balanced chemical equation to represent the use of hydrogen fuel.

Energy, Energy

Plants absorb energy when they carry out photosynthesis.

What happens to energy during chemical reactions?

Changes in energy are a part of all chemical reactions. Chemical reactions can either release energy or absorb energy. Energy is needed to break chemical bonds in the reactants. As new bonds form in the products, the reactants release energy. Reactions are described by the overall change in energy between the products and reactants.

Energy Can Be Absorbed

A chemical reaction that requires an input of energy is called an **endothermic reaction**. The energy taken in during an endothermic reaction is absorbed from the surroundings, usually as heat. This is why endothermic reaction mixtures often feel cold.

Photosynthesis is an example of an endothermic process that absorbs light energy. In photosynthesis, plants use energy from the sun to change carbon dioxide and water to oxygen and the sugar glucose. Overall, more energy is absorbed during photosynthesis than is released to the surroundings. Some of the absorbed energy is stored in the products: oxygen and glucose.

Energy Can Be Released

A chemical reaction in which energy is released to the surroundings is called an **exothermic reaction**. Exothermic reactions can give off energy in several forms. For example, you feel warmth and see a glow when a candle burns. Burning is an exothermic reaction. The products of the reaction are lower in energy than the reactants. Some of the energy in the bonds of the reactants changes to energy as heat and light. Exothermic reaction mixtures often feel warm when heat is released to the surroundings.

12 List Name three everyday exothermic chemical reactions.

_____

_____

_____

_____

Burning a candle releases energy as heat and light.

Energy Is Always Conserved

The **law of conservation of energy** states that energy cannot be created or destroyed. However, energy can change form. The total amount of energy does not change in endothermic or exothermic reactions. For example, light energy from the sun changes into energy stored in chemical bonds during photosynthesis.

Methane (CH_4) burns when it reacts with oxygen (O_2). This reaction produces carbon dioxide (CO_2) and water (H_2O), as shown below. The reaction of methane and oxygen is exothermic. Burning methane releases energy as heat and light into the surroundings. This energy was first stored in the chemical bonds of the reactants. The energy that was stored in the bonds of the reactants is equal to the energy released plus the energy stored in the bonds of the products. The total amount of all of the types of energy is the same before and after every chemical reaction.

Active Reading

13 Describe What happens to the energy absorbed during an endothermic reaction?

_____

_____

_____

_____

_____

Exothermic Reaction of Methane and Oxygen

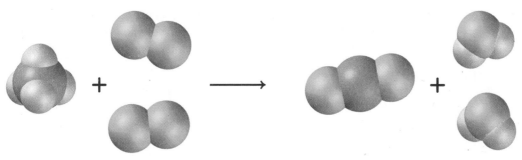

Stored energy of reactants = Stored energy of products and released energy

---

14 Compare Complete the Venn diagram to compare endothermic and exothermic reactions.

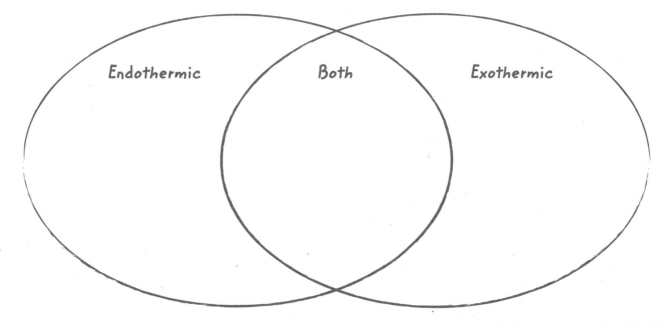

Endothermic   Both   Exothermic

The Need for Speed

Active Reading

15 Identify As you read, underline factors that affect reaction rate.

What affects the rates of reactions?

Some chemical reactions occur in less than a second. Others may take days. The rate of a reaction describes how fast the reaction occurs. For a reaction to occur, particles of the reactants must collide. Reaction rates are affected by how often the particles collide. Factors that affect reaction rates include concentration, surface area, temperature, and the presence of a catalyst.

Changing the Rate of Reaction

Decreased Rate	Increased Rate	Factors That Affect Reaction Rates

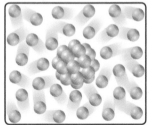 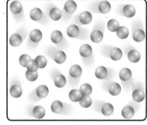

Concentration At higher concentrations, there are more reactants in a given volume. The reactants are more likely to collide and react. The reaction rate is higher when reactant concentration is higher.

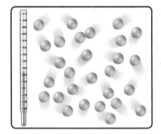 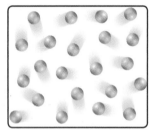

Surface Area The reaction rate increases when more reactant particles are exposed to one another. Crushing or grinding solids increases their surface area and the reaction rate.

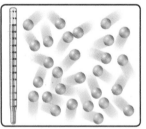

Temperature Reactions usually occur faster at higher temperatures. Particles move faster at higher temperatures. Because the reactant particles move more quickly, they are more likely to collide and react.

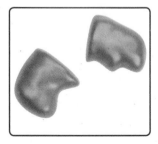 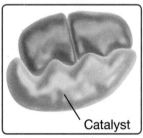

Catalyst

Catalysts A catalyst is a substance that changes the rate of a chemical reaction without being used up or changed very much. Catalysts can increase reaction rate by bringing together reactants. Enzymes are a type of catalyst found in living things.

Enzymes

Enzymes that increase the rates of reactions keep your body going. They help digest food so your body has the energy it needs. They also help build the molecules your body needs to grow.

Energy

All living things need energy to function. This energy is released when food molecules break down. Enzymes speed up reactions so energy is readily available.

Medical Conditions

Problems with enzymes can cause medical conditions or changes in the body. Albinism, a lack of pigment, occurs when a certain enzyme in animals does not work the way it should work.

Cleaners

Enzymes are not only found in living things. They can be used outside of the body, too. The enzymes in some cleaners help break down substances such as grease.

Extend

Inquiry

16 Describe Explain how enzymes affect reactions.

17 Research Lactose intolerance is a condition that occurs when people are unable to digest milk products. Investigate the cause of lactose intolerance. Write a summary of your findings.

18 Design Create a project that explains how lactose intolerance affects people and why it occurs. Present your project as a written report, a poster, or an oral report.

Visual Summary

To complete this summary, fill in the blanks with the correct word or phrase. Then, use the key below to check your answers. You can use this page to review the main concepts of the lesson.

Bonds are broken and formed during chemical reactions to produce new substances.

19 One sign of a chemical reaction is the formation of a solid _____.

A chemical equation uses symbols to show the relationship between the products and the reactants.

$$C + O_2 \longrightarrow CO_2$$

20 A balanced chemical equation shows that chemical reactions follow the law of conservation of _____.

Chemical Reactions

Exothermic reactions release energy to the surroundings, and endothermic reactions absorb energy from the surroundings.

21 The total amount of energy before and after a chemical reaction is _____.

Reaction rate is affected by reactant concentration, temperature, surface area, and catalysts.

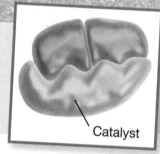

Catalyst

22 A _____ is not changed much by a chemical reaction.

23 The rate of reaction is _____ at higher temperatures because particles collide more often.

24 Design Write a procedure for how you would measure the effect of reactant concentration on the reaction rate.

Lesson Review

Vocabulary

Draw a line to connect the following terms to their definitions.

1 reactant

2 product

A a substance that is produced by a chemical reaction

B a substance that participates in a chemical reaction

Key Concepts

3 Describe What happens to the atoms in the reactants during a chemical reaction?

_____

_____

_____

4 Explain How does a balanced chemical equation show that mass is never lost or gained in a chemical reaction?

_____

_____

_____

_____

_____

5 Relate Describe four ways you could increase the rate of a chemical reaction.

_____

_____

_____

_____

_____

6 Compare How do exothermic and endothermic reactions differ?

_____

_____

Critical Thinking

Use this diagram to answer the following questions.

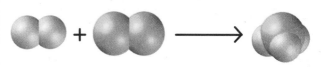

7 Model The reactants in the above reaction are hydrogen (H_2) and nitrogen (N_2). The product is ammonia (NH_3). In the space below, write a balanced chemical equation that represents the reaction.

8 Analyze This reaction releases energy as heat. Explain whether the reaction is exothermic or endothermic and whether it obeys the law of conservation of energy.

_____

_____

_____

_____

_____

9 Evaluate Two colorless solutions are mixed together. Bubbles form as the solution is stirred. Give two possible explanations for this result.

_____

_____

_____

_____

_____

10 Apply The chemical formula of glucose is $C_6H_{12}O_6$. What are the names of the elements in glucose, and how many atoms of each element are present in a glucose molecule?

_____

_____

_____

My Notes

Balancing Chemical Equations

A chemical equation is an expression that shows how substances interact during a chemical change. Chemical equations must be balanced so that they show the same number of each type of atom before and after the reaction. Balanced chemical equations support the law of conservation of mass.

> Subscripts show how many atoms of an element are present. Here, the subscript *2* indicates that two atoms of aluminum are present in this compound.

Tutorial

Use the following steps to balance a chemical equation.

> The chemical symbol *Al* shows that aluminum atoms are in this compound.

$$Al_2(SO_4)_3$$

> Parentheses are used to group atoms together. The chemical formula $Al_2(SO_4)_3$ describes a compound that contains two Al atoms and three $-SO_4$ groups per unit.

1 Identify how many atoms of each element are in each chemical formula.

The example at the right shows how to read the parts of a chemical formula.

2 Compare the number of each type of atom in the reactants to the number of each type of atom in the products.

Reactants are the substances that participate in a chemical reaction. Their chemical formulas are written on the left side of a chemical equation. Products are the substances formed in a reaction. Their chemical formulas are written on the right. Reactants are separated from products by an arrow called a *yields sign*.

$$Al_2(SO_4)_3 + HCl \longrightarrow AlCl_3 + H_2SO_4$$

Reactants	Products
Aluminum = 2	Aluminum = 1
Chlorine = 1	Chlorine = 3
Hydrogen = 1	Hydrogen = 2
Oxygen = 12	Oxygen = 4
Sulfur = 3	Sulfur = 1

3 Add coefficients to balance the atoms in the reactants with the atoms in the products.

In a balanced chemical equation, the number of each atom in the reactants equals the number of each atom in the products. Coefficients are numbers greater than 1 that are placed in front of a chemical formula. Coefficients balance the number of atoms on each side of the equation.

4 Check your work.

Are there equal numbers of each type of atom on both sides of the yields sign? To find the number of each type of atom, multiply the coefficient by the subscripts.

$$Al_2(SO_4)_3 + 6HCl \longrightarrow 2AlCl_3 + 3H_2SO_4$$

Reactants	Products
Aluminum = 2	Aluminum = 2
Chlorine = 6	Chlorine = 6
Hydrogen = 6	Hydrogen = 6
Oxygen = 12	Oxygen = 12
Sulfur = 3	Sulfur = 3

You Try It!

Acid precipitation can cause a lake to become acidic and unsuitable for living things. One way to reduce the acidity is to add a base. The chemical equation below shows the reaction that takes place when the base calcium hydroxide reacts with sulfuric acid in acid precipitation. Use the skills you've reviewed to balance this chemical equation.

The acidity of a lake can be adjusted by adding a base.

---

1 Identify how many atoms of each element are present in each chemical formula.

Complete the table at the right by identifying the number of each type of atom in the reactants and in the products. (Hint: You may refer to the periodic table to find the name of unfamiliar elements.)

$$Ca(OH)_2 + H_2SO_4 \longrightarrow CaSO_4 + H_2O$$

Reactants	Products
Calcium = 1	Calcium = 1

---

2 Compare the number of each type of atom in the reactants to the number of each type of atom in the products.

Compare the number of atoms in the reactants to the atoms in the products. Which elements are not balanced on both sides of the equation?

---

3 Add coefficients to balance the chemical equation.

Add coefficients in front of the chemical formulas at the right to balance the chemical equation.

$$\_\_Ca(OH)_2 + \_\_H_2SO_4 \longrightarrow \_\_CaSO_4 + \_\_H_2O$$

Reactants	Products

4 Check your work.

Are there equal numbers of each type of atom on both sides of the yields sign? Record the number of each type of atom in the table.

Unit 2 ⟨Big Idea⟩ The atomic structure of an element determines the properties of the element and determines how the element interacts with other elements.

Lesson 1
ESSENTIAL QUESTION
How do we know what parts make up the atom?

Describe how the development of the atomic theory has led to the modern understanding of the atom and its parts.

Lesson 2
ESSENTIAL QUESTION
How are elements arranged on the periodic table?

Describe the relationship between the arrangement of elements on the periodic table and the properties of those elements.

Lesson 3
ESSENTIAL QUESTION
How are chemical reactions modeled?

Use balanced chemical equations to model chemical reactions.

Think Outside the Book

2 Synthesize Choose one of these activities to help synthesize what you have learned in this unit.

☐ Using what you learned in lessons 1 and 2, explain how the structure of the atom is related to the periodic table by making a poster presentation. Include captions and labels.

☐ Using what you learned in lessons 1 and 3, describe the structure of atoms and how the atom's bonds can be broken to create new substances.

Connect ESSENTIAL QUESTIONS
Lessons 1 and 3

1 Compare What happens to atoms during chemical reactions?

_____

_____

_____

_____

Unit 2 Review

Name _____

Vocabulary

Fill in each blank with the term that best completes the following sentences.

1 A(n) _____ is a chemical reaction in which energy is released to the surroundings.

2 The _____ is the number of protons in the nucleus of an atom of that element.

3 A(n) _____ is the smallest particle of an element that has the chemical properties of that element.

4 _____ are elements that have some properties of metals and some properties of nonmetals.

5 A(n) _____ is the process in which atoms are rearranged to produce new substances.

Key Concepts

Read each question below, and circle the best answer.

6 The chart below gives the atomic number and mass number of two elements.

	Element A	Element B
Atomic number	10	9
Mass number	20	19

How many protons does Element B have?

A 10

C 9

B 20

D 19

7 All atoms of a given element contain

A the same number of protons but a different number of neutrons.

B the same number of neutrons but a different number of protons.

C the same number of neutrons and protons.

D different numbers of neutrons and protons.

8 Below is a square that represents one element of the periodic table.

20

Ca

Calcium

40.08

What information is in this square of the periodic table, from top to bottom?

A average atomic mass, chemical symbol, chemical name, atomic number

B atomic number, chemical symbol, chemical name, average atomic mass

C average atomic mass, chemical symbol, chemical name, proton number

D atomic number, chemical symbol, chemical name, proton number

9 The diagram below is one model of an atom. By whom was this model of an atom proposed?

Atom

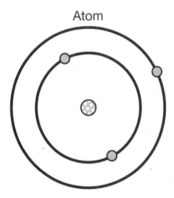

A Thomson   **C** Rutherford

B Dalton   **D** Bohr

10 What are the columns and the rows of the periodic table called?

A periods and energy levels   **C** atomic numbers and periods

B groups and periods   **D** groups and atomic numbers

11 Which action can speed up the rate of a chemical reaction?

A removing a catalyst

B lowering the reactant concentration

C lowering the temperature

D breaking a reactant into smaller pieces

12 A chemical reaction is shown below.

$$Fe + H_2O \rightarrow Fe_3O_4 + H_2$$

What are the products in the equation?

A Fe_3O_4 only

B Fe only

C Fe and H_2O

D Fe_3O_4 and H_2

13 Which of the following occurrences indicates that a chemical reaction has taken place?

A An odor is produced by burning a sugar cube.

B A puddle is produced by melting an ice cube.

C A loud noise is produced by crushing a can.

D A shard of glass is produced by breaking a bottle.

Critical Thinking

Answer the following questions in the space provided.

14 List three properties of metals that nonmetals typically do not have.

_____

_____

Describe where metals and nonmetals are found on the periodic table.

_____

_____

What is the name for elements that have some properties of metals and some properties of nonmetals?

_____

_____

15 What does it mean to balance an equation?

_____

Why does an equation need to be balanced?

_____

_____

_____

How is a coefficient used to balance an equation?

_____

_____

_____

Connect **ESSENTIAL QUESTIONS**
Lessons 2 and 3

Answer the following question in the space provided.

16 Use the periodic table to identify the chemical symbols and find which elements make up the following substances.

$$CH_4$$
$$2O_2$$
$$CO_2$$
$$H_2O$$

The following chemical equation shows the reaction of methane and oxygen to form carbon dioxide and water.

$$CH_4 + 2O_2 \rightarrow CO_2 + H_2O$$

Balance the above reaction by writing in the correct coefficient(s).

How does a balanced equation demonstrate the law of conservation of mass?

_____

_____

Cells

Big Idea

All living things are made up of one or more cells.

7.LS1.1, 7.LS1.2, 7.LS1.3, 7.LS1.4

Colorized picture of the organelles of a cell through a modern microscope

What do you think?

As microscopes have become more powerful, our understanding of cells and their functions has also increased. What kinds of questions would you use a microscope to answer?

Cells seen through an early microscope

Seeing through Microscopes

Microscopes have come a long way. Today, we can see the details of the surface of metals at the atomic level. Microscopes have allowed us to study our world at some of the smallest levels.

Circa 1000 CE
Although people may have used rock crystals to magnify things thousands of years ago, it wasn't until about 1000 CE that people were able to form and polish clear-glass partial spheres. Placing these reading stones on top of a page made it easier to read the words.

Reading stones magnify the words on a page.

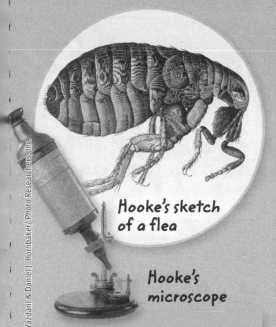

Hooke's sketch
of a flea

Hooke's
microscope

1665
Robert Hooke was interested
in many areas of science.
In 1665, Hooke invented a
light microscope to look at
small creatures, like fleas.
Hooke's microscope was
similar to a telescope, but it
also had a way to shine light
on the object.

1931
Ernst Ruska developed the
electron microscope, which
shows much greater detail
than do light microscopes.
The electron microscope uses
an electron beam instead of
light to show things as small
as the structure of viruses.
Ruska received the Nobel Prize
in Physics in 1986 for
his breakthrough.

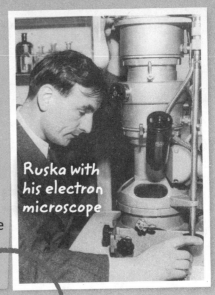

Ruska with
his electron
microscope

Atoms at platinum's
surface

1981
The scanning tunneling
microscope changed again
the way scientists look at
things. Using this microscope,
we can look at images of
surfaces at the atomic level.
The microscope uses a beam
of electrons to map a surface.
This information is collected
and processed so that it can be
viewed on a computer screen.

What's in a Microscope?

① Think About It

A What characteristics do different
microscopes have?

_____

_____

_____

_____

_____

B Why are microscopes used?

_____

_____

_____

_____

_____

② Conduct Research

Choose a specific kind of microscope and research
how it is used, whether it is used to view live or
dead samples, and its range of magnification.

_____

_____

_____

_____

_____

_____

Take It Home

With an adult, prepare an oral presentation
for your class on the microscope that you
have researched. See *ScienceSaurus*® for
more information about microscopes.

Lesson 1

The Characteristics of Cells

ESSENTIAL QUESTION

What are living things made of?

By the end of this lesson, you should be able to explain the components of the scientific theory of cells.

7.LS1.1

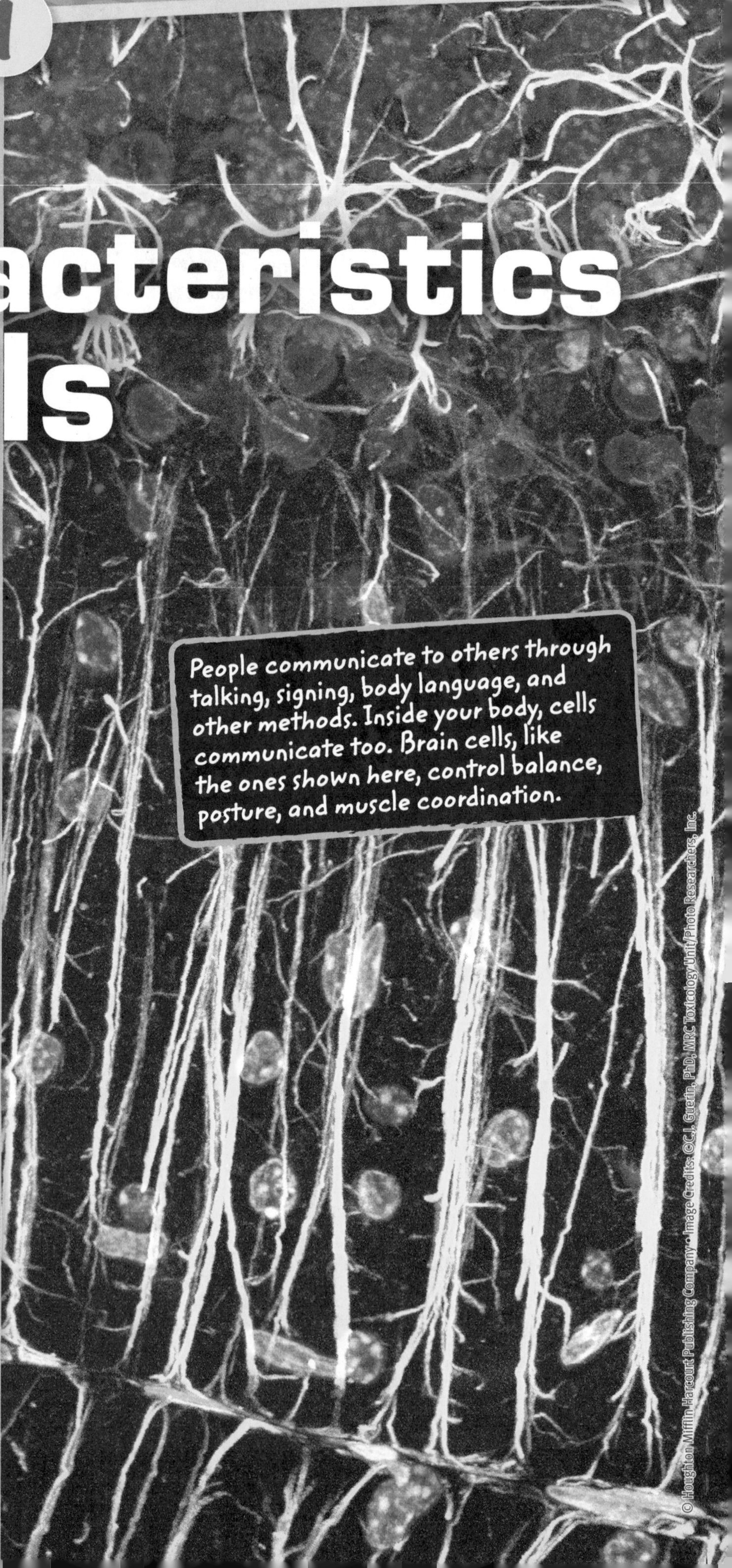

People communicate to others through talking, signing, body language, and other methods. Inside your body, cells communicate too. Brain cells, like the ones shown here, control balance, posture, and muscle coordination.

Lesson Labs

Quick Labs
- How Do Tools that Magnify Help Us Study Cells?
- Investigating Cell Size

Exploration Lab
- Using a Microscope to Explore Cells

Engage Your Brain

1 Predict Check T or F to show whether you think each statement is true or false.

T   F

☐   ☐   All living things are made up of one or more cells.

☐   ☐   Rocks are made up of cells.

☐   ☐   All cells are the same size.

☐   ☐   Cells perform life functions for living things.

2 Model Develop and construct a two-dimensional model of what you think a cell looks like. Describe any parts you include in your model, and explain their functions.

Active Reading

3 Synthesize Many English words have their roots in other languages. Use the Greek words below to make an educated guess about the meanings of the words *prokaryote* and *eukaryote*. Here *kernel* refers to the nucleus, where genetic material is contained in some cells.

Word part	Meaning
pro-	before
eu-	true
karyon	kernel

Vocabulary Terms

- cell
- organism
- cell membrane
- cytoplasm
- organelle
- nucleus
- prokaryote
- eukaryote

4 Apply As you learn the definition of each vocabulary term in this lesson, create your own sketches of a prokaryotic cell and a eukaryotic cell and label the parts in each cell.

prokaryote:

_____

_____

eukaryote:

_____

_____

Cell-ebrate!

What is a cell?

Like all living things, you are made up of cells. A **cell** is the smallest functional and structural unit of all living organisms. An **organism** is any living thing. All organisms are made up of cells. Some organisms are just one cell. Others, like humans, contain trillions of cells. An organism carries out all of its own life processes.

Robert Hooke was the first person to describe cells. In 1665, he built a microscope to look at tiny objects. One day, he looked at a thin slice of cork from the bark of a cork tree. The cork looked as if it was made of little boxes. Hooke named these boxes *cells*, which means "little rooms" in Latin.

Active Reading

5 Identify As you read, underline the reasons why cells are important.

Visualize It!

6 Compare Look at the photos of the three different cells. What do the cells have in common?

_____

_____

_____

_____

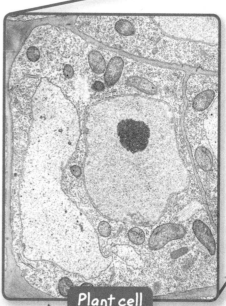

Plant cell

Bacterial cell

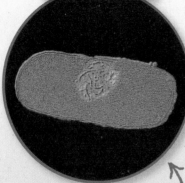

Plant cells range in size from 10 μm to 100 μm. They can be much larger than animal cells.

Bacterial cells are up to 1000 times smaller than human cells.

The average size of a human cell is 10 μm. It would take about 50 average human cells to cover the dot on this letter i.

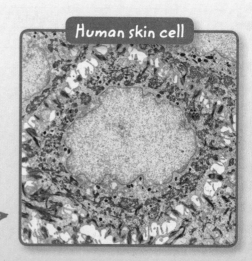
Human skin cell

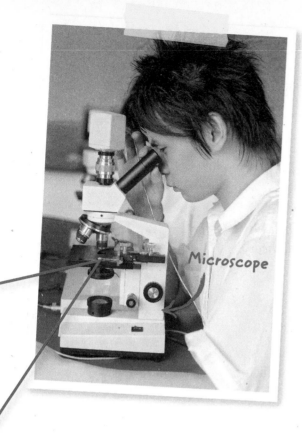

Microscope

Why are most cells small?

Most cells are too small to be seen without a microscope. Cells are small because their size is limited by their outer surface area. Cells take in food and get rid of wastes through their outer surface. As a cell grows, it needs more food and produces more waste. Therefore, more materials pass through its outer surface. However, as a cell grows, the cell's volume increases faster than the surface area. If a cell gets too large, the cell's surface area will not be large enough to take in enough nutrients or pump out enough wastes. The ratio of the cell's outer surface area to the cell's volume is called the *surface area-to-volume ratio*. Smaller cells have a greater surface area-to-volume ratio than larger cells.

Do the Math

Here's an example of how to calculate the surface area-to-volume ratio of the cube shown at the right.

Sample Problem

A Calculate the surface area.

surface area of cube =

number of faces × area of one face

surface area of cube = $6(2 \, cm \times 2 \, cm)$

surface area of cube = $24 \, cm^2$

B Calculate the volume.

volume of cube = side × side × side

volume of cube = $2 \, cm \times 2 \, cm \times 2 \, cm$

volume of cube = $8 \, cm^3$

C Calculate the surface area-to-volume ratio. A ratio is a comparison between numbers. It can be written by placing a colon between the numbers being compared.

surface area : volume = $24 \, cm^2 : 8 \, cm^3$

surface area : volume = $3 \, cm^2 : 1 \, cm^3$

You Try It

7 Calculate What is the surface area-to-volume ratio of a cube whose sides are 3 cm long?

A Calculate the surface area.

B Calculate the volume.

C Calculate the surface area-to-volume ratio.

Cell *Hall of Fame*

What is the cell theory?

Scientific knowledge often results from combining the work of several scientists. For example, the discoveries of Matthias Schleiden (muh•THY•uhs SHLY•duhn), Theodor Schwann (THEE•oh•dohr SHVAHN), and Rudolf Virchow (ROO•dawlf VIR•koh) led to one very important theory called the *cell theory*. The cell theory lists three basic characteristics of all cells and organisms:

- All organisms are made up of one or more cells.
- The cell is the basic unit of all organisms.
- All cells come from existing cells.

The cell theory is fundamental to the study of organisms, medicine, heredity, evolution, and all other aspects of life science.

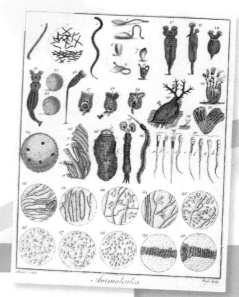

Animalcules

Visualize It!

8 Provide As you read, fill in the missing events on the timeline.

Model of Hooke's microscope

1673
Anton van Leeuwenhoek made careful drawings of the organisms he observed.

1665
Robert Hooke sees tiny, box-like spaces when using a microscope like this to observe thin slices of cork. He calls these spaces cells.

1858
Rudolf Virchow _____
_____
_____
_____
_____.

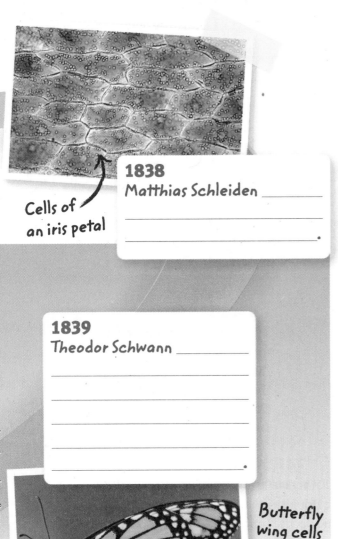

9 Explain How can microscopes help you see cells? First, think of a good place to collect a sample of cells. Then, in a paragraph, describe how to prepare a microscope slide to observe those cells.

Cells of an iris petal

1838
Matthias Schleiden _____
_____
_____.

1839
Theodor Schwann _____
_____
_____
_____
_____
_____.

Butterfly wing cells

This iris and butterfly are multicellular organisms made up of many cells.

All Organisms Are Made Up of One or More Cells

Anton van Leeuwenhoek (AN•tahn VAN LAY•vuhn•huk) was the first person to describe actual living cells when he looked at a drop of pond water under a microscope. These studies made other scientists wonder if all living things were made up of cells. In 1838, Matthias Schleiden concluded that plants are made of cells. Then in 1839, Theodor Schwann determined that all animal tissues are made of cells. He concluded that all organisms are made up of one or more cells.

Organisms that are made up of just one cell are called *unicellular organisms*. The single cell of a unicellular organism must carry out all of the functions for life. Organisms that are made up of more than one cell are called *multicellular organisms*. The cells of multicellular organisms often have specialized functions.

The Cell is the Basic Unit of All Organisms

Based on his observations about the cellular make up of organisms, Schwann made another conclusion. He determined that the cell is the basic unit of all living things. Thus, Schwann wrote the first two parts of the cell theory.

All Cells Come from Existing Cells

In 1858, Rudolf Virchow, a doctor, proposed that cells could form only from the division of other cells. Virchow then added the third part of the cell theory that all cells come from existing cells.

Active Reading

10 Summarize What is the cell theory?

_____
_____
_____
_____
_____

On the Cellular

What parts do all cells have in common?

Different cells vary in size and shape. However, all cells have some parts in common, including cell membranes, cytoplasm, organelles, and DNA. These different parts help the cell to carry out all life activities.

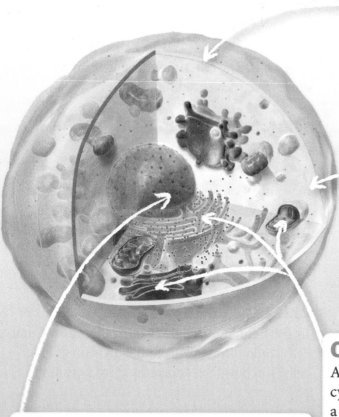

Cell Membrane

A **cell membrane** is a protective layer that covers a cell's surface and acts as a barrier between the inside of a cell and the cell's environment. It also controls materials, such as water and oxygen, that move into and out of a cell.

Cytoplasm

The region enclosed by the cell membrane that includes the fluid and all of the *organelles* of the cell is called the **cytoplasm** (SY•tuh•plaz•uhm).

Organelles

An **organelle** is a small body in a cell's cytoplasm that is specialized to perform a specific function. Cells can have one or more types of organelles. Most, but not all, organelles have a membrane.

DNA

Deoxyribonucleic acid, or DNA, is genetic material that provides instructions for all cell processes. Organisms inherit DNA from their parent or parents. In some cells, the DNA is contained in a membrane-bound organelle called the **nucleus**. In other types of cells, the DNA is not contained in a nucleus.

Think Outside the Book Inquiry

12 Research Research organelles. Write a paragraph about one organelle that explains how that organelle's structure and function contribute to the life activities of a cell and organism of your choice. Then develop and construct a simple model that you can use to identify its structure and function.

What are the two types of cells?

Although cells have some basic parts in common, there are some important differences. The way that cells store their DNA is the main difference between the two cell types.

 **Active Reading**

13 Identify As you read, underline the differences between prokaryotes and eukaryotes.

Prokaryotic

A **prokaryote** (proh•KAIR•ee•oht) is a single-celled organism that does not have a nucleus or membrane-bound organelles. Its DNA is located in the cytoplasm. Prokaryotic cells contain organelles called *ribosomes* that do not have a membrane. Some prokaryotic cells have hairlike structures called *flagella* that help them move. Prokaryotes, which include all bacteria and archaea, are smaller than eukaryotes.

Eukaryotic

A **eukaryote** (yoo•KAIR•ee•oht) is an organism made up of cells that contain their DNA in a nucleus. Eukaryotic cells contain membrane-bound organelles, as well as ribosomes. Not all eukaryotic cells are the same. Animals, plants, protists, and fungi are eukaryotes. All multicellular organisms are eukaryotes. Most eukaryotes are multicellular. Some eukaryotes, such as amoebas and yeasts, are unicellular.

Visualize It!

14 Identify Use the list of terms below to fill in the blanks with the matching cell parts in each cell. Some terms are used twice.

DNA in cytoplasm
DNA in nucleus
Cytoplasm
Cell membrane
Organelles

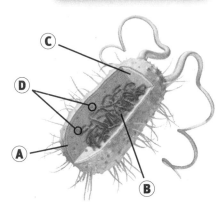

Prokaryotic

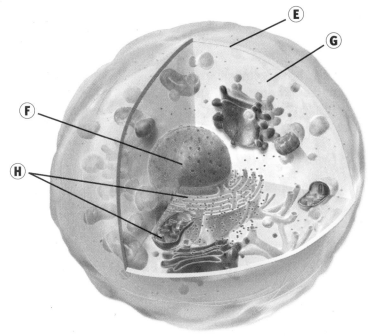

Eukaryotic

A _____

B _____

C _____

D _____

E _____

F _DNA in nucleus_

G _____

H _____

Visual Summary

To complete this summary, fill in the blanks with the correct word or phrase. Then use the key below to check your answers. You can use this page to review the main concepts of the lesson.

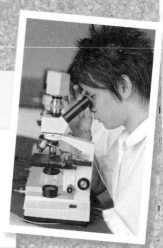

Cells and Cell Theory

A cell is the smallest unit that can perform all the processes necessary for life.

15 The cell of a(n) _____ organism must carry out all of its life functions; an organism made up of more than one cell is called a _____ organism.

The cell theory lists three basic principles of all cells and organisms.

16 All cells come from existing _____ .

All cells have a cell membrane, cytoplasm, organelles, and DNA.

17 The organelle that contains DNA in eukaryotic cells is called a(n) _____ .

Eukaryotic

Prokaryotic

Answers: 15 unicellular, multicellular; 16 cells; 17 nucleus

18 Relate Choose an organism that you are familiar with, and explain how the three parts of the cell theory relate to that organism.

Lesson Review

Vocabulary

Fill in the blank with the term that best completes the following sentences.

1 The _____ is the smallest functional and structural unit of all living things.

2 All cells are surrounded by a(n) _____.

3 A living thing is called a(n) _____.

Key Concepts

4 Describe Discuss two ways that all cells are alike.

_____

_____

_____

_____

_____

5 List What are the main ideas of the cell theory?

_____

_____

_____

_____

_____

_____

6 Compare How do prokaryotes differ from eukaryotes? How are they similar?

_____

_____

_____

_____

_____

_____

_____

Critical Thinking

Use this figure to answer the following questions.

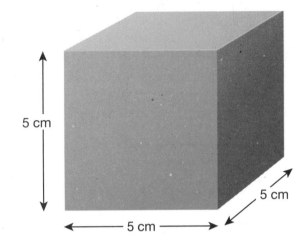

7 Apply What is the surface area-to-volume ratio of this cube?

_____

_____

8 Apply Cells are not as large as this cube. Explain why in terms of a cell's surface area-to-volume ratio.

_____

_____

_____

_____

_____

9 Compare How is the structure of a unicellular organism different from the structure of a multicellular organism? How does this difference affect cellular function in each organism?

_____

_____

_____

_____

_____

_____

_____

My Notes

Chemistry of Life

ESSENTIAL QUESTION

What are the building blocks of organisms?

By the end of this lesson, you should be able to discuss the chemical makeup of living things.

These fungi are bioluminescent, which means they produce light from chemical reactions in their bodies. The light attracts insects that disperse the fungi's spores.

Engage Your Brain

1 Describe Fill in the blank with the word or phrase that you think correctly completes the following sentences.

The chemical formula for _____

is H_2O. The *H* stands for hydrogen and the

_____ stands for oxygen.

If you don't get enough water, you might

_____

_____

2 Relate What do you think you are made of?

_____

_____

_____

_____

_____

Active Reading

3 Synthesize You can often define an unknown word if you know the meaning of its word parts. Use the word parts and sentence below to make an educated guess about the meaning of the word *atom*.

Word part	Meaning
a–	not
tom	to cut

Example sentence
Air is mostly made up of oxygen and nitrogen <u>atoms</u>.

Vocabulary Terms
- atom
- molecule
- lipid
- protein
- carbohydrate
- nucleic acid
- phospholipid

4 Identify This list contains the key terms you'll learn in this lesson. As you read, circle the definition of each term.

atom:

_____

_____

It's Elementary

What are atoms and molecules?

Think about where you live. The streets are lined with many types of buildings. But these buildings are made from a lot of the same materials, such as bricks, glass, wood, and steel. Similarly, all cells are made from the same materials. The materials in cells are made up of atoms that can join together to form molecules.

Atoms Are the Building Blocks of Matter

The matter that you encounter every day, both living and nonliving, is made up of basic particles called **atoms.** Not all atoms are the same. There are nearly one hundred types of atoms that occur naturally on Earth. These different types of atoms are known as *elements*. Each element has unique properties. For example, oxygen is a colorless gas made up of oxygen atoms. The element gold is a shiny metal made up of gold atoms. Just six elements make up most of the human body. These and other elements are important for cell processes in all living things.

Active Reading

5 Relate How do atoms relate to cells?

_____

_____

_____

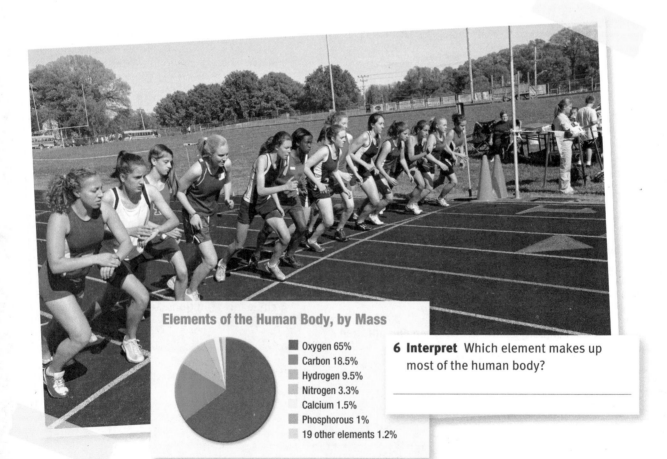

Elements of the Human Body, by Mass

- Oxygen 65%
- Carbon 18.5%
- Hydrogen 9.5%
- Nitrogen 3.3%
- Calcium 1.5%
- Phosphorous 1%
- 19 other elements 1.2%

6 Interpret Which element makes up most of the human body?

_____

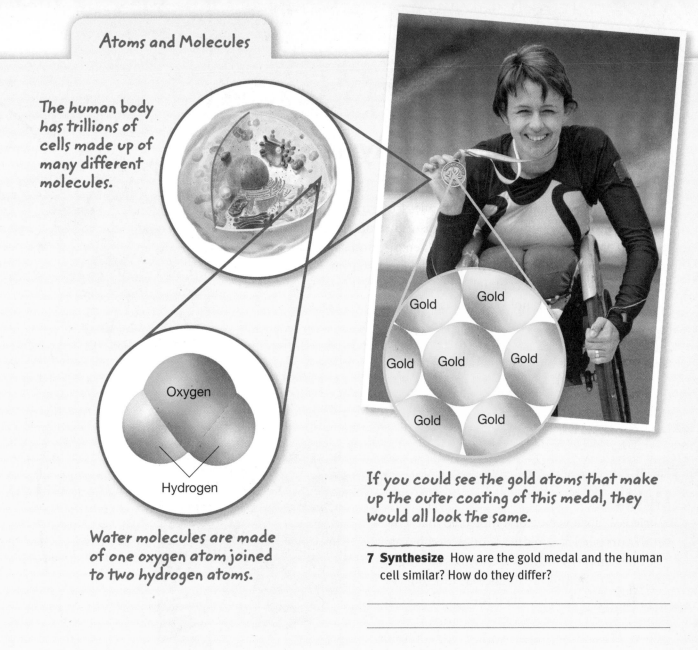

The human body has trillions of cells made up of many different molecules.

Oxygen

Hydrogen

Water molecules are made of one oxygen atom joined to two hydrogen atoms.

Gold Gold
Gold Gold Gold
Gold Gold

If you could see the gold atoms that make up the outer coating of this medal, they would all look the same.

7 Synthesize How are the gold medal and the human cell similar? How do they differ?

_____

_____

_____

Molecules Are Made of Two or More Atoms

A **molecule** is a group of atoms that are held together by chemical bonds. For example, the molecule of water shown above is made of one oxygen atom bonded to two hydrogen atoms. If you separated the oxygen and hydrogen atoms, then you would no longer have a water molecule.

Some molecules are made up of only one type of atom. For example, a molecule of oxygen gas is made of two oxygen atoms. Other molecules contain different types of atoms. A substance made up of atoms of two or more elements joined by chemical bonds is called a *compound*. Most of the molecules found in cells are also compounds.

Cell Fuel

What are some important types of molecules in cells?

Organisms need certain types of molecules for growth, repair, and other life processes. For example, organisms use nutrients such as lipids, proteins, and carbohydrates for energy and as building materials. You get these nutrients from the food you eat. Nucleic acids are molecules that contain instructions for cell functions. Each of these types of molecules has a role in cell processes.

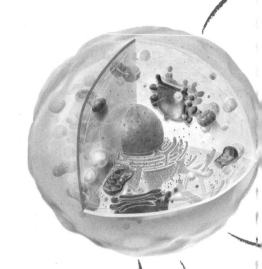

 **Active Reading**

8 Identify What are some examples of nutrients?

_____

_____

_____

Lipids

A **lipid** is a fat molecule or a molecule that has similar properties. Lipids do not mix with water. They have many jobs in cells, such as storing energy. Fats and oils are lipids that store energy that organisms can use when they need it. Your cells get lipids from foods such as olive oil and fish. Waxes and steroids are other types of lipids.

Proteins

A **protein** is a molecule made up of smaller molecules called *amino acids*. When you eat foods high in proteins, such as peanut butter and meat, the proteins are broken down into amino acids. Amino acids are used to make new proteins. Proteins are used to build and repair body structures and to regulate body processes. Proteins called *enzymes* (EHN•zymz) help chemical processes happen in cells.

9 Describe What are the building blocks of proteins?

_____

Carbohydrates

Molecules that include sugars, starches, and fiber are called **carbohydrates**. Cells use carbohydrates as a source of energy and for energy storage. Cells break down carbohydrates to release the energy stored in them. Carbohydrates contain carbon, hydrogen, and oxygen atoms. Simple carbohydrates, such as table sugar, are made up of one sugar molecule or a few sugar molecules linked together. Complex carbohydrates, such as starch, are made of many sugar molecules linked together. Pasta, made from grains, is a good source of complex carbohydrates.

Nucleic Acids

A **nucleic acid** is a molecule that carries information in cells. Nucleic acids are made up of smaller molecules called *nucleotides* (NOO•klee•oh•TYDZ). Deoxyribonucleic acid, or DNA, is one type of nucleic acid that is found in all cells. DNA contains the information that cells need to make molecules, such as proteins. The order of nucleotides in DNA reads like a recipe. Each nucleotide tells the cell the order of amino acids needed to build a certain protein.

DNA

10 Summarize Fill in the table with a function of each nutrient in the cell.

Nutrient	Function in the cell
Lipids	
Proteins	
Carbohydrates	
Nucleic acids	

Waterworks

What are phospholipids?

All cells are surrounded by a cell membrane. The cell membrane helps protect the cell and keep the internal conditions of the cell stable. A lipid that contains phosphorus is called a **phospholipid** (FOSS•foh•LIH•pyd). Phospholipids form much of the cell membrane. The head of a phospholipid molecule is attracted to water. The tail repels water, or pushes it away. Because there is water inside and outside the cell, the phospholipids form a double layer. One layer lines up so that the heads face the outside of the cell. A second layer of phospholipids line up so the heads face the inside of the cell. The tails from both layers face each other, forming the middle of the cell membrane. Molecules, such as water, are regulated into and out of a cell through the cell membrane.

Active Reading **11 Explain** Describe how phospholipids form a barrier between water inside the cell and water outside the cell.

_____

_____

_____

_____

Visualize It!

12 Identify Write *attracts* next to the end of the phospholipid that attracts water. Write *repels* next to the end that repels water.

Cell membrane

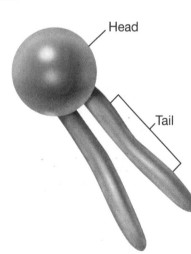

Phospholipid molecule

Head

Tail

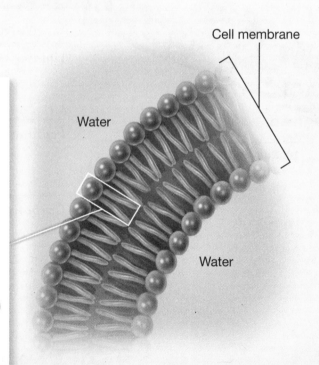

Water

Water

Why is water important?

Many cell processes require water, which makes up nearly two-thirds of the mass of the cell. Thus, water is an important nutrient for life. Water moves through the cell membrane by a process called *osmosis*. Osmosis depends on the concentration of the water inside and outside of the cell. Pure water has the highest concentration of water molecules. If the water concentration inside the cell is lower than the water concentration outside the cell, then water will move into the cell. If the environment outside a cell has a low concentration of water, such as in a salty solution, water will move out of the cell.

Losing too much water can cause a cell to shrivel and die.

The right balance of water allows a cell to function normally.

If too much water enters a cell, it may swell up and burst.

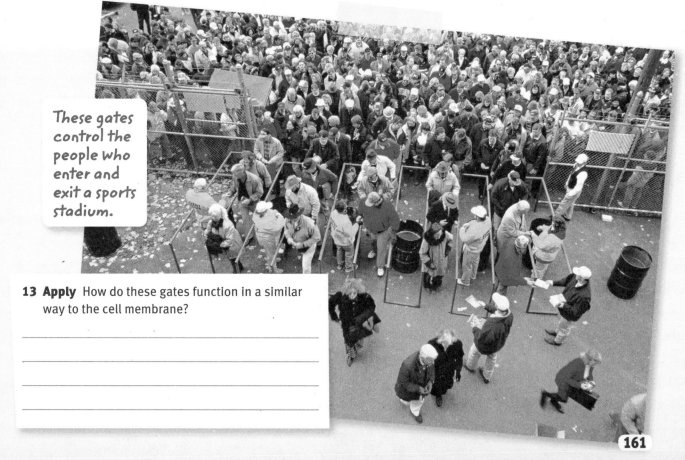

These gates control the people who enter and exit a sports stadium.

13 Apply How do these gates function in a similar way to the cell membrane?

_____

_____

_____

_____

Visual Summary

To complete this summary, circle the correct word and fill in the blanks with the correct word or phrase. Then, use the key below to check your answers. You can use this page to review the main concepts of the lesson.

Cell Chemistry

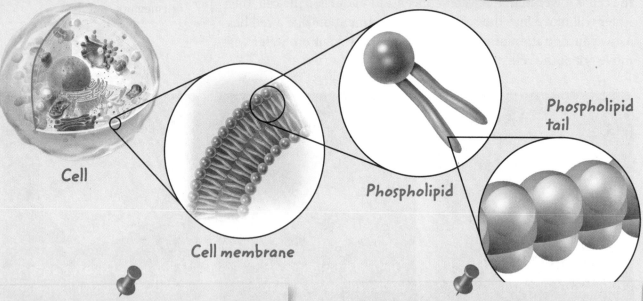

Cell

Cell membrane

Phospholipid

Phospholipid tail

Cells are made up of atoms and molecules.

15 A cell membrane is made of phospholipid atoms / molecules.

16 The tail of the phospholipid is made up of carbon and hydrogen atoms / molecules.

Cells use different molecules for life processes.

17 List four types of molecules important for cell processes.

_____

_____

_____

18 Water moves into and out of a cell through the

_____ .

Answers: 15 molecules; 16 atoms; 17 lipids, carbohydrates, proteins, nucleic acids; 18 cell membrane

19 **Relate** Explain how atoms and molecules are important to cell processes.

Lesson Review

Vocabulary

Fill in the blank with the term that best completes the following sentences.

1 The smallest unit of an element is a(n)

_____.

2 A(n) _____ is a group of atoms joined by chemical bonds.

Key Concepts

3 Contrast What is the difference between atoms and molecules?

_____

_____

_____

_____

4 Identify What are the functions of proteins in organisms?

_____

_____

_____

_____

5 List Name four important types of molecules found in cells.

_____

_____

_____

_____

6 Describe How does the structure of the cell membrane help the cell regulate water?

_____

_____

_____

_____

_____

_____

Critical Thinking

Use this diagram to answer the following questions.

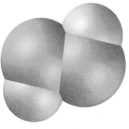

7 Identify Is this an atom or a molecule? Explain.

_____

_____

_____

_____

_____

8 Recognize The red spheres represent oxygen atoms, and the blue spheres represent hydrogen atoms. Is this substance a compound? Explain.

_____

_____

_____

_____

_____

_____

9 Summarize Why is water important in cells?

_____

_____

_____

_____

_____

_____

My Notes

Cell Structure and Function

ESSENTIAL QUESTION

What are the different parts that make up a cell?

By the end of this lesson, you should be able to compare the structure and function of cell parts in plant and animal cells.

→ 7.LS1.1

Cells have many parts. This part is called a Golgi complex. It functions like a shipping facility, packaging and distributing proteins and other materials for use in the cell.

Lesson Labs

Quick Labs
- Comparing Cells
- Making a 3-D Cell Model
- Cell Walls and Wilting

Engage Your Brain

1 Predict Check T or F to show whether you think each statement is true or false.

T	F	
☐	☐	All cells have the same structure and function.
☐	☐	Prokaryotes do not have a nucleus.
☐	☐	Plant cells are the same as animal cells.
☐	☐	All organisms are multicellular.

2 Relate How does the structure of this umbrella relate to its function?

_____

_____

_____

_____

_____

Active Reading

3 Synthesis You can often define an unknown word if you know the meaning of its word parts. Use the word parts and sentence below to make an educated guess about the meaning of the word *chloroplast*.

Word part	Meaning
chloro-	green
plast	structure

Example sentence
Plant cells have <u>chloroplasts</u>, which contain a green pigment used for making their own food.

Vocabulary Terms

- **cytoskeleton**
- **mitochondrion**
- **ribosome**
- **endoplasmic reticulum**
- **Golgi complex**
- **cell wall**
- **vacuole**
- **chloroplast**
- **lysosome**

4 Apply As you learn the definition of each vocabulary term in this lesson, create your own definition or sketch to help you remember the meaning of the term.

chloroplast:

_____

_____

_____

_____

Lesson 3 Cell Structure and Function **165**

Being Eu-nique

What are the characteristics of eukaryotic cells?

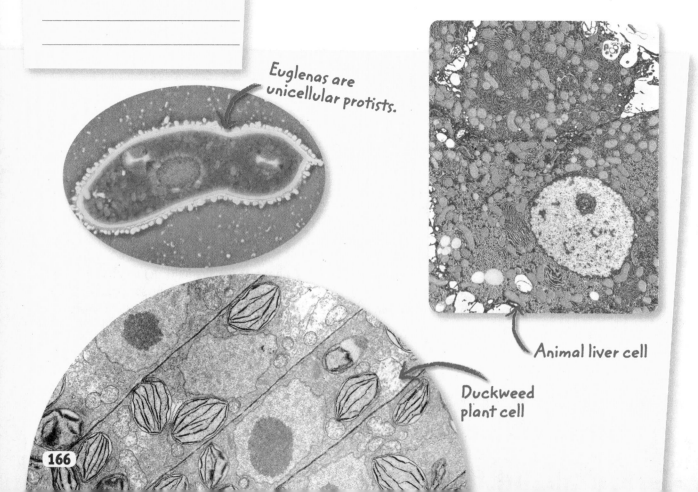
Active Reading

5 Identify As you read, underline the characteristics of eukaryotic cells.

All organisms are made up of one or more cells, but what kinds of cells? There are two types of organisms: prokaryotes and eukaryotes. Prokaryotes are made up of a single prokaryotic cell. Eukaryotes are made up of one or more eukaryotic cells. Prokaryotic cells do not have a nucleus or membrane-bound organelles. Eukaryotic cells have membrane-bound organelles, including a nucleus.

Eukaryotic cells can differ from each other depending on their *structure* and *function*. A cell's structure is the arrangement of its parts. A cell's function is the activity the parts carry out. For example, plant cells and animal cells have different parts that have different functions for the organism. This is what make plants and animals so different from each other. Even cells within the same organism can differ from each other depending on their function. Most of the cells in multicellular organisms are specialized to perform a specific function. However, all eukaryotic cells share some characteristics. They all have a nucleus, membrane-bound organelles, and parts that protect and support the cell.

Visualize It!

6 Apply A euglena is a unicellular organism. Why is it a eukaryote like the plant and animal cells shown here?

_____

_____

_____

_____

Euglenas are unicellular protists.

Animal liver cell

Duckweed plant cell

Parts that Protect and Support the Cell

Every cell is surrounded by a cell membrane. The cell membrane acts as a barrier between the inside of a cell and the cell's environment. This membrane protects the cell and regulates what enters and leaves the cell.

The cytoplasm is the region between the cell membrane and the nucleus that includes fluid and all of the cell organelles. Throughout the cytoplasm of eukaryotic cells is a **cytoskeleton**. The cytoskeleton is a network of protein filaments that gives shape and support to cells. The cytoskeleton is also involved in cell division and in movement. It may help parts within the cell to move. Or it may form structures that help the whole organism to move.

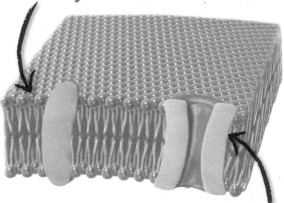

The cell membrane is a double layer of phospholipids. Water molecules and some gas molecules can pass through the cell membrane.

Other larger materials must pass through protein channels in the membrane.

7 Describe What are two functions of the cell membrane?

_____

_____

_____

_____

Genetic Material in the Nucleus

The nucleus is an organelle in eukaryotic cells that contains the cell's genetic material. Deoxyribonucleic acid, or DNA, is stored in the nucleus. DNA is genetic material that contains information needed for cell processes, such as making proteins. Proteins perform most actions of a cell. Although DNA is found in the nucleus, proteins are not made there. Instead, instructions for how to make proteins are stored in DNA. These instructions are sent out of the nucleus through pores in the nuclear membrane. The nuclear membrane is a double layer. Each layer is similar in structure to the cell membrane.

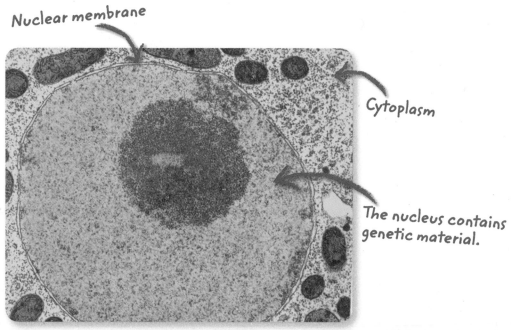

Nuclear membrane

Cytoplasm

The nucleus contains genetic material.

Part-iculars

What organelles are found in plant and animal cells?

Even though plant and animal cells are microscopic, they are very complex. They have many parts that function to keep the cell alive. Many of these parts are membrane-bound organelles that perform a specific function.

Mitochondria

Organisms need energy for all life's activities and processes. Cells carry out such activities and processes for growth and repair, movement of materials into and out of the cell, and chemical processes. Cells get energy by breaking down food using a process called *cellular respiration*. Cellular respiration occurs in an organelle called the **mitochondrion** (my•TOH•kahn•dree•ahn). In cellular respiration, cells use oxygen to release energy stored in food. For example, cells break down the sugar glucose to release the energy stored in the sugar. The mitochondria then transfer the energy released from the sugar to a molecule called *adenosine triphosphate*, or ATP. Cells use ATP to carry out cell processes.

Mitochondria have their own DNA and they have two membranes. The outer membrane is smooth. The inner membrane has many folds. Folds increase the surface area inside the mitochondria where cellular respiration occurs.

8 Explain Why are mitochondria called the powerhouses of cells?

_____

_____

_____

Ribosomes

Proteins control most chemical reactions of cells and provide structural support for cells and tissues. Some proteins are even exported out of the cell for other functions throughout the body. Making, packaging, and transporting proteins requires many organelles. The **ribosome** is the cell organelle that makes proteins by putting together chains of amino acids using instructions encoded in the cell's DNA. An amino acid is any of about 20 different carbon-based molecules that are used to make proteins. Almost all cells have ribosomes, which are the smallest organelles.

Ribosomes are not enclosed in a membrane. In prokaryotes, the ribosomes are suspended freely in the cytoplasm. In eukaryotes, some ribosomes are free, and others are attached to another cell organelle called the *endoplasmic reticulum*.

9 Describe How do ribosomes make proteins?

_____

_____

_____

© Houghton Mifflin Harcourt Publishing Company • Image Credits: (r) ©Jose Luis Calvo/Shutterstock

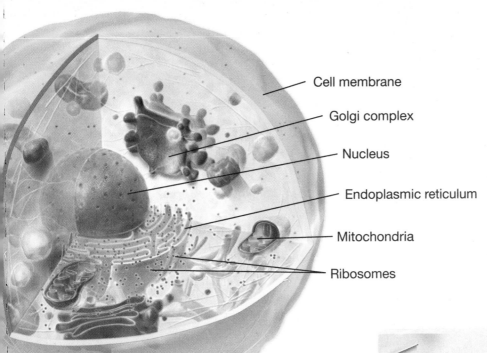

Cell membrane

Golgi complex

Nucleus

Endoplasmic reticulum

Mitochondria

Ribosomes

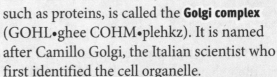

Golgi complex

Golgi Complex

The membrane-bound organelle that packages and distributes materials, such as proteins, is called the **Golgi complex** (GOHL•ghee COHM•plehkz). It is named after Camillo Golgi, the Italian scientist who first identified the cell organelle.

The Golgi complex is a system of flattened membrane sacs. Lipids and proteins from the ER are delivered to the Golgi complex where they may be modified to do different jobs. The final products are enclosed in a piece of the Golgi complex's membrane. This membrane pinches off to form a small bubble, or vesicle. The vesicle transports its contents to other parts of the cell or out of the cell.

11 Describe What is the function of the Golgi complex?

_____
_____
_____

Endoplasmic Reticulum

In the cytoplasm is a system of membranes near the nucleus called the **endoplasmic reticulum** (ehn•doh•PLAHZ•mick rhett•ICK•yoo•luhm), or ER. The ER assists in the production, processing, and transport of proteins and in the production of lipids. The ER is either smooth or rough. Rough ER has ribosomes attached to its membrane, while smooth ER does not. Ribosomes on the rough ER make many of the cell's proteins. Some of these proteins move through the ER to different places in the cell. The smooth ER makes lipids and breaks down toxic materials that could damage the cell.

10 Compare How does rough ER differ from smooth ER in structure and function?

_____
_____
_____

© Houghton Mifflin Harcourt Publishing Company • Image Credits:(l) ©CNRI/SPL/Photo Researchers, Inc.; (r) ©SPL/Photo Researchers, Inc

Now Showing:
The Plant Cell

What additional parts are found in plant cells?

Think about some ways that plants are different from animals. Plants don't move around, and some have flowers. Plant cells do have a cell membrane, cytoskeleton, nucleus, mitochondria, ribosomes, ER, and a Golgi complex, just like animal cells do. In addition, plant cells have a cell wall, a large central vacuole, and chloroplasts.

Cell Wall

In addition to the cell membrane, plant cells have a **cell wall**. The cell wall is a rigid structure that surrounds the cell membrane, identified by the yellow line around the plant cell in this photo. Cell walls provide support for and protection to the cell. Plants don't have a skeleton like many animals do, so they get their shape from the cell wall. The cells of fungi, archaea, bacteria, and some protists also have cell walls.

Large Central Vacuole

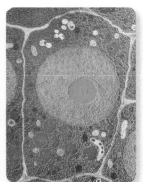

A **vacuole** (VAK•yoo•ohl) is a fluid-filled vesicle found in the cells of most animals, plants, and fungi. A vacuole may contain enzymes, nutrients, water, or wastes. Plant cells also have a large central vacuole that stores water. A central vacuole full of water helps support the cell. Plants may wilt when the central vacuole loses water.

13 Compare How do large central vacuoles differ from vacuoles?

_____

_____

_____

14 Identify Label these cell parts on the plant cell shown here:
- Mitochondrion
- Golgi complex
- Nucleus
- Endoplasmic reticulum
- Ribosomes
- Cell wall
- Cell membrane
- Cytoskeleton

Large central vacuole

F _____

G _____

A _____

B _____

C _____

D _____

E _____

H _____

Chloroplast

Chloroplasts

Animals must eat food to provide their cells with energy. However, plants, and some protists, can make their own food using photosynthesis. These organisms have **chloroplasts** (KLOHR•oh•plahstz), which are cell organelles where photosynthesis occurs. Photosynthesis is the process by which cells use sunlight, carbon dioxide, and water to make sugar and oxygen. Chloroplasts are green because they contain a green pigment called *chlorophyll* (KLOHR•oh•fill). Chlorophyll absorbs the energy in sunlight. This energy is used to make sugar, which is then used by mitochondria to make ATP. Chloroplasts have two outer membranes.

15 Describe What is the role of chlorophyll inside chloroplasts?

_____

_____

_____

Think Outside the Book Inquiry

16 Describe Cyanobacteria and green algae are similar to plants. Choose one of these organisms and explain why they are similar to plants but are not classified as plants.

Introducing:
The Animal Cell

What additional part is found in animal cells?

Animal cells are eukaryotic cells that contain a nucleus and are surrounded by a cell membrane. They contain many of the same organelles as most plant cells, including mitochondria, ribosomes, ER, and a Golgi complex. Most animal cells also contain a membrane-bound organelle called a *lysosome*.

Active Reading **17 Recognize** As you read, underline the function of lysosomes.

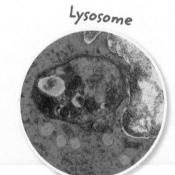

Lysosome

Lysosomes

Cell organelles called **lysosomes** (LY•soh•zohmz) contain digestive enzymes, which break down worn-out or damaged organelles, waste materials, and foreign invaders in the cell. Some of these materials are collected in vacuoles. A lysosome attaches to the vacuole and releases the digestive enzymes inside. Some of these materials are recycled and reused in the cell. For example, a human liver cell recycles half of its materials each week.

18 Compare How are lysosomes similar to vacuoles?

_____

_____

_____

_____

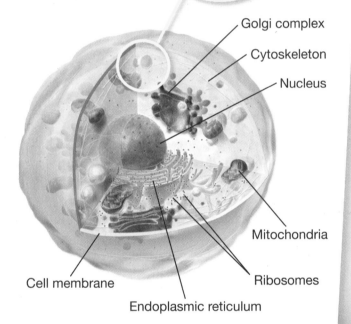

Golgi complex

Cytoskeleton

Nucleus

Mitochondria

Ribosomes

Endoplasmic reticulum

Cell membrane

19 Model Construct a two-dimensional model of each cell organelle identified in the *Structure* column. Complete the *Function* column for each structure. (The first one has been done for you.) Then put check marks in the last two columns to identify whether the cell structure can usually be found in plant cells, animal cells, or both kinds of cells.

Structure	Function	In plant cell?	In animal cell?
Nucleus	Contains the genetic material, called DNA. The DNA is like computer code that controls the cell's processes, such as making protein.		
Endoplasmic reticulum			
Golgi complex			
Ribosome			
Chloroplast			
Mitochondrion			
Large central vacuole			
Lysosome			

Visual Summary

To complete this summary, fill in the blanks to identify the organelles in each cell. Then, use the key below to check your answers. You can use this page to review the main concepts of the lesson.

Compare
Plant Cells and Animal Cells

Structures in plant cells

20 _____

21 _____

Structures in animal cells

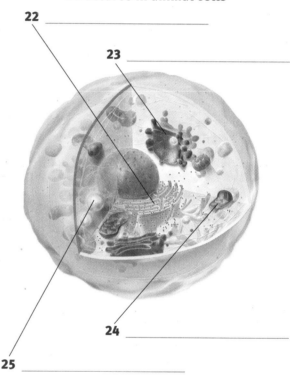

22 _____

23 _____

24 _____

25 _____

Plants and animals are eukaryotes. The structures inside a eukaryotic cell work together to keep the cell and the entire organism alive.

Answers: 20 large central vacuole; 21 cell wall; 22 endoplasmic reticulum; 23 Golgi complex; 24 mitochondrion; 25 lysosome

26 Summarize How do eukaryotic cells differ from each other?

Lesson Review

Vocabulary

Circle the term that best completes the following sentences.

1 A *Golgi complex / ribosome* makes proteins that are transported through the endoplasmic reticulum.

2 The *nucleus / large central vacuole* contains genetic material of a eukaryotic cell.

3 The *cell membrane / cytoplasm* acts as a barrier between the inside of a cell and the cell's environment.

4 The organelle in which photosynthesis takes place is the *cell wall / chloroplast*.

Key Concepts

5 Recognize What do all eukaryotic cells have in common?

_____

_____

_____

_____

_____

6 Compare How are the functions of the cytoskeleton and the cell wall similar?

_____

_____

_____

_____

7 Contrast What structures are found in plant cells that are not found in animal cells?

_____

_____

_____

Critical Thinking

Use this diagram to answer the following questions.

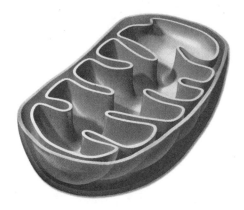

8 Identify What is this organelle?

_____

9 Explain How does its structure affect its function?

_____

_____

_____

_____

_____

_____

10 Compare Which cells contain this organelle: plant cells, animal cells, or both?

_____

11 Apply Explain the function of ribosomes and why cells need them.

_____

_____

_____

_____

_____

_____

My Notes

Making Predictions

Scientists try to answer questions about the world by developing hypotheses, making predictions, and conducting experiments to test those predictions. To make a prediction, a scientist will analyze a general idea and then predict specific results. Predictions often take the form of "if–then" statements. For example, "If living organisms are made of small units called cells, then we predict that we will see cells if we look at organisms up close under a microscope."

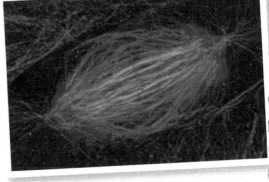

A dividing frog cell showing microtubules (green) and DNA (blue)

Tutorial

For an organism to grow and reproduce, chromosomes must replicate and cells must divide. The following steps will teach you how to make predictions from hypotheses about the role of protein fibers, called microtubules, in cell division.

Question: How do chromosomes move and separate during cell division?

Hypothesis: Microtubules play an important role in the movement of the chromosomes during cell division.

Prediction: If microtubules were inhibited during cell division, then chromosomes would not be able to move and separate from each other during cell division.

Observations: When microtubules are exposed to a drug that blocks microtubule formation, movement of chromosomes is inhibited and cell division stops.

What is the hypothesis? A hypothesis is a plausible answer to a scientific question. Form a hypothesis based on prior experience, background knowledge, or your own observations.

What would we expect or predict to see if the hypothesis were true? When scientists summarize their data, they look for observations and measurements that will support their hypothesis.

Does the prediction match the observations? If the data matches the predictions generated by the hypothesis, then the hypothesis is supported. Sometimes errors occur during the scientific investigation, which can lead to incorrect results. There is also the possibility that correct data will not match the hypothesis. When this happens, generate a new hypothesis.

You Try It!

Scientists often propose hypotheses about the causes of events they observe. Read the following scenario, and answer the questions that follow.

Scenario: A cell biologist has three cell cultures of human skin cells. The cells in each culture are taken from the same cell line. Each cell culture is placed in a solution for observation. The cells in culture A are growing faster than the cells in cultures B and C.

Question: Why are the cells in culture A growing at a faster rate than the cells in cultures B and C?

Hypothesis 1: The waste level is higher in cultures B and C than in culture A.

Hypothesis 2: The nutrient levels are higher in culture A than in cultures B and C.

1 Making Predictions Read each of the hypotheses above and then make a prediction for each about what might be observed.

Hypothesis 1:

_____

_____

_____

Hypothesis 2:

_____

_____

_____

2 Testing a Hypothesis Identify a possible experiment for each hypothesis that you can perform or observations that you can make to find out whether the hypothesis is supported.

Hypothesis 1:

_____

_____

_____

Hypothesis 2:

_____

_____

_____

3 Predicting Outcomes Fill in the two tables below with plausible data that supports each hypothesis.

Culture	Waste level	Rate of growth (cells/hour)
A		
B		
C		

Culture	Nutrient level	Rate of growth (cells/hour)
A		
B		
C		

Take It Home

Find a recent newspaper or magazine article that makes a conclusion based on a scientific study. Carefully evaluate the study and identify the predictions that were tested in the study. Bring the article to class and be prepared to discuss your analysis of the article.

The Diversity of Cells

ESSENTIAL QUESTION

How are organisms classified?

By the end of this lesson, you should be able to describe how science classifies living things, sorting each organism into groups based on its cellular structure and other features.

7.LS1.3

Two-thirds of ocean life remains undiscovered. As scientists encounter new life, they will classify each organism to learn more about how their discoveries relate to what is already known.

Lesson Labs

Quick Labs
- Observing Bacteria
- What Do Protists Look Like?

Field Lab
- Culturing Bacteria from the Environment

 Engage Your Brain

1 Predict Check T or F to show whether you think each statement is true or false.

T   F

☐ ☐ All multicellular organisms have specialized cells.

☐ ☐ Taxonomy is the science of describing, classifying, and naming living things.

☐ ☐ Kingdoms are the highest level of classification.

☐ ☐ Bacteria are eukaryote-celled organisms.

☐ ☐ Only organisms in the domain Plantae produce their own food through photosynthesis.

2 Analyze The orchid mantis below is so well camouflaged that you might mistake it for a flower! Write down how the orchid mantis is similar to and different from other animals.

_____

_____

 Active Reading

3 Synthesis You can use word parts to understand unfamiliar vocabulary. Use the prefix below to make an educated guess about the meaning of the word *microorganism*.

Prefix	Meaning
micro-	small

microorganism:

_____

_____

_____

Vocabulary Terms

- Bacteria
- Archaea
- Eukarya
- Eubacteria
- Archaebacteria
- kingdom
- Protista
- Fungi
- Plantae
- Animalia

4 Identify As you read, place a question mark next to any words that you don't understand. When you finish reading the lesson, go back and review the text that you marked. If the information is still confusing, consult a classmate or a teacher.

All Sorts of Cells

What are living things made of?

All living things are made of cells. Some, like bacteria (bak•TIR•ee•uh), are *unicellular* organisms. Unicellular organisms are made of a single cell. This single cell contains everything the organism needs to carry out the same seven processes that keep plants and animals alive.

Most of these unicellular organisms are so small that you need a microscope to see them. Organisms that can be seen only through a microscope are called *microorganisms*.

Amoeba

Spirogyra

An amoeba is an example of a simple unicellular organism. Amoebas can move in a crawling fashion by changing their shape.

A spirogyra is a simple multicellular organism. Spirogyras can be split into pieces, and each piece will grow into a complete organism.

Is life simple or complex?

Unicellular organisms are also called *simple* organisms. Biologists call such organisms simple because they are simple in structure. Simple organisms can also be *multicellular*. These simple multicellular organisms are made up of more than one cell, but the cells are all identical or very similar.

Other multicellular organisms are *complex*. Complex organisms have a diversity of *specialized* cells. The average human body has over 37 trillion cells, but all of these cells belong to one of only about 200 different kinds of specialized cells. Specialized cells differ in structure, size, or shape. For example, the largest cell in the human body is the female egg, and the smallest cell is the male sperm.

Specialized cells also differ in function. For example, white blood cells protect the body against germs, whereas red blood cells carry oxygen to all parts of the body.

Complex organisms have a diversity of cells. Groups of specialized cells come together to form a tissue, such as muscle tissue or bone tissue. Different tissues then group together to form organs. Specialized cells, tissue, and organs all have unique structures and functions that serve the organism.

5 Apply Why do you think new spirogyra can be grown from pieces of an existing organism?

_____

_____

_____

How do scientists keep track of living things?

Active Reading

6 Identify As you read, underline the levels of classification.

There are millions of living organisms on Earth, and each one has a unique cellular structure and cellular organization. To keep track of all of these living things, science *classifies* them based on the characteristics that the various organisms share. The science of describing, classifying, and naming living things is called *taxonomy*. Classification helps scientists answer questions such as:

- What characteristics do different organisms have in common?
- What makes an organism unique?
- How are living things related to each other?

Scientists use an eight-level system to classify living things. From most general to most specific, the levels of classification are domain, kingdom, phylum, class, order, family, genus, and species.

Visualize It!

7 Apply How does the number of organisms in each level change as you move closer to the species level?

_____

_____

_____

Classifying Organisms

Domain **Domain Eukarya** includes all protists, fungi, plants, and animals.

Kingdom **Kingdom Animalia** includes all animals.

Phylum Animals in **Phylum Chordata** have a hollow nerve cord in their backs. Some have a backbone.

Class Animals in **Class Mammalia**, or mammals, have a backbone and nurse their young.

Order Animals in **Order Carnivora** are mammals that have special teeth for tearing meat.

Family Animals in **Family Canidae** are canines. They are carnivores with nonretractable claws.

Genus Animals in **Genus *Canis*** are dog-like carnivores. They have prominent canine teeth.

Species The **Species *Canis familiaris***, or domestic dog, has unique traits that other members of genus *Canis* do not have.

From domain to species, each level of classification contains a smaller group of organisms.

Cell Royalty: Domains and Kingdoms

What are the three domains?

A domain represents the largest differences among organisms. These differences are found in the cellular structure of organisms. The three domains are **Bacteria**, **Archaea** (ar•KEE•uh), and **Eukarya** (yoo•KAIR•ee•uh). Some scientists in other countries use a five-kingdom system instead of the more standard six-kingdom system. In the five-kingdom system, Eubacteria and Archaebacteria are not separate kingdoms. Instead, all of the organisms in those two kingdoms are classified in kingdom Monera.

8 Compare How are organisms in the domains Eubacteria and Archaebacteria similar? How are they different?

_____

_____

_____

Cell Type	Prokaryote	
Domain	Bacteria	Archaea
Kingdom	**Eubacteria (yoo•bak•TEER•ee•uh)** The only kingdom in the domain Bacteria is Eubacteria. Kingdom Eubacteria contains unicellular organisms that have a cell wall, but no nucleus or organelles. Eubacteria can be found in soil, in water, and even in the bodies of plants and animals.	**Archaebacteria (ahr•kee•bak•TEER•ee•uh)** All organisms in the domain Archaea belong to the kingdom Archaebacteria. Organisms in kingdom Archaebacteria differ from those in kingdom Eubacteria both in their genetics and in the makeup of their cell walls. Archaebacteria can survive in extreme and harsh environments, such as salt lakes, hot springs, and thermal vents.
Number of Cells	Unicellular	Unicellular
Cellular Structure	Simple E. coli bacteria are a large and diverse group of eubacteria. Although most strains of E. coli are harmless, others can make you very sick.	Simple Organisms from the genus Methanosarcina live in oxygen-deprived areas, such as ground water and the digestive tracts of animals, and produce methane.

What are the kingdoms?

Kingdom (KING•duhm) is the second highest taxonomic rank. It is the rank below domain. Kingdoms used to be the highest level, but then scientists noticed that organisms in two of the kingdoms were very different from organisms in the four other kingdoms. As a result, science created a new taxonomic rank and called it a *domain*.

9 Evaluate Do cells have similarities and differences across all the kingdoms? If so, what are they? Use evidence or examples to support your answer.

_____

_____

_____

Eukaryote			
Eukarya			
Protista (proh•TIS•tuh)	**Fungi** (FUHN•jy)	**Plantae** (PLAN•tee)	**Animalia** (an•uh•MEY•lee•uh)
A protist is any eukaryote organism that is not an animal, plant, or fungi. Protist cells may or may not have cell walls or chloroplasts. Protists can acquire nutrients by photosynthesis, absorption, or both.	Organisms in kingdom Fungi are made of cells with cell walls but no chloroplasts. Fungi acquire nutrients through absorption, and they are the major decomposers of nature.	The cells of organisms in kingdom Plantae have a cell wall and chloroplasts. These organisms, which acquire nutrients through photosynthesis, are the source of food for most living creatures on Earth.	Animalia have cells with cell membranes but no cell walls or chloroplasts. Animalia acquire nutrients through ingestion. All Animalia need oxygen for metabolism.
Mostly unicellular, but some multicellular	*Unicellular/ Multicellular*	*Multicellular*	*Multicellular*
Simple	*Complex*	*Complex*	*Complex*
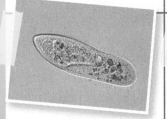			
Paramecium are unicellular organisms found in ponds, swamps, and other bodies of water.	Mushrooms are multicellular organisms that can grow almost anywhere.	Most cactuses live in habitats that are subject to drought.	The red fox is the largest fox and lives across the entire Northern Hemisphere.

Sorting it Out

What are the kinds of organisms?

There are many different types of organisms. Organisms can be organized according to whether they have unicellular or multicellular, and prokaryote or eukaryote structures.

Visualize It!

10 Identify Fill in the blanks with the missing kingdoms.

A _____

Halobacterium

You would have to travel to the Great Salt Lake or the Dead Sea to find organisms in genus *Halobacterium* because they live where many other organisms can't survive. The prokaryote cells of genus *Halobacterium* thrive in environments with very high concentrations of salt. Such cells are easy to spot because of their red, or sometimes orange, color. *Halobacterium* organisms are decomposers that feed on dead matter and wastes.

Procyon lotor

You probably know *Procyon lotor* by its more common name, raccoon. This complex multicellular organism acquires its nutrients through ingestion. You can identify *Procyon lotor* by the mask it wears on its face and its extremely dexterous front paws. Most raccoons live in forests, but due to habitat destruction, some live in urban areas where they are considered pests.

B _____

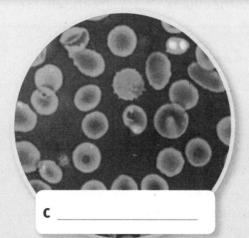

C _____

Plasmodium falciparum

Plasmodium falciparum is a unicellular eukaryote organism with a simple unicellular structure that causes the disease malaria. It is transmitted by the female mosquito. In fact, without the mosquito, there would be no *Plasmodium falciparum* because this organism only reproduces in the mosquito's gut. Of all the malarial parasites, it is the deadliest. Although there are treatments for malaria, there is no vaccine.

Penicillium chrysogenum

If you have ever had to take an antibiotic for a bacterial infection, then you probably have *Penicillium chrysogenum* to thank for getting better. This multicellular eukaryote is a decomposer that is used to produce penicillin. Penicillin was discovered in 1928, when Alexander Fleming noticed that some bacteria he was culturing would not grow near this decomposer.

D _____

E _____

Iris germanica

Iris germanica is a complex multicellular organism whose cells have cell walls. These organisms produce their own food through photosynthesis. While native to central and southern Europe, *Iris germanica* now grows all over the world. The iris is the state flower of Tennessee.

Vibrio cholerae

The natural habitat of *Vibrio cholerae* is brackish or salt water. It is a unicellular prokaryote organism. Some strains of *Vibrio cholerae* cause the disease cholera. It is estimated that up to 4 million people suffer from cholera each year. Cholera infections are most commonly caused by tainted water that people drink. Most people who are infected with cholera live in undeveloped countries with poor drinking water.

F _____

Active Reading

11 Identify As you read, underline the characteristics of each organism that will help you identify its kingdom.

Visual Summary

To complete this summary, check the box that indicates true or false. Then, use the key below to check your answers. You can use this page to review the main concepts of the lesson.

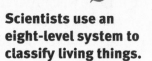

Organisms have a diversity of cells and cellular structures.

    T **F**

12 ☐ ☐ All organisms are multicellular.

13 ☐ ☐ All multicellular organisms are complex.

Scientists use an eight-level system to classify living things.

    T **F**

14 ☐ ☐ The science of describing, classifying, and naming living things is called *taxonomy*.

15 ☐ ☐ Kingdoms have more organisms than any other level.

Scientists use cellular structure to classify organisms.

    T **F**

16 ☐ ☐ Plantae get their nutrients through photosynthesis.

17 ☐ ☐ Only organisms in kingdom Plantae have chloroplasts.

Domains are divided into kingdoms.

    T **F**

18 ☐ ☐ Every domain has more than one kingdom.

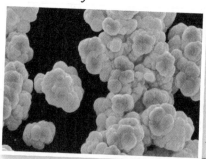

Answers: 12 F, 13 F, 14 T, 15 F, 16 T, 17 F, 18 F

19 Summarize Why do scientists classify living organisms?

© Houghton Mifflin Harcourt Publishing Company • Image Credits: (tl) ©Rimantas Abromas/Shutterstock; (bl) ©Jimbycat/Getty Images; (br) ©Power and Syred/Science Source

Lesson Review

Vocabulary

Fill in the blanks with the term that best completes the sentences.

1 A(n) _____ has fewer organisms than a domain, but it has more organisms than a phylum.

2 The four kingdoms of eukaryotes are _____, _____, _____, and _____.

3 Prokaryote-celled organisms belong to either the _____ or _____ kingdoms.

Key Concepts

4 List Name the eight levels of classification from most general to most specific.

_____

_____

_____

_____

_____

_____

5 Identify What two words are used to describe the number of cells in an organism?

_____

_____

_____

_____

6 Compare What do complex organisms have that makes them different from simple organisms?

_____

_____

_____

_____

7 Explain Describe how scientists determine which kingdom an organism belongs to.

_____

_____

_____

_____

Critical Thinking

8 Explain What do you need to know in order to determine the domain to which an organism belongs?

_____

_____

_____

_____

_____

_____

9 Synthesize How are plants and animals the same? How are they different?

_____

_____

_____

_____

_____

_____

10 Classify A scientist finds an organism that has a single cell without a nucleus. This organism was found in pond water. In which kingdom does it belong? Explain.

_____

_____

_____

_____

_____

_____

My Notes

Levels of Cellular Organization

ESSENTIAL QUESTION

How are living things organized?

By the end of this lesson, you should be able to describe the different levels of organization in living things.

➤ 7.LS1.4

The eye of a green iguana is an organ made of millions of cells and many layers of tissues.

🖐 Lesson Labs

Quick Labs
• Evaluating Specialization
• Observing Plant Organs

Exploration Lab
• The Organization of Organisms

🧠 Engage Your Brain

1 Describe Fill in the blank with the word or phrase you think correctly completes the following sentences.

Your body has many organs, such as a

heart and _____.

Plant organs include stems and

_____.

Animal and plant organs are organized into organ systems, much like you organize your

homework in _____.

2 Explain How is the structure of a hammer related to its function?

_____
_____
_____
_____
_____

✏️ Active Reading

3 Relate Many scientific words, such as *organ* and *tissue,* also have everyday meanings. Use context clues to write your own definition for each underlined word.

It is helpful to use a <u>tissue</u> when sneezing to prevent the spread of droplets carrying bacteria.

tissue:

_____
_____
_____

An <u>organ</u> can be very difficult to play.

organ:

_____
_____
_____

Vocabulary Terms

• organism   • organ system
• tissue   • structure
• organ   • function

4 Apply As you learn the definition of each vocabulary term in this lesson, create your own definition or sketch to help you remember the meaning of the term.

Body Building

How are living things organized?

Active Reading

5 Identify As you read, underline the characteristics of unicellular and multicellular organisms.

An **organism** is a living thing that can carry out life processes by itself. *Unicellular organisms* are made up of just one cell that performs all of the functions necessary for life. Unicellular organisms do not have levels of organization. Having only one cell has advantages and disadvantages. For example, unicellular organisms need fewer resources and some can live in harsh conditions, such as hot springs and very salty water. However, a disadvantage of being unicellular is that the entire organism dies if the single cell dies.

Into Cells

Multicellular organisms are made up of more than one cell. These cells are grouped into different levels of hierarchical organization, including tissues, organs, and organ systems. The cells that make up a multicellular organism, such as humans and plants, are specialized to perform specific functions. Many multicellular organisms reproduce through sexual reproduction, during which a male sex cell fertilizes a female sex cell. The single cell that results from fertilization divides repeatedly. This cell division forms the basic tissues of an embryo, which further develop into all of the specialized tissues and organs within a multicellular organism. Other characteristics of multicellular organisms include a larger size and a longer lifespan than unicellular organisms.

There are some disadvantages to being multicellular. Multicellular organisms need more resources than do unicellular organisms. Also, the cells of multicellular organisms are specialized for certain jobs, which means that cells must depend on each other to perform all of the functions that an organism needs to live.

Humpback whales are multicellular organisms.

Diatoms are microscopic unicellular organisms that live in water.

Into Tissues

A **tissue** is a group of similar cells that perform a common function. Humans and many other animals are made up of four basic types of tissue: nervous, epithelial, connective, and muscle. Nervous tissue functions as a messaging system within the body. Epithelial tissue is protective and forms boundaries, such as skin. Connective tissue, including bones and blood, holds parts of the body together and provides support and nourishment to organs. Muscle tissue helps produce movement.

Plants have three types of tissue: transport, protective, and ground. Transport tissue moves water and nutrients through the plant. Protective tissue protects the outside of the plant. Ground tissue provides internal support and storage and absorbs light energy to make food in photosynthesis (foh•toh•SIN•thuh•sis).

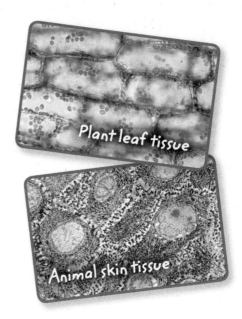
Plant leaf tissue

Animal skin tissue

6 Compare Fill in the Venn diagram to compare the functions of animal tissues and plant tissues. What functions do they share?

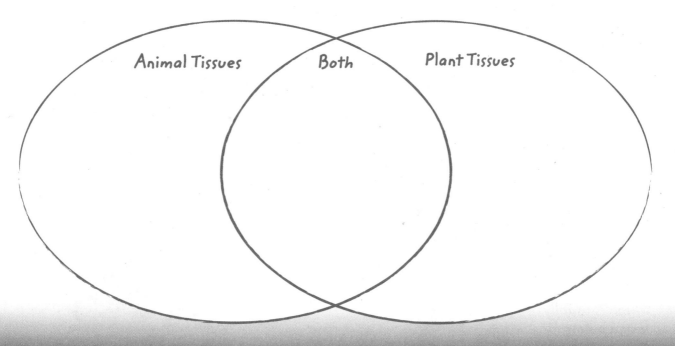

Animal Tissues   Both   Plant Tissues

Visualize It!

7 Apply In which organism shown on the opposite page are cells organized into tissues? Explain your answer.

_____

_____

_____

_____

_____

Into Organs

A structure made up of a collection of tissues that carries out a specialized function is called an **organ**. The stomach is an organ that breaks down food for digestion. Different types of tissues work together to accomplish this function. For example, nervous tissue sends messages to the stomach's muscle tissue to tell the muscle tissue to contract. When the muscle tissue contracts, food and stomach acids are mixed, and the food breaks down.

Plants also have organs that are made up of different tissues working together. For example, a leaf is an organ that contains protective tissue to reduce water loss, ground tissue for photosynthesis, and transport tissue to move nutrients from leaves to stems. Stems and roots are organs that function to transport and store water and nutrients in the plant. The trunk of most trees is a stem. Roots are usually below the ground.

Active Reading

8 Apply How do organs relate to cells and tissues?

_____

_____

_____

Two organ systems in plants include the shoot system, which includes stems and leaves, and the root system, which is usually found below the ground.

Plant cell

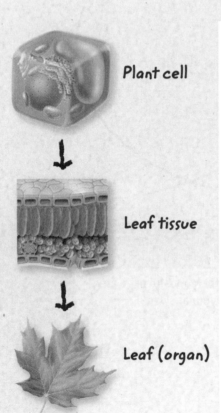
Leaf tissue

Leaf (organ)

Visualize It!

9 Identify Label the organ system shown in the tree below. Then draw and label the tree's root system.

The digestive system is an organ system found in most animals, including humans.

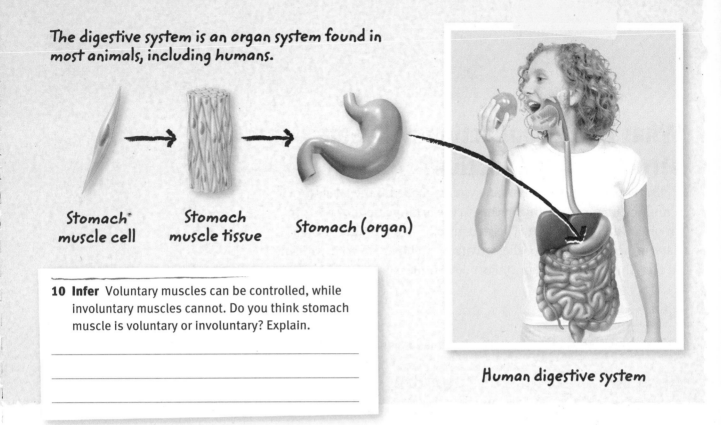

Stomach muscle cell → Stomach muscle tissue → Stomach (organ)

Human digestive system

10 Infer Voluntary muscles can be controlled, while involuntary muscles cannot. Do you think stomach muscle is voluntary or involuntary? Explain.

_____

_____

_____

Into Organ Systems

An **organ system** is a group of organs that work together to perform body functions. Each organ system has a specific job to do for the organism. For example, the stomach works with other organs of the digestive system to digest and absorb nutrients from food. Other organs included in the digestive system are the esophagus and the small and large intestines.

Humans are made up of many organ systems. All of the systems have specific functions to keep the body alive.

Think Outside the Book Inquiry

11 Illustrate Research an organ system of the human body other than the digestive system and draw a diagram that shows the organizational hierarchy from cell to organism.

What's Your Function?

What is the connection between structure and function?

Cells, tissues, organs, and organ systems make up the structure of a multicellular organism. **Structure** is the arrangement of parts in an organism or an object. The structure of a cell, tissue, or organ determines its **function**, or the activity of each part in an organism. In fact, the structure of any object determines its function.

Active Reading

12 Recognize As you read, underline examples of multicellular structures.

Structure Determines Function

Cells, tissues, and organs vary in structure. For example, bone cells look different from plant leaf cells. A lung differs from a stomach because they have different functions. Cells, tissues, and organs are specialized to perform specific functions. For example, a lung is an organ made up of cells and tissues that work together to help you breathe. The lungs are made up of millions of tiny air sacs called *alveoli* (singular, *alveolus*). The large number of alveoli increases the surface area of the lungs to let enough oxygen and carbon dioxide move between the lungs and the blood.

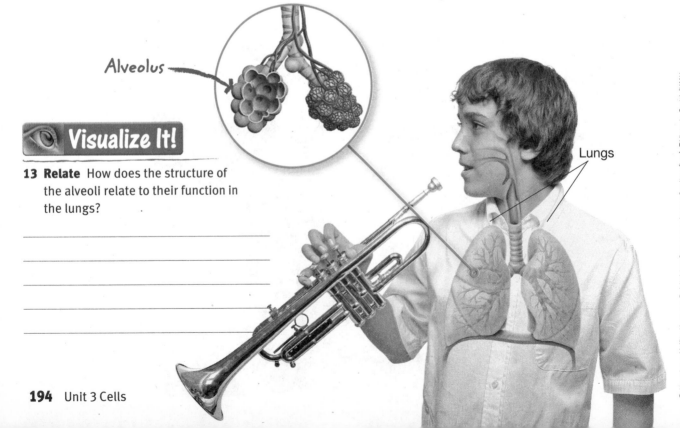

Alveolus

Lungs

Visualize It!

13 Relate How does the structure of the alveoli relate to their function in the lungs?

_____

_____

_____

_____

_____

WEIRD SCIENCE

Odd Bodies

With millions of different organisms that exist on Earth, it's no wonder there are so many different body structures. Some organisms have special structures that can help them eat—or not be eaten!

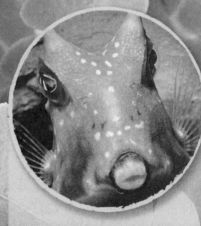

Can't Touch This!
Named for its prickly body, the spiny katydid doesn't make much of a meal for its predator. Male katydids sing loudly at night to attract female katydids. The singing can also attract predators, such as bats, who hunt for food at night. Its spines provide the katydid with some protection from being eaten.

Blow on Your Food
The longhorn cowfish is a marine organism that lives on the sandy ocean bottom at depths up to 50 m. Its permanently puckered mouth helps the cowfish find food. The cowfish blows jets of water into the sand to find and feed on tiny organisms.

Night Vision
The tarsier's huge eyes provide excellent vision for hunting insects at night. Its eyes average 16 mm in diameter, but the tarsier's overall body size ranges from 85 mm to 165 mm. In comparison, your eyes would be the size of apples! When the tarsier spots its prey, it leaps through the air to pounce on it. The tarsier's long fingers help it grasp branches when it's on the move.

Extend

Inquiry

14 Relate How does the body structure of each of these organisms contribute to a particular function?

15 Contrast How do structures in living organisms compare with structures of nonliving things such as construction cranes, buildings, ships, airplanes, or bridges?

16 Imagine Describe an organism that might live in an extreme environment such as inside a volcano, deep in the ocean, or in an icy cave. What type of organism is it? What special structures would it have in order to survive in that environment?

Systems at Work

What tasks do systems perform to meet the needs of cells?

Complex organisms are made up of many systems. These systems work together to perform actions needed by cells to function properly. Whether it is a bone cell or a skin cell, each cell in the organism needs to receive nutrients, exchange carbon dioxide and oxygen, and have waste products taken away.

A unicellular organism must perform all functions necessary for life, such as getting nutrients, exchanging gases, and removing wastes. The functions must be performed by a single cell, because there is no opportunity for cell specialization.

Multicellular organisms face different challenges. Multicellular organisms have different cell types that can work together in groups to perform specific functions. Groups of cells that work together form tissues. Groups of tissues that work together form organs, and groups of organs that work together form systems. Systems work with other systems. In most animals, the digestive, respiratory, and excretory systems interact with the circulatory system to maintain healthy cells. A circulatory system delivers nutrients to body cells and carries away wastes. It carries oxygen to cells and removes carbon dioxide.

Some plants have a vascular system that transports water and nutrients to and from cells throughout the plant. Xylem and phloem are tissues that make up the vascular system. Xylem transports water from roots to cells. Phloem transports nutrients made in leaf cells to all parts of the plant.

Active Reading

17 Compare How do unicellular organisms and multicellular organisms compare in meeting their needs to stay alive?

_____

_____

_____

_____

_____

Visualize It!

18 Analyze This diagram shows the xylem and phloem that make up the plant's vascular system. How does a vascular system serve the needs of plant cells?

_____

_____

_____

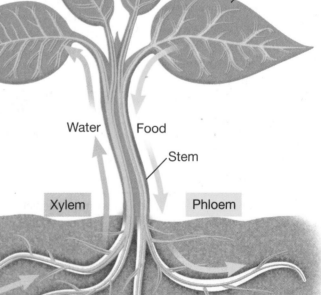

Leaf

Water   Food

Stem

Xylem   Phloem

Roots

Delivering Nutrients

The digestive system in most animals breaks down food mechanically and chemically. In most animals, the digestive system works with a circulatory system. In the small intestine, nutrients are absorbed through thousands of finger-like projections in the wall of the small intestine, called villi, and then into the blood vessels of the circulatory system. Once in the blood, the nutrients are delivered to cells throughout the body.

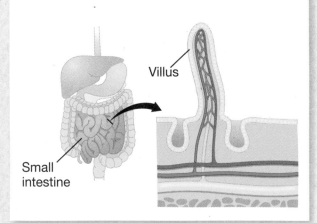

Villus

Small intestine

Delivering Oxygen

In animals, taking in oxygen is a function of the respiratory system. Depending on the animal, oxygen enters a body through skin, gills, spiracles, or lungs. There, it comes in contact with the circulatory system. Oxygen enters the bloodstream and is carried to the cells of the body. Once in the cells, oxygen is used to release energy from nutrients from digestion.

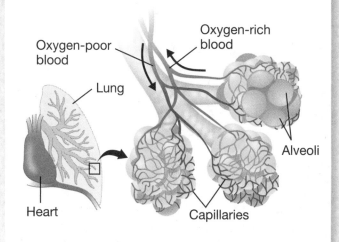

Oxygen-poor blood

Oxygen-rich blood

Lung

Alveoli

Heart

Capillaries

Removing Wastes

Skin, lungs, the digestive system, and the kidneys all have processes for removing waste products from the body. Sweat evaporates from the skin. Solid wastes and some water move out as part of the digestive system. Carbon dioxide and some water are breathed out through the respiratory system. In humans, the largest amount of excess water and waste products from cells is carried by the blood to the kidneys. There, wastes are filtered out of the blood through a complex series of tubules in the kidneys and leave the body as urine.

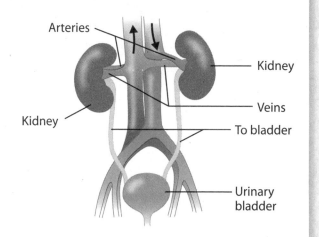

Arteries

Kidney

Veins

Kidney

To bladder

Urinary bladder

👁 Visualize It!

19 Synthesize Notice that oxygen-poor blood (blue) and oxygen-rich blood (red) are shown in all three diagrams. Describe the role of blood in the transportation of materials throughout the body.

_____

_____

_____

_____

_____

_____

Visual Summary

To complete this summary, fill in the blanks with the correct word. Then, use the key below to check your answers. You can use this page to review the main concepts of the lesson.

Cellular Organization

All organisms are made up of one or more cells.

T F

20 ☐ ☐ A plant is a unicellular organism.

The structures of cells, tissues, and organs determine their functions.

T F

21 ☐ ☐ The protective tissue on a leaf has a structure that keeps the moisture in the leaf from drying out.

Multicellular organisms are hierarchically organized into tissues, organs, and organ systems.

T F

22 ☐ ☐ This leaf is an example of a plant organ.

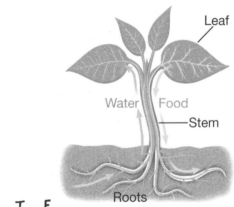

Leaf

Water   Food

Stem

Roots

T F

23 ☐ ☐ A plant obtains water from its environment through the root system.

Answers: 20 False; 21 True; 22 True; 23 True

24 **Synthesize** How do cells, tissues, organs, and organ systems work together in a multicellular organism?

Lesson Review

Vocabulary

Fill in the blank with the term that best completes the following sentences.

1 Animals have four basic types of

_____: nervous, epithelial, muscle, and connective.

2 Together, the esophagus, stomach, and

intestines are part of a(n) _____.

Key Concepts

3 Describe What are the levels of hierarchical organization in multicellular organisms?

_____

_____

_____

_____

_____

_____

4 Analyze Discuss two benefits of multicellular organisms' having some specialized cells rather than all the cells being the same.

_____

_____

_____

_____

_____

5 Relate How do the structures in an organism relate to their functions?

_____

_____

_____

_____

_____

_____

Critical Thinking

Use the figure to answer the next two questions.

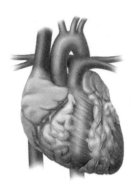

Human heart

6 Apply What level of hierarchical organization is shown here?

_____

7 Relate How does this level of hierarchical organization relate to cells? To organ systems?

_____

_____

_____

_____

_____

_____

_____

8 Analyze Explain why a circulatory system is important in meeting the needs of all cells throughout an animal's body.

_____

_____

_____

_____

_____

_____

_____

My Notes

Homeostasis and Cell Processes

ESSENTIAL QUESTION

How do organisms maintain homeostasis?

By the end of this lesson, you should be able to explain the important processes that organisms undergo to maintain stable internal conditions.

7.LS1.2

These American alligators are warming themselves in the sun. Temperature is one factor that an organism can control to maintain stable internal conditions.

Lesson Labs

Quick Labs
- Investigate Microorganisms
- Homeostasis and Adaptations

Exploration Lab
- Diffusion

Engage Your Brain

1 Explain How is this person able to stay on the skateboard?

_____

_____

2 Describe Fill in the blanks with the word or phrase that you think correctly completes the following sentences.

Eating _____ provides your body with nutrients it needs for energy.

Cells can _____ to make more cells.

Trucks, airplanes, and trains are used to _____ people and supplies from one place to another.

Active Reading

3 Synthesis You can often define an unknown word if you know the meaning of its word parts. Use the word parts and sentence below to make an educated guess about the meaning of the word *photosynthesis*.

Word part	Meaning
photo-	light
synthesis	to make

Example sentence
Plants use a process called <u>photosynthesis</u> to make their own food.

Vocabulary Terms

- homeostasis
- photosynthesis
- cellular respiration
- mitosis
- passive transport
- diffusion
- osmosis
- active transport
- endocytosis
- exocytosis

4 Identify As you read, place a question mark next to any words that you don't understand. When you finish reading the lesson, go back and review the text that you marked. If the information is still confusing, consult a classmate or a teacher.

photosynthesis:

_____

_____

Stayin' Alive

What is homeostasis?

We all feel more comfortable when our surroundings are ideal—not too hot, not too cold, not too wet, and not too dry. Cells are the same way. However, a cell's environment is constantly changing. **Homeostasis** (hoh•mee•oh•STAY•sis) is the maintenance of a constant internal state in a changing environment. In order to survive, your cells need to be able to obtain and use energy, make new cells, exchange materials, and eliminate wastes. Homeostasis ensures that cells can carry out these tasks in a changing environment.

Active Reading **6 Summarize** What are four things that cells can do to maintain homeostasis?

_____

_____

_____

Visualize It!

7 Apply Think about how this girl is feeling after she exercises. What things can you see that are helping to keep her body temperature stable?

_____

_____

Balance in Organisms

All cells need energy and materials in order to carry out life processes. A unicellular organism exchanges materials directly with its environment. The cell membrane and other parts of the cell regulate what materials get into and out of the cell. This is one way that unicellular organisms maintain homeostasis.

Cells in multicellular organisms must work together to maintain homeostasis for the entire organism. Multicellular organisms have systems that transport materials to cells from other places in the organism. For example, the main transport system in your body is your cardiovascular system. The cardiovascular system includes the heart, blood vessels, and blood. The heart pumps blood through branched blood vessels that come close to every cell in the body. Blood carries materials to the cells and carries wastes away from the cells. Other multicellular organisms have transport systems, too. For example, many plants have two types of vascular tissues that work together as a transport system. *Xylem* is the tissue that transports water and minerals from the roots to the rest of the plant. Another tissue called *phloem* transports food made within plant cells.

Active Reading

8 Compare As you read, underline how unicellular organisms and multicellular organisms exchange materials.

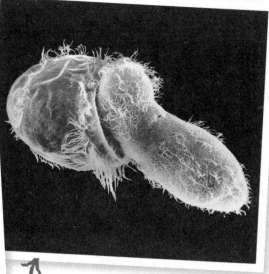

A unicellular organism, **Didinium**, is eating another unicellular organism, called a **Paramecium**.

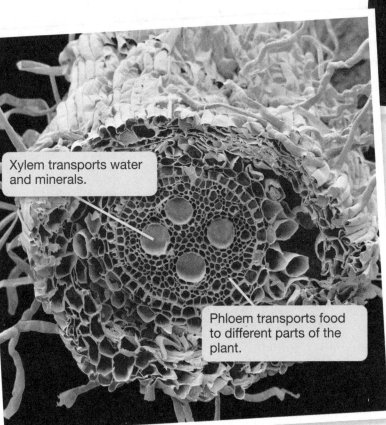

Xylem transports water and minerals.

Phloem transports food to different parts of the plant.

Plants have two types of vascular tissue that they use to transport materials.

© Houghton Mifflin Harcourt Publishing Company • Image Credits: (t) ©Biophoto Associates/Photo Researchers, Inc.; (b) ©Steve Gschmeissner/Photo Researchers, Inc.

Get Growing!

How do cells get energy?

Cells need energy to perform cell functions. Cells get energy by breaking down materials, such as food, in which energy is stored. Breaking down food also provides raw materials the cell needs to make other materials for cell processes.

Photosynthesis

The sun provides the energy for plants to grow and make food. Plants use sunlight to change carbon dioxide and water into sugar and oxygen. This process by which plants, algae, and some bacteria make their own food is called **photosynthesis**. Inside plant and algal cells are special cell organelles, called *chloroplasts*, where photosynthesis takes place.

Cellular Respiration

All living things need food to produce energy for cell processes. The process by which cells use oxygen to produce energy from food is called **cellular respiration**. Plants, animals, and most other organisms use cellular respiration to get energy from food.

Nearly all the oxygen around us is made by photosynthesis. Animals and plants use oxygen during cellular respiration to break down food. Cellular respiration also produces carbon dioxide. Plants need carbon dioxide to make sugars. So, photosynthesis and respiration are linked, each one depending on the products of the other.

Plants provide the food for nearly all living things on land. Some organisms eat plants for food. Other organisms eat animals that eat plants.

9 Synthesize Fill in the blanks with the materials that are involved in photosynthesis and cellular respiration.

Photosynthesis	_____ + carbon dioxide $\xrightarrow{\text{sunlight}}$ _____ + oxygen
Cellular respiration	sugar + _____ $\longrightarrow$ water + _____ + energy

How do cells divide?

Cells grow, divide, and die. Some cells divide more often than others. For example, cells in the skin are constantly dividing to replace those that have died or are damaged. Some cells, such as nerve cells, cannot divide to produce new cells once they are fully formed. Multicellular organisms grow by adding more cells. These new cells are made when existing cells divide.

The Cell Cycle

Cell division in eukaryotes is a complex process. Before a cell can divide, its deoxyribonucleic acid (DNA) is copied. Then, the DNA copies are sorted into what will become two new cells. In order to divide up the DNA evenly between the new cells, the DNA needs to be packaged. The packages are called *chromosomes* (croh•moh•SOHMS). Equal numbers of chromosomes are separated, and the nucleus splits to form two identical nuclei. This process is called **mitosis**. Then, the rest of the cell divides, resulting in two identical cells. Because the two new cells have DNA identical to that found in the original cell, all the cells in an organism have the same genetic material.

Active Reading

10 Explain Why is it important for DNA to be copied before cell division?

_____

_____

_____

_____

Visualize It!

11 Compare How do new cells form in plants and animal?

_____

_____

_____

_____

When a plant cell divides, a cell plate forms and the cell splits into two cells.

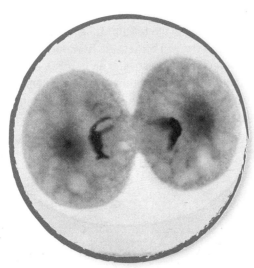

In animal cells, the cell membrane pinches inward through the cell to form two new cells.

Move It!

How do cells exchange materials?

What would happen to a factory if its supply of raw materials never arrived or it couldn't get rid of its garbage? Like a factory, an organism must be able to obtain materials for energy, make new materials, and get rid of wastes. The exchange of materials between a cell and its environment takes place at the cell's membrane. Cell membranes are *semi-permeable* because they allow only certain particles to cross into or out of the cell.

Passive Transport

The movement of particles across a cell membrane without the use of energy by the cell is called **passive transport**. Passive transport aids homeostasis because, along with active transport, it helps to maintain a constant internal state in a changing environment. For example, when a tea bag is added to a cup of water, the molecules in the tea will eventually spread throughout the water. **Diffusion** is the movement of molecules from high concentrations to low concentrations. Some nutrients move into a cell by diffusion. Some waste products move out of the cell by diffusion. **Osmosis** is the diffusion of water through a semi-permeable membrane. Many molecules are too large to diffuse through the cell membrane. Some of these molecules enter and exit cells through protein channels embedded in the cell membrane. When molecules move through these protein channels from areas of higher concentration to areas of lower concentration, the process usually requires no energy.

Active Reading

12 Relate As you read, underline the similarity between diffusion and osmosis.

13 Conduct an Investigation Pour boiling hot water into a clear teacup. Place a tea bag in the teacup. Take notes on what happens, and then describe what you witnessed. How dark is the water after five minutes? After ten minutes? After an hour? Does it keep getting darker and darker? Explain how this experiment demonstrates the role of passive transport in homeostasis. (Keep in mind the role of the paper that holds the tea.)

_____

_____

_____

_____

_____

Active Transport

Cells often need to move materials across the cell membrane from areas of low concentration into areas of higher concentration. This is the opposite direction of passive transport. **Active transport** is the movement of particles against a concentration gradient and requires the cell to use energy. Some large particles that do not fit through the protein channels may require active transport across the cell membrane by processes called *endocytosis* and *exocytosis*.

Visualize It!

14 Identify Place a check mark next to the box that describes diffusion. Explain your answer.

_____

_____

_____

_____

Chemical energy

Passive transport moves materials into and out of a cell to areas of lower concentration. ☐

Active transport uses energy to move materials into and out of a cell to areas of higher concentration. ☐

Endocytosis

The process by which a cell uses energy to surround a particle and enclose the particle in a vesicle to bring the particle into the cell is called **endocytosis** (en•doh•sye•TOH•sis). Vesicles are sacs formed from pieces of the cell membrane. Unicellular organisms, such as amoebas, use endocytosis to capture smaller organisms for food.

The cell comes into contact with a particle.

The cell membrane begins to wrap around the particle.

15 Describe What is happening in this step?

_____

_____

_____

_____

Exocytosis

When particles are enclosed in a vesicle and released from a cell, the process is called **exocytosis** (ek•soh•sye•TOH•sis). Exocytosis is the reverse process of endocytosis. Exocytosis begins when a vesicle forms around particles within the cell. The vesicle fuses to the cell membrane and the particles are released outside of the cell. Exocytosis is an important process in multicellular organisms.

Large particles that must leave the cell are packaged in vesicles.

16 Describe What is happening in this step?

_____

_____

_____

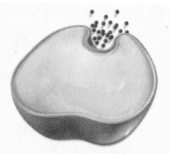

The cell releases the particles to the outside of the cell.

How do organisms maintain homeostasis?

As you have read, cells can obtain energy, divide, and transport materials to maintain stable internal conditions. In multicellular organisms, the cells must work together to maintain homeostasis for the entire organism. For example, when some organisms become cold, the cells respond in order to maintain a normal internal temperature. Muscle cells will contract to generate heat, a process known as shivering.

Some animals adapt their behavior to control body temperature. For example, many reptiles bask in the sun or seek shade to regulate their internal temperatures. When temperatures become extremely cold, some animals hibernate. Animals such as ground squirrels are able to conserve their energy during the winter when food is scarce.

Some trees lose all their leaves around the same time each year. This is a seasonal response. Having bare branches during the winter reduces the amount of water loss. Leaves may also change color before they fall. As autumn approaches, chlorophyll, the green pigment used for photosynthesis, breaks down. As chlorophyll is lost, other yellow and orange pigments can be seen.

The leaves of some trees change colors when the season changes.

Active Reading

17 Identify As you read, underline the different ways that organisms can respond to changes in the environment.

Visualize It!

18 Describe How is this boy's body responding to the cold weather?

_____

_____

_____

Visual Summary

To complete this summary, fill in the blanks with the correct word or phrase. Then use the key below to check your answers. You can use this page to review the main concepts of the lesson.

Cells need energy to perform cell functions.

19 Food is made during _____.
Energy is produced from food during

_____.

Cell division allows organisms to grow and repair damaged parts.

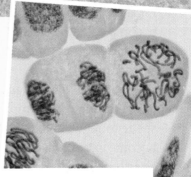

20 _____ occurs when cells divide to form two new nuclei that are identical to each other.

Maintaining Homeostasis: Balance In Organisms

Materials move into and out of cells through the cell membrane.

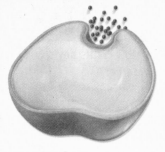

21 _____ uses energy to release particles from a cell.

Organisms respond to changes in the environment.

22 The change in leaf color on these trees is one way the trees maintain _____.

Answers: 19 photosynthesis; cellular respiration, 20 Mitosis; 21 Active transport; 22 homeostasis

23 Summarize Explain why organisms need to maintain homeostasis.

210 Unit 3 Cells

© Houghton Mifflin Harcourt Publishing Company • Image Credits: (tl) ©Ocean/Corbis; (tr) ©M.I. Walker/SPL/Photo Researchers, Inc.; (br) ©Digital Vision

Lesson Review

Vocabulary

In your own words, define the following terms.

1 homeostasis

_____

_____

2 endocytosis

_____

_____

_____

Key Concepts

3 Compare What is the difference between passive and active transport?

_____

_____

_____

4 List List four things that cells do to maintain homeostasis.

_____

_____

_____

_____

5 Describe What happens during mitosis?

_____

_____

_____

6 Apply How do the cells in your body get energy?

_____

_____

_____

_____

_____

Critical Thinking

Use the graphs to answer the next two questions.

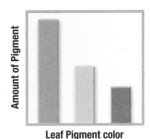

Summer

Fall

Amount of Pigment

Leaf Pigment color

Amount of Pigment

Leaf Pigment color

7 Compare How do the amounts of green pigment, chlorophyll, differ from summer to fall?

_____

_____

_____

8 Infer How do you think the change in chlorophyll levels is a response to changes in the length of day from summer to fall?

_____

_____

_____

_____

_____

_____

_____

9 Explain Why is homeostasis important for cells as well as for an entire organism?

_____

_____

_____

_____

My Notes

Analyzing Technology

Skills
✓ Identify risks
✓ Identify benefits
Evaluate cost of technology
Evaluate environmental impact
Propose improvements
Propose risk reduction
Plan for technology failures
✓ Compare technology
✓ Communicate results

Objectives
• Identify different resources for nutritional values.
• Compare the nutritional value of common foods.

Analyzing Nutrients

Technology includes products, processes and systems developed to meet people's needs. Therefore, food is a kind of technology. Food supplies materials, called *nutrients*, that the body needs to perform its life functions. Your body gets nutrients from the food that you eat and the beverages that you drink. Each nutrient plays a role in keeping your body healthy. To make good decisions about what to eat, use nutrition guidelines such as the ChooseMyPlate.gov recommendations and the Nutrition Facts panels and ingredient labels on food packages.

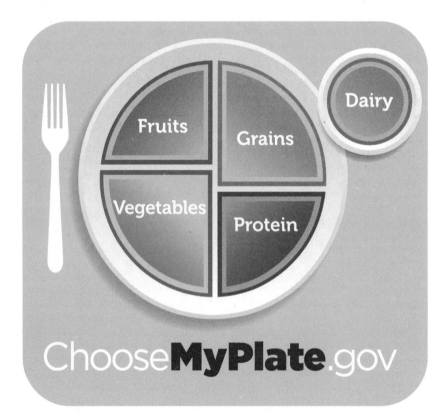

The MyPlate image was designed to help people make healthy food choices. As shown on the MyPlate icon, a healthy meal should be made up primarily of fruits and vegetables. The rest should be made up of lean protein, whole grains, and low-fat dairy products.

1 Infer According to the MyPlate icon, what kinds of food should you eat to maintain a healthy body?

_____

_____

What's in Your Food?

Nutrients are listed on food labels by amounts and as percentages of Daily Values. The Daily Value (DV) of a nutrient is the recommended amount that a person should consume in a day. The percentage of the DV of a nutrient tells you what percentage of the recommended amount is provided by one serving of the food if your diet contains 2,000 Calories. A Calorie is a measurement of the amount of energy your body gets from a food. Your body gets energy from carbohydrates, proteins, and fats. So when is the amount of a nutrient in a food item low, and when is it high? If a food item has less than 5% of the DV of a nutrient, the Food and Drug Administration (FDA) says it's low in that nutrient. If the item has more than 20% of the DV of a nutrient, the FDA says it's high in that nutrient.

2 Calculate If a person consumes an entire can of this product, what percentage of his or her Daily Value of saturated fat would he or she consume?

_____

_____

_____

_____

Fat Builds cell membranes, excess linked with heart disease

Sodium Needed for nerve function, excess linked with heart and kidney disease

Dietary Fiber Lowers risk of diabetes and heart disease

Protein Important for heart, brain, kidney, muscles

Vitamin A Important for eyes, skin

Calcium Important for bones, teeth, heart

Vitamin C Helps body absorb iron

Iron Vital for red blood cells

Nutrition Facts

Serving Size 8 ounces   Servings in can 2

Amount Per Serving

Calories 155   Calories from Fat 93

	% Daily Value*
Total Fat 11g	**16%**
Saturated Fat 3g	**15%**
Trans Fat	
Polyunsaturated Fat 5g	
Monounsaturated Fat 3g	
Cholesterol 0mg	**0%**
Sodium 148mg	**6%**
Potassium 45mg	**1%**
Total Carbohydrate 14g	**5%**
Dietary Fiber 1g	**5%**
Sugars 1g	
Protein 2g	

Vitamin A	0%	•	Vitamin C	9%
Calcium	1%	•	Iron	3%

* Percent Daily Values are based on a 2,000 calorie diet. Your Daily Values may be higher or lower depending on your calorie needs.

 You Try It! ⟶

Now it's your turn to compare the nutritional value of some food items.

You Try It!

Now it's your turn to use a Pugh chart and to compare the nutritional value of some common food items. You will analyze which foods are most likely to provide better nutrition, which allows you to make objective comparisons.

You Will Need

✓ Make a list of 5 common foods that you like to eat, including some that you think are healthy and some that you think are not very healthy.

(1) Identify Risks

Using Nutrition Facts labels from Internet or supermarket resources, find out what nutrients are in each food on your list. Which foods are high in nutrients that are associated with health risks, such as saturated fat and cholesterol? Are there other health risks in these foods—for example, few healthy nutrients, or too many calories based on your recommended daily allowance? Use the information you find to fill in the table.

Food item	Unhealthy nutrients	Other health risks
1		
2		
3		
4		
5		

(2) Identify Benefits

Now use the same resources to identify which foods from your list are high in nutrients associated with health benefits. Are there other benefits you should consider for your foods? Use your information to fill in the table.

Food item	Healthy nutrients	Other health benefits
1		
2		
3		
4		
5		

(3) Compare Technologies

Now make a Pugh chart to compare nutritional values numerically. Write the names of the five foods you chose in the top row of the chart below. Fill in the boxes under each food item, ranking the food on a scale of 1–5, based on how it compares to the other foods for each nutrient.

Key for Ranking:

Each food is assigned 1 if it has the least of the listed nutrient and a 5 if it has the most.

1 = lowest

5 = highest

Fiber				
Protein				
Vitamin A				
Calcium				
Vitamin C				
Iron				
Total				

(4) Communicate Results

Summarize your comparison of your food items, and interpret the information. Which of your foods has the highest total? Which has the lowest? What do your results tell you about the nutritional value of these foods?

_____

_____

_____

_____

_____

Unit 3 〈 **Big Idea** 〈 All living things are made up of one or more cells.

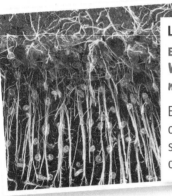

Lesson 1

ESSENTIAL QUESTION
What are living things made of?

Explain the components of the scientific theory of cells.

Lesson 2

ESSENTIAL QUESTION
What are the building blocks of organisms?

Discuss the chemical makeup of living things.

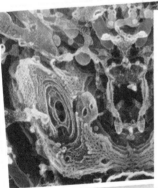

Lesson 3

ESSENTIAL QUESTION
What are the different parts that make up a cell?

Compare the structure and function of cell parts in plant and animal cells.

Lesson 4

ESSENTIAL QUESTION
How are organisms classified?

Describe how science classifies living things sorting them into groups.

Lesson 5

ESSENTIAL QUESTION
How are living things organized?

Describe the different levels of organization in living things.

Lesson 6

ESSENTIAL QUESTION
How do organisms maintain homeostasis?

Explain the important processes that organisms undergo to maintain stable internal conditions.

Connect **ESSENTIAL QUESTIONS**
Lessons 3 and 6

1 Synthesize Explain the role of a cell membrane and how it aids in maintaining homeostasis.

_____

_____

_____

_____

Think Outside the Book

2 Synthesize Choose one of the activities to help synthesize what you learned in this unit.

☐ Using what you learned in lessons 2 and 3, choose a plant or an animal, and create a poster that shows its levels of hierarchical organization from a single cell to the whole organism. Include a diagram of a cell and one example of the organism's tissues, organs, and organ systems.

☐ Using what you learned in lesson 4, create a slide presentation on the classification of cells according to kingdoms. Incorporate images of organisms representing each kingdom.

Unit 3 Review

Name _____

Vocabulary

Check the box to show whether each statement is true or false.

T	F	
☐	☐	**1** Scientists use taxonomy to classify organisms into domains and kingdoms.
☐	☐	**2** A molecule is made up of atoms that are joined together.
☐	☐	**3** A eukaryote has cells that do not contain a nucleus, whereas a prokaryote has cells that have a nucleus.
☐	☐	**4** A cell organelle that is found in animal cells but usually not in plant cells is a lysosome.
☐	☐	**5** A tissue is a group of similar cells that perform a common function.

Key Concepts

Read each question below, and circle the best answer.

6 Prem finds an unusual object on the forest floor. After he examines it under a microscope and performs several lab tests, he concludes that the object is a living thing. Which of the following observations most likely led to Prem's conclusion?

A The object contained carbon.

B Prem saw cells in the object.

C The object had a green color.

D Prem saw minerals inside the object.

7 Which of the following substances must animal cells take in from the environment to maintain homeostasis?

A DNA

B oxygen

C chlorophyll

D carbon dioxide

Unit 3 Review continued

8 Juana made the following table.

Organelle	Function
Mitochondrion	Cellular respiration
Ribosome	DNA synthesis
Chloroplast	Photosynthesis
Endoplasmic reticulum	Makes proteins and lipids
Golgi complex	Packages proteins

In her table, Juana listed several cell organelles and their functions, but she made an error. Which of the organelles shown in the table is listed with the wrong function?

A mitochondrion
B ribosome
C chloroplast
D Golgi complex

9 Which molecule can mix with water and is also a source of energy and a storage area for energy in the body?

A lipid
B chlorophyll
C nucleic acid
D carbohydrate

10 Which method of material exchange uses up energy?

A osmosis
B diffusion
C active transport
D passive transport

11 Consider a multicellular organism whose cells have cell walls, but not chloroplasts. What kingdom does it belong to, based on its cellular characteristics?

A Plantae
B Protista
C Fungi
D Eubacteria

12 What organ system in animals performs a similar function as the xylem and phloem of plants?

   A digestive system

   B excretory system

   C respiratory system

   D circulatory system

13 Which statement correctly tells why the cells of unicellular and multicellular organisms divide?

   A The cells of unicellular organisms divide to reproduce; those of multicellular organisms divide to replace cells and to grow.

   B The cells of unicellular organisms divide to replace cells and to grow; those of multicellular organisms divide to reproduce.

   C The cells of both kinds of organisms divide to reproduce.

   D The cells of both kinds of organisms divide to replace cells and to grow.

14 The following picture shows *E. coli* cells, a species of bacterium.

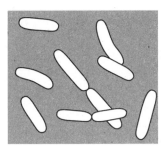

Which of the following statements correctly compares the cells shown in the picture with a human cell?

   A Both types of cells divide by mitosis.

   B Human cells contain proteins, but *E. coli* cells do not.

   C Both cells contain ribosomes and a cell membrane.

   D Human cells contain DNA, but *E. coli* cells do not.

15 A plant leaf is an organ that traps light energy to make food. In what way is an animal stomach similar to a plant leaf?

A Both organs make food.

B Both organs are made up of only one kind of cell.

C Both organs are made up of several kinds of tissues.

D Both organs take in oxygen and release carbon dioxide.

16 The following table shows the surface-area-to-volume ratio of four cube-shaped cell models.

Cell Model	Surface Area	Volume	Surface-Area-to-Volume Ratio
A	6 cm^2	1 cm^3	6 : 1 = 6
B	24 cm^2	8 cm^3	24 : 8 = 3
C	54 cm^2	27 cm^3	54 : 27 = 2
D	96 cm^2	64 cm^3	96 : 64 = 1.5

Cells are small, and their surface area is large in relation to their volume. This is an important feature for the proper transport of both nutrients and water into and out of the cell. Which of the four model cells do you think will be best able to supply nutrients and water to its cell parts?

A cell model A

B cell model B

C cell model C

D cell model D

17 Cells of a multicellular organism are specialized. What does this statement mean?

A Cells of a multicellular organism are adapted to perform specific functions.

B Cells of a multicellular organism perform all life functions but not at the same time.

C Cells of a multicellular organism are specialized because they have a complex structure.

D Cells of a multicellular organism can perform all the life functions the organism needs to survive.

Name _____

Critical Thinking

Answer the following questions in the space provided.

18 The following diagram shows a cell that Dimitri saw on his microscope slide.

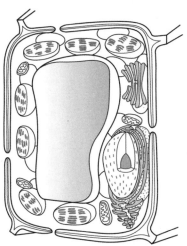

Dimitri's teacher gave him an unlabeled slide of some cells and asked him to identify whether the cells were plant cells or animal cells. Dimitri examined the slide under a microscope and concluded that the cells were plant cells.

How did Dimitri reach his conclusion? Is his conclusion correct? What life process can these cells carry out that a cell from another kind of multicellular organism cannot?

_____

_____

_____

_____

_____

19 There are many ways to categorize cells. Cells can be simple or complex, and unicellular or multicellular. Why are living things organized according to their cellular structure?

_____

_____

_____

_____

_____

_____

20 One of the characteristics of living things is that they respond to external changes in their environment so that their internal environment stays as stable as possible. Why must an organism do this? Name an environmental change that an animal must respond to in order to keep a stable internal environment. What might happen to an organism if it could not adapt to an external change?

_____

_____

_____

_____

Connect **ESSENTIAL QUESTIONS**
Lessons 2, 5, and 6

Answer the following question in the space provided.

21 Use the following picture showing the vascular system of some plants.

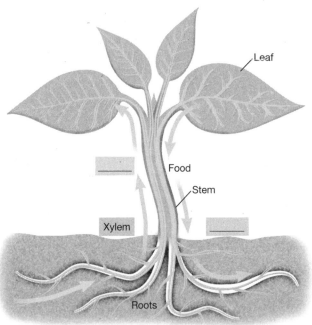

Two of the labels on the diagram are missing. What are the missing labels? Describe the process that plants use to transport water and nutrients to and from cells.

_____

_____

_____

_____

_____

© Houghton Mifflin Harcourt Publishing Company

The Cycling of Matter and Energy

Big Idea

All living things need matter and energy to survive.

7.LS1.9, 7.LS2.1

All living and nonliving things are made of matter. Energy helps living organisms use matter in life processes, such as eating, breathing, growing, and reproducing.

What do you think?

Mealy parrots and cattleya orchids are both found in the Amazon rainforest. How do organisms like these get and use matter and energy?

CITIZEN SCIENCE

Design for Living

British ecologist Arthur Tansley often gets credit for coining the word *ecosystem*. In fact, British botanist Arthur Roy Clapham came up with the term when Tansley asked him for a word to describe both the physical and biological parts of an environment.

1 Think About It

How can matter and energy leave one ecosystem and move to another ecosystem?

_____

_____

_____

_____

_____

_____

_____

Seaweed cannot survive outside of water for very long. When matter is taken out of its ecosystem, this interferes with the balance of organisms.

② Ask A Question

How does matter and energy move through an ecosystem?

Design your own ecosystem. Remember to include both living and nonliving features.

Write it!

Make a list of all the things in your ecosystem.

_____

_____

_____

_____

_____

③ Apply Your Knowledge

A What does your ecosystem need in order to function successfully?

_____

_____

_____

B Which of the things you listed above are examples of matter? Which are examples of energy?

_____

_____

_____

_____

C How do matter and energy move through your ecosystem?

_____

_____

_____

_____

Take It Home

Plant two bean plants or marigolds in separate pots. Place one of the pots in a sunny location. Place the other pot in a closet. Provide both plants with the same amount of water and fertilizer. Check both plants daily, noting their size and overall health. Record your observations for one month. What do your findings tell you?

Photosynthesis and Cellular Respiration

ESSENTIAL QUESTION

How do cells get and use energy?

By the end of this lesson, you should be able to explain how cells capture and release energy.

7.LS1.9

Sunflowers capture light energy and change it to chemical energy, but people need to eat to get energy.

✋ **Lesson Labs**

Quick Labs
- Plant Cell Structures
- Investigate Carbon Dioxide

S.T.E.M. Lab
- Investigate Rate of Photosynthesis

Engage Your Brain

1 Predict Check T or F to show whether you think each of the following statements is true or false.

T	F	
☐	☐	All living things must eat other living things for food.
☐	☐	Plants can make their own food.
☐	☐	Plants don't need oxygen, only carbon dioxide.
☐	☐	Animals eat plants or other animals that eat plants.
☐	☐	Many living things need oxygen to release energy from food.

2 Infer Look at the photo. Describe the differences between the plants. What do you think caused these differences?

_____

_____

_____

_____

_____

_____

_____

 ## Active Reading

3 Synthesize You can often define an unknown word if you know the meaning of its word parts. Use the word parts and sentence below to make an educated guess about the meaning of the term *chlorophyll*.

Word part	Meaning
chloro-	green
-phyll	leaf

Example sentence
Chlorophyll is a pigment that captures light energy.

chlorophyll:

_____

_____

Vocabulary Terms

- photosynthesis
- cellular respiration
- chlorophyll

4 Apply As you learn the definition of each vocabulary term in this lesson, write your own definition or make a sketch to help you remember the meaning of the term.

Energize!

How do the cells in an organism function?

Active Reading 5 **Identify** As you read, underline sources of energy for living things.

How do you get the energy to run around and play soccer or basketball? How does a tree get the energy to grow? All living things, from the tiniest single-celled bacterium to the largest tree, need energy. Cells must capture and use energy or they will die. Cells get energy from food. Some living things can make their own food. Many living things get their food by eating other living things.

Your cells use energy all the time, whether you are active or not.

Cells Need Energy

Growing, moving, and other cell functions use energy. Without energy, a living thing cannot replace cells, build body parts, or reproduce. Even when a living thing is not very active, it needs energy. Cells constantly use energy to move materials into and out of the cell. They need energy to make different chemicals. And they need energy to get rid of wastes. A cell could not survive for long if it did not have the energy for all of these functions.

Active Reading 6 **Relate** Why do living things need energy at all times?

_____

_____

_____

Cells Get Energy from Food

The cells of all living things need chemical energy. Food contains chemical energy. Food gives living things the energy and raw materials needed to carry out life processes. When cells break down food, the energy of the chemical bonds in food is released. This energy can be used or stored by the cell. The atoms and molecules in food can be used as building blocks for the cell.

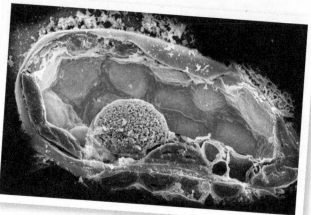

Plant cells make their own food using energy from the sun.

Living things get food in different ways. In fact, they can be grouped based on how they get food. Some living things, such as plants and many single-celled organisms, are called *producers* (proh•DOO•suhrz). Producers can make their own food. Most producers use energy from the sun. They capture and store light energy from the sun as chemical energy in food. A small number of producers, such as those that live in the deepest parts of the ocean, use chemicals to make their own food. Producers use most of the food they produce for energy. The unused food is stored in their bodies.

Many living things, such as people and other animals, are *consumers* (kun•SOO•muhrz). Consumers must eat, or consume, other living things to get food. Consumers may eat producers or other consumers. The cells of consumers break down food to release the energy it contains. A special group of consumers is made up of *decomposers* (dee•cum•POH•zhurhz). Decomposers break down dead organisms or the wastes of other organisms. Fungi and many bacteria are decomposers.

7 Compare Use the Venn diagram below to describe how producers and consumers get energy.

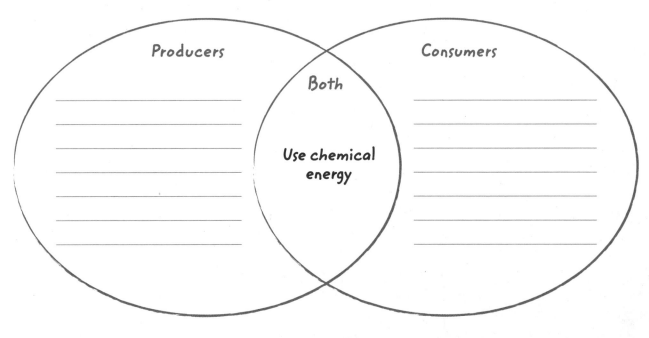

Producers

Both

Consumers

Use chemical energy

Cooking with Chloroplasts

How do plant cells make food?

Nearly all life on Earth gets energy from the sun. Plants make food with the energy from the sun. So, plants use energy from the sun directly. Animals use energy from the sun indirectly when they eat a plant or another animal.

In a process called **photosynthesis** (foh•toh•SYN•thuh•sys), plants use energy from sunlight, carbon dioxide, and water to make sugars. It is a cycling of matter and flow of energy into and out of organisms. Plants capture light energy from the sun and change it to chemical energy in sugars. These sugars are made from water and carbon dioxide. In addition to sugars, photosynthesis also produces oxygen gas. The oxygen gas is given off into the air.

Active Reading

8 Identify What is the source of energy for nearly all life on Earth?

_____

_____

Visualize It!

Photosynthesis In many plants, photosynthesis takes place in the leaf. Chlorophyll, which is located in chloroplasts, captures light energy from the sun. This light energy is converted to chemical energy in sugars.

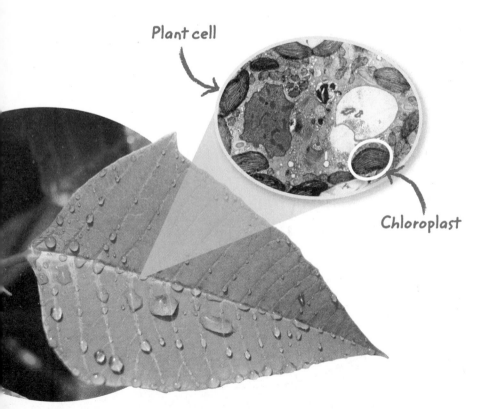

Plant cell

Chloroplast

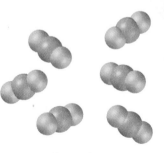

Water

Carbon dioxide

Capturing Light Energy

Energy from sunlight powers the process of photosynthesis. The light energy is converted to chemical energy, which is stored in the bonds of the sugar molecules made during photosynthesis.

Photosynthesis takes place in organelles called *chloroplasts* (KLOHR•oh•plahstz). These organelles are found only in the cells of plants and other organisms that undergo photosynthesis. They are not found in animal or fungal cells. Chloroplasts contain a green pigment called **chlorophyll** (KLOHR•oh•fill). Chlorophyll captures energy from sunlight. This energy is used to combine carbon dioxide (CO_2) and water (H_2O), forming the sugar glucose ($C_6H_{12}O_6$) and oxygen gas (O_2). Photosynthesis is a series of reactions summarized by the following chemical equation:

$$6CO_2 + 6H_2O + \text{light energy} \rightarrow C_6H_{12}O_6 + 6O_2$$

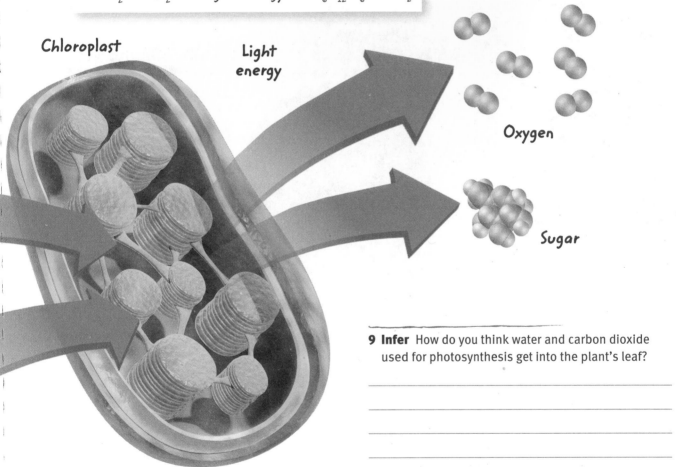

Chloroplast

Light energy

Oxygen

Sugar

9 Infer How do you think water and carbon dioxide used for photosynthesis get into the plant's leaf?

_____

_____

_____

_____

Storing Chemical Energy

Glucose (GLOO•kohs) is a sugar that stores chemical energy. It is the food that plants make. Plant cells break down glucose for energy. Excess sugars are stored in the body of the plant. They are often stored as starch in the roots and stem of the plant. When another organism eats the plant, the organism can use these stored sugars for energy.

Mighty Mitochondria

How do cells get energy from food?

When sugar is broken down, energy is released. It is stored in a molecule called *adenosine triphosphate* (ATP). ATP powers many of the chemical reactions that enable cells to survive. The process of breaking down food to produce ATP is called **cellular respiration** (SELL•yoo•lahr ress•puh•RAY•shuhn). Cellular respiration is another way in which matter is cycled and energy is flowed into and out of organisms.

Mitochondria are found in both plant cells and animal cells.

Mitochondrion

Cellular Respiration During cellular respiration, cells use oxygen gas to break down sugars and release energy.

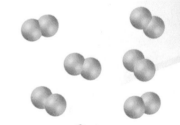

Oxygen

Using Oxygen

Cellular respiration takes place in the cytoplasm and cell membranes of prokaryotic cells. In eukaryotic cells, cellular respiration takes place in organelles called *mitochondria* (singular, *mitochondrion*). Mitochondria are found in both plant and animal cells. The starting materials of cellular respiration are glucose and oxygen.

In eukaryotes, the first stage of cellular respiration takes place in the cytoplasm. Glucose is broken down into two 3-carbon molecules. This releases a small amount of energy. The next stage takes place in the mitochondria. This stage requires oxygen. Oxygen enters the cell and travels into the mitochondria. As the 3-carbon molecules are broken down, energy is captured and stored in ATP.

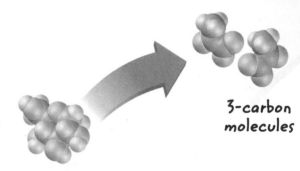

Sugar from photosynthesis

3-carbon molecules

Releasing Energy

The products of cellular respiration are chemical energy (ATP), carbon dioxide, and water. The carbon dioxide formed during cellular respiration is released by the cell. In many animals, the carbon dioxide is carried to the lungs and exhaled during breathing.

Some of the energy produced during cellular respiration is released as heat. However, much of the energy produced during cellular respiration is transferred to ATP. ATP can be carried throughout the body. When ATP is broken down, the energy released is used for cellular activities. The steps of cellular respiration can be summarized by the following equation:

$$C_6H_{12}O_6 + 6O_2 \rightarrow 6CO_2 + 6H_2O + \text{chemical energy (ATP)}$$

Think Outside the Book **Inquiry**

11 **Identify** With a partner, construct a scientific explanation to describe the processes of cellular respiration and photosynthesis in the cycling of matter and flow of energy into and out of organisms. Make sure to base your scientific explanation on compiled evidence.

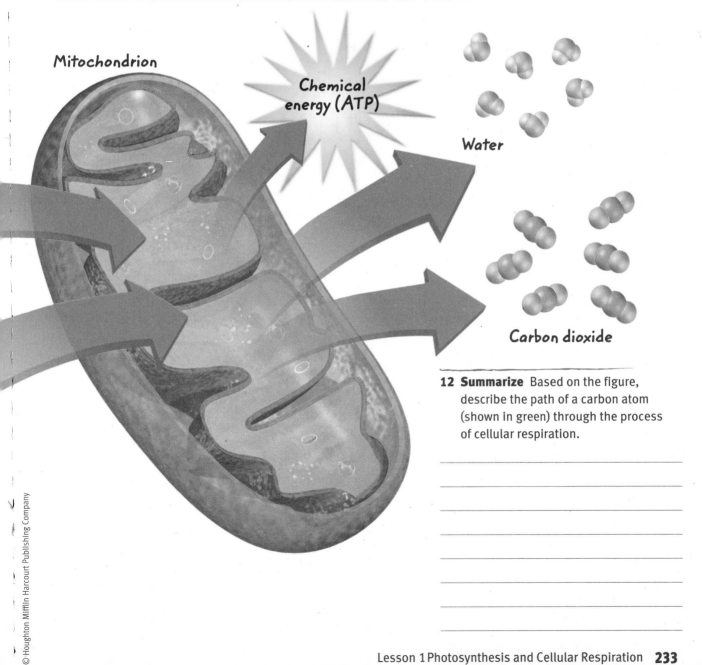

Mitochondrion

Chemical energy (ATP)

Water

Carbon dioxide

12 **Summarize** Based on the figure, describe the path of a carbon atom (shown in green) through the process of cellular respiration.

_____

_____

_____

_____

_____

_____

Merry-Go-Round!

How are photosynthesis and cellular respiration connected?

Most of the oxygen in the atmosphere was made during photosynthesis. Nearly all organisms use this oxygen during cellular respiration. They produce carbon dioxide and release it into the environment. In turn, plants use the carbon dioxide to make sugars. So, photosynthesis and respiration are linked, each depending on the products of the other.

A _____ energy

👁 Visualize It!

13 Synthesize Fill in the missing labels, and draw in the missing molecules.

D _____

Used in

Produces

Chloroplast
(in plant cells)

Oxygen

Carbon dioxide

B _____

Produces

Used in

Mitochondrion
(in plant and animal cells)

14 Summarize How are the starting materials and products of cellular respiration and photosynthesis related?

_____

_____

_____

C _____ energy

© Houghton Mifflin Harcourt Publishing Company

Out of Air

When there isn't enough oxygen, living things can get energy by anaerobic respiration (AN•uh•roh•bick ress•puh•RAY•shuhn). *Anaerobic* means "without oxygen." Like cellular respiration, anaerobic respiration produces ATP. However, it does not produce as much ATP as cellular respiration. Even so, anaerobic respiration is another way to cycle matter and flow energy into and out of organisms.

Rising to the Top

Fermentation is a type of anaerobic respiration. Many yeasts rely on fermentation for energy. Carbon dioxide is a product of fermentation. Carbon dioxide causes bread to rise, and gives it air pockets.

Feel the Burn!

The body uses anaerobic respiration during hard exercise, such as sprinting. This produces lactic acid, which can cause muscles to ache after exercise.

Extend

Inquiry

15 Compare What products do both cellular and anaerobic respiration have in common?

16 Research Yeast is an important ingredient when baking bread. If you were making two loaves of bread, one with the correct amount of yeast and the other with only half of the required amount of yeast, what do you think will happen to the one with only half of the required amount of yeast? Research the effects that yeast has on anaerobic respiration when baking bread. Write a scientific explanation about how the use of yeast in fermentation uses anaerobic respiration to help the bread rise.

17 Compare Research and compare cellular respiration and fermentation. How are they similar? How do they differ? Summarize your results by doing one of the following:
- make a poster
- draw a comic strip
- write a brochure
- make a table

Visual Summary

To complete this summary, check the box that indicates true or false. Then, use the key below to check your answers. You can use this page to review the main concepts of the lesson.

Cells get and use energy

Living things need energy to survive.

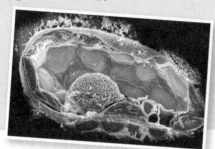

	T	F	
18	☐	☐	Organisms get energy from food.
19	☐	☐	A producer eats other organisms.

Plants make their own food.

	T	F	
20	☐	☐	Photosynthesis is the process by which plants make their own food.
21	☐	☐	Chlorophyll captures light energy during photosynthesis.

Cells release energy from food during cellular respiration.

	T	F	
22	☐	☐	Carbon dioxide is required for cellular respiration.
23	☐	☐	Cellular respiration takes place in chloroplasts.

Photosynthesis and cellular respiration are interrelated.

	T	F	
24	☐	☐	The products of photosynthesis are the starting materials of cellular respiration.

Answers: 18 T; 19 F; 20 T; 21 T; 22 F; 23 F; 24 T

25 Identify Describe how the cells in your body get energy and then use that energy.

Lesson Review

Lesson 1

Vocabulary

Fill in the blank with the term that best completes the following sentences.

1 _____ takes place in organelles called *chloroplasts*.

2 Light energy is captured by the green pigment _____.

3 Cells use oxygen to release energy during _____.

Key Concepts

Use the figure to answer the following questions.

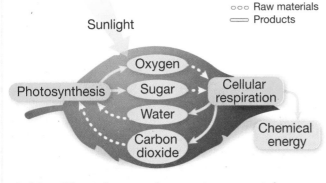

4 Identify What are the starting materials and products of photosynthesis and cellular respiration?

_____

_____

_____

_____

5 Relate What does the diagram above reveal about the connections between photosynthesis and cellular respiration?

_____

_____

_____

_____

6 Contrast How do plants and animals get their energy in different ways?

_____

_____

_____

_____

Critical Thinking

7 Infer Does your body get all its energy from the sun? Explain.

_____

_____

_____

_____

_____

8 Synthesize Could cellular respiration happen without photosynthesis? Explain your reasoning.

_____

_____

_____

_____

_____

9 Apply Plants don't move around, so why do they need energy?

_____

_____

_____

_____

_____

My Notes

Energy and Matter in Ecosystems

ESSENTIAL QUESTION

How do energy and matter move through ecosystems?

By the end of this lesson, you should be able to explain the flow of energy and the cycles of matter in ecosystems.

7.LS2.1

Living things get energy from food. Plants can make their own food, but people have to eat other organisms.

238

Engage Your Brain

1 Predict Organisms get energy from food. Underline the organisms in the list below that get food by eating other organisms.

Lizard	Butterfly
Pine tree	Cactus
Grass	Mountain lion
Salamander	Bluebird
Turtle	Moss

2 Diagram An ecosystem is made up of all living and nonliving things in an environment. Choose a nearby ecosystem, and draw a diagram below of the flow of energy from the sun to the organisms in the ecosystem.

 Active Reading

3 Apply Many scientific words, such as *energy*, also have everyday meanings. Use context clues to write your own definition for each meaning of the word *energy*.

You could feel the <u>energy</u> in the crowd during the homecoming game.

_____

_____

When she had the flu, Eliza slept all day because she felt completely drained of <u>energy</u>.

_____

_____

The brightly colored painting was full of <u>energy</u>.

_____

_____

Vocabulary Terms

- **matter**
- **energy**
- **ecosystem**
- **law of conservation of energy**
- **law of conservation of mass**
- **energy pyramid**
- **water cycle**
- **nitrogen cycle**
- **carbon cycle**

4 Apply As you learn the definition of each vocabulary term in this lesson, create your own definition or sketch to help remember the meaning of the term.

Soak Up the Sun

How do organisms get energy and matter?

To live, grow, and reproduce, all organisms need matter and energy. **Matter** describes anything that has mass and takes up space. Organisms use matter in chemical processes, such as digestion and breathing. For these processes to occur, organisms need energy. **Energy** is the ability to do work and enables organisms to use matter in life processes. Organisms have different ways of getting matter and energy from their environment.

Active Reading

5 Identify As you read, underline the characteristics of producers and consumers.

From the Sun

Organisms called *producers* use energy from their surroundings to make their own food. In most ecosystems, the sun is the original source of energy. Producers, like most plants and algae, use sunlight to convert water and carbon dioxide into sugars. In a few ecosystems, producers use chemical energy instead of light energy to make food. Producers take in matter, such as carbon dioxide, nitrogen, and water from air and soil.

From Other Organisms

Consumers are organisms that get energy by eating producers or other consumers. They get materials such as carbon, nitrogen, and phosphorus from the organisms they eat. So, consumers take in both energy and matter when they eat other organisms.

Roots help trees get matter, such as water and nutrients, from the soil.

6 Infer Use this table to identify where producers and consumers get energy and matter.

Type of organism	How it gets energy	How it gets matter
Producer		
Consumer		

What happens to energy and matter in ecosystems?

Energy and matter are constantly moving through ecosystems. An **ecosystem** is a specific community of organisms and their physical environment. Organisms need energy and matter for many functions, such as moving, growing, and reproducing. Some producers use carbon dioxide and water to make sugars, from which they get energy. They also collect materials from their environment for their life processes. Consumers get energy and matter for their life processes by eating other organisms. During every process, some energy is lost as heat. And, matter is returned to the physical environment as wastes or when organisms die.

Biotic vs. Abiotic Factors in the Ecosystem

To understand the cycling of matter in the ecosystem, you must first understand the biotic and abiotic factors in an ecosystem. Abiotic factors, such as sunlight and temperature, are required for living things to survive. Biotic factors, such as plants and nitrogen, are all the living things in an ecosystem. The ecosystem needs both biotic and abiotic factors to be balanced.

Energy and Matter Are Conserved

The **law of conservation of energy** states that energy cannot be created or destroyed. Energy changes forms. Some producers change light energy from the sun to chemical energy in sugars. When sugars are used, some energy is given off as heat. Much of the energy in sugars is changed to another form of chemical energy that cells can use for life functions. The **law of conservation of mass** states that mass cannot be created or destroyed. Instead, matter moves through the environment in different forms.

Energy and Matter Leave Ecosystems

Ecosystems do not have clear boundaries, so energy and matter can leave them. Matter and energy can leave an ecosystem when organisms move. For example, some birds feed on fish in the ocean. When birds fly back to land, they take the matter and energy from the fish out of the ocean. Matter and energy can leave ecosystems in moving water and air. Even though the matter and energy enter and leave an ecosystem, they are never destroyed.

7 Analyze How might energy and matter leave the ecosystem shown in the picture above?

_____

_____

_____

_____

_____

8 Compare Use the Venn diagram to relate how energy and matter move through ecosystems.

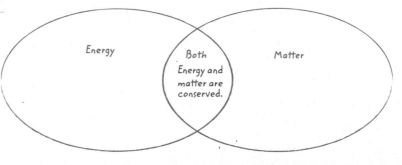

Energy   Both Energy and matter are conserved.   Matter

© Houghton Mifflin Harcourt Publishing Company • Image Credits: ©Gary Crabbe/Alamy

How does energy move through an ecosystem?

Energy enters most ecosystems as sunlight, which some producers use to make food. Primary consumers, such as herbivores, get energy by consuming producers. Secondary consumers, such as carnivores, get energy by eating primary consumers, and so on up the food chain. An organism uses most of the energy it takes in for life processes. However, some energy is lost to the environment as heat. A small amount of energy is stored within an organism. Only this stored energy can be used by a consumer that eats the organism.

An **energy pyramid** is a tool that can be used to trace the flow of energy through an ecosystem. The pyramid's shape shows that there is less energy and fewer organisms at each level. At each step in the food chain, energy is lost to the environment. Because less energy is available, fewer organisms can be supported at higher levels. The bottom level—the producers—has the largest population and the most energy. The other levels are consumers. At the highest level, consumers will have the smallest population because of the limited amount of energy available to them.

Visualize It!

9 Analyze Describe how energy flows through each level in this energy pyramid. Is all the matter and energy from one level transferred to the next level?

_____

_____

_____

_____

_____

_____

_____

_____

Tertiary consumers

The amount of energy available and population size decrease as you go up the energy pyramid.

Secondary consumers

Primary consumers

Producers

How does matter move through an ecosystem?

Matter cycles through an ecosystem. For example, water evaporates from Earth's surface into the atmosphere and condenses to form clouds. After forming clouds, water falls back to Earth's surface, completing a cycle.

Carbon and nitrogen also cycle through an ecosystem. Producers take in compounds made of carbon and nitrogen from the physical environment. They use these compounds for life processes. Primary consumers get matter by consuming producers.

Secondary consumers eat primary consumers. The matter in primary consumers is used in chemical processes by secondary consumers. In this way, carbon and nitrogen flow from producers through all levels of consumers.

Consumers do not use all of the matter that they take in. Some of the matter is turned into waste products. Decomposers, such as bacteria and fungi, break down solid waste products and dead organisms, returning matter to the physical environment. Producers can then reuse this matter for life processes, starting the cycling of matter again.

All of these cycles can take place over large areas. Matter leaves some ecosystems and enters other ecosystems. For example, water that evaporates from a lake in the middle of a continent can later fall into an ocean. Because matter can enter and leave an ecosystem, it is called an *open system*.

Active Reading **10 Identify** What is the role of decomposers in cycling matter?

_____

_____

_____

Visualize It!

11 Analyze Describe how water is moving through the ecosystem on this page.

_____

_____

_____

_____

_____

_____

What is the water cycle?

The movement of water between the oceans, atmosphere, land, and living things is known as the **water cycle**. Three ways water can enter the atmosphere are evaporation, transpiration, and respiration. During *evaporation*, the sun's heat causes water to change from liquid to vapor. Plants release water vapor from their leaves in *transpiration*. Organisms release water as waste during *respiration*.

In *condensation*, the water vapor cools and returns to liquid. The water that falls from the atmosphere to land and bodies of water is *precipitation*. Rain, snow, sleet, and hail are forms of precipitation. Most precipitation falls into the ocean. The precipitation that falls on land and flows into streams and rivers is called *runoff*. Some precipitation seeps into the ground and is stored underground in spaces between or within rocks. This water, called *groundwater*, will slowly flow back into the soil, streams, rivers, and oceans.

© Houghton Mifflin Harcourt Publishing Company

Active Reading

12 Explain How does water from the atmosphere return to Earth's surface?

_____

_____

_____

_____

_____

_____

Visualize It!

13 Label Use the terms *evaporation*, *transpiration*, and *respiration* to correctly complete the diagram. Be sure the arrow for each term leads from the proper source.

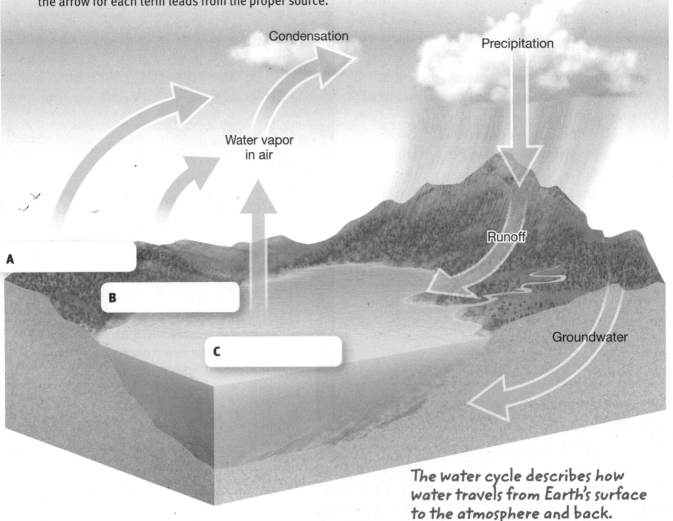

Condensation

Precipitation

Water vapor in air

Runoff

Groundwater

A

B

C

The water cycle describes how water travels from Earth's surface to the atmosphere and back.

What is the nitrogen cycle?

Organisms need nitrogen to build proteins and DNA for new cells. The movement of nitrogen between the environment and living things is called the **nitrogen cycle**. Most of Earth's atmosphere is nitrogen gas. But most organisms cannot use nitrogen gas directly. However, bacteria in the soil are able to change nitrogen gas into forms that plants can use. This process is called *nitrogen fixation*. Lightning can also fix nitrogen into usable compounds. Plants take in and use fixed nitrogen. Consumers can then get the nitrogen they need by eating plants or other organisms.

When organisms die, decomposers break down their remains. Decomposition releases a form of nitrogen into the soil that plants can use. Finally, certain types of bacteria in the soil can convert nitrogen into a gas, which is returned to the atmosphere.

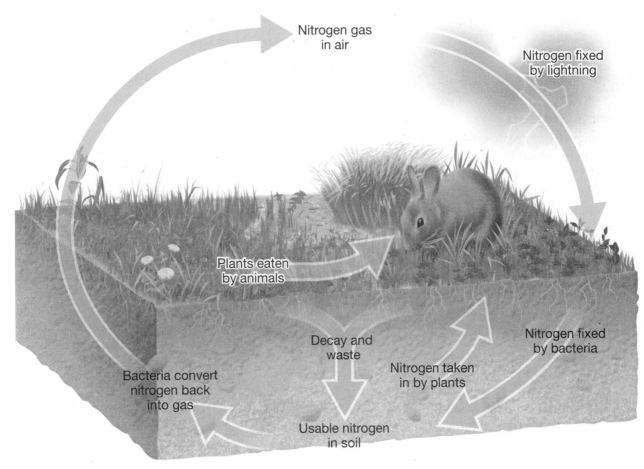

Nitrogen gas in air

Nitrogen fixed by lightning

Plants eaten by animals

Decay and waste

Nitrogen taken in by plants

Nitrogen fixed by bacteria

Bacteria convert nitrogen back into gas

Usable nitrogen in soil

In the nitrogen cycle, nitrogen gas is converted into usable nitrogen by bacteria and lightning. Plants take in the usable nitrogen. Consumers get the nitrogen they need from the organisms they eat.

Visualize It! Inquiry

14 Hypothesize What would happen to the ecosystem if there were no nitrogen-fixing bacteria?

_____

_____

_____

_____

What is the carbon cycle?

Carbon is an important building block of organisms. It is found in sugars, which store the chemical energy that organisms need to live. It also is found in the atmosphere (as carbon dioxide gas), in bodies of water, in rocks and soils, in organisms, and in fossil fuels. Carbon moves through organisms and between organisms and the physical environment in the **carbon cycle**.

What is the oxygen cycle?

Oxygen makes up about 20% of the atmosphere. It works with the carbon cycle in that photosynthesis creates oxygen, then plants and animals breathe in that oxygen and breathe out carbon dioxide, which is needed for photosynthesis to occur, and the process begins all over again.

Active Reading 15 **List** Identify five places where carbon may be found.

_____

_____

_____

Respiration

Photosynthesis

Photosynthesis

During photosynthesis, producers in the water and on land take in light energy from the sun and use carbon dioxide and water to make sugars. These sugars contain carbon and store chemical energy. Oxygen gas is also a product of photosynthesis.

Respiration

Cellular respiration occurs in producers and consumers on land and in water. During respiration, sugars are broken down to release energy. The process uses oxygen gas. Energy, carbon dioxide, and water are released.

carbon in organisms

carbon dioxide dissolved in water

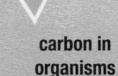
Visualize It!

16 Relate Briefly describe how carbon enters and exits a consumer, such as the sheep shown in this diagram.

_____

_____

_____

_____

_____

_____

Think Outside the Book Inquiry

17 Model Choose a biotic item and an abiotic item. Develop a two-dimensional model that depicts how carbon and oxygen are used to cycle through the ecosystem, thus creating energy for other parts of the ecosystem.

Combustion

Combustion is the burning of materials, including wood and fossil fuels. Burning once-living things releases carbon dioxide, water, heat, and other materials into the environment. It may also produce pollution.

carbon dioxide in air

Combustion

Photosynthesis

Respiration

carbon in organisms

Decomposition

Decomposition is the breakdown of dead organisms and wastes. Decomposers get energy from this material by respiration. Decomposition returns carbon dioxide, water, and other nutrients to the environment.

Decomposition

carbon in fossil fuels

Fossil Fuels

Fossil fuels formed from decomposing organisms that were buried deeply millions of years ago. Fossil fuels are burned during combustion, releasing carbon dioxide into the air.

Think Outside the Book Inquiry

18 Apply With a partner, choose an ecosystem with which you are familiar. Make a diagram of how carbon cycles in the ecosystem and how energy flows through it. Be sure to label your diagram.

Visual Summary

To complete this summary, fill in the blanks with the correct word or phrase. Then use the key below to check your answers. You can use this page to review the main concepts of the lesson.

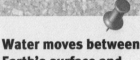

Energy and Matter in Ecosystems

Organisms get energy and matter from different sources.

19 Many _____ get energy from sunlight.

20 _____ get energy by eating other organisms.

Water moves between Earth's surface and the atmosphere in the water cycle.

21 Water that flows over the surface of the ground is called _____.

Nitrogen moves from the atmosphere, to organisms, and back to the atmosphere in the nitrogen cycle.

22 _____ is the process by which bacteria turn nitrogen gas into compounds plants can use.

Carbon cycles through organisms, into the physical environment, and back again.

23 Dead organisms that were buried may turn into _____ after millions of years.

24 Carbon from this material reenters the atmosphere by _____.

Answers: 19 producers; 20 Consumers; 21 runoff; 22 Nitrogen fixation; 23 fossil fuels; 24 combustion

25 **Explain** If energy and matter cannot be destroyed, what happens to energy and matter when an organism is eaten?

Lesson Review

Vocabulary

Fill in the blanks with the term that best completes the following sentences.

1 The ability to do work is called _____.

2 _____ is anything that has mass and takes up space.

3 A(n) _____ can be used to trace the flow of energy through an ecosystem.

Key Concepts

4 Describe Explain the difference between a producer, a consumer, and a decomposer.

_____

_____

_____

5 Compare How are the law of conservation of energy and the law of conservation of mass similar?

_____

_____

_____

_____

_____

6 Explain Why do organisms need nitrogen?

_____

_____

_____

_____

Critical Thinking

7 Analyze In an ecosystem, which would have a larger population: producers or primary consumers? Explain.

_____

_____

_____

Use the graph to answer the following questions.

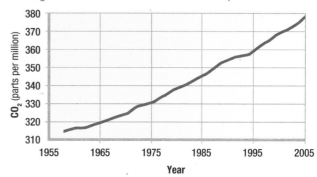

Average Carbon Dioxide Levels at Mauna Loa, Hawaii

Source: *NOAA 2004*

8 Analyze What process of the carbon cycle is likely causing the increase in carbon dioxide levels shown in the graph above?

_____

_____

9 Identify What is the most likely source of the increase in carbon dioxide in the atmosphere shown in the graph above?

_____

_____

10 Evaluate If people planted huge numbers of trees and other plants, how might the carbon dioxide levels in the graph above change? Explain your answer.

_____

_____

_____

_____

_____

11 Apply Water is traveling up a tree carrying nutrients. Use the water cycle to explain how that water later becomes groundwater.

_____

_____

_____

_____

_____

My Notes

Interpreting Models

Many people use models to share an understanding of how things work. A model could be a representation of an object, an idea, or even a process or system. Models are used to describe and explain things that cannot be experienced directly. They can include physical replicas, diagrams, mathematical representations, or computer simulations. Models are often used when conducting scientific research. They help scientists develop questions and explanations, generate data that can be used to make predictions, and communicate ideas to others. A scientific model has the same meaning to everyone who uses it.

Tutorial

Systems models help scientists show the relationships between components of a system, or between interconnected processes that make up a cycle. Consider how a scientist might develop a model to represent the water cycle.

Visuals
Visuals are used in models to quickly communicate information. Scientists often use pictures and images to relay complex concepts. Here the image of a raining cloud provides a visual that represents the process of precipitation.

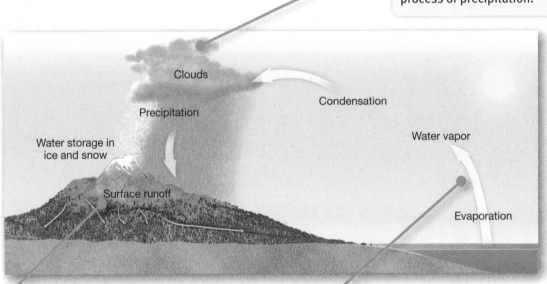

Elements
The elements in a model are all the different components that make it up. Elements might be physical objects, such as water, clouds, or the sun. Elements can also be steps in a process, or interconnected processes, such as those shown here.

Interactions
The interactions in a model represent the way in which the different elements connect or relate to each other. Interactions are often represented by arrowed lines, which indicate the flow within the system or process.

You Try It!

Look at the following model and answer the questions below to evaluate whether the model clearly illustrates how carbon and nitrogen move through an ecosystem.

Decomposers break down waste products and dead organisms, returning carbon and nitrogen to the physical world.

Producers take in carbon and nitrogen from the physical world.

Physical World

Decomposers acquire carbon and nitrogen by absorbing the waste products of consumers.

Primary consumers get carbon and nitrogen by consuming producers.

1 Identifying Elements What are the elements in the process represented by the model?

_____

_____

_____

_____

2 Interpreting Interactions How do the different elements in the model connect or relate to each other? Support your explanation with an example from the model.

_____

_____

_____

_____

3 Analyzing Visuals What visuals have been used in the model? How do the visuals help inform your understanding of the model?

_____

_____

_____

Take It Home

Think of an ecosystem that interests you. Research the producers, consumers, and decomposers found in it. Develop a model to represent how energy and matter cycle through that ecosystem. Bring your model to class and be prepared to interpret it for your classmates.

Lesson 1

ESSENTIAL QUESTION
How do cells get and use energy?

Explain how cells capture and release energy.

Lesson 2

ESSENTIAL QUESTION
How do energy and matter move through ecosystems?

Explain the flow of energy and the cycles of matter in ecosystems.

Connect ESSENTIAL QUESTIONS
Lessons 1 and 2

1 Synthesize Explain how photosynthesis works to produce energy for Earth's ecosystems.

_____

_____

_____

_____

Think Outside the Book

2 Synthesize Choose one of the activities to help synthesize what you learned in this unit.

☐ Using what you learned in lessons 1 and 2, choose a biome or an aquatic ecosystem and draw or make a collage of an energy pyramid that might be found in it. Label each tier of the energy pyramid and identify the species shown.

☐ Using what you learned in lessons 1 and 2, draw a diagram of cellular respiration and photosynthesis. Identify how the processes use oxygen, energy, carbon dioxide, and water.

Name _____

Vocabulary

Check the box to show whether each statement is true or false.

T	F	
☐	☐	**1** <u>Photosynthesis</u> is the process in which cells use oxygen to break down food and release stored energy.
☐	☐	**2** The <u>law of conservation of energy</u> states that energy can be both created and destroyed.
☐	☐	**3** <u>Chlorophyll</u> captures energy from sunlight.
☐	☐	**4** The <u>law of conservation of mass</u> states that matter moves through the environment in different forms.
☐	☐	**5** The process of breaking down food to produce adenosine triphosphate is called <u>cellular respiration</u>.

Key Concepts

Read each question below, and circle the best answer.

6 Where do producers, such as trees, get the energy needed to survive?

A sun

B air

C organisms they eat

D remains of organisms

7 Below is an energy pyramid diagram.

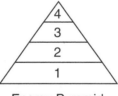

Energy Pyramid

Why is the level at 4 so much smaller than the level at 1?

A Organisms gain energy as the food chain moves up the pyramid.

B Fewer organisms are supported as you move down the pyramid.

C Only the energy that is used is available to organisms at a higher level.

D Only the energy that is stored is available to organisms at a higher level.

8 Below is a diagram of the carbon cycle.

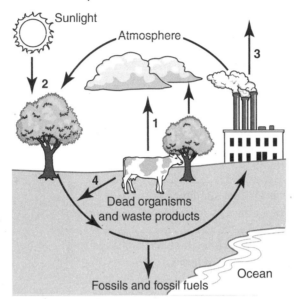

Which number corresponds to combustion and the release of CO_2, water, and the loss of energy as heat into the environment?

A 1

C 3

B 2

D 4

9 What element can be changed by lightning into a form that plants can use?

A oxygen

C phosphorous

B carbon

D nitrogen

10 The following diagram shows a common cell organelle.

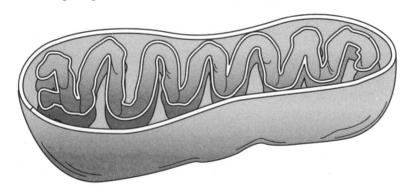

What process takes place in the organelle shown?

A photosynthesis

C cellular respiration

B protein synthesis

D packaging of proteins

Critical Thinking

Answer the following questions in the space provided.

11 Explain how photosynthesis and cellular respiration are related. Give examples of how the processes work together.

_____

_____

_____

_____

_____

_____

_____

_____

12 Combustion, decomposition, and fossil fuels all play important roles in which cycle of matter? Explain their roles and how they are connected with each other.

_____

_____

_____

_____

_____

_____

_____

Unit 4 Review continued

Answer the following question in the space provided.

13 The following picture shows the process of photosynthesis.

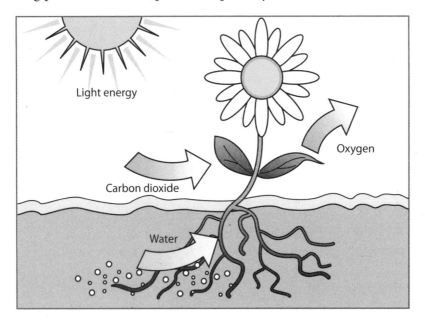

In which plant organ and organelle does photosynthesis take place? One of the products of photosynthesis is missing from the diagram. What is this missing product? Describe the role of this substance in cells. How do animals get this substance?

_____

_____

_____

_____

_____

Reproduction, Survival, and Heredity

Big Idea

Characteristics from parents are passed to offspring in predictable ways.

7.LS1.6, 7.LS1.7, 7.LS1.8, 7.LS3.1, 7.LS3.2, 7.LS3.3

What do you think?

Every organism—including orange trees and dogs— shares traits with its offspring. How are qualities passed on from generation to generation?

Unit 5
Reproduction, Survival, and Heredity

© Houghton Mifflin Harcourt Publishing Company • Image Credits: (br) ©Science Source/Photo Researchers, Inc.; (tr) ©Cheryl Power/SPL/Photo Researchers, Inc.

CITIZEN SCIENCE

Pass It On

Heredity was a mystery that scientists worked to crack over hundreds of years. The modern field of genetics is vital to the understanding of hereditary diseases. The study of genetics can also predict which traits will be passed from parent to offspring.

1856–1863

Many people consider Gregor Mendel to be the father of modern genetics. His famous pea plant experiments, conducted from 1856–1863, helped to illustrate and establish the laws of inheritance.

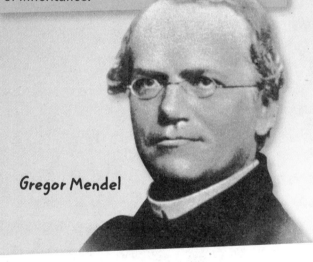

Gregor Mendel

Which traits do you think Mendel might have examined in pea plants? What traits might a fruit or vegetable plant inherit from a parent plant?

_____

_____

_____

_____

_____

Pairs of chromosomes viewed under a microscope

Fruit fly

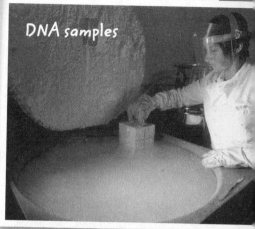

DNA samples

1882
Walther Flemming discovered chromosomes while observing the process of cell division. He didn't know it, but chromosomes pass characteristics from parents to offspring.

1908
Thomas Hunt Morgan was the first to actually realize that chromosomes carry traits. Morgan's fruit fly studies established that genes are located on chromosomes. Scientists still use fruit flies in research today.

2003
Our DNA carries information about all of our traits. In fact, the human genome is made up of 20,000–25,000 genes! In 2003, the Human Genome Project successfully mapped the first human genome.

Take It Home Making Trait Predictions

See *ScienceSaurus*® for more information about genes and heredity.

① Think About It

Different factors influence appearance. Family members may look similar in some ways but different in others. What factors influence a person's appearance?

_____

_____

_____

_____

② Ask Some Questions

Can you spot any physical traits that people in your family share? Do you think any of them may have made it easier for your ancestors to survive in a particular environment?

_____

_____

_____

③ Make a Plan

A Consider the traits that are most distinctive in your family. How can you trace the way these traits have been passed through the family? Design an investigation of hereditary characteristics in your family.

_____

_____

_____

_____

B Describe how these characteristics might be the same or different as they are passed on to offspring. What factors might influence this? Make notes here, and illustrate your descriptions on a separate sheet of paper.

_____

_____

_____

Mitosis

ESSENTIAL QUESTION

How do cells divide?

By the end of this lesson, you should be able to relate the process of mitosis to its functions in single-celled and multicellular organisms.

▬ **7.LS1.8**

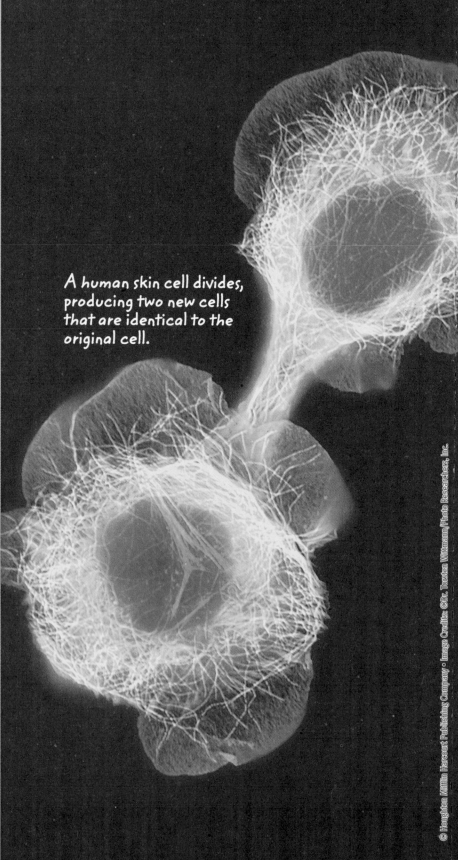

A human skin cell divides, producing two new cells that are identical to the original cell.

✋ **Lesson Labs**

Quick Labs
• Modeling Mitosis
• Mitosis Flipbooks
• DNA, Chromosomes, and Cell Division

Exploration Lab
• Stages of the Cell Cycle

Engage Your Brain

1 Predict Check T or F to show whether you think each statement is true or false.

T　F

☐　☐　Single-celled organisms can reproduce by cell division.

☐　☐　The only function of cell division is reproduction.

☐　☐　In multicellular organisms, cell division can help repair injured areas.

☐　☐　Cell division produces two cells that are different from each other.

2 Infer An old sequoia tree weighs many tons and has billions of cells. These trees start out as tiny seeds. Predict how these trees get so large.

_____

_____

_____

_____

✏️ Active Reading

3 Synthesize You can often define an unknown word if you know the meaning of its word parts. Use the word parts and sentence below to make an educated guess about the meaning of the word *cytokinesis*.

Word part	Meaning
cyto-	hollow vessel
-kinesis	division

Example sentence
When a dividing cell undergoes <u>cytokinesis</u>, two cells are produced.

cytokinesis:

_____

_____

_____

Vocabulary Terms

• DNA
• chromosomes
• cell cycle
• interphase
• mitosis
• cytokinesis

4 Apply As you learn the definition of each vocabulary term in this lesson, write your own definition or make a sketch to help you remember the meaning of the term.

Splitsville!

Why do cells divide?

Cell division happens in all organisms. Cell division takes place for different reasons. For example, single-celled organisms reproduce through cell division. In multicellular organisms, cell division is involved in growth, development, and repair, as well as reproduction.

Reproduction

Cell division is important for asexual reproduction, which involves only one parent organism. In single-celled organisms, the parent divides in two, producing two identical offspring. In single-celled and some multicellular organisms, offspring result when a parent organism buds, producing offspring. In multicellular organisms, reproduction by cell division can include plant structures such as runners and plantlets.

Growth and Repair

One characteristic of all living things is that they grow. You are probably bigger this year than you were last year. Your body is made up of cells. Although cells themselves grow, most growth in multicellular organisms happens because cell division produces new daughter cells.

Cell division also produces cells for repair. If you cut your hand or break a bone, the damaged cells are replaced by new daughter cells that form during cell division.

 **Visualize It!**

5 Apply Take a look at the photos below. Underneath each photo, describe the role of cell division in what is taking place.

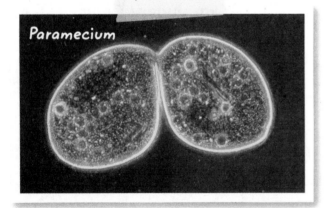
Paramecium

Starfish

Role of cell division:

_____

_____

_____

Role of cell division:

_____

_____

_____

What happens to genetic material during cell division?

The genetic material in cells is called DNA (deoxyribonucleic acid). A **DNA** molecule contains the information that determines the traits that a living thing inherits and needs to live. It contains instructions for an organism's growth, development, and activities. In eukaryotes, DNA is found in the nucleus.

During most of a cell's life cycle, DNA, along with proteins, exists in a complex material called *chromatin* (KROH•muh•tin). Before cell division, DNA is duplicated, or copied. Then, in an early stage of cell division, the chromatin is compacted into visible structures called **chromosomes** (KROH•muh•sohmz). A duplicated chromosome consists of two identical structures called *chromatids* (KROH•muh•tidz). The chromatids are held together by a *centromere* (SEN•truh•mir).

6 Describe What happens to DNA before cell division?

_____

_____

_____

_____

Chromosome
A duplicated chromosome has two chromatids, which are held together by a centromere.

Centromere

Chromatid

A chromosome is made of compacted chromatin.

Chromatin
Chromatin is made up of DNA and proteins.

Protein

DNA

DNA
DNA is found in the nucleus of a eukaryotic cell.

Visualize It!

7 Analyze What happens to chromatin in the early stages of cell division?

_____

_____

_____

Around and Around

What are the stages of the cell cycle?

The life cycle of an organism includes birth, growth, reproduction, and death. The life cycle of a eukaryotic cell, called the **cell cycle**, can be divided into three stages: interphase, mitosis, and cytokinesis. During the cell cycle, a parent cell divides into two new cells. The new daughter cells are genetically identical to the parent.

 **Active Reading**

8 Identify As you read, underline the main characteristics of each stage of the cell cycle.

Interphase

The part of the cell cycle during which the cell is not dividing is called **interphase** (IN•ter•fayz). A lot of activity takes place in this stage of the cell's life. The cell grows to about twice the size it was when it was first produced. It also produces various organelles. The cell engages in normal life activities, such as transporting materials into the cell and getting rid of wastes.

Changes that occur during interphase prepare a cell for division. Before a cell can divide, DNA must be duplicated. This ensures that, after cell division, each new daughter cell gets an exact copy of the genetic material in the original cell.

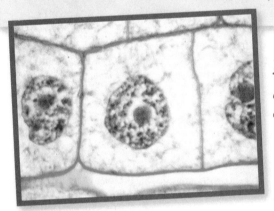

During interphase, the cell carries out normal life activities.

INTERPHASE

Active Reading

9 Describe What happens during interphase?

_____

_____

_____

_____

_____

Mitosis

In eukaryotic cells, **mitosis** (my•TOH•sis) is the part of the cell cycle during which the nucleus divides. Prokaryotes do not undergo mitosis because they do not have a nucleus. Mitosis results in two nuclei that are identical to the original nucleus. So, the two new daughter cells formed after cell division are genetically identical. During mitosis, chromosomes condense from chromatin. When viewed with a microscope, chromosomes are visible inside the nucleus. At the end of mitosis, the cell has two identical sets of chromosomes in two separate nuclei.

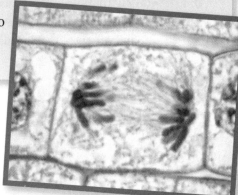

During mitosis, the cell's nucleus divides into two identical nuclei.

MITOSIS

Prophase

Metaphase

Anaphase

Telophase

CYTOKINESIS

Cytokinesis

Cytokinesis (sy•toh•kuh•NEE•sis) is the division of the parent cell's cytoplasm. Cytokinesis begins during the last step of mitosis. During cytokinesis, the cell membrane pinches inward between the new nuclei. Eventually, it pinches all the way, forming two complete cells.

In a cell that has a cell wall, such as a plant cell, a cell plate forms. The cell plate becomes cell membranes that separate the new cells. New cell walls form where the plate was.

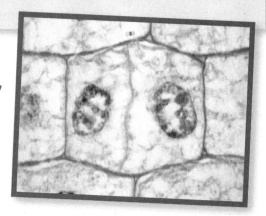

During cytokinesis, the cytoplasm divides and two new cells are produced.

 **Visualize It!**

10 Interpret Based on this diagram, in what stage does a cell spend most of its time?

Phasing Out

What are the phases of mitosis?

Mitosis has four phases: prophase (PROH•fayz), metaphase (MET•uh•fayz), anaphase (AN•uh•fayz), and telophase (TEE•luh•fayz). By the end of these phases, the cell will have two identical nuclei and cytokinesis will begin.

Active Reading

11 Identify As you read, underline the major events that take place in each phase of mitosis.

During interphase, DNA is duplicated.

Prophase

During prophase, the chromatin in the nucleus of a cell condenses and becomes visible under a microscope. Each chromosome consists of two chromatids held together by a centromere. The membrane around the nucleus breaks down.

Prophase

Metaphase

Metaphase

During metaphase, chromosomes line up in the middle of the cell. Centromeres of the chromosomes are the same distance from each side of the cell.

Anaphase

Anaphase

During anaphase, the chromatids separate. They are pulled to opposite sides of the cell. Each side of the cell ends up with a complete set of chromosomes.

12 Model With a small group, write
a play that acts out the steps
of mitosis. Trade your play with
another group, and perform the
play for your classmates.

Both new cells
start the cycle
again.

After mitosis,
cytokinesis
results in two new
daughter cells.

Telophase

Telophase

The last phase of mitosis is telophase. A new
nuclear membrane forms around each group
of chromosomes. So, the cell now has two
identical nuclei. The chromosomes become less
condensed. Cytokinesis begins during this phase.

13 Apply Use the table below to draw a picture for
each step of the cell cycle.

Step	Drawing
Interphase	
Mitosis: Prophase	
Mitosis: Metaphase	
Mitosis: Anaphase	
Mitosis: Telophase	
Cytokinesis	

Visual Summary

To complete this summary, fill in the blanks with the correct word or phrase. Then, use the key below to check your answers. You can use this page to review the main concepts of the lesson.

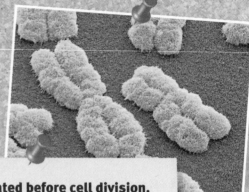

During the cell cycle, cells divide to produce two identical cells.

14 Three reasons that cells divide are

_____

_____

_____

DNA is duplicated before cell division.

15 Loose chromatin is compacted into

_____ ,

each of which has two

_____ that are

held together by a centromere.

Mitosis

The cell cycle is the life cycle of a cell.

16 They lack nuclei, so prokaryotes do not undergo _____.

17 The cell produces organelles during _____ .

18 _____ results in the formation of two new cells.

Answers: 14 reproduction, growth, repair; 15 chromosomes, chromatids; 16 mitosis; 17 interphase; 18 Cytokinesis

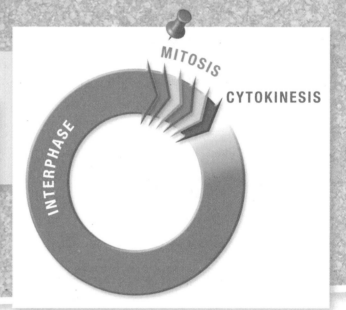

19 Summarize Briefly describe the four phases of mitosis.

Lesson Review

Vocabulary

Fill in the blanks with the term that best completes the following sentences.

1 _____ provides the information for cell growth and function.

2 The cell spends most of its time in the _____ stage of the cell cycle.

3 After _____ , the nucleus of the parent cell has divided into two new nuclei.

4 A _____ is the condensed, visible form of chromatin.

Key Concepts

5 Relate What happens in a cell during interphase?

_____

_____

_____

_____

6 Explain Construct an explanation about the function of mitosis for multicellular organisms. How does the production of genetically identical daughter cells help with growth and repair?

_____

_____

_____

_____

7 Explain Why is it important for DNA to be duplicated before mitosis?

_____

_____

_____

_____

_____

Critical Thinking

Use the figures below to answer the questions that follow.

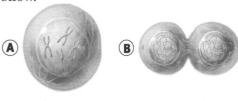

8 Sequence Starting with prophase, what is the correct order of the four diagrams above?

_____

9 Identify What phase is shown in each of the diagrams above?

_____

_____

_____

_____

10 Describe What is happening to the cell in diagram B?

_____

_____

_____

11 Predict What would happen if the cell went through mitosis but not cytokinesis?

_____

_____

_____

_____

My Notes

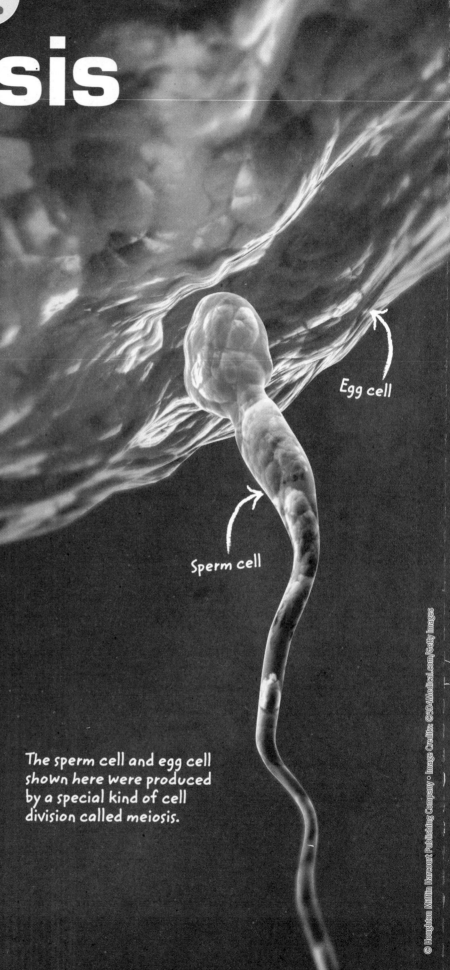

Meiosis

ESSENTIAL QUESTION

How do cells divide for sexual reproduction?

By the end of this lesson, you should be able to describe the process of meiosis and its role in sexual reproduction.

7.LS3.2

Egg cell

Sperm cell

The sperm cell and egg cell shown here were produced by a special kind of cell division called meiosis.

Engage Your Brain

1 Predict Check T or F to show whether you think each statement is true or false.

T F

☐ ☐ The offspring of sexual reproduction have fewer chromosomes than their parents have.

☐ ☐ During sexual reproduction, two cells combine to form a new organism.

☐ ☐ Sex cells are produced by cell division.

☐ ☐ Sex cells have half the normal number of chromosomes.

2 Calculate Organisms have a set number of chromosomes. For example, humans have 46 chromosomes in body cells and half that number (23) in sex cells. In the table below, fill in the number of chromosomes for different organisms.

Organism	Full set of chromosomes	Half set of chromosomes
Human	46	23
Fruit fly		4
Chicken		39
Salamander	24	
Potato	48	

Active Reading

3 Synthesize You can often define an unknown word if you know the meaning of its word parts. Use the word parts and the sentence below to make an educated guess about the meaning of the term *homologous*.

Word part	Meaning
homo-	same
-logos	word, structure

Example sentence
Homologous chromosomes are a pair of chromosomes that look similar and have the same genes.

homologous:

_____

_____

Vocabulary Terms

- homologous chromosomes
- meiosis

4 Apply As you learn the definition of each vocabulary term in this lesson, write your own definition or make a sketch to help you remember the meaning of the term.

Number Off!

How do sex cells differ from body cells?

Before sexual reproduction can take place, each parent produces sex cells. *Sex cells* have half of the genetic information that body cells have. Thus, when the genetic information from two parents combines, the offspring have a full set of genetic information. The offspring will have the same total number of chromosomes as each of its parents.

Active Reading **5 Relate** Describe sex cells.

_____

_____

Chromosome Number

In body cells, most chromosomes are found in pairs that have the same structure and size. These **homologous chromosomes** (huh•MAHL•uh•guhs KROH•muh•sohmz) carry the same genes. A homologous chromosome pair may have different versions of the genes they carry. One chromosome pair is made up of *sex chromosomes*. Sex chromosomes control the development of sexual characteristics. In humans, these chromosomes are called X and Y chromosomes. Cells with a pair of every chromosome are called *diploid* (DIP•loyd). Many organisms, including humans, have diploid body cells.

This photo shows the 23 chromosome pairs in a human male. Body cells contain all of these chromosomes. Sex cells contain one chromosome from each pair.

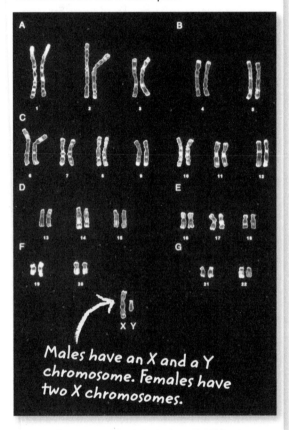

Males have an X and a Y chromosome. Females have two X chromosomes.

Visualize It! (Inquiry)

6 Predict The cell shown is a body cell that has two pairs of homologous chromosomes. Use the space to the right to draw a sex cell for the same organism.

Body cell   Sex cell

Why do organisms need sex cells?

Most human body cells contain 46 chromosomes. Think about what would happen if two body cells were to combine. The resulting cell would have twice the normal number of chromosomes. A sex cell is needed to keep this from happening.

Sex cells are also known as *gametes* (GAM•eetz). Gametes contain half the usual number of chromosomes—one chromosome from each homologous pair and one sex chromosome. Cells that contain half the usual number of chromosomes are known as *haploid* (HAP•loyd).

Gametes are found in the reproductive organs of plants and animals. An egg is a gamete that forms in female reproductive organs. The gamete that forms in male reproductive organs is called a sperm cell.

How are sex cells made?

You know that body cells divide by the process of mitosis. Mitosis produces two new daughter cells, each containing exact copies of the chromosomes in the parent cell. Each new cell has a full set of chromosomes. But to produce sex cells, a different kind of cell division is needed.

Meiosis

A human egg and a human sperm cell each have 23 chromosomes. When an egg is joined with, or *fertilized* by, a sperm cell, a new diploid cell is formed. This new cell has 46 chromosomes, or 23 pairs of chromosomes. One set is from the mother, and the other set is from the father. The newly formed diploid cell may develop into an offspring. **Meiosis** (my•OH•sis) is the type of cell division that produces haploid sex cells such as eggs and sperm cells.

 Visualize It!

For the example of fertilization shown, the egg and sperm cells each have one chromosome.

**Egg cell
(female gamete)**

Haploid

**Sperm cell
(male gamete)**

Haploid

Fertilization ──►

**Fertilized egg cell
(zygote)**

Diploid

7 Summarize Based on the figure, describe the process of fertilization.

_____

_____

_____

What are the stages of meiosis?

Meiosis results in the formation of four haploid cells. Each haploid cell has half the number of chromosomes found in the original cell. Meiosis has two parts: meiosis I and meiosis II.

Meiosis I

Remember that homologous chromosomes have the same genes, but they are not exact copies of each other. Before meiosis I begins, each chromosome is duplicated, or copied. Each half of a duplicated chromosome is called a *chromatid* (KROH•muh•tid). Chromatids are connected to each other by *centromeres* (SEN•truh•mirz). Duplicated chromosomes are drawn in an **X** shape. Each side of the **X** represents a chromatid, and the point where they touch is the centromere.

During meiosis I, pairs of homologous chromosomes and sex chromosomes split apart into two new cells. These cells each have one-half of the chromosome pairs and their duplicate chromatids. The steps of meiosis I are shown below.

8 Sequence As you read, underline what happens to chromosomes during meiosis.

Duplicated homologous chromosomes

Half of a homologous chromosome pair

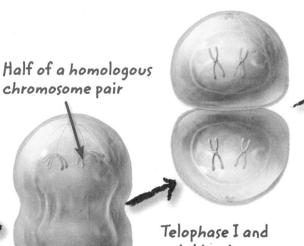

Prophase I
The chromosomes are copied before meiosis begins. The duplicated chromosomes, each made up of two chromatids, pair up.

Metaphase I
After the nuclear membrane breaks down, the chromosome pairs line up in the middle of the cell.

Anaphase I
The chromosomes separate from their partners, and then move to opposite ends of the cell.

Telophase I and cytokinesis
The nuclear membranes re-form, and the cell divides into two cells. The chromatids are still joined.

9 Contrast How does meiosis II differ from meiosis I?

_____

_____

_____

_____

Telophase II and cytokinesis
The nuclear membranes re-form and the cells divide. Four new haploid cells are formed. Each has half the usual number of chromosomes.

Centromere

Chromatid

Anaphase II
The chromatids are pulled apart and move to opposite sides of the cell.

Metaphase II
The chromosomes line up in the middle of each cell.

Prophase II
The chromosomes are not copied again before meiosis II. The nuclear membrane breaks down.

Think Outside the Book

10 Summarize Work with a partner to make a poster that describes all the steps of meiosis.

Meiosis II

Meiosis II involves both of the new cells formed during meiosis I. The chromosomes of these cells are not copied before meiosis II begins. Both of the cells divide during meiosis II. The steps of meiosis II are shown above.

Meiosis II results in four haploid sex cells. In male organisms, these cells develop into sperm cells. In female organisms, these cells become eggs. In females of some species, three of the cells are broken down and only one haploid cell becomes an egg.

11 Identify At the end of meiosis II, how many cells have formed?

_____

How does meiosis compare to mitosis?

The processes of meiosis and mitosis are similar in many ways. However, they also have several very important differences.

- Only cells that will become sex cells go through meiosis. All other cells divide by mitosis.
- During meiosis, chromosomes are copied once, and then the nucleus divides twice. During mitosis, the chromosomes are copied once, and then the nucleus divides once.
- The cells produced by meiosis contain only half of the genetic material of the parent cell—one chromosome from each homologous pair and one sex chromosome. The cells produced by mitosis contain exactly the same genetic material as the parent—a full set of homologous chromosomes and a pair of sex chromosomes.

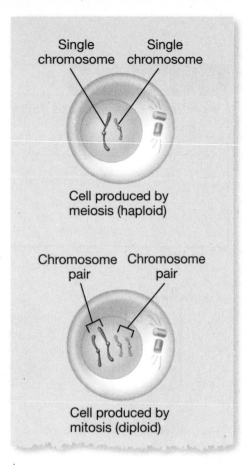

Single chromosome   Single chromosome

Cell produced by meiosis (haploid)

Chromosome pair   Chromosome pair

Cell produced by mitosis (diploid)

12 Summarize Using the table below, compare meiosis and mitosis.

Characteristic	Meiosis	Mitosis
Number of nuclear divisions		
Number of cells produced		
Number of chromosomes in new cells (diploid or haploid)		
Type of cell produced (body cell or sex cell)		
Steps of the process		

Down Syndrome

Down syndrome is a genetic disease. It is usually caused by an error during meiosis. During meiosis, the chromatids of chromosome 21 do not separate. So, a sex cell gets two copies of chromosome 21 instead of one copy. When this sex cell joins with a normal egg or sperm, the fertilized egg has three copies of chromosome 21 instead of two copies.

Beating the Odds

Down syndrome causes a number of health problems and learning difficulties, but many people with Down syndrome have fulfilling lives.

1 2 3 4 5

6 7

11 12

One Too Many

Someone who has Down syndrome has three copies of chromosome 21 instead of two copies.

18

19 20 21 22

Extend

Inquiry

13 Identify What type of error in meiosis causes Down syndrome?

14 Investigate Research the characteristics of Down syndrome. How can some of the difficulties caused by the disorder be overcome?

15 Recommend Research the Special Olympics. Then make an informative brochure, poster, or oral presentation that describes how the Special Olympics gives people with Down syndrome and other disabilities the chance to compete in sports.

Visual Summary

To complete this summary, fill in the blanks with the correct word or phrase. Then use the key below to check your answers. You can use this page to review the main concepts of the lesson.

Meiosis

Meiosis produces haploid cells that can become sex cells.

16 List the steps of meiosis I.

_____

_____

_____

_____

17 List the steps of meiosis II.

_____

_____

_____

Sex cells have half as many chromosomes as body cells.

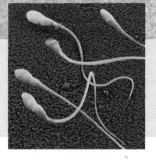

18 Sex cells produced by males are called _____, and sex cells produced by females are called _____.

Mitosis and meiosis have similarities and differences.

Single chromosome

Single chromosome

Cell produced by meiosis (haploid)

Chromosome pair

Chromosome pair

Cell produced by mitosis (diploid)

19 During _____, chromosomes are copied once and the nucleus divides twice.

20 During _____, chromosomes are copied once and the nucleus divides once.

Answers: 16 prophase I, metaphase I, anaphase I, telophase I and cytokinesis; 17 prophase II, metaphase II, anaphase II, telophase II and cytokinesis; 18 sperm cells, eggs; 19 meiosis, 20 mitosis

21 Summarize Briefly describe what happens during meiosis I and meiosis II.

Lesson Review

Vocabulary

Fill in the blanks with the term that best completes the following sentences.

1 _____ chromosomes are found in body cells but not sex cells.

2 The process of _____ produces haploid cells.

Key Concepts

3 Compare How does the number of chromosomes in sex cells compare with the number of chromosomes in body cells?

_____

_____

_____

4 Identify What is the function of meiosis?

_____

_____

5 List Identify the steps of meiosis.

_____

_____

_____

_____

_____

6 Compare How are mitosis and meiosis alike and different? Compare the resulting daughter cells in each process.

_____

_____

_____

_____

_____

_____

Critical Thinking

Use the figure to answer the following questions.

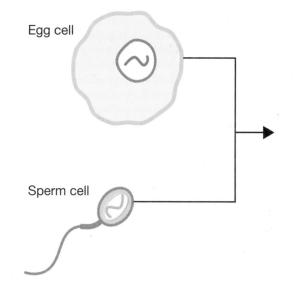

Egg cell

Sperm cell

7 Identify By what process did these cells form?

_____

8 Identify How many chromosomes does a body cell for the organism shown have?

_____

9 Predict Draw a picture of the cell that would form if the sperm cell fused with the egg cell. What is this cell called?

10 Synthesize What would happen if meiosis did not occur?

_____

_____

_____

_____

My Notes

Michael Coble

GENETICIST

Michael Coble's interest in genetics began when, as young child, he learned about Gregor Mendel's discoveries. While Coble was in college, his interest increased due to a science project in which he had to find dominant and recessive genes in fruit flies. Little did Coble know at the time that his work in genetics would lead him to solve one of history's greatest mysteries: What happened to Russia's royal family, the Romanovs, during the Russian revolution?

The whole family had supposedly been executed in 1918. However, many people believed there was a chance that at least one of the children had escaped.

Coble says that "since 1918, over 200 individuals have claimed to be one of the five 'surviving' Romanov children." Fueling the mystery was the fact that there were no remains in the Romanovs' grave for two of the children.

However, in 2007, a grave with the remains of two people was found. Coble and his team used the DNA evidence to identify the remains as the missing Romanov children.

Coble continues his work in genetics today. He says, "It is very rewarding to know that something you were involved with will be used for finding criminals, exonerating the innocent, or helping to identify missing persons."

If the bands of DNA on the film line up correctly, you have a match.

Dr. Coble solved the mystery of Princess Anastasia and the other Romanov children.

Social Studies Connection

Research Find out more about what happened to the Romanovs, including the mystery around Princess Anastasia. Put together a slideshow or a video to report your findings.

JOB BOARD

Genetic Counselor

What You'll Do: Analyze a family's risk factors for inherited conditions and disorders

Where You Might Work: At a doctor's office, a health clinic, or a hospital

Education: A graduate degree in genetic counseling

Other Job Requirements: Certification from the American Board of Genetic Counseling

Plant Nursery Manager

What You'll Do: Grow plants from seeds, cuttings, or by other methods. Manage a plant-related business or organization.

Where You Might Work: At a botanical garden, a garden center, or a plant nursery

Education: A degree in plant science and/or business management

Other Job Requirements: A green thumb!

MULTIPLE Births

Not so rare anymore

Dr. Brian Kirshon and his medical team made history in December 1998. They delivered the world's first known set of surviving octuplets. Octuplets are a very rare type of multiple birth in which the mother carries eight fetuses in her uterus at once. There have been only 19 recorded instances of octuplets. Only two of those sets survived past birth—the first in 1998, and another in 2009. Considering how rare octuplets are, how is it possible that two pairs were born so recently?

The birth rate for twins increased by 70% from 1980 to 2004. In 2006, the birth rate for twins was up to 32 for every 1,000 births. The birth rate in 2006 for having triplets or a larger birth was 153 for every 100,000 births.

What's going on? Doctors point to modern fertility drugs and treatments. In addition, many women are now waiting until later in life to have children. This increases the chance of having a multiple birth.

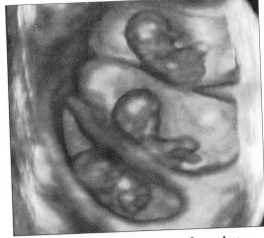

3D ultrasound image of triplets

Sexual and Asexual Reproduction

ESSENTIAL QUESTION

How do organisms reproduce?

By the end of this lesson, you should be able to describe asexual and sexual reproduction and list the advantages and disadvantages of each.

7.LS1.7

The female wolf spider carries her young on her back for a short time after they hatch.

 **Lesson Labs**

Quick Labs
• Reproduction and Diversity
• Egg vs. Sperm
• Create a Classification System

Field Lab
• Investigate Asexual Reproduction

Engage Your Brain

1 Predict Check T or F to show whether you think each statement is true or false.

T	F	
☐	☐	Reproduction requires two parents.
☐	☐	Some organisms reproduce by cell division.
☐	☐	New plants can grow from parts of a parent plant, such as roots and stems.
☐	☐	Offspring of two parents always look like one of their parents.

2 Describe How is the young wolf in the photo below similar to its mother?

_____

_____

_____

_____

Active Reading

3 Synthesize You can often define an unknown word if you know the meaning of its word parts. Use the word parts and sentence below to make an educated guess about the meaning of the word *reproduction*.

Word part	Meaning
re-	again
produce	to make
-ion	act or process

Example sentence
Flowers are plant organs that are used for reproduction.

reproduction:

_____

_____

Vocabulary Terms

• asexual reproduction
• sexual reproduction
• fertilization

4 Apply As you learn the definition of each vocabulary term in this lesson, write your own definition or make a sketch to help you remember the meaning of the term.

One Becomes Two

What is asexual reproduction?

An individual organism does not live forever. The survival of any species depends on the ability to reproduce. Reproduction passes on genetic information to new organisms. Reproduction involves various kinds of cell division.

Most single-celled organisms and some multicellular organisms reproduce asexually. In **asexual reproduction** (ay•SEHK•shoo•uhl ree•pruh•DUHK•shuhn), one organism produces one or more new organisms that are identical to itself. These organisms live independently of the original organism. The organism that produces the new organism or organisms is called a *parent*. Each new organism is called an *offspring*. The parent passes on all of its genetic information to the offspring. So, the offspring produced by asexual reproduction are genetically identical to their parents. They may differ only if a genetic mutation happens.

Active Reading

5 Relate Describe the genetic makeup of the offspring of asexual reproduction.

_____

_____

_____

Dandelions usually reproduce asexually. The dandelions in this field may all be genetically identical!

Think Outside the Book (Inquiry)

6 Summarize Research five organisms that reproduce asexually. Make informative flashcards that describe how each organism reproduces asexually. When you have finished, trade flashcards with a classmate to learn about five more organisms.

How do organisms reproduce asexually?

Organisms reproduce asexually in many ways. In prokaryotes, which include bacteria and archaea, asexual reproduction happens by cell division. In eukaryotes, which include single-celled and multicellular organisms, asexual reproduction is a more involved process. It often involves a type of cell division called *mitosis* (my•TOH•sis). Mitosis produces genetically identical cells.

Binary Fission

Binary fission (BY•nuh•ree FISH•uhn) is the form of asexual reproduction in prokaryotes. It is a type of cell division. During binary fission, the parent organism splits in two, producing two new cells. Genetically, the new cells are exactly like the parent cell.

Budding

During *budding,* an organism develops tiny buds on its body. A bud grows until it forms a new full-sized organism that is genetically identical to the parent. Budding is the result of mitosis. Eukaryotes such as single-celled yeasts and multicellular hydras reproduce by budding.

Spores

A *spore* is a specialized cell that can survive harsh conditions. Both prokaryotes and eukaryotes can form spores. Spores are produced asexually by one parent. Spores are light and can be carried by the wind. Under the right conditions, a spore develops into an organism, such as a fungus.

Vegetative Reproduction

Some plants are able to reproduce asexually by *vegetative reproduction*. Mitosis makes vegetative reproduction possible. New plants may grow from stems, roots, or leaves. Runners are above-ground stems from which a new plant can grow. Tubers are underground stems from which new plants can grow. Plantlets are tiny plants that grow along the edges of a plant's leaves. They drop off the plant and grow on their own.

 Visualize It!

7 Infer Pick one of the pictures below. Describe how the type of asexual reproduction can help the organism reproduce quickly.

_____

_____

_____

Bacteria reproduce by binary fission.

Hydras reproduce by budding.

Spores can survive for long periods in harsh conditions.

New potato plants can grow from tubers.

Two Make One

What is sexual reproduction?

Most multicellular organisms can reproduce sexually. In **sexual reproduction** (SEHK•shoo•uhl ree•pruh•DUHK•shuhn), two parents each contribute a sex cell to the new organism. Half the genes in the offspring come from each parent. So, the offspring are not identical to either parent. Instead, they have a combination of traits from each parent.

Active Reading

8 Identify As you read, underline the names of the male and female sex cells.

Fertilization

Usually, one parent is male and the other is female. Males produce sex cells called *sperm cells.* Females produce sex cells called *eggs.* Sex cells are produced by a type of cell division called *meiosis* (my•OH•sis). Sex cells have only half of the full set of genetic material found in body cells.

A sperm cell and an egg join together in a process called **fertilization** (fer•tl•i•ZAY•shuhn). When an egg is fertilized by a sperm cell, a new cell is formed. This cell is called a *zygote* (ZY•goht). It has a full set of genetic material. The zygote develops into a new organism. The zygote divides by mitosis, which increases the number of cells. This increase in cells produces growth. You are the size that you are today because of mitosis.

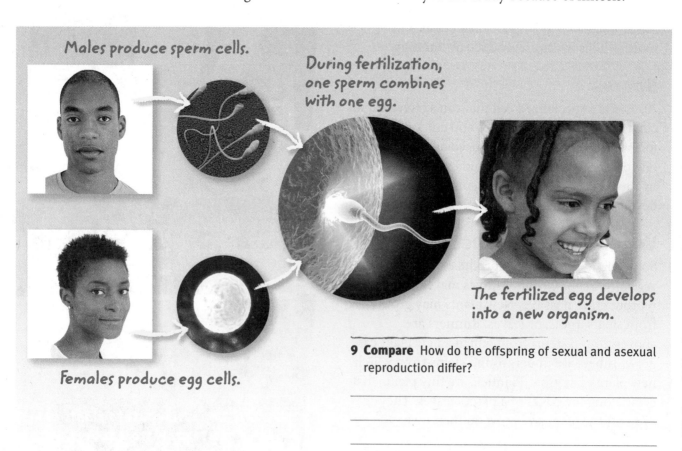

Males produce sperm cells.

During fertilization, one sperm combines with one egg.

The fertilized egg develops into a new organism.

Females produce egg cells.

9 Compare How do the offspring of sexual and asexual reproduction differ?

_____

_____

_____

Odd Reproduction

It may seem like only single-celled organisms undergo asexual reproduction. However, many multicellular organisms reproduce asexually.

Original starfish arm

Newly grown body and arms

Appearing Act
Some organisms, such as aphids, reproduce asexually by *parthenogenesis*. A female produces young without fertilization.

Falling to Pieces
Tapeworms can reproduce asexually by *fragmentation*. Each segment of the worm can become a new organism if it breaks off of the worm.

Seeing Stars
Organisms such as starfish reproduce asexually by *regeneration*. Even a small part of the starfish can grow into a new organism.

Extend

Inquiry

10 Identify Which types of asexual reproduction involve part of an organism breaking off?

11 Investigate Research the advantages and disadvantages of a type of reproduction shown on this page.

12 Hypothesize A female shark was left alone in an aquarium tank. She was not pregnant when placed in the tank. Scientists were surprised one morning to find a baby shark in the tank. Form a hypothesis about what type of reproduction took place in this scenario.

Added Advantage

What are the advantages of each type of reproduction?

Organisms reproduce asexually, sexually, or both. Each type of reproduction has advantages. For example, sexual reproduction involves complex structures, such as flowers and other organs. These are not needed for asexual reproduction. But the offspring of sexual reproduction may be more likely to survive in certain situations. Read on to find out more about the advantages of each.

13 Compare Use the Venn diagram below to compare asexual and sexual reproduction.

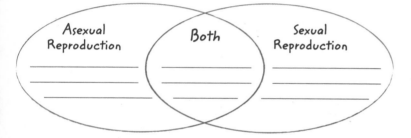

Asexual Reproduction   Both   Sexual Reproduction

Visualize It!

14 Evaluate Study the two photos above and compare the characteristics of each set of offspring with those of their parents. Were the offspring in photo A created by sexual reproduction or asexual reproduction? What about photo B? How do you know? Include evidence to support your statements.

_____

_____

_____

Advantages of Asexual Reproduction

Asexual reproduction has many advantages. First, an organism can reproduce very quickly. Offspring are identical to the parent. This ensures that any favorable traits the parent has are passed on to offspring. Also, a parent organism does not need to find a partner to reproduce. Finally, all offspring—not just females—are able to produce more offspring.

15 List Identify four advantages of asexual reproduction.

_____

_____

_____

_____

Cholla cactuses reproduce asexually by vegetative reproduction. They drop off small pieces that grow into new plants.

Cats reproduce sexually. Offspring are similar to, but not exactly like, their parents.

Advantages of Sexual Reproduction

Sexual reproduction is not as quick as asexual reproduction. Nor does it produce as many offspring. However, it has advantages. First, it increases genetic variation. Offspring have different traits that improve the chance that at least some offspring will survive. This is especially true if the environment changes. Offspring are not genetically identical to their parents. So, they may have a trait that the parents do not have, making them more likely to survive.

16 Explain How can increased genetic variation help some offspring survive?

_____

_____

_____

Advantages of Using Both Types of Reproduction

Some organisms can use both types of reproduction. For example, when conditions are favorable, many plants and fungi will reproduce asexually. Doing so lets them spread quickly and take over an area. When the environment changes, these organisms will switch to sexual reproduction. This strategy increases the chance that the species will survive. Because of genetic variation, at least some of the offspring may have traits that help them make it through the environmental change.

17 Compare In the table below, place check marks in the appropriate boxes to identify characteristics of sexual or asexual reproduction. Then, write a statement to summarize the advantages and disadvantages of both types of reproduction.

	Quick	Increases chance of survival in changing environments	Produces genetic variation	Doesn't need a partner	Requires complex structures
Asexual reproduction					
Sexual reproduction					

_____

_____

Visual Summary

To complete this summary, circle the correct word that completes each statement. Then use the key below to check your answers. You can use this page to review the main concepts of the lesson.

Asexual reproduction involves one parent.

Reproduction

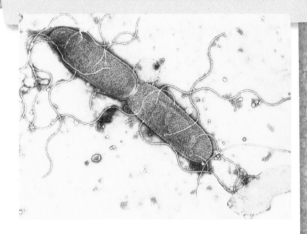

18 The offspring of asexual reproduction are genetically identical / similar to the parent organisms.

19 Prokaryotes reproduce by budding / binary fission.

20 Specialized reproductive structures called runners / spores can survive harsh conditions.

21 A benefit of asexual reproduction is that it is fast / slow.

Sexual reproduction involves two parents.

22 Male organisms produce sex cells called eggs / sperm cells.

23 Male and female sex cells join during fertilization / meiosis.

24 Sexual reproduction increases genetic variation / similarity.

Answers: 18 identical; 19 binary fission; 20 spores; 21 fast; 22 sperm cells; 23 fertilization; 24 variation

25 Explain How do both asexual reproduction and sexual reproduction enable the survival of a species?

Lesson Review

Vocabulary

Fill in the blanks with the term that best completes the following sentences.

1 After _____ , the zygote develops into a larger organism.

2 An advantage of _____ reproduction is the ability to reproduce quickly.

3 The offspring of _____ reproduction are more likely to survive changes in the environment.

Key Concepts

4 Identify What are some advantages of asexual and sexual reproduction?

_____

_____

_____

_____

_____

5 Compare In sexual reproduction, how do the offspring compare to the parents?

_____

_____

_____

6 Identify List four types of asexual reproduction.

_____

_____

_____

7 Explain Why do some organisms use both types of reproduction?

_____

_____

_____

Critical Thinking

Use the graph to answer the following questions.

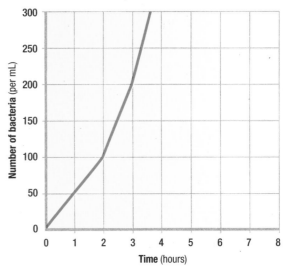

Growth of a Bacterial Population Over Time

8 Infer What type of reproduction is most likely taking place?

_____

_____

9 Analyze Which advantage of reproduction does the graph show? Explain.

_____

_____

_____

_____

10 Predict How might the graph change if the environmental conditions of the bacteria suddenly change? Explain.

_____

_____

_____

_____

_____

_____

My Notes

Adaptations and Survival

ESSENTIAL QUESTION

How do organisms adapt to their environment?

By the end of this lesson, you should be able to describe how structural and behavioral adaptations help plants and animals survive and reproduce.

7.LS1.6

The habit of living together in groups is an important adaptation that increases animals' chances of survival in unforgiving environments.

Engage Your Brain

1 Predict Match the plant or animal on the left with the trait on the right that has helped the organism obtain food, water, or protection.

cactus   toxins in skin

polar bear   stems that store water

poison dart frog   roots close to the soil surface

water lily   ability to tolerate body temperatures up to 107 °C

rose   white fur

camel   thorns

2 Infer Fill in the blank with the word that you think correctly completes the following sentences.

The _____ of an elephant can be used to help the animal survive by allowing it to pick up food and drink water.

The bright _____ of a peacock helps it attract a mate in order to reproduce.

The _____ of a cat are positioned at the front of its head so it can focus on its prey.

The Venus flytrap attracts insects with its scent and bright _____.

In dry forests, trees have thick _____ to limit the loss of water by evaporation.

Active Reading

3 Synthesize You can often define an unknown word if you know the meaning of its word parts. Use the word parts and sentence below to make an educated guess about the meaning of the word *mutation*.

Word part	Meaning
mutare	to change
-ion	act or process

Example sentence
A <u>mutation</u> is beneficial to an organism if it helps that organism thrive in its habitat.

Vocabulary Terms
- adaptation
- variation
- mutation
- evolution
- natural selection
- structural adaptation
- behavioral adaptation
- exaptation
- vestigial adaptation

4 Apply As you learn the definition of each vocabulary term in this lesson, write your own definition or make a sketch to help you remember the meaning of the term.

mutation:

_____

_____

_____

Stayin' Alive!

Why do adaptations occur?

All plants and animals have *adaptations*. **Adaptations** are traits that make it more likely that an organism will be able to survive and reproduce in its habitat. The thick fur of a polar bear is an adaptation that keeps the bear warm in freezing temperatures. A chameleon's ability to change color to avoid predators is an adaptation. Adaptations are usually a response to changes in the habitat. These habitat changes lead to gradual changes in the traits of a species over time.

 **Visualize It!**

5 Analyze How do you think the cactus has adapted to avoid being eaten by animals?

_____

_____

_____

Genetic Variation

Within any single species, there is great genetic **variation**, or difference in traits. Flowers have a variety of scents; certain beetles are green while others are brown. Some variations may not be beneficial, but those that do aid survival are likely to be passed on from generation to generation. If green beetles are more likely to be eaten by predators than brown beetles, more brown beetles will survive and reproduce. Their offspring will have the helpful trait—their brown color.

Mutations

A **mutation**, or random change in an organism's genes, is the cause of all variation. When a habitat changes, some mutations may improve a species' ability to survive in its new environment. The new trait, for example, might make it easier for the animal or plant to defend against predators.

Evolution

A mutation can be helpful or harmful, or it may be neither. A helpful mutation will be passed down from one generation to the next. It eventually becomes a typical trait of the entire species, or an adaptation. Adaptations, however, do not take place overnight; they generally develop over a long period of time and over many generations. This gradual change in traits in a species is called **evolution**. A scientist named Charles Darwin first proposed this theory in the nineteenth century. Darwin's theory of evolution explains the process that produces this gradual change.

Natural Selection

Evolution works by natural selection. The term **natural selection** refers to the competition among organisms that are trying to survive. Some organisms are better adapted to their habitats than others, and it is these organisms that survive and reproduce. On the other hand, those organisms that are not well adapted to their habitats may die out. The traits that help a species survive are passed on to future generations, and the unhelpful traits eventually disappear. Over generations, the adaptive traits become more common in the population. Eventually, most of the individuals in a species have the adaptation.

Active Reading 6 **Describe** What happens when a mutation is passed down from one generation to the next?

_____

_____

_____

_____

_____

Think Outside the Book (Inquiry)

7 **Research** Research a person in history that contributed to science, such as Charles Darwin. Describe how that person's contribution turned into a scientific theory or fact that we use today to study adaptations and survival.

The Survival Apps

How does adaptation aid survival?

Structural adaptations and *behavioral adaptations* help plants and animals improve the probability of survival, which in turn affects their probability of reproductive success.

Structural Adaptations

A **structural adaptation** is a change in some physical part of an organism. A duck's webbed feet and a cactus's spines are both structural adaptations. These traits help the organism survive in its habitat.

Over time, habitats may change. As a result of a change, a certain species of bird may have only one food source, which is buried beneath the bark of trees. Birds with sharply pointed beaks can extract the food by drilling holes in the bark. Over time, only the well-fed birds will survive and pass their pointed-beak gene on to the next generations. This sharply pointed beak has become a structural adaptation.

Behavioral Adaptations

A **behavioral adaptation** allows an animal to survive by changing the way an organism acts. Behavioral adaptations can be *instinctive*, meaning that an organism is born with that pattern of behavior. However, some are *learned*, which means they must be taught to behave a certain way.

Instinctive behavioral adaptations include swarming, hibernating, and migrating. Hunting is an example of learned behavior. Lion cubs follow their mother on hunts. They watch her stalk and pounce on her prey. During playtime, they practice this stalking and pouncing behavior.

Visualize It!

8 Identify Look at the images. Which animals are exhibiting instinctive behavior? And learned behavior?

_____

_____

Visualize It!

9 Infer The following organisms have some kind of adaptation that helps them survive in their habitats. Complete the chart by determining whether the adaptation is structural or behavioral.

Description	Structural or Behavioral Adaptation?
Elephant trunks	
Penguins that live in groups	
Bats that migrate	
Thorns on a rosebush	

296 Unit 5 Reproduction, Survival, and Heredity

Exaptations

An **exaptation** (egs·ap·TAY·zhuhn) is an adaptation resulting from natural selection for a particular purpose. Eventually, this adaptation takes on a different function. For example, feathers were probably adaptations that originally kept an animal warm. Only later were feathers a useful adaptation that made flight possible. Feathers are thus an adaption for warmth and an exaptation for flight.

Vestigial Adaptations

Some adaptations can become useless over time. These adaptations are called *vestigial*. **Vestigial adaptations** (ve·STIJ·ee·uhl ad·ap·TAY·shuhnz) do not disappear, but they no longer serve the original purpose. Biologists believe the human appendix is a vestigial structure. This organ aids in the digestion of cellulose, and was probably useful when grass was a large part of the human diet.

Coadaptation and Co-Extinction

Sometimes, pairs of organisms adapt together in such a way that they meet one another's needs. This kind of mutually beneficial adaptation is called *coadaptation*. For example, in its caterpillar stage, the lycaenid butterfly secretes a nectar-like substance from a special gland that attracts some species of ants. The ants then swarm over the caterpillar and protect it from other predators.

However, coadaptation can have disadvantages. It can lead to co-extinction. *Co-extinction* is the loss of a species due to the extinction of another species. The extinction of the California parakeet led to the co-extinction of six species of mites that had a coadaptive relationship with the bird.

Visualize It!

10 Identify Which organisms in the photos have a vestigial structure? What is the structure, and why do you think it is vestigial?

_____

_____

Active Reading

11 Describe How do lycaenid butterflies have coadaptive relationships with ants?

_____

_____

_____

_____

Leave Me Alone!

How do organisms adapt?

Organisms adapt for four reasons: to obtain food, water, or nutrients; to cope with physical conditions such as temperature; to defend against threats; and to reproduce and rear young. Common forms of structural adaptations include *camouflage*, *mimicry*, *chemical defense*, and *body coverings and parts*. *Migration* and *hibernation* are behavioral adaptations.

Active Reading

12 Identify As you read, underline the way each type of structural adaptation works.

Mimicry and Camouflage

Mimicry is an adaptation that lets an organism disguise itself to look or sound like another organism that a predator will ignore. Camouflage is a form of mimicry. Camouflage allows a plant or animal to blend in with their surroundings to hide from predators and prey.

The bee orchid is a flower that uses mimicry to attract bees for pollination by looking like a female bee.

Wasp

Clearwig moth

The octopus releases black ink to escape from predators.

Visualize It!

13 Apply Which of the insects above is the mimic and which is the model? Why?

_____

_____

_____

Chemical Defense

Some animals and plants poison their predators or give off a chemical defense when attacked, like venom, ink, and sprays. Chemical defenses are meant to disorient predators or harm them enough so that they no longer disturb the animal or plant.

Body Coverings and Parts

Body coverings and parts, such as skin, scales, feathers, and bark, are all evolutionary adaptations.

Body coverings protect organisms in diverse environments, such as water, land, and sky. Trees have protective bark that can help them survive the high temperatures of wildfires. Many organisms have specialized body parts that serve specific purposes. Jellyfish, for example, have tentacles with stinging cells to catch their prey.

Migration

Migration is a seasonal round trip from one habitat to another. Seasonal changes can reduce a habitat's food and water supplies, so some animals must move to stay alive. Some animals, like bats, travel only short distances. However, snow geese can travel 5,000 miles from the Arctic to the southern United States.

Hibernation

Some animals remain in the same habitat even when seasonal changes reduce their food supply. *Hibernation* is an extended period of deep sleep during the winter. The animal uses very little energy, so it can survive without a lot of food.

Animals such as skunks, bees, bears, and snakes look for a safe place to hibernate. Before hibernating, some animals may prepare by eating extra food and storing it as body fat. This stored fat delivers energy if they need it later.

 Visualize It!

14 Identify Write the correct form of structural adaptation for each organism.

A _____

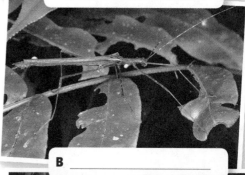

B _____

C _____

D _____

Visualize It!

15 Compare Compare and contrast migration and hibernation. Use the Venn diagram to show how they are different and similar.

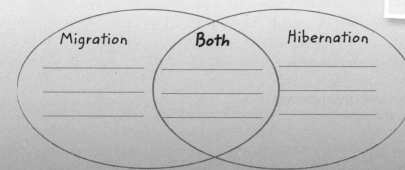

Migration   Both   Hibernation

Visual Summary

To complete this summary, circle the correct word or phrase. Then, use the key below to check your answers. You can use this page to review the main concepts of the lesson.

Adaptation

Animals and plants make changes that may help them survive in their environments.

16 When a plant or animal faces a change in its habitat, sometimes a mutation / migration takes place that enables it to function better in its new environment.

Adaptations help plants and animals improve their probability of survival and reproduction.

17 A structural / behavioral adaptation is a change in the way an organism acts. A structural / behavioral adaptation is a change in some physical part of an organism.

Mimicry and camouflage are common forms of adaptation.

18 Adaptations develop in the organism so it can more easily cope with physical conditions such as temperature / learn by instinct.

Answers: 16 mutation; 17a behavioral; 17b structural; 18 cope with physical conditions such as temperature

19 **Summarize** Choose a plant or animal to focus on. Develop an argument based on evidence and scientific reasoning to explain how behavioral and structural adaptations affect the chances of survival and reproduction of that plant or animal.

Lesson Review

Vocabulary

Fill in the blanks with the term that best completes the following sentences.

1 _____ are adaptations that have become useless.

2 Two organisms that adapt in a way that meets each other's needs is a demonstration of _____.

3 Camouflage is a form of _____, which is an adaptation in which an organism looks or sounds like another living organism.

4 The _____ that helps an individual to survive in its particular habitat is a feature that is likely to be passed on from generation to generation.

Key Concepts

5 Identify What are the different ways organisms adapt?

_____

_____

_____

6 Identify What are some examples of structural and behavioral adaptations?

_____

_____

_____

7 Compare How are the chances of surviving and reproducing for an individual with an adaptation to a recent change in its environment higher than the chances of an individual without that adaptation?

_____

_____

_____

Critical Thinking

Use this photo to answer the following questions.

8 Describe Describe the camel's environment.

_____

_____

9 Analyze Name two things the camel must be able to do to survive in this environment.

_____

_____

_____

10 Synthesize Explain how the camel's behavioral and structural adaptations enable it to survive and reproduce in its environment.

_____

_____

_____

_____

My Notes

Heredity

ESSENTIAL QUESTION

How are traits inherited?

By the end of this lesson, you should be able to analyze the inheritance of traits in individuals.

Members of the same family share certain traits. Can you think of some traits that family members share?

Lesson Labs

Quick Labs
• Dominant Alleles
• What's the Difference between a Dominant Trait and a Recessive Trait?

Engage Your Brain

1 Predict Check T or F to show whether you think each statement is true or false.

T   F

☐   ☐   Siblings look similar because they each have some traits of their parents.

☐   ☐   Siblings always have the same hair color.

☐   ☐   Siblings have identical DNA.

2 Describe Do you know any identical twins? How are they similar? How are they different?

_____

_____

_____

_____

_____

 Active Reading

3 Infer Use context clues to write your own definition for the words *exhibit* and *investigate*.

Example sentence
A person with brown hair may also <u>exhibit</u> the trait of brown eye color.

exhibit:

_____

_____

Example sentence
Gregor Mendel began to <u>investigate</u> the characteristics of pea plants.

investigate:

_____

_____

Vocabulary Terms

• heredity
• gene
• allele
• genotype
• phenotype
• dominant
• recessive
• incomplete dominance
• codominance

4 Identify This list contains the key terms you'll learn in this lesson. As you read, circle the definition of each term.

Give Peas a Chance

What is heredity?

Imagine a puppy. The puppy has long floppy ears like his mother has, and the puppy has dark brown fur like his father has. How did the puppy get these traits? The traits are a result of information stored in the puppy's genetic material. The passing of genetic material from parents to offspring is called **heredity**.

What did Gregor Mendel discover about heredity?

The first major experiments investigating heredity were performed by a monk named Gregor Mendel. Mendel lived in Austria in the 1800s. Before Mendel became a monk, he attended a university and studied science and mathematics. This training served him well when he began to study the inheritance of traits among the pea plants in the monastery's garden. Mendel studied seven different characteristics of pea plants: plant height, flower and pod position, seed shape, seed color, pod shape, pod color, and flower color. A *characteristic* is a feature that has different forms in a population. Mendel studied each pea plant characteristic separately, always starting with plants that were true-breeding for that characteristic. A true-breeding plant is one that will always produce offspring with a certain trait when allowed to self-pollinate. Each of the characteristics that Mendel studied had two different forms. For example, the color of a pea could be green or yellow. These different forms are called *traits*.

Characteristics of Pea Plants

Characteristic	Traits	
Seed color		
Seed shape		
Pod color		
Flower position		

5 **Apply** Is flower color a characteristic or a trait?

_____

_____

Traits Depend on Inherited Factors

In his experiments with seed pod color, Mendel took two sets of plants, one true-breeding for plants that produce yellow seed pods and the other true-breeding for plants that produce green seed pods. Instead of letting the plants self-pollinate as they do naturally, he paired one plant from each set. He did this by fertilizing one plant with the pollen of another plant. Mendel called the plants that resulted from this cross the first generation. All of the plants from this first generation produced green seed pods. Mendel called this trait the *dominant* trait. Because the yellow trait seemed to recede, or fade away, he called it the *recessive* trait.

Then Mendel let the first-generation plants self-pollinate. He called the offspring that resulted from this self-pollination the second generation. About three-fourths of the second-generation plants had green seed pods, but about one-fourth had yellow pods. So the trait that seemed to disappear in the first generation reappeared in the second generation. Mendel hypothesized that each plant must have two heritable "factors" for each trait, one from each parent. Some traits, such as yellow seed pod color, could only be observed if a plant received two factors—one from each parent—for yellow pod color. A plant with one yellow factor and one green factor would produce green pods because producing green pods is a dominant trait. However, this plant could still pass on the yellow factor to the next generation of plants.

6 Identify As you read, underline Mendel's hypothesis about how traits are passed from parents to offspring.

 **Visualize It!**

7 Apply Which pod color is recessive?

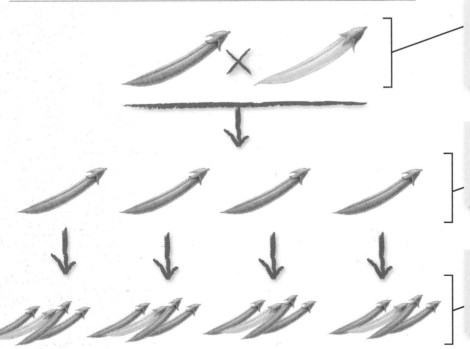

Parent plants Mendel crossed true-breeding green-pod plants with true-breeding yellow-pod plants.

First generation All of the first generation plants had green pods. Mendel let these plants self-pollinate.

Second generation About three-fourths of the second generation had green pods, and one-fourth had yellow pods.

It's in Your Genes!

How are traits inherited?

Mendel's experiments and conclusions have been the basis for much of the scientific thought about heredity. His ideas can be further explained by our modern understanding of the genetic material DNA. What Mendel called "factors" are actually segments of DNA known as genes!

Genes are made up of DNA.

Genes Are Passed from Parents to Offspring

Genes are segments of DNA found in chromosomes that give instructions for producing a certain characteristic. Humans, like many other organisms, inherit their genes from their parents. Each parent gives one set of genes to the offspring. The offspring then has two versions, or forms, of the same gene for every characteristic—one version from each parent. The different versions of a gene are known as **alleles** (uh•LEELZ). Genes are often represented by letter symbols. Dominant alleles are shown with a capital letter, and recessive alleles are shown with a lowercase version of the same letter. An organism with two dominant or two recessive alleles is said to be *homozygous* for that gene. An organism that has one dominant and one recessive allele is *heterozygous*.

Humans have 23 pairs of chromosomes.

In humans, cells contain pairs of chromosomes. One chromosome of each pair comes from each of two parents. Each chromosome contains sites where specific genes are located.

A gene occupies a specific location on both chromosomes in a pair.

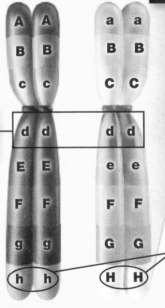

Alleles are alternate forms of the same gene.

8 Apply Circle a gene pair for which this person is heterozygous.

This girl has dimples.

This girl does not have dimples.

Genes Influence Traits

The alternate forms of genes, called alleles, determine the traits of all living organisms. The combination of alleles that you inherited from your parents is your **genotype** (JEEN•uh•typ). Your observable traits make up your **phenotype** (FEEN•uh•typ). The phenotypes of some traits follow patterns similar to the ones that Mendel discovered in pea plants. That is, some traits are dominant over others. For example, consider the gene responsible for producing dimples, or creases in the cheeks. This gene comes in two alleles: one for dimples and one for no dimples. If you have even one copy of the allele for dimples, you will have dimples. This happens because the allele for producing dimples is dominant. The **dominant** allele contributes to the phenotype if one or two copies are present in the genotype. The no-dimples allele is recessive. The **recessive** allele contributes to the phenotype only when two copies of it are present. If one chromosome in the pair contains a dominant allele and the other contains a recessive allele, the phenotype will be determined by the dominant allele. If you do not have dimples, it is because you inherited two no-dimples alleles—one from each parent. This characteristic shows *complete dominance,* because one trait is completely dominant over another. However, not all characteristics follow this pattern.

Active Reading

11 **Identify** What is the phenotype of an individual with one allele for dimples and one allele for no dimples?

_____

_____

Many Genes Can Influence a Single Trait

Some characteristics, such as the color of your skin, hair, and eyes, are the result of several genes acting together. Different combinations of alleles can result in different shades of eye color. Because there is not always a one-to-one relationship between a trait and a gene, many traits do not have simple patterns of inheritance.

A Single Gene Can Influence Many Traits

Sometimes, one gene influences more than one trait. For example, a single gene causes the tiger shown below to have white fur. If you look closely, you will see that the tiger also has blue eyes. The gene that affects fur color also influences eye color.

Many genetic disorders in humans are linked to a single gene but affect many traits. For example, the genetic disorder sickle cell anemia occurs in individuals who have two recessive alleles for a certain gene. This gene carries instructions for producing a protein in red blood cells. When a person has sickle cell anemia alleles, the body makes a different protein. This protein causes red blood cells to be sickle or crescent shaped when oxygen levels are low. Sickle-shaped blood cells can stick in blood vessels, sometimes blocking the flow of blood. These blood cells are also more likely to damage the spleen. With fewer healthy red blood cells, the body may not be able to deliver oxygen to the body's organs. All of the traits associated with sickle cell anemia are due to a single gene.

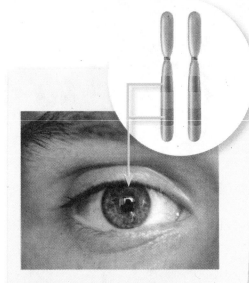

Visualize It!

12 Identify How many genes are responsible for eye color in this example?

_____

_____

This single gene affects the tiger's fur color and eye color.

The Environment Can Influence Traits

Sometimes, the environment influences an organism's phenotype. For example, the arctic fox has a gene that is responsible for coat color. This gene is affected by light. In the winter, there are fewer hours of daylight, and the hairs that make up the arctic fox's coat grow in white. In the summer, when there are more daylight hours, the hairs in the coat grow in brown. In this case, both genes and the environment contribute to the organism's phenotype. The environment can influence human characteristics as well. For example, your genes may make it possible for you to grow to be tall, but you need a healthy diet to reach your full height potential.

Traits that are learned in one's environment are not inherited. For example, your ability to read and write is an acquired trait—a skill you learned. You were not born knowing how to ride a bike, and if you have children, they will not be born knowing how to do it either. They will have to learn the skill just as you did.

 **Active Reading**

13 Identify Give an example of an acquired trait.

_____

_____

In the summer, the arctic fox has a brown coat.

In the winter, the arctic fox has a white coat.

14 Predict What advantage does white fur give the arctic fox in winter?

_____

_____

_____

Bending the Rules

What are the exceptions to complete dominance?

The characteristics that Mendel chose to study demonstrated complete dominance, meaning that heterozygous individuals show the dominant trait. Some human traits, such as freckles and dimples, follow the pattern of complete dominance, too. However, other traits do not. For traits that show incomplete dominance or codominance, one trait is not completely dominant over another.

Incomplete Dominance

In **incomplete dominance**, each allele in a heterozygous individual influences the phenotype. The result is a phenotype that is a blend of the phenotypes of the parents. One example of incomplete dominance is found in the snapdragon flower, shown below. When a true-breeding red snapdragon is crossed with a true-breeding white snapdragon, all the offspring are pink snapdragons. Both alleles of the gene have some influence. Hair texture is an example of incomplete dominance in humans. A person with one straight-hair allele and one curly-hair allele will have wavy hair.

Active Reading

15 **Identify** As you read, underline examples of incomplete dominance and codominance.

Visualize It!

16 **Analyze** How can you tell that these snapdragons do not follow the pattern of complete dominance?

_____

_____

_____

_____

Pink snapdragons are produced by a cross between a red snapdragon and a white snapdragon.

Codominance

For a trait that shows **codominance**, both of the alleles in a heterozygous individual contribute to the phenotype. Instead of having a blend of the two phenotypes, heterozygous individuals have both of the traits associated with their two alleles. An example of codominance is shown in the genes that determine human blood types. There are three alleles that play a role in determining a person's blood type: *A, B,* and *O.* The alleles are responsible for producing small particles on the surface of red blood cells called antigens. The *A* allele produces red blood cells coated with A antigens. The *B* allele produces red blood cells coated with B antigens. The *O* allele does not produce antigens. The *A* and *B* alleles are codominant. So, someone with one *A* allele and one *B* allele will have blood cells that are coated with A antigens and B antigens. This person would have type AB blood.

Think Outside the Book **Inquiry**

17 Research Blood type is an important factor when people give or receive blood. Research the meanings of the phrases "universal donor" and "universal recipient." What are the genotypes of each blood type?

Active Reading **18 Identify** What antigens coat the red blood cells of a person with type AB blood?

_____

Visualize It!

19 Predict The color of these imaginary fish is controlled by a single gene. Sketch or describe their offspring if the phenotypes follow the pattern of complete dominance, incomplete dominance, or codominance.

 X

Complete dominance (Blue is dominant to yellow.)	Incomplete dominance	Codominance

Visual Summary

To complete this summary, circle the correct word or phrase. Then use the key below to check your answers. You can use this page to review the main concepts of the lesson.

Heredity

Gregor Mendel studied patterns of heredity in pea plants.

20 Traits that seemed to disappear in Mendel's first-generation crosses were dominant / recessive traits.

Inherited genes influence the traits of an individual.

21 An individual with the genotype BB is heterozygous / homozygous.

Phenotypes can follow complete dominance, incomplete dominance, or codominance.

22 When these imaginary fish cross, their offspring are all green. This is an example of codominance / incomplete dominance.

Answers: 20 recessive; 21 homozygous; 22 incomplete dominance

23 **Apply** If a child has blonde hair and both of her parents have brown hair, what does that tell you about the allele for blonde hair?

312 Unit 5 Reproduction, Survival, and Heredity

Lesson Review

Vocabulary

Draw a line to connect the following terms to their definitions.

1 heredity

2 gene

3 phenotype

A an organism's appearance or other detectable characteristic

B a section of DNA that contains instructions for a particular characteristic

C the passing of genetic material from parent to offspring

Key Concepts

4 Describe What did Mendel discover about genetic factors in pea plants?

_____

_____

_____

_____

_____

_____

5 Describe What is the role of DNA in determining an organism's traits?

_____

_____

_____

_____

6 Apply Imagine that a brown horse and a white horse cross to produce an offspring whose coat is made up of some brown hairs and some white hairs. Which pattern of dominance is this an example of?

7 Identify Give an example of a trait that is controlled by more than one gene.

_____

_____

Use this diagram to answer the following questions.

8 Identify What is the genotype at the Q gene?

_____

9 Apply For which genes is this individual heterozygous?

_____

Critical Thinking

10 Describe Marfan syndrome is a genetic disorder caused by a dominant allele. Describe how Marfan syndrome is inherited.

_____

_____

_____

11 Describe Jenny, Jenny's mom, and Jenny's grandfather are all good basketball players. Give an example of an inherited trait and an acquired trait that could contribute to their skill at basketball.

_____

_____

_____

_____

My Notes

Interpreting Tables

Visual displays, such as diagrams, tables, or graphs, are useful ways to show data collected in an experiment. A table is the most direct way to communicate this information. Tables are also used to summarize important trends in scientific data. Making a table may seem easy. However, if tables are not clearly organized, people will have trouble reading them. Below are a few strategies to help you improve your skills in interpreting scientific tables.

Tutorial

Use the following instructions to study the parts of a table about heredity in Brittanies and to analyze the data shown in the table.

Offspring from Cross of Black Solid and Liver Tricolor Brittanies		
Color	**Pattern**	**Number of Offspring**
orange and white	solid	1
black and white	solid	1
	tricolor	3
liver and white	solid	1
	tricolor	3

Reading the Title
Every table should have an informative title. By reading the title of the table to the left, we know that the table contains data about the offspring of a cross between a black solid Brittany and a liver tricolor Brittany.

Summarizing the Title
Sometimes it is helpful to write a sentence to summarize a table's title. For example, you could write, "This table shows how puppies that are the offspring of a black solid Brittany and a liver tricolor Brittany might look."

Analyzing the Headings
Row and column headings describe the data in the cells. Headings often appear different from the data in the cells, such as being larger, bold, or being shaded. The row headings in the table to the left organize three kinds of data: the coat color of the puppies, the coat pattern of the puppies, and the number of puppies that have each combination of coat color and pattern.

Describing the Data
In complete sentences, record the information that you read in the table. For example, you could write, "There are five different kinds of offspring. Tricolor puppies are most common, and puppies with a solid coat pattern are least common. There are twice as many tricolor puppies as solid puppies."

Analyzing the Data
Now that you have seen how the table is organized, you can begin to look for trends in the data. Which combinations are most common? Which combinations are least common?

You Try It!

The table below shows the characteristics of Guinea pig offspring. Look at the table, and answer the questions that follow.

Characteristics of Guinea Pig Offspring from Controlled Breeding			
Hair Color	Coat Texture	Hair Length	Number of Guinea Pigs
black	rough	short	27
		long	9
	smooth	short	9
		long	3
white	rough	short	9
		long	3
	smooth	short	3
		long	1

1 Summarizing the Title Circle the title of the table. Write a one-sentence description of the information shown in the table.

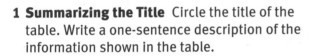

2 Analyzing the Headings Shade the column headings in the table. What information do they show? How many combinations of hair color, coat texture, and hair length are shown?

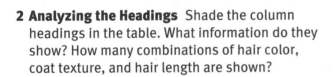

3 Analyzing the Data Circle the most common type of Guinea pig. Box the least common type of Guinea pig. Write sentences to describe the characteristics of each.

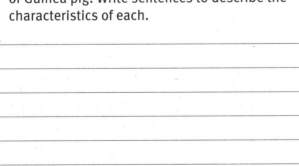

4 Applying Mathematics Calculate the total number of Guinea pig offspring. Write this total at the bottom of the table. What percentage of the total number of Guinea pigs has short hair? What percentage of the total number of Guinea pigs has long hair?

5 Observing Trends Based on your data from Step 4, which characteristic is dominant in Guinea pigs: long hair or short hair?

6 Applying Concepts What is one advantage of displaying data in tables? What is one advantage of describing data in writing?

Take It Home

With an adult, practice making tables. You can categorize anything that interests you. Make sure your table has a title and clearly and accurately organizes your data using headings. If possible, share your table with your class.

Punnett Squares and Pedigrees

ESSENTIAL QUESTION

How are patterns of inheritance studied?

By the end of this lesson, you should be able to explain how patterns of heredity can be predicted by Punnett squares and pedigrees.

— **7.LS3.3**

These cattle are bred for their long, curly hair, which keeps them warm in cold climates. This trait is maintained by careful breeding of these animals.

🖐 Lesson Labs

Quick Labs
• Gender Determination
• Interpreting Pedigree Charts
• Completing a Punnett Square

S.T.E.M. Lab
• Matching Punnett Square Predictions

Engage Your Brain

1 Infer Why do you think that children look like their parents?

_____

_____

_____

_____

_____

_____

_____

_____

_____

2 Apply Color or label each circle with the color that results when the two paints mix. As you read the lesson, think about how this grid is similar to and different from a Punnett square.

✏ Active Reading

3 Apply Use context clues to write your own definition for the words *occur* and *outcome*.

Example sentence
Tools can be used to predict the likelihood that a particular genetic combination will <u>occur</u>.

occur:

_____

_____

Example sentence
A Punnett square can be used to predict the <u>outcome</u> of a genetic cross.

outcome:

_____

_____

Vocabulary Terms
• **Punnett square**   • **ratio**
• **probability**   • **pedigree**

4 Apply As you learn the definition of each vocabulary term in this lesson, create your own definition or sketch to help you remember the meaning of the term.

Squared Away

How are Punnett squares used to predict patterns of heredity?

When Gregor Mendel studied pea plants, he noticed that traits are inherited in patterns. One tool for understanding the patterns of heredity is a diagram called a *Punnett square*. A **Punnett square** is a graphic used to predict the possible genotypes of offspring in a given cross. Each parent has two alleles for a particular gene. An offspring receives one allele from each parent. A Punnett square shows all of the possible allele combinations in the offspring.

The Punnett square below shows how alleles are expected to be distributed in a cross between a pea plant with purple flowers and a pea plant with white flowers. The top of the Punnett square shows one parent's alleles for this trait (*F* and *F*). The left side of the Punnett square shows the other parent's alleles (*f* and *f*). Each compartment within the Punnett square shows an allele combination in potential offspring. You can see that in this cross, all offspring would have the same genotype (*Ff*). Because purple flower color is completely dominant to white flower color, all of the offspring would have purple flowers.

Active Reading

5 Identify In a Punnett square, where are the parents' alleles written?

_____

_____

_____

_____

This Punnett square shows the possible offspring combinations in pea plants with different flower colors.

Key:

F Purple flower allele

f White flower allele

Genotype: FF
Phenotype: purple flower

Genotype: ff
Phenotype: white flower

One parent's alleles

	F	F
f	Ff	Ff
f	Ff	Ff

The other parent's alleles

6 Apply Fill in the genotypic and phenotypic data of the parents and offspring in this Punnett square. Sketch the resulting offspring possibilities in the white boxes below. (Hint: Assume complete dominance.)

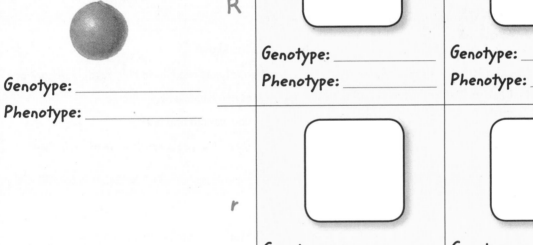

Key:

R Round pea allele

r Wrinkled pea allele

Genotype: _____

Phenotype: _____

	R	r
R	Genotype: _____ Phenotype: _____	Genotype: _____ Phenotype: _____
r	Genotype: _____ Phenotype: _____	Genotype: _____ Phenotype: _____

Genotype: _____

Phenotype: _____

7 Analyze What does each compartment of the Punnett square represent?

_____

_____

_____

_____

_____

_____

_____

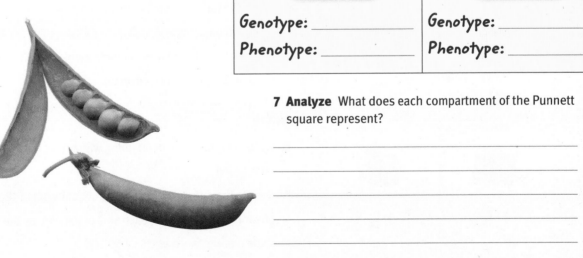

How can a Punnett square be used to make predictions about offspring?

A Punnett square does not tell you what the exact results of a certain cross will be. A Punnett square only helps you find the probability that a certain genotype will occur. **Probability** is the mathematical chance of a specific outcome in relation to the total number of possible outcomes.

Probability can be expressed in the form of a **ratio** (RAY•shee•oh), an expression that compares two quantities. A ratio written as 1:4 is read as "one to four." The ratios obtained from a Punnett square tell you the probability that any one offspring will get certain alleles. Another way of expressing probability is as a *percentage*. A percentage is like a ratio that compares a number to 100. A percentage states the number of times a certain outcome might happen out of a hundred chances.

1:4 is the ratio of red squares to total squares.

Do the Math   Sample Problem

In guinea pigs, the dominant *B* allele is responsible for black fur, while the recessive *b* allele is responsible for brown fur. Use the Punnett square to find the probability of this cross resulting in offspring with brown fur.

	B	b
b	Bb	bb
b	Bb	bb

Identify

A. What do you know?

Parent genotypes are Bb and bb. Possible offspring genotypes are Bb and bb.

B. What do you want to find out?

Probability of the cross resulting in offspring with brown fur

Plan

C. Count the total number of offspring allele combinations: 4

D. Count the number of allele combinations that will result in offspring with brown fur: 2

Solve

E. Write the probability of offspring with brown fur as a ratio: 2:4

F. Rewrite the ratio to express the probability out of 100 offspring by multiplying each side of the ratio by the same number (such as 25): 50:100

G. Convert the ratio to a percentage: 50%

Answer: 50% chance of offspring with brown fur

Do the Math **You Try It**

8 Calculate This Punnett square shows a cross between two *Bb* guinea pigs. Predict the dominant and recessive alleles to be transmitted from the parent to offspring. What is the probability of the cross resulting in offspring with black fur?

	B	b
B	BB	Bb
b	Bb	bb

Identify

A. What do you know?

B. What do you want to find out?

Plan

C. Count the total number of offspring allele combinations:

D. Count the number of allele combinations that will result in offspring with black fur:

Solve

E. Write the probability of offspring with black fur as a ratio:

F. Rewrite the ratio to express the probability out of 100 offspring by multiplying each side of the ratio by the same number:

G. Convert the ratio to a percentage:

Answer:

9 Graph In the cross above, what is the ratio of each of the possible genotypes? Show your results by filling in the pie chart at the right. Fill in the key with color or shading to show which pieces of the chart represent the different genotypes.

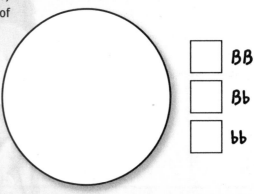

☐ BB

☐ Bb

☐ bb

How can a pedigree trace a trait through generations?

A pedigree is another tool used to study patterns of inheritance. A **pedigree** traces the occurrence of a trait through generations of a family. Pedigrees can be created to trace any inherited trait—even hair color!

Pedigrees can be useful in tracing a special class of inherited disorders known as *sex-linked disorders*. Sex-linked disorders are associated with an allele on a sex chromosome. Many sex-linked disorders, such as hemophilia and colorblindness, are caused by an allele on the X chromosome. Women have two X chromosomes, so a woman can have one allele for colorblindness without being colorblind. A woman who is heterozygous for this trait is called a *carrier,* because she can carry or pass on the trait to her offspring. Men have just one X chromosome. In men, this single chromosome determines if the trait is present.

The pedigree below traces a disease called *cystic fibrosis.* Cystic fibrosis causes serious lung problems. Carriers of the disease have one recessive allele. They do not have cystic fibrosis, but they are able to transmit, or pass, the recessive allele on to their children when reproduction occurs. If a child receives a recessive allele from each parent, then the child will have cystic fibrosis. Other genetic conditions follow a similar pattern.

Think Outside the Book Inquiry

10 Design Create a pedigree chart that traces the occurrence of dimples in your family or in the family of a friend. Collect information for as many family members as you can.

Visualize It!

Pedigree for Cystic Fibrosis

	Males ⬜ Females ◯
	⬜—◯ Vertical lines connect children to their parents.
	◼ or ● A solid square or circle indicates that the person has a certain trait.
	◨ or ◖ A half-filled square or circle indicates that the person is a carrier of the trait.

11 Analyze Does anyone in the third generation have cystic fibrosis? Explain.

_____

_____

_____

12 Calculate What is the probability that the child of two carriers will have cystic fibrosis?

_____

_____

_____

Saving the European Mouflon

The European mouflon is an endangered species of sheep. Scientists at the University of Teramo in Italy used genetic tools and techniques to show how the population of mouflon could be preserved.

Maintaining Genetic Diversity

When a very small population of animals interbreeds, there is a greater risk that harmful genetic conditions can appear in the animals. This is one issue that scientists face when trying to preserve endangered species. One way to lower this risk is to be sure that genetically similar animals do not breed.

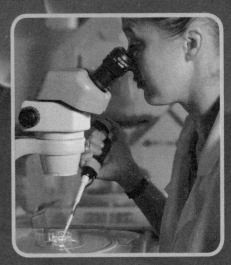

Genetics to the Rescue!

Researchers combined the sperm and eggs of genetically dissimilar European mouflons in a laboratory. The resulting embryo was implanted into a mother sheep. By controlling the combination of genetic material, scientists hope to lower the risk of inherited disorders.

Extend

Inquiry

13 Explain Why are small populations difficult to preserve?

14 Research Research another population of animals that has been part of a captive breeding program.

15 Describe Describe these animals and the results of the breeding program by doing one of the following:
- make a poster
- write a song
- write a short story
- draw a graphic novel

Visual Summary

To complete this summary, fill in the blanks with the correct word or phrase. Then use the key below to check your answers. You can use this page to review the main concepts of the lesson.

Punnett squares can be used to make predictions about possible offspring.

	F	F
f	Ff	Ff
f	Ff	Ff

16 A Punnett square shows combinations of different _____ received from each parent.

Pedigrees trace a trait through generations.

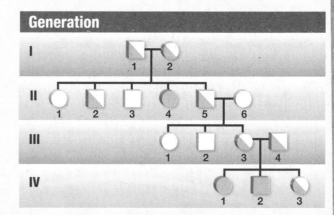

Generation

17 An allele responsible for a _____ is found on a sex chromosome.

Answers: 16 alleles; 17 sex-linked disorder

18 **Compare** How is a heterozygous individual represented in the Punnett square and pedigree shown above?

Lesson Review

Vocabulary

Circle the term that best completes the following sentences.

1 A *Punnett square / ratio* is a tool that can be used to predict the genotypes of potential offspring in a given cross.

2 The results from a Punnett square can be used to find the *pedigree / probability* that a certain allele combination will occur in offspring.

3 A mathematical expression that compares one number to another is called a *pedigree / ratio*.

Key Concepts

Use this diagram to answer the following questions.

	G	G
g	Gg	Gg
g	Gg	Gg

4 Analyze What is gene G responsible for in these fruit flies?

_____

_____

5 Analyze What is the ratio of heterozygous offspring to total offspring in the Punnett square?

_____

6 Define What is a sex-linked disorder?

_____

_____

_____

_____

Critical Thinking

7 Infer Imagine a pedigree that traces an inherited disorder found in individuals with two recessive alleles for gene D. The pedigree shows three siblings with the genotypes *DD*, *Dd*, and *dd*. Did the parents of these three children have the disorder? Explain.

_____

_____

_____

8 Explain A *Bb* guinea pig crosses with a *Bb* guinea pig, and four offspring are produced. All of the offspring are black. Explain how this could happen.

_____

_____

_____

_____

9 Synthesize You are creating a pedigree to trace freckles, a recessive trait, in a friend's family. You find out which of her family members have freckles and which do not. When you complete the pedigree, what can you learn about members of your friend's family that you could not tell just by looking at them?

_____

_____

_____

_____

My Notes

DNA Structure and Function

ESSENTIAL QUESTION

What is DNA?

By the end of this lesson, you should be able to describe the structure and main functions of DNA.

7.LS3.1

This is a DNA strand from the nucleus of an amphibian egg. The DNA and mRNA molecules create the feathery appearance.

Lesson Labs

Quick Labs
- Modeling DNA
- Building a DNA Sequence
- Mutations Cause Diversity

Exploration Lab
- Extracting DNA

Engage Your Brain

1 Predict Check T or F to show whether you think each statement is true or false.

T	F	
☐	☐	DNA is found in the cells of all living things.
☐	☐	All DNA mutations are harmful.
☐	☐	The cell can make copies of its DNA.

2 Describe DNA is sometimes called the *blueprint of life*. Why do you think that is?

_____
_____
_____
_____
_____
_____

Active Reading

3 Synthesize Many English words have their roots in other languages. Use the Latin words below to make an educated guess about the meanings of the words *replication* and *mutation*.

Latin word	Meaning
mutare	to change
replicare	to repeat

Example sentence
DNA can undergo <u>mutation</u>.

mutation:

_____
_____

Example sentence
Before cell division, DNA <u>replication</u> occurs.

replication:

_____
_____

Vocabulary Terms

- DNA
- nucleotide
- replication
- mutation
- RNA
- ribosome

4 Identify This list contains the key terms you'll learn in this lesson. As you read, circle the definition of each term.

Cracking the CODE

ATTAGCGATCACTAAATTAGC

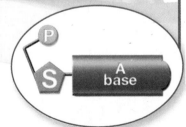

Active Reading

5 Identify As you read, underline the meaning of the word *code*.

What is DNA?

The genetic material of a cell contains information needed for the cell's growth and other activities. It also determines the inherited characteristics of an organism. The genetic material in cells is contained in a molecule called deoxyribonucleic (dee•OK•see•ry•boh•noo•KLAY•ik) acid, or **DNA** for short. You could compare the information in DNA to the books in your local library. You might find a book describing how to bake a cake or one describing how to play your favorite video game. The books, however, don't actually do any of those things—you do. Similarly, the "books" that make up the DNA "library" carry the information that a cell needs to function, grow, and divide. However, DNA doesn't do any of those things. Proteins do most of the work of a cell and also make up much of the structure of a cell.

Scientists describe DNA as containing a code. A *code* is a set of rules and symbols used to carry information. For example, your computer uses a code of ones and zeroes that is translated into numbers, letters, and graphics on a computer screen. To understand how DNA functions as a code, you first need to learn about the structure of the DNA molecule.

DNA Timeline

Review this timeline to learn about some of the important scientific contributions to our understanding of DNA.

1875	1900	1925

1869 Friedrich Miescher identifies a substance that will later be known as DNA.

1919 Phoebus Levene publishes a paper on nucleic acids. His research helps scientists determine that DNA is made up of sugars, phosphate groups, and four nitrogen-containing bases: adenine, thymine, guanine, and cytosine. Bases are often referred to by their first letter: A, T, C, or G. Each base has a different shape.

6 Analyze In this model, what do *P, S,* and *A base* represent?

_____

_____

How was DNA discovered?

The discovery of the structure and function of DNA did not happen overnight. Many scientists from all over the world contributed to our current understanding of this important molecule. Some scientists discovered the chemicals that make up DNA. Others learned how these chemicals fit together. Still others determined the three-dimensional structure of the DNA molecule. The timeline below shows some of the key steps in this process of discovery.

An image of DNA produced by using x-rays.

1951 Rosalind Franklin and Maurice Wilkins make images of DNA using x-rays. When an x-ray passes through the molecule, the ray bends and creates a pattern that is captured on film.

1953 James Watson and Francis Crick use Chargaff's rules and the x-ray images of DNA to conclude that DNA looks like a long, twisted ladder. They build a large-scale model of DNA using simple materials from their laboratory.

1950

1975

1950 Erwin Chargaff observes that the amount of guanine always equals the amount of cytosine, and the amount of adenine equals the amount of thymine. His findings are now known as *Chargaff's rules*.

1952 Alfred Hershey and Martha Chase perform experiments with viruses to confirm that DNA, not proteins, carries genetic information.

Unraveling DNA

DNA is found in the nucleus of eukaryotic cells.

What does DNA look like?

The chemical components that make up DNA are too small to be observed directly. But experiments and imaging techniques have helped scientists to infer the shape of DNA and the arrangement of its parts.

The Shape of DNA Is a Double Helix

The structure of DNA is a twisted ladder shape called a *double helix*. The two sides of the ladder, often referred to as the DNA backbone, are made of alternating sugars and phosphate groups. The rungs of the ladder are made of a pair of bases, each attached to one of the sugars in the backbone.

Active Reading **8 Describe** Where are phosphate groups found in a DNA molecule?

_____

_____

The DNA molecule has a double-helix shape.

Visualize It!

9 Compare Explain how the double-helix structure of DNA is like a spiral staircase.

_____

_____

_____

_____

_____

DNA Is Made Up of Nucleotides

A base, a sugar, and a phosphate group make a building block of DNA known as a **nucleotide**. This chemical unit joins with others, and they repeat to form the DNA molecule. There are four different nucleotides in DNA, identified by their bases: adenine (A), thymine (T), cytosine (C), and guanine (G). Because of differences in size and shape, adenine always pairs with thymine (A-T) and cytosine always pairs with guanine (C-G). These paired, or *complementary*, bases fit together like two pieces of a puzzle.

The order of the nucleotides in DNA is a code that carries information. The DNA code is read like a book. *Genes* are segments of DNA that relate to a certain trait. Each gene has a starting point and an ending point, with the DNA code being read in one direction. The bases A, T, C, and G form the alphabet of the code. The code stores information about which proteins the cells should build. The types of proteins your body makes determine your traits.

10 Apply Place boxes around the bases that pair with each other.

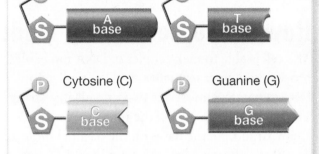

11 Devise The bases are often referred to simply by their initials—A, T, C, and G. The phrase "all tigers can growl" may help you remember them. Think of another phrase that uses words starting with A, T, C, and G that could help you remember the bases. Write your phrase below.

_____

_____

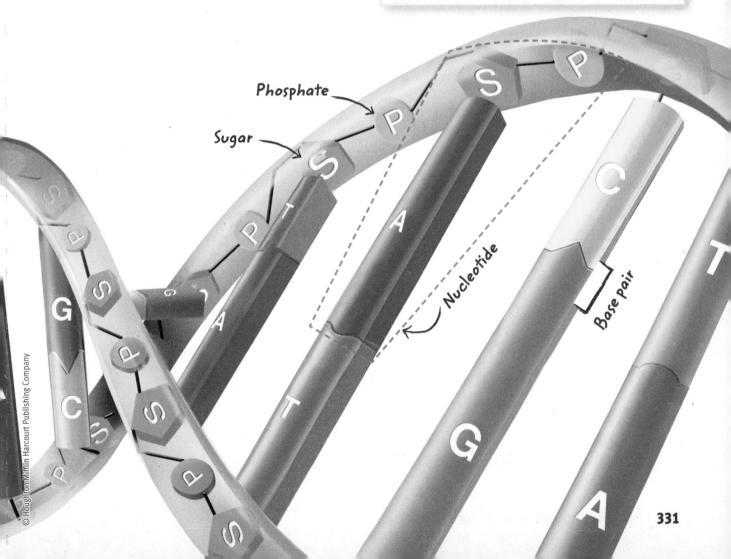

Phosphate

Sugar

Nucleotide

Base pair

331

How are copies of DNA made?

The cell is able to make copies of DNA molecules through a process known as **replication**. During replication, the two strands of DNA separate, almost like two threads in a string being unwound. The bases on each side of the molecule are used as a pattern for a new strand. As the bases on the original molecule are exposed, complementary nucleotides are added. For example, an exposed base containing adenine attaches to a nucleotide containing thymine. When replication is complete, there are two identical DNA molecules. Each new DNA molecule is made of one strand of old DNA and one strand of new DNA.

Visualize It!

12 Apply Fill in the blanks to complete the labels on this model of replicating DNA.

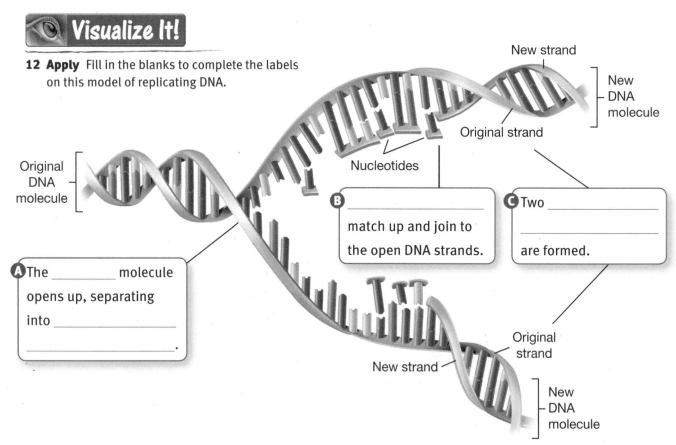

New strand

New DNA molecule

Original strand

Nucleotides

B _____ match up and join to the open DNA strands.

C Two _____ _____ are formed.

Original DNA molecule

A The _____ molecule opens up, separating into _____ _____.

New strand

Original strand

New DNA molecule

When are copies of DNA made?

Before a cell divides, it copies the DNA so that each new daughter cell will have a complete set of instructions. Our cells can replicate DNA in just a few hours. How? Replication begins in many places along the DNA strand. So, many groups of proteins are working to replicate your DNA at the same time.

Mutation

What are mutations?

Changes in the number, type, or order of bases on a piece of DNA are known as **mutations**. Sometimes, a base is left out. This kind of change is known as a *deletion*. Or, an extra base might be added. This kind of change is an *insertion*. The most common mutation happens when one base replaces another. This kind of change is known as a *substitution*.

How do mutations happen? Given the large number of bases in an organism's DNA, it is not surprising that random errors can occur during replication. However, DNA can also be damaged by physical or chemical agents called *mutagens*. Ultraviolet light and the chemicals in cigarette smoke are examples of mutagens.

Cells make proteins that can fix errors in DNA. But sometimes a mistake isn't corrected, and it becomes part of the genetic code. Structural changes to genes on chromosomes can result in good, bad, or neutral changes to the structure and function of the organism. Thus mutations to DNA may be beneficial, neutral, or harmful. A *genetic disorder* results from mutations that harm the normal function of a cell. Some of these disorders, such as Tay-Sachs disease and sickle-cell anemia, are *inherited*, or passed on from parent to offspring. Other genetic disorders result from mutations that occur during a person's lifetime. Most cancers fall into this category.

Visualize It!

13 Apply Place a check mark in the box to indicate which type of mutation is being shown.

Original sequence

Ⓐ

☐ deletion   ☐ insertion   ☐ substitution

Ⓑ

☐ deletion   ☐ insertion   ☐ substitution

Ⓒ

☐ deletion   ☐ insertion   ☐ substitution

This snake has albinism, a condition in which the body cannot make the pigments that give color to the skin and eyes.

14 Explain Albinism is an inherited genetic disorder. Explain what is meant by "inherited genetic disorder."

_____

_____

_____

15 Hypothesize Do you think the inherited traits were beneficial, harmful, or neutral for the individual animals? Explain your reasoning.

A mutation to the DNA of some bears living in the Arctic resulted in them having thicker coats. They passed on this gene to their offspring.

_____

_____

A dog's DNA has given it two different eye colors, but it sees as well as any other dog.

_____

_____

Protein Factory

What is the role of DNA and RNA in building proteins?

Imagine that you are baking cookies. You have a big cookbook that contains the recipe. If you take the book with you into the kitchen, you risk damaging the book and losing important instructions. You only need one page from the book, so you copy the recipe on a piece of paper and leave the cookbook on the shelf. This process is similar to the way that the cell uses DNA to build proteins. First, some of the information in the DNA is copied to a separate molecule called ribonucleic acid, or **RNA**. Then, the copy is used to build proteins. Not all the instructions are needed all the time. In eukaryotes, the DNA is protected inside the cell's nucleus.

Like DNA, RNA has a sugar-phosphate backbone and the bases adenine (A), guanine (G), and cytosine (C). But instead of thymine (T), RNA contains the base uracil (U). Also, the sugar found in RNA is different from the one in DNA. There are three types of RNA: messenger RNA, ribosomal RNA, and transfer RNA. Each type of RNA has a special role in making proteins.

Active Reading **16 Identify** As you read, number the sentences that describe the steps of transcription.

Transcription: The Information in DNA Is Copied to Messenger RNA

When a cell needs a set of instructions for making a protein, it first makes an RNA copy of the necessary section of DNA. This process is called *transcription*. Transcription involves DNA and messenger RNA (mRNA). Only individual genes are transcribed, not the whole DNA molecule. During transcription, DNA is used as a template to make a complementary strand of mRNA. The DNA opens up where the gene is located. Then RNA bases match up to complementary bases on the DNA template. When transcription is complete, the mRNA is released and the DNA molecule closes.

DNA

RNA

Protein

RNA uses the genetic information stored in DNA to build proteins.

mRNA

Cell nucleus

A During transcription, DNA is used as a template to make a complementary strand of mRNA. In eukaryotes, the mRNA then exits the nucleus.

Translation: The Information in Messenger RNA Is Used to Build Proteins

Once the mRNA has been made, it is fed through a protein assembly line within a ribosome. A **ribosome** is a cell organelle made of ribosomal RNA (rRNA) and protein. As mRNA passes through the ribosome, transfer RNA (tRNA) molecules deliver amino acids to the ribosome. Each group of three bases on the mRNA strand codes for one amino acid. So the genetic code determines the order in which amino acids are brought to the ribosome. The amino acids join together to form a protein. The process of making proteins from RNA is called *translation*.

B A ribosome attaches to an mRNA strand at the beginning of a gene.

tRNA

Amino acid

Ribosome

C A tRNA molecule enters the ribosome. Three bases on the tRNA match up to three complementary bases on the mRNA strand. The bases on the mRNA strand determine which tRNA and amino acid move into the ribosome.

Chain of amino acids

Chain of amino acids released

D The tRNA transfers its amino acid to a growing chain. Then, the tRNA is released. The ribosome moves down the mRNA and the process repeats.

E Once the ribosome reaches the end of the gene, the chain of amino acids is released.

17 Apply Fill in the table below by placing check marks in the appropriate boxes and writing the product of transcription and translation.

Process	What molecules are involved?				What is the product?
Transcription	☐ DNA	☐ mRNA	☐ tRNA	☐ ribosome	
Translation	☐ DNA	☐ mRNA	☐ tRNA	☐ ribosome	

Visual Summary

To complete this summary, fill in the blanks with the correct word or phrase. Then use the key below to check your answers. You can use this page to review the main concepts of the lesson.

DNA Structure and Function

DNA has a double-helix shape and is made up of nucleotides.

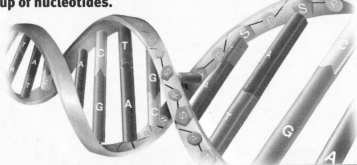

18 The four bases in DNA nucleotides are

_____

_____

_____.

The cell can make copies of DNA.

19 DNA replication happens before cells _____.

DNA can mutate.

20 Three types of DNA mutations are

_____

_____.

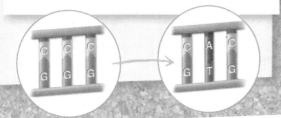

DNA and RNA are involved in making proteins.

21 The two processes involved in making proteins from the DNA code are

22 Explain How could a mutation in the DNA affect what proteins are made by the cell?

Lesson Review

Vocabulary

Fill in the blanks with the term that best completes the following sentences.

1 A(n) _____ of DNA consists of a sugar, a phosphate, and a nitrogen-containing base.

2 A(n) _____ is a change in the base sequence of a DNA molecule.

Key Concepts

Draw a line to connect the following scientists to their contributions to our understanding of DNA.

3 Erwin Chargaff

4 Rosalind Franklin and Maurice Wilkins

5 James Watson and Francis Crick

A took x-ray images of DNA molecule

B proposed a double-helix model of DNA

C found that the amount of adenine equals the amount of thymine and that the amount of guanine equals the amount of cytosine

6 Identify How does the structure of RNA differ from the structure of DNA?

_____

_____

_____

_____

7 Identify When does DNA replication occur?

_____

_____

8 Describe Name the three types of RNA and list their roles in making proteins.

_____

_____

_____

_____

_____

_____

9 Identify What can cause DNA mutations?

_____

_____

_____

Critical Thinking

Use this diagram to answer the following questions.

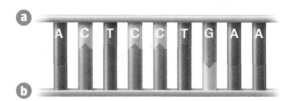

a
A C T C C T G A A
b

10 Describe What is the sequence of bases on DNA strand *b*, from left to right?

_____

11 Apply This segment of DNA is transcribed to form a complementary strand of mRNA. The mRNA then undergoes translation. How many amino acids would the RNA code for?

_____

12 Infer After many cell divisions, a segment of DNA has more base pairs than it originally did. Explain what has happened.

_____

_____

_____

13 Explain Why must DNA replicate?

_____

_____

_____

_____

_____

_____

My Notes

Identifying Variables

When you are analyzing or designing a scientific experiment, it is important to identify the variables in the experiment. Usually, an experiment is designed to discover how changing one variable affects another variable. In a scientific investigation, the independent variable is the factor that is purposely changed. The dependent variable is the factor that changes in response to the independent variable.

Tutorial

Use the following strategies to help you identify the variables in an experiment.

Reading a Summary
The published results of an experiment usually include a brief summary. You should be able to identify the variables from it. In the summary to the left, the independent variable is the DNA of the corn plants, and the dependent variable is the height of the plants.

Summary: We genetically modified corn plants to increase growth in low-light conditions.

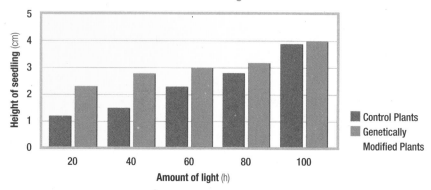

Effect of Genetic Modifications on Corn Seedling Growth

Control Plants
Genetically Modified Plants

Analyzing a Graph Making a graph can be a very effective way to show the relationship between variables. For a line graph, the independent variable is usually shown on the *x*-axis, or the horizontal axis. The dependent variable is usually shown on the *y*-axis, or the vertical axis.

Describing the Data When you read a graph, describing the information in complete sentences can help you to identify the variables. For example, you could write, "In the first 80 hours, the genetically modified corn plants grew much more quickly than the control plants grew. But by 100 hours, both kinds of plants were about the same height. This shows that the effect of the independent variable was greatest during the first 80 hours of plant growth."

Identifying the Effects of Variables Look closely at the graph. Notice that the genetically modified seedlings grew more quickly than the control seedlings, but the effects were greatest in the early part of the experiment. A variable's effect is not always constant throughout an experiment.

© Houghton Mifflin Harcourt Publishing Company • Image Credits: (b) ©Chris Knapton/Photo Researchers, Inc.

You Try It!

The passage below describes the process of gel electrophoresis.
Use the description to answer the question that follows.

> During gel electrophoresis, DNA is broken into separate fragments.
> These fragments are added to a gel. When an electric current is
> applied to the gel, the fragments travel different distances through
> the gel. The size of the DNA fragments determines how far they
> travel. Smaller fragments travel farther than larger fragments do.
> Scientists can use these data to identify unknown samples of DNA.

1 Reading a Summary Identify the variables described in
the passage.

_____

_____

The graph below shows the results of DNA
analysis using gel electrophoresis. Look at the
graph and answer the questions that follow.

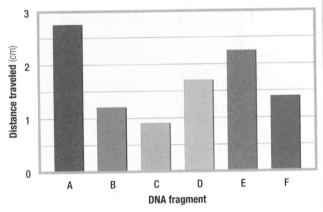

Distance Traveled by DNA Fragments

2 Analyzing a Graph Which variables are shown
in the graph? Circle the axis that shows the
dependent variable.

_____

_____

3 Analyzing the Data What is the relationship
between the size of the DNA fragments and the
distance they traveled? Circle the DNA fragment
that is the smallest.

_____

_____

4 Applying Mathematics Calculate the average
distance that the DNA fragments traveled. How
much farther than the average distance did the
smallest DNA fragment travel?

5 Applying Concepts Why is it important to limit
the number of variables in an experiment?

_____

_____

_____

_____

_____

Take It Home

**With an adult, plan and conduct a simple
experiment that includes an independent
variable and a dependent variable. Record
your results and graph your data if possible.
Then share your results with the class.**

Unit 5 — Big Idea

Characteristics from parents are passed to offspring in predictable ways.

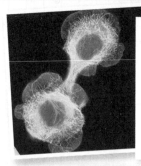

Lesson 1
ESSENTIAL QUESTION
How do cells divide?

Relate the process of mitosis to its functions in single-celled and multicellular organisms.

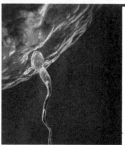

Lesson 2
ESSENTIAL QUESTION
How do cells divide for sexual reproduction?

Describe the process of meiosis and its role in sexual reproduction.

Lesson 3
ESSENTIAL QUESTION
How do organisms reproduce?

Describe sexual and asexual reproduction and list the advantages and disadvantages of each.

Lesson 4
ESSENTIAL QUESTION
How do organisms adapt to their environment?

Describe how structural and behavioral adaptations help organisms to survive and reproduce.

Lesson 5
ESSENTIAL QUESTION
How are traits inherited?

Analyze the inheritance of traits in individuals.

Lesson 6
ESSENTIAL QUESTION
How are patterns of inheritance studied?

Explain how patterns of heredity can be predicted by Punnett squares and pedigrees.

Lesson 7
ESSENTIAL QUESTION
What is DNA?

Describe the structure and main functions of DNA.

Connect — ESSENTIAL QUESTIONS
Lessons 1 and 2

1 Synthesize How are meiosis and mitosis similar? How are they different?

_____

_____

_____

Think Outside the Book

2 Synthesize Choose one of these activities to help synthesize what you have learned in this unit.

☐ Using what you learned in lessons 2, 3, 5, and 7, develop a computer slideshow presentation to explain how genes are passed down from parents to offspring.

☐ Using what you learned in lessons 1, 5 and 7, create a poster that shows the structure and functions of DNA, as well as its roles in cell division and in determining an organism's traits.

Unit 5 Review

Name _____

Vocabulary

Fill in each blank with the term that best completes the following sentences.

1 The genetic material of all cells is _____ .

2 A(n) _____ compares or shows the relationship between two quantities.

3 A(n) _____ is a change in the way an organism acts that helps it to survive.

4 _____ is the process of cell division that results in the formation of cells with half the usual number of chromosomes.

5 The type of reproduction that results in offspring that are genetically identical to the single parent is known as _____ reproduction.

Key Concepts

Read each question below, and circle the best answer.

6 A mouse breeder crosses a black-furred mouse with a white-furred mouse. All of the offspring have gray fur. What kind of inheritance pattern explains how fur color is inherited in mice?

A sex-linked

B codominance

C complete dominance

D incomplete dominance

7 What process does a multicellular organism use to replace its damaged body cells?

A mitosis

B meiosis

C replication

D transcription

8 The following diagram shows one way a mutation can form during DNA replication.

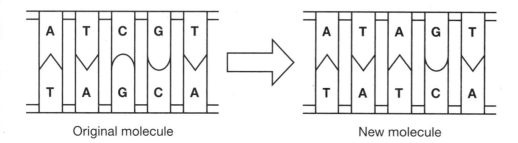

Original molecule → New molecule

What kind of mutation has occurred during the DNA replication shown in the diagram?

A deletion

C substitution

B insertion

D transcription

9 How does a sex cell differ from a body cell?

A A sex cell does not contain chromosomes.

B A sex cell contains homologous chromosomes.

C A sex cell has the same number of chromosomes as a body cell.

D A sex cell has half the amount of genetic material as a body cell.

10 How do the chromosomes at the end of meiosis I compare with the chromosomes at the end of meiosis II?

A Chromosomes have one chromatid at the end of both meiosis I and meiosis II.

B Chromosomes have two chromatids at the end of both meiosis I and meiosis II.

C Chromosomes have one chromatid at the end of meiosis I and two chromatids at the end of meiosis II.

D Chromosomes have two chromatids at the end of meiosis I and one chromatid at the end of meiosis II.

11 The following table shows the percentage of each base in a sample of DNA.

Base	Percentage of total bases
A	12%
C	38%
T	12%
G	38%

Which of the following statements explains the data in the table?

A A pairs only with C, and T pairs only with G.

B A pairs only with T, and C pairs only with G.

C DNA is made up of nucleotides that consist of a sugar, a phosphate, and a base.

D The bases in DNA are arranged in the interior of a double helix, like rungs of a ladder.

12 Which of the following is an advantage of asexual reproduction?

A It is a slow process.   **C** The organism can increase in number quickly.

B Two parents are needed.   **D** It introduces genetic diversity in the offspring.

13 The diagram below shows a cross that is similar to one of Mendel's pea plant crosses.

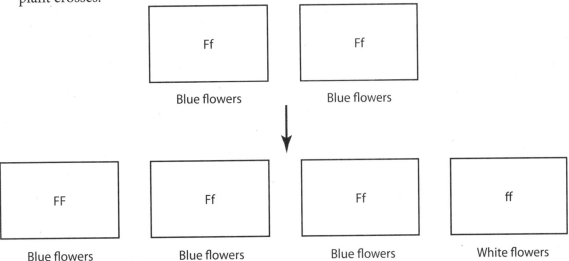

How is blue flower color inherited in the cross shown?

A as a codominant trait   **C** as a dominant trait

B as a recessive trait   **D** as an incompletely dominant trait

14 Which of the following statements correctly describes the function of cell division in unicellular organisms?

A Cell division allows the organism to grow.

B Cell division allows the organism to reproduce.

C Cell division allows the organism to produce sex cells.

D Cell division allows the organism to repair damage to the cell.

15 Which statement about zygotes, which form by fertilization, is correct?

A Zygotes have a full set of chromosomes, receiving half from each parent.

B Zygotes have half the set of chromosomes from one parent only.

C Zygotes have two full sets of chromosomes, one set from each parent.

D Zygotes have half the set of chromosomes, one-fourth from each parent.

16 The diagram shows a cell during the anaphase stage of mitosis.

Justin's teacher showed him this slide of a stage of mitosis. He noticed the slide contains two homologous pairs of chromosomes. How would this diagram be different if it showed anaphase I of meiosis instead of anaphase of mitosis?

A Each chromosome would still have two chromatids.

B The chromosomes would look the same as in mitosis.

C You would be able to see DNA in the chromosomes during meiosis.

D Homologous chromosomes would be moving to the same end of the cell.

17 If the sequence of bases in one strand of DNA is ATTCGAC, what will be the base sequence on the strand that is formed during replication?

A ATTCGAC   **C** UAAGCUG

B TAAGCTG   **D** AUUCGAC

Critical Thinking

Answer the following questions in the space provided.

18 Describe the major steps of gene transcription and translation. What molecules and organelles are involved in the processes?

_____

_____

_____

_____

_____

19 Jake made a pedigree to trace the traits of straight and curly hair in his family.

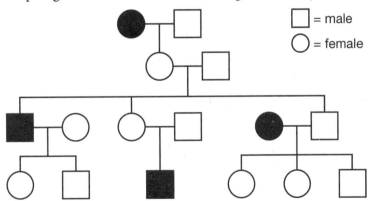

☐ = male

◯ = female

A shaded circle or square in Jake's pedigree represents a person with straight hair. Is straight hair controlled by a dominant allele or a recessive allele? What led to your conclusion? How do you know that straight hair is not sex-linked?

_____

_____

_____

_____

_____

_____

_____

Unit 5 Review continued

20 The polar bear is found in ice-covered areas of the Northern Hemisphere. It has thick fur, 4 inches of fat underneath its skin, and webbed feet. It primarily eats seals. Another species of bear, the sun bear, lives in the tropical rain forest. It has short hair, strong legs, and an extra long tongue. Its diet consists mainly of insects and honey found in trees. Explain how and why each of these bears developed their particular traits. Be sure to mention the concepts of adaptation and survival.

_____

_____

_____

_____

Connect ESSENTIAL QUESTIONS
Lessons 5 and 6

Answer the following question in the space provided.

21 The following diagram shows a Punnett square made to predict the earlobe shape of the offspring of two parents.

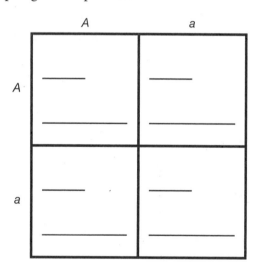

A stands for the trait of free-hanging earlobes and *a* stands for the trait of attached earlobes. Write the genotype of each offspring on the first line in each box of the Punnett square. What will be the phenotype of each offspring? Write either *attached* or *free-hanging* on the second line in each box. Describe how the trait of free-hanging earlobes is inherited. What is the expected ratio of free-hanging earlobes to attached earlobes in the offspring?

_____

_____

_____

_____

_____

_____

Human Body Systems

Houghton Mifflin Harcourt Publishing Company • Image Credits: (bkgd) ©Scott Camazine / Photo Researchers, Inc.; (br) ©Yellow Dog Productions/The Image Bank/Getty Images

Big Idea

The human body is made up of systems that carry out unique functions and work together to maintain equilibrium and support life.

7.LS1.5, 7.ETS2.1

A brain scan can show whether the brain is functioning normally.

What do you think?

In the Middle Ages, people dug up and dissected the dead to learn about the body. Today, technology like the MRI scanner allows us to study the living body. How does the living body work?

A patient must stay still to get an accurate MRI scan.

Unit 6
Human Body Systems

CITIZEN SCIENCE

Muscles at Work

Design a test for muscle endurance or strength.

① Define The Problem

Unlike many things that wear out with use, our muscles actually get stronger the more often they are used. Doing different kinds of exercises helps different groups of muscles. But how can you tell if you are improving? How can you tell how strong a group of muscles is?

Muscles become larger as they become stronger.

It takes practice and training to develop the strength to hold your body up like this.

② Think About It

Design a test for a group of muscles.

Choose a group of muscles that you would like to work with. Then, come up with one or two simple exercises that can be done to show either how strong the muscles are or how well they are able to work continuously. Place a time limit on your tests so that the tests don't take too long.

Check off the points below as you use them to design your test.

☐ The kind of action the muscles can do.

☐ To do the test safely, remember to isolate the group of muscles. (Research how to do an exercise safely.)

☐ The equipment you will need for the test.

③ Plan and Test Your Design

A Write out how you will conduct your test in the space below. Check your plan with your teacher before proceeding.

_____

_____

_____

_____

_____

_____

B Conduct the test on yourself. Have a classmate time you, help you count, or make any other measurements that you might need help with. Briefly state your findings.

_____

_____

_____

_____

_____

Take It Home

Do the same exercises at home for two weeks. Do strength training exercises every second day to avoid injury. Do continuous movement exercises, such as running, every day. Then, conduct your test again. See if there is any improvement. Report your findings to the class. See *ScienceSaurus*® for more information about muscular systems.

Introduction to Body Systems

ESSENTIAL QUESTION

How do the body systems work together to maintain homeostasis?

By the end of this lesson, you should be able to describe how the body is a large system that is made up of smaller subsystems, including how they work together to maintain homeostasis.

7.LS1.5

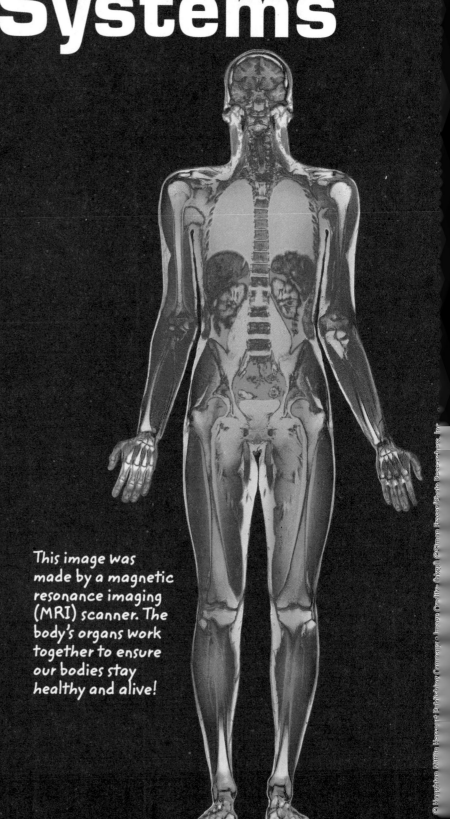

This image was made by a magnetic resonance imaging (MRI) scanner. The body's organs work together to ensure our bodies stay healthy and alive!

Engage Your Brain

1 Predict Check T or F to show whether you think each statement is true or false.

T | F
☑ | ☐ Your muscles provide a framework that supports and protects your body.
☑ | ☐ When you breathe in and out, you're using your lungs.
☑ | ☐ Your nervous system gets rid of wastes from your body.
☑ | ☐ When you eat food, it enters your digestive system.

2 Identify Draw a diagram of your body showing at least four organs. As you read the lesson, write down the organ system that each organ is a part of.

 ## Active Reading

3 Synthesize You can often define an unknown word if you know the meaning of its word parts. Use the word parts and sentence below to make an educated guess about the meaning of the word *homeostasis*.

Greek word	Meaning
homoios	same
stasis	standing

Example Sentence
In order to maintain <u>homeostasis</u>, the cardiovascular system and the respiratory system work together to move oxygen-carrying blood around the body.

Vocabulary Term

• homeostasis

4 Apply As you learn the definition of the vocabulary term in this lesson, make a sketch that shows the meaning of the term or an example of that term. Next to your drawing, write your own definition of the term.

homeostasis:

_____

_____

_____

What do the body systems do?

The human body is one large system that is made up of smaller systems. Sometimes these systems are called subsystems, because they support the overall functioning of the body. These systems work together to maintain equilibrium and support life. Equilibrium means balance. The body must be in balance in order to stay healthy and strong. The body also needs energy to run and move. Energy is needed to reproduce, get rid of waste, and protect the body. Body systems, also called *organ systems*, help the body do all of these things. They also coordinate all the functions of the body.

Groups of organs that work together form body systems. Nerves detect a stimulus in the environment and send a signal through the spinal cord to the brain. The brain sends a signal to respond. Without all the parts, the system would not work. Some organs work in more than one body system.

Active Reading **5 Identify** As you read about body systems on these pages, underline the main function of each body system.

The **respiratory system** gathers oxygen from the environment and gets rid of carbon dioxide from the body. The exchange, called respiration, occurs in the lungs.

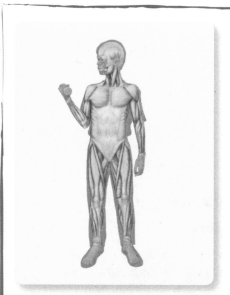

The **muscular system** allows movement of body parts. It works with the skeletal system to help with locomotion, which helps you move.

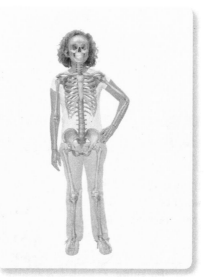

The **skeletal system** is made up of bones, ligaments, and cartilage. It supports the body and protects important organs. It also makes blood cells.

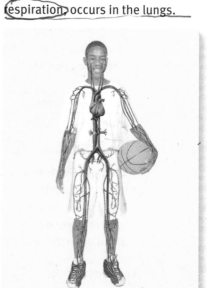

The **cardiovascular system** moves blood through the body. The heart is the pump for this system. Blood flows through blood vessels.

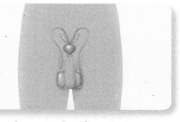

The **male reproductive system** produces sperm and delivers it to the female reproductive system.

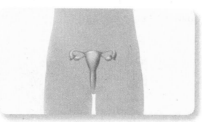

The **female reproductive system** produces eggs and nourishes a developing fetus.

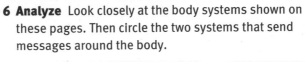

6 Analyze Look closely at the body systems shown on these pages. Then circle the two systems that send messages around the body.

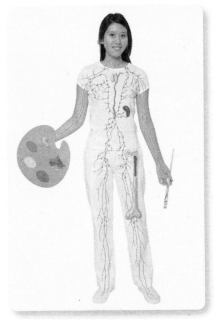

The lymphatic system returns leaked fluid back to the blood. As a major part of the immune system, it has cells that help get rid of invading bacteria and viruses.

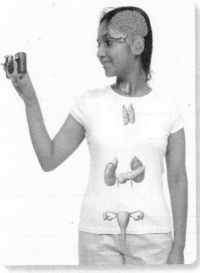

The endocrine system makes chemical messages. These messages help to regulate conditions inside the body. They also influence growth and development.

The integumentary system is the protective covering of the body. It includes the skin, hair, and nails. As part of the immune system, the skin acts as a barrier that protects the body from infection.

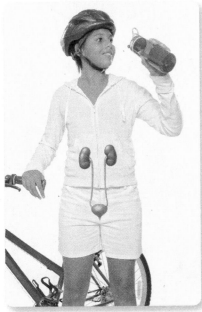

The excretory system gets rid of the body's wastes. The urinary system, shown here, removes wastes from blood. The skin, lungs, and digestive system also remove waste in a process called *excretion*.

The digestive system breaks down food into nutrients that can be used by the body. The stomach breaks down food into tiny pieces. Nutrients are absorbed in the small intestine. This is called *digestion*.

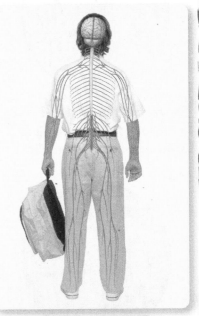

The nervous system collects information and responds to it by sending electrical messages. This information may come from outside or inside the body. The brain is the center of the nervous system.

A Closer Look

How are structure and function linked?

Even though animals may look very different on the outside, on the inside, their cells, tissues, and organs look very similar. This is because these structures do the same basic job. For example, a frog's heart, a bird's heart, and a human's heart all have the same function, to pump blood around the body. They are all made of the same type of muscle tissue, which is made up of the same type of muscle cells. The structure of the hearts is similar, too. Though their shape may be a little different from each other, they are all muscular pumps that push blood around the body.

The shapes and sizes of cells are related to their function. For example, sperm cells have long tails that are used to move. Nerve cells are long and thin to send messages long distances. Surface skin cells are broad and flat. The diagram below shows how skin cells form the skin, which covers and protects the body.

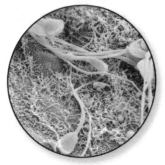

Sperm cells can "swim." They have long tails that whip around to move the cells.

Skin is made up of different cells in many layers. The epidermis is the outer layer of skin. The dermis is the second layer of skin and contains glands, hair follicles, and blood vessels.

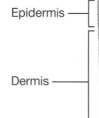

Epidermis

Dermis

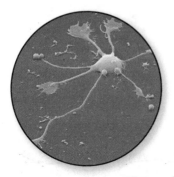

Nerve cells have long, thin branches to send electrical messages between the brain and far-away body parts.

Inquiry

7 Infer Muscle cells can get longer and shorter. How does this ability fit in with their job in the body?

Depending on what the muscl does, it might need to either be shorter or longer to do their job in the body.

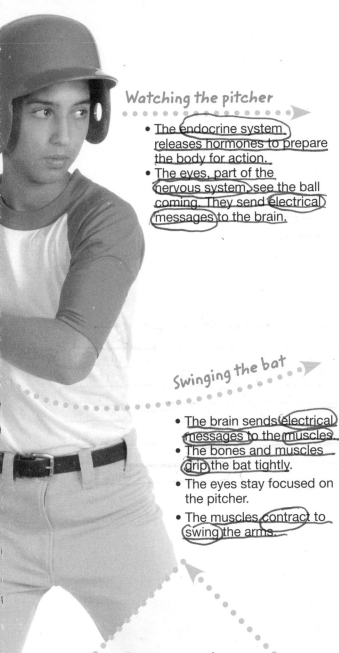

Watching the pitcher

- The endocrine system releases hormones to prepare the body for action.
- The eyes, part of the nervous system, see the ball coming. They send electrical messages to the brain.

Swinging the bat

- The brain sends electrical messages to the muscles.
- The bones and muscles grip the bat tightly.
- The eyes stay focused on the pitcher.
- The muscles contract to swing the arms.

Running the bases

- The muscles and bones help the legs move quickly.
- The heart, which is part of the cardiovascular system, pumps quickly to move blood from the lungs to the body.
- The muscles use oxygen from the blood to keep moving.

How do body systems work together?

Our body systems can do a lot, but they can't work alone! Almost everything we need for our bodies to work properly requires many body systems to work together. For example, when the nervous system senses danger, the endocrine system releases hormones that cause the heart to beat faster to deliver more oxygen through the circulatory system to muscles. In this example, the muscular and skeletal systems, often called the *musculoskeletal system*, worked together to avoid danger.

Active Reading **8 Identify** As you read the captions on the left, underline examples of body systems working together.

Body Systems Share Organs

Many organs are part of several body systems. Reproductive organs are part of the reproductive system and part of the endocrine system. The liver works in the digestive system, but it is also part of the excretory system. The heart is part of the muscular system and the cardiovascular system. Blood vessels, too, are shared. For example, blood vessels transport chemical messages from the endocrine system and cells from the lymphatic and cardiovascular systems.

Body Systems Communicate

There are two basic ways cells communicate: by electrical messages and by chemical messages. Nerve cells transfer information between the body and the spinal cord and brain. Nerves pass electrical messages from one cell to the next along the line. The endocrine system sends chemical messages through the bloodstream to certain cells.

9 Explain The body is made up of many different systems. Explain how these systems work together to support digestion, respiration, excretion, circulation, sensation, and motion.

These systems all work together to make your body function correctly through sending messages to different parts of your body.

Lesson 1 Introduction to Body Systems **355**

Keeping the Balance

What is homeostasis?

Cells need certain conditions to work properly. They need food and oxygen and to have their wastes taken away. If body conditions were to change too much, cells would not be able to do their jobs. **Homeostasis** (hoh•mee•oh•STAY•sis) is the maintenance of a constant internal environment when outside conditions change. Responding to change allows all systems to work properly.

Responding to Change

If the external environment changes, body systems work together to keep conditions stable within the body. For example, if body cells were to get too cold, they would not work properly and they could die. So, if the brain senses the body temperature is getting too low, it tells the muscles to shiver. Shivering muscles release energy as heat, which warms the body. Your brain will also tell you to put on a sweater!

Maintaining Equilibrium

To maintain homeostasis, the body has to recognize that conditions are changing and then respond in the right way. In order to work, organ systems need to communicate properly. The electrical messages of the nervous system and chemical signals of the endocrine system tell the body what changes to make. If the body cannot respond properly to the internal messages or to an external change, a disease may develop.

Too cold   Just right   Too hot

A thermostat keeps an even temperature in a room by turning the heater off when it gets too warm, and on when it gets too cold. Your body does the same thing, but in a different way.

Visualize It!

10 Relate How does the body react when the outside temperature gets too hot?

_____

_____

_____

© Houghton Mifflin Harcourt Publishing Company • Image Credits: (cl) ©INSADCOPhotography/Alamy; (c) ©BLOOMimage/Getty images; (cr) ©ABSODELS/Getty Images; (b) ©Tetra Images/Getty Images

What can go wrong with homeostasis?

If one body system does not work properly, other body systems can be affected. For example, body cells that do not get enough energy or nutrients cannot work properly. A lack of food harms many systems and may cause disease or even death. The presence of toxins or pathogens also can disrupt homeostasis. Toxins can prevent cells from carrying out life processes and pathogens can break down cells. Problems also occur if the body's messages do not work, or if those messages are not sent when or where they are needed. Many diseases that affect homeostasis are hereditary.

Active Reading

11 Identify As you read this page, underline what can happen if homeostasis is disrupted.

Structure or Function Diseases

Problems with the structure or function of cells, tissues, or organs can affect the body. For example, diabetes is a disease that affects cell function. Certain changes in body cells stop them from taking glucose in from the blood as they normally do. If cells cannot get energy in the form of glucose, they cannot work properly.

Pathogens and Disease

When the body cannot maintain homeostasis, it is easier for pathogens to invade the body. Pathogens can also cause a disruption in homeostasis. For example, tuberculosis is a lung disease caused by bacteria. It weakens the lungs and body. Weakened lungs cannot take in oxygen well. Low oxygen levels affect the whole body.

12 Apply Alcoholism is a disease that disrupts homeostasis. Below are three body systems that are affected by alcohol. The effects on the nervous system are filled in. In the space provided, predict what might happen when the function of the two remaining systems is affected.

Body systems affected	What are the effects?
Nervous system	Disrupts proper functioning of the brain. The brain cannot respond properly to internal or external messages.
Digestive system	
Reproductive system	

Alcoholism can damage the structure and function of the liver and reduce its ability to remove toxins from the blood.

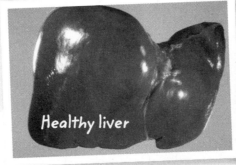
Healthy liver

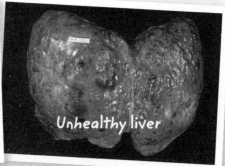
Unhealthy liver

Visual Summary

To complete this summary, fill in the blanks with the correct word or phrase. Then use the key below to check your answers. You can use this page to review the main concepts of the lesson.

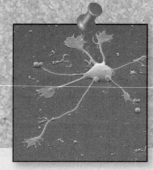

Body systems each have specific jobs.

13 The _____ system brings oxygen into the blood and releases carbon dioxide from the body.

The structure of cells, tissues, and organs are linked to their functions.

14 The long, thin cells of the _____ system help transmit electrical messages around the body.

The muscular heart pushes _____ around the body.

Body Systems and Homeostasis

Body systems work together, which allows the body to work properly.

15 The _____ and _____ systems work together to allow the player to swing the bat.

The body maintains homeostasis by adjusting to change.

16 If body temperature goes up, the _____ senses the change and will work to reduce the body temperature to normal.

Answers: 13 respiratory; 14 nervous; blood; 15 nervous; muscular (either order) 16 brain

17 Explain How might disruption of the respiratory system affect homeostasis of the body?

Lesson Review

Vocabulary

Use a term from the lesson to complete each sentence below.

1 _____ is maintaining stable conditions inside the body.

2 A group of organs that work together is called a(n) _____ .

Key Concepts

3 Compare How are the functions of the skeletal and muscular systems related?

_____

_____

_____

4 Identify What body system receives information from inside and outside the body and responds to that information?

_____

_____

5 Explain How is skin part of the integumentary system and the excretory system?

_____

_____

_____

_____

6 Describe What are the basic needs of all cells in the body?

_____

_____

7 Relate Give an example of how a cell's structure relates to its function in the body.

_____

_____

_____

Critical Thinking

Use the graph to answer the following questions.

Body Temperature Over Time

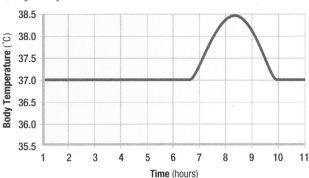

8 Analyze Is the body in homeostasis during the entire time shown in the graph? Explain your answer.

_____

_____

_____

9 Predict What would happen to the body if the body temperature continued to decrease during the tenth hour instead of leveling off?

_____

_____

_____

10 Apply The body loses water and salts in sweat. Explain why drinking large volumes of plain water after exercising may affect the salt balance in the body.

_____

_____

_____

_____

_____

My Notes

The Skeletal and Muscular Systems

By working together, your muscular and skeletal systems allow you to do many things such as stand up, sit down, type a note, or run a race.

ESSENTIAL QUESTION

How do your skeletal and muscular systems work?

By the end of this lesson, you should be able to explain how the skeletal and muscular systems work together to allow movement of the body.

7.LS1.5

Lesson Labs

Quick Labs
- Power in Pairs
- Speed of a Reflex

Exploration Lab
- A Closer Look at Muscles

 **Engage Your Brain**

1 Identify Circle the terms that best complete the following sentences.

The *skeletal / muscular* system is responsible for supporting the body.

Bones are part of your *skeletal / muscular* system.

Your heart is made up of *bone / muscle* tissue.

You can increase your flexibility by stretching your *bones / muscles*.

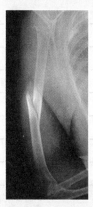

2 Infer This x-ray shows a broken arm. How might this injury affect your ability to move?

_____

_____

_____

_____

 **Active Reading**

3 Synthesize You can often identify functions of a body part if you know what its name means. Use the Latin words below and context clues to make an educated guess about a function of *ligaments* and *tendons*.

Latin word	Meaning
ligare	to tie
tendere	to stretch

Example Sentence
<u>Ligaments</u> are found at the ends of bones.

ligament:

_____

Example Sentence
<u>Tendons</u> connect muscles to bones.

tendon:

_____

Vocabulary Terms

- skeletal system
- muscular system
- ligament
- tendon
- joint

4 Apply As you learn the definition of each vocabulary term in this lesson, create your own definition or sketch it to help you remember the meaning of the term.

What's Inside?

What are the main functions of the skeletal system?

When you hear the word *skeleton*, you might think of the dry, white bones that you see in the models in your science class. You might think your bones are lifeless, but they are very much alive. The **skeletal system**, one of the major subsystems of the body, is the organ system that supports and protects the body and allows it to move. Its other jobs include storing minerals and producing red blood cells. The human skeleton is inside the body, so it is called an *endoskeleton*.

 **Active Reading**

5 Identify As you read, underline the main functions of the skeletal system.

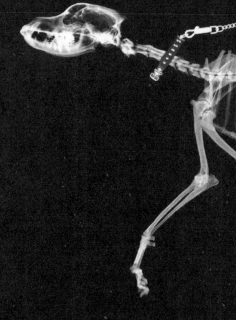

Visualize It!

6 Relate How might a suit of armor be a good analogy for a function of the skeletal system?

_____

_____

_____

_____

Protection

Bones provide protection to organs. For example, your ribs protect your heart and lungs, your vertebrae protect your spinal cord, and your skull protects your brain.

Storage

The hard outer layer of bone, called *compact bone*, stores important minerals such as calcium. These minerals are necessary for nerves and muscles to work properly.

Support

Bones provide support for your body and make it possible for you to sit or stand upright. If you did not have bones, you would be a mass of soft tissue, like a slug. However, unlike a slug, you would not be able to move around without your bones.

Movement

Bones play an important role in movement (also known as locomotion) by providing a place for muscles to attach. Muscles pull on bones to move the body. Without bones, muscles could not do their job of moving the body.

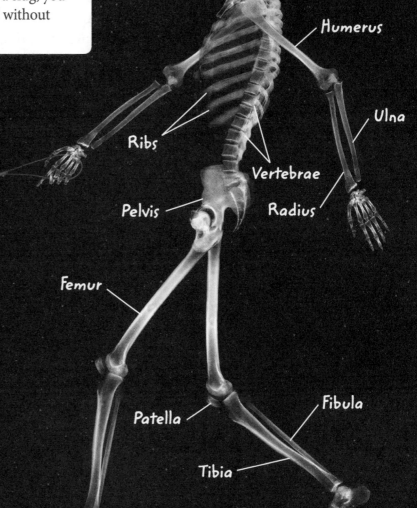

Skull

Clavicle

Humerus

Ulna

Ribs

Vertebrae

Radius

Pelvis

Femur

Fibula

Patella

Tibia

Blood Cell Production

At the center of bones, such as the long bones in the man's and dog's legs, is soft tissue called *marrow*. Red marrow, a type of marrow that makes blood cells, is found mostly in flat bones, such as the ribs, pelvis, and skull. The red and white blood cells shown here are made in the red bone marrow.

Supporting Life

The skeletal system supports life by providing a framework for the body and protecting vital organs. This also maintains equilibrium, or balance, by storing minerals and producing red blood cells, which are needed to keep people alive and healthy.

No Bones About It!

What are the parts of the skeletal system?

Bones, ligaments, and cartilage make up your skeletal system. The skeletal system is divided into two parts. The skull, vertebrae, and ribs make up the *axial skeleton*, which supports the body's weight and protects internal organs. The arms, legs, shoulders, and pelvis make up the *appendicular skeleton*, which allows for most of the body's movement.

Bones

Bones are alive! They have blood vessels that supply nutrients and nerves, which signal pain. The body of a newborn baby has about 300 bones, but the average adult has only 206 bones. As a child grows, some bones fuse together.

Ligaments

The tough, flexible strand of connective tissue that holds bones together is a **ligament**. Ligaments allow movement, and are found at the end of bones. Some ligaments, such as the ones on your vertebrae, prevent too much movement of bones.

7 Compare How does the axial skeleton differ from the appendicular skeleton?

_____

_____

_____

_____

Cartilage

Cartilage is a strong, flexible, and smooth connective tissue found at the end of bones. It allows bones to move smoothly across each other. The tip of your nose and your ears are soft and bendy because they contain only cartilage. Cartilage does not contain blood vessels.

What are bones made of?

Bones are hard organs made of minerals and connective tissue. If you looked inside a bone, you would notice two kinds of bone tissue. One kind, called *compact bone*, is dense and does not have any visible open spaces. Compact bone makes bones rigid and hard. Tiny canals within compact bone contain blood capillaries. The other kind of bone tissue, called *spongy bone*, has many open spaces. Spongy bone provides most of the strength and support for a bone. In long bones, such as those of the arm or the leg, an outer layer of compact bone surrounds spongy bone and another soft tissue called *marrow*.

Active Reading **8 Identify** As you read, underline the name of a protein found in bone.

Minerals

Calcium is the most plentiful mineral in bones. The minerals in bones are deposited by bone cells called *osteoblasts*. Minerals, such as calcium, make the bones strong and hard.

Connective Tissue

The connective tissue in bone is made mostly of a protein called *collagen*. Minerals make the bones strong and hard, but the collagen in bones allows them to be flexible enough to withstand knocks and bumps. Otherwise, each time you bumped a bone, it would crack like a china cup.

Marrow

Bones also contain a soft tissue called *marrow*. There are two types of marrow. Red marrow is the site of platelet and red and white blood cell production. Red marrow is in the center of flat bones such as the ribs. Yellow marrow, which is found in the center of long bones such as the femur, stores fat.

Bones, such as the femur shown here, are made mostly of connective tissue. They also contain minerals such as calcium.

Ligament

Spongy bone

Compact bone

Marrow

Blood vessels

Cartilage

9 Summarize In the chart below, fill in the main functions of each part of the skeletal system.

Structure	Function
Spongy bone	
Compact bone	
Cartilage	
Ligaments	

How do bones grow?

The skeleton of a fetus growing inside its mother's body does not contain hard bones. Instead, most bones start out as flexible cartilage. When a baby is born, it still has a lot of cartilage. As the baby grows, most of the cartilage is replaced by bone.

The bones of a child continue to grow. The long bones lengthen at their ends, in areas called *growth plates*. Growth plates are areas of cartilage that continue to make new cells. Bone cells called *osteocytes* move into the cartilage, hardening it and changing it into bone. Growth continues into adolescence and sometimes even into early adulthood. Most bones harden completely after they stop growing. Even after bones have stopped growing, they can still repair themselves if they break.

This baby's skeleton has more cartilage than his older brother's skeleton has.

Bone Connections

How are bones connected?

The place where two or more bones connect is called a **joint**. Some joints allow movement of body parts, others stop or limit movement. Just imagine how difficult it would be to do everyday things such as tying your shoelaces if you could not bend the joints in your arms, legs, neck, or fingers!

Joints

Bones are connected to each other at joints by strong, flexible ligaments. The ends of the bone are covered with cartilage. Cartilage is a smooth, flexible connective tissue that helps cushion the area in a joint where bones meet. Some joints allow little or no movement. These *fixed joints* can be found in the skull. Other joints, called *movable joints*, allow movement of the bones.

Your joints allow you to do everyday tasks easily.

Some Examples of Movable Joints

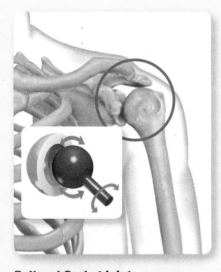

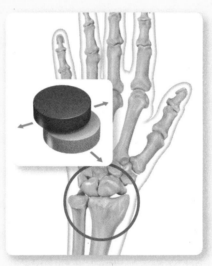

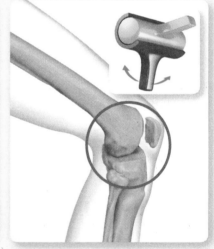

Ball and Socket joint
Shoulders and hips are ball-and-socket joints. Ball-and-socket joints allow one of the bones of the joint to rotate in a large circle.

Gliding joint
Wrists and ankles are gliding joints. Gliding joints allow a great deal of flexibility in many directions.

Hinge joint
Knees and elbows are hinge joints. Hinge joints work like door hinges, allowing bones to move back and forth.

 Inquiry

10 **Apply** Some joints, such as the ones in your skull, do not move at all. Why do you think it is important that skull joints cannot move?

_____

_____

_____

_____

What are some injuries and disorders of the skeletal system?

Sometimes the skeletal system can become injured or diseased. Injuries and diseases of the skeletal system affect the body's support system and ability to move. Hereditary factors may play a role in the incidence of diseases, such as osteoporosis and arthritis.

Active Reading

11 Identify As you read, underline the characteristics of each injury and disease.

Fractures

Bones may be fractured, or broken. Bones can be broken by a high-force impact such as a fall from a bike. A broken bone usually repairs itself in six to eight weeks.

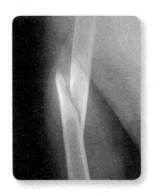

Sprains

A sprain is an injury to a ligament that is caused by stretching a joint too far. The tissues in the sprained ligament can tear and the joint becomes swollen and painful to move. Sprains are common sports injuries.

12 Apply How could someone sprain a ligament?

_____

_____

_____

_____

_____

Osteoporosis

Osteoporosis is a disease that causes bone tissue to become thin. The bones become weak and break more easily. It is most common among adults who do not get enough calcium in their diet. What you eat now can affect your risk of developing osteoporosis later in life.

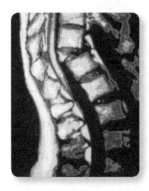

13 Infer Why is it important to get enough calcium in your diet?

_____

_____

_____

_____

Arthritis

Arthritis is a disease that causes joints to swell, stiffen, and become painful. It may also cause the joint to become misshapen, as shown in the photo. A person with arthritis finds it difficult to move the affected joint. Arthritis can be treated with drugs that reduce swelling.

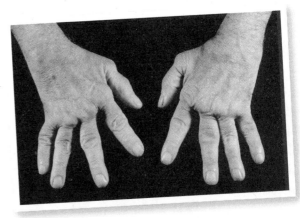

Keep Moving!

What are the main functions of the muscular system?

Muscles pump blood through your body, enable you to breathe, hold you upright, and allow you to move. All animals, except the simplest invertebrates, have muscles for movement. The **muscular system**, one of the major subsystems of the body, is mostly made of the muscles that allow your body to move and be flexible. Other muscles move materials inside your body, which helps maintain equilibrium. *Muscle* is the tissue that contracts and relaxes, making movement, or locomotion, possible. Muscle tissue is made up of muscle cells. Muscle cells contain special proteins that allow them to shorten and lengthen.

Active Reading **14 Identify** How do muscles make movement possible?

_____

_____

_____

What are the three types of muscles?

Your body has three kinds of muscle tissue: *skeletal muscle, smooth muscle,* and *cardiac muscle.* Each muscle type has a specific function in your body.

You are able to control the movement of skeletal muscle, so it is called *voluntary muscle.* You are not able to control the movement of smooth muscle or cardiac muscles. Muscle action that is not under your control is *involuntary.* Smooth muscle and cardiac muscle are called *involuntary muscles.*

Smooth Muscle

Smooth muscle is found in internal organs and blood vessels. It helps move materials through the body. Arteries and veins contain a layer of smooth muscle that can contract and relax. This action controls blood flow through the blood vessel. Smooth muscle movement in your digestive system helps move food through your intestines. Smooth muscle is involuntary muscle.

Working Together

The skeletal system often works together with the muscular system, and is known as the musculoskeletal system. Muscles help bones move, so without the musculoskeletal system, locomotion would not be possible. A healthy musculoskeletal system helps maintain the body's equilibrium, supports the frame of your body, and allows you to maintain a healthy life.

Smooth muscle cells are spindle-shaped. They are fat in the middle with thin ends.

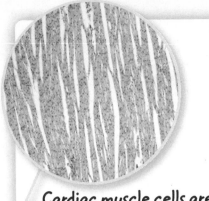

Cardiac Muscle

Cardiac muscle is the tissue that makes up the heart. Your heart never gets tired like your skeletal muscle can. This is because cardiac muscle cells are able to contract and relax. In order to supply lots of energy to the cells, cardiac muscle cells contain many mitochondria. Your cardiac muscles do not stop moving your entire lifetime!

The contractions of cardiac muscle push blood out of the heart and pump it around the body. Cardiac muscle is involuntary; you cannot consciously stop your heart from pumping.

Cardiac muscle cells are long, thin, and branched.

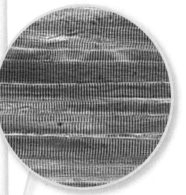

Skeletal Muscle

Skeletal muscle is attached to your bones and allows you to move. You have control over your skeletal muscle. For example, you can bring your arm up to your mouth to take a bite from an apple. The tough strand of tissue that connects a muscle to a bone is called a **tendon**. When a muscle contracts, or shortens, the attached bones are pulled closer to each other. For example, when the bicep muscle shortens, the arm bends at the elbow.

Most skeletal muscles work in pairs around a joint, as shown below. One muscle in the pair, called a *flexor*, bends a joint. The other muscle, the *extensor*, straightens the joint. When one muscle of a pair contracts, the other muscle relaxes to allow movement of the body part. Muscle pairs are found all around the body.

Skeletal muscle cells are long and thin with stripes, or striations.

 **Visualize It!**

15 Apply What would happen to the arm if the flexor was not able to contract?

_____

_____

_____

_____

_____

_____

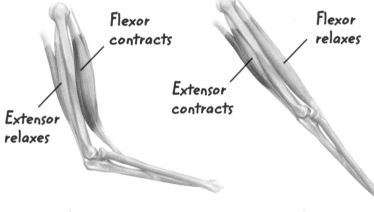

Flexor contracts

Extensor relaxes

The biceps muscle is the flexor that contracts to bend the arm.

Flexor relaxes

Extensor contracts

The triceps muscle is the extensor that contracts to straighten the arm.

 **Visualize It!**

16 Compare How do the three muscle tissue types look similar and different?

_____

_____

_____

_____

_____

Move It or Lose It!

What are some injuries and disorders of the muscular system?

Like other systems, the muscular system can suffer injury or disease. As a result, muscles may lose normal function. Some muscle diseases are hereditary. Diseases that affect muscle function can also affect other body systems. For example, myocarditis is an inflammation of the heart muscle that can cause heart failure and harm the cardiovascular system.

Muscle Strain and Tears

A *strain* is a muscle injury in which a muscle is overstretched or torn. This can happen when muscles have not been stretched properly or when they are overworked. Strains cause the muscle tissue to swell and can be painful. Strains and tears need rest to heal.

Muscular Dystrophy

Muscular dystrophy is a hereditary disease that causes skeletal muscle to become weaker over time. It affects how muscle proteins form. A person with muscular dystrophy has poor balance and difficulty walking or doing other everyday activities.

Tendinitis

Tendons connect muscles to bones. Tendons can become inflamed or even torn when muscles are overused. This painful condition is called *tendinitis*. Tendinitis needs rest to heal. It may also be treated with medicines that reduce swelling.

---

17 Contrast What is the difference between a muscle strain and tendinitis?

_____

_____

_____

Physical therapy can help people gain full use of their muscles and joints after an injury.

Think Outside the Book

18 Plan With a classmate, research the recommendations for regular physical activity. Then design a poster to show how people can fit 30–60 minutes of physical activity into their daily lives.

What are some benefits of exercise?

Exercising is one of the best things you can do to keep your body healthy. *Exercise* is any activity that helps improve physical fitness and health. Exercise benefits the muscular system by increasing strength, endurance, and flexibility. Exercise helps other body systems, too. It helps keep your heart, blood vessels, lungs, and bones healthy. Exercise also reduces stress, helps you sleep well, and makes you feel good.

Exercises that raise your heart rate to a certain level for at least 60 minutes improve the fitness of the heart. A fit heart is a more efficient pump. It can pump more blood around the body with each beat. It is also less likely to develop heart disease. Good muscle strength and joint flexibility may help a person avoid injuries. Weight training helps bones stay dense and strong. Dense, strong bones are less likely to break. Thirty to sixty minutes of physical activity every day can help improve the health of people of all ages, from children to older adults.

Active Reading **19 Identify** As you read, underline the characteristics of anaerobic and aerobic exercise.

Muscle Strength

Resistance exercise helps improve muscle strength by building skeletal muscle and increasing muscle power. Resistance exercise involves short bursts of intense effort lasting no more than a few minutes. Resistance exercises are also called *anaerobic exercises* because the muscle cells contract without using oxygen. Lifting weights and doing pushups are examples of anaerobic exercises.

Muscle Endurance

Endurance exercises allow muscles to contract for a longer time without getting tired. Endurance exercises are also called *aerobic exercises* because the muscle cells use oxygen when contracting. Aerobic exercises involve moderately intense activity from about 30 to 60 minutes at a time. Some examples of aerobic exercises are walking, jogging, bicycling, skating, and swimming.

Flexibility

Can you reach down and touch your toes? If a joint can move through a wide range of motions, it has good flexibility. *Flexibility* refers to the full range of motion of a joint. Stretching exercises help improve flexibility of a joint. Having good flexibility can help prevent ligament, tendon, and muscle injuries. Stretching after aerobic or anaerobic exercises may also help prevent injuries.

© Houghton Mifflin Harcourt Publishing Company • Image Credits: ©Andersen Ross/Digital Vision/Getty Images

Visual Summary

To complete this summary, fill in the blanks with the correct word or phrase. Then, use the key below to check your answers. You can use this page to review the main concepts of the lesson.

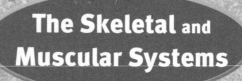

The skeletal system supports and protects the body and allows for movement.

20 The three main parts of the skeletal system are bones, _____ , and _____ .

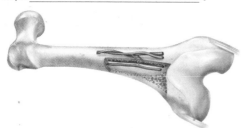

Joints connect two or more bones.

21 The shoulder is an example of a _____ joint.

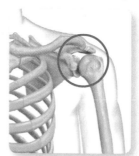

The muscular system allows for movement and flexibility.

22 Muscles work in _____ to move body parts.

Exercise benefits the body in many ways.

23 Aerobic exercises improve muscle _____ .

Anaerobic exercises improve muscle _____ .

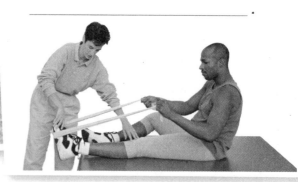

Answers: 20 cartilage; ligaments; 21 ball and socket; 22 pairs; 23 endurance; strength

24 **Synthesize** Explain why you need both muscles and bones to move your body.

Lesson Review

Vocabulary

Draw a line to connect the following terms to their definitions.

1 skeletal system

2 ligament

3 muscular system

4 joint

5 tendon

A A group of muscles that allows you to move and that moves materials inside your body

B a place where two or more bones connect

C bones, cartilage, and the ligaments that hold bones together

D tough strands of tissue that connect muscles to bones

E a type of tough, flexible connective tissue that holds bones together

Key Concepts

6 List What are the functions of the skeletal system?

_____

_____

_____

7 Analyze What are bones made of?

_____

_____

8 Explain How do muscles work in pairs to move the body?

_____

_____

_____

_____

9 Identify What bone disease is caused by a lack of calcium in the diet?

_____

Critical Thinking

Use this graph to answer the following questions.

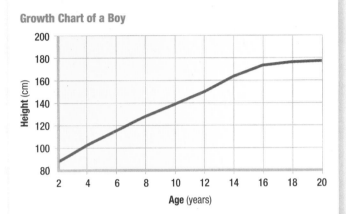

Growth Chart of a Boy

10 Analyze At which points on this graph is bone growing at the fastest rate?

_____

_____

_____

11 Infer At which times on this graph would you expect that the boy's growth plates have stopped creating new bone?

_____

_____

_____

12 Apply If aerobic exercise improves heart strength so that it pumps more blood with each beat, what likely happens to the heart rate as the cardiac muscle gets stronger? Explain your answer.

_____

_____

_____

_____

_____

_____

My Notes

The Circulatory and Respiratory Systems

ESSENTIAL QUESTION

How do the circulatory and respiratory systems work?

By the end of this lesson, you should be able to relate the structures of the circulatory and respiratory systems to their functions in the human body.

7.LS1.5

This micrograph shows red blood cells inside a blood vessel in the lung. The blood cells are picking up oxygen to bring to the rest of the body.

Engage Your Brain

1 Identify Check T or F to show whether you think each statement is true or false.

T **F**

☐ ☐ Air is carried through blood vessels.

☐ ☐ The cardiovascular system does not interact with any other body system.

☐ ☐ The respiratory system gets rid of carbon dioxide from the body.

☐ ☐ Smoking cigarettes can lead to lung disease.

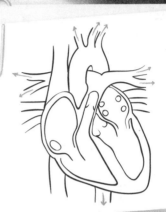

2 Identify What is the name of the organ, shown here, that makes the "lub-dub" sound in your chest?

_____

3 Infer What is the function of this organ?

_____

_____

_____

Active Reading

4 Synthesize You can sometimes tell a lot about the structure of an unknown object by understanding the meaning of its name. Use the meaning of the Latin word and the sentence below to write your own definition of *capillary*.

Latin word	Meaning
capillaris	thin and hairlike

Example Sentence
Oxygen that is carried by blood cells moves across the capillary wall and into body cells.

capillary:

_____

_____

_____

Vocabulary Terms

• cardiovascular system
• blood
• lymphatic system
• lymph
• lymph node
• artery
• capillary
• vein
• respiratory system
• pharynx
• larynx
• trachea
• bronchi
• alveoli

5 Apply As you learn the definition of each vocabulary term in this lesson, create your own definition or sketch to help you remember the meaning of the term.

Go with the Flow!

What is the circulatory system?

Active Reading

6 Identify As you read, underline the functions of the cardiovascular system and the lymphatic system.

When you hear the term *circulatory system*, what do you think of? If you said, "Heart, blood, and blood vessels," you are half right. The term *circulatory system* is actually a subsystem that describes both the cardiovascular system and the lymphatic system. Both systems work closely together to move fluids around your body and protect it from disease, which helps you stay healthy. Moving blood helps keep all parts of your body warm. In these ways, the two systems help maintain equilibrium in the body.

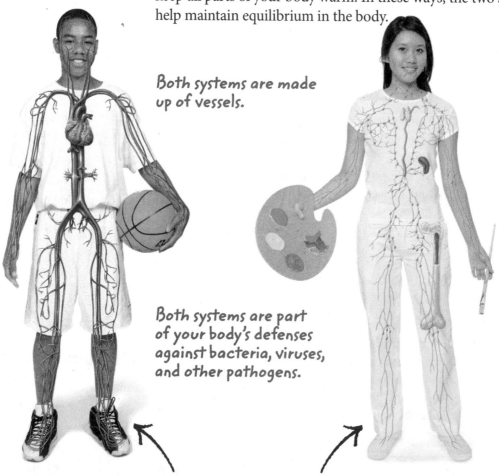

Both systems are made up of vessels.

Both systems are part of your body's defenses against bacteria, viruses, and other pathogens.

The Cardiovascular System

Your heart, blood, and blood vessels make up your **cardiovascular system**, which transports blood around your body. **Blood** is the fluid that carries gases, nutrients, and waste through the body. The cardiovascular system is a closed circulatory system; the blood is carried in vessels that form a closed loop. The blood maintains homeostasis by transporting hormones, nutrients, and oxygen to cells and by carrying waste away from cells.

The Lymphatic System

The **lymphatic system** is a group of organs and tissues that collect the fluid that leaks from blood and returns it to the blood. The leaked fluid is called **lymph**. The lymphatic system is an open circulatory system, so lymph can move in and out of the vessels. The lymphatic system is also part of the body's defenses against disease. Certain lymph vessels in the abdomen move fats from the intestine and into the blood.

7 Compare Fill in the Venn diagram to compare the structures and functions of both of these systems. You can add more details as you read more about these systems in this lesson.

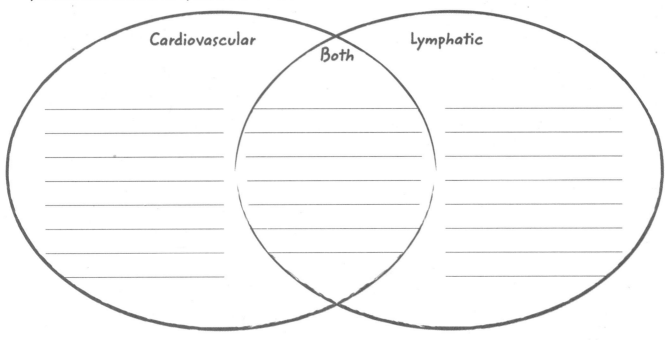

Cardiovascular   Both   Lymphatic

How do the systems work together?

Every time your heart pumps, a little fluid is forced out of the thin walls of the tiniest blood vessels, called *capillaries*. Most of this fluid is reabsorbed by the capillaries, and the remaining fluid is collected by lymph capillaries. *Lymph capillaries* absorb fluid, particles, such as dead cells, and pathogens from around body cells. The lymph capillaries carry the fluid, now called *lymph,* to larger lymph vessels. Lymph is returned to the cardiovascular system when it drains into blood vessels at the base of the neck.

The lymphatic system is the place where certain blood cells, called *white blood cells,* mature. Some of these white blood cells stay in the lymphatic system where they attack invading pathogens.

Active Reading

8 Synthesize How does returning leaked fluid from the blood help maintain homeostasis and support life?

_____

_____

_____

_____

_____

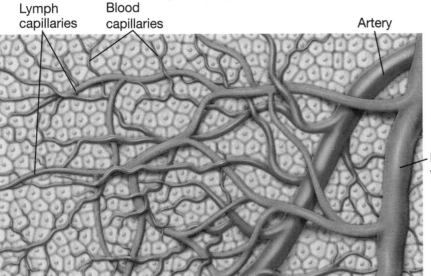

Lymph capillaries   Blood capillaries   Artery

Lymphatic vessel

The fluid that leaks from blood capillaries moves into lymph capillaries and is eventually returned to the blood.

Node Doubt!

What are the parts of the lymphatic system?

As you have read, lymph vessels collect and return fluids that have leaked from the blood. In addition to these vessels, several organs and tissues are part of the lymphatic system.

Active Reading

9 Identify As you read these pages, underline the main function of each part of the lymphatic system.

Lymph Nodes

As lymph travels through lymph vessels, it passes through lymph nodes. **Lymph nodes** are small, bean-shaped organs that remove pathogens and dead cells from lymph. Lymph nodes are concentrated in the armpits, neck, and groin. Infection-fighting blood cells, called *white blood cells,* are found in lymph nodes. When bacteria or other pathogens cause an infection, the number of these blood cells may multiply greatly. The lymph nodes fill with white blood cells that are fighting the infection. As a result, some lymph nodes may become swollen and painful. Swollen lymph nodes might be an early clue of an infection.

Lymph node

Lymph Vessels

Lymph vessels are the thin-walled vessels of the lymphatic system. They carry lymph back to lymph nodes. From the lymph nodes, the fluid is returned to the cardiovascular system through the lymph vessels. The vessels have valves inside them to stop lymph from flowing backward.

Bone Marrow

Bones—part of your skeletal system—are very important to your lymphatic system. *Bone marrow* is the soft tissue inside of bones where blood cells are produced.

Tonsils

Tonsils are small lymphatic organs at the back of the throat and tongue. The tonsils at the back of the throat are the most visible. Tonsils help defend the body against infection. White blood cells in the tonsil tissues trap pathogens. Tonsils in the throat sometimes get infected. An infection of the tonsils is called *tonsillitis*. When tonsils get infected, they may become swollen, as shown here.

Thymus

The *thymus* is an organ in the chest. Some white blood cells made in the bone marrow finish developing in the thymus. From the thymus, the white blood cells travel through the lymphatic system to other areas of the body. The thymus gets smaller as a person gets older. This organ is also a part of the endocrine system.

Spleen

The *spleen* is the largest lymphatic organ. It stores white blood cells and also allows them to mature. As blood flows through the spleen, white blood cells attack or mark pathogens in the blood. If pathogens cause an infection, the spleen may also release white blood cells into the bloodstream.

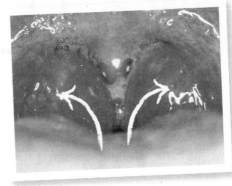

Swollen tonsils

Visualize It!

10 Predict A bad case of tonsillitis can sometimes affect a person's breathing. How is this possible?

_____

_____

_____

What are some disorders of the lymphatic system?

Lymphoma is a type of cancer that often begins in a lymph node. It can cause a swelling in the node called a *tumor*. There are many different types of lymphomas. Another disorder of the lymph system is lymphedema (lim•fih•DEE•muh). Lymphedema is a swelling of body tissues caused by a blockage or injury to lymph vessels. Lymph vessels are unable to drain lymph from a certain area, and that area becomes swollen. Filariasis is a disease caused by threadlike worms called *nematodes*. The nematodes may enter lymphatic vessels and block them, preventing lymph from moving around the body. Bubonic plague is a bacterial infection of the lymphatic system. The bacteria can enter the body through the bite of an infected flea. The bacteria grow inside lymph nodes, causing the nodes to swell.

Active Reading

11 Identify As you read, underline the names of the lymphatic system diseases discussed here.

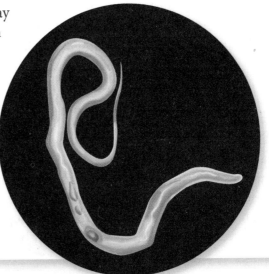

A person gets infected with filarial worms by being bitten by an infected fly. Filariasis is rare in the United States, but it is common in some developing countries.

The Heart of the Matter

What are the parts of the cardiovascular system?

Your cardiovascular system is the organ system that carries nutrients, gases, and hormones to body cells and waste products from body cells. It also helps keep the different parts of your body at an even temperature. Your cardiovascular system is made up of the heart, blood vessels, and blood.

Heart

The heart is the pump that sends blood around the body. Your heart is about the size of your fist and is almost in the center of your chest. When heart muscle contracts, it squeezes the blood inside the heart. This squeezing creates a pressure that pushes blood through the body.

Your heart has a left side and a right side. The two sides are separated by a thick wall. The right side of the heart pumps oxygen-poor blood to the lungs. The left side pumps oxygen-rich blood to the body. Each side has an upper chamber and a lower chamber. Each upper chamber is called an *atrium*. Each lower chamber is called a *ventricle*. Blood enters the atria and is pumped down to the ventricles. Flaplike structures called *valves* are located between the atria and the ventricles and in places where large vessels are attached to the heart. As blood moves through the heart, these valves close to prevent blood from going backward. The "lub-dub" sound of a beating heart is caused by the valves closing.

Blood

Blood is a type of connective tissue that is part of the cardiovascular system. It serves as a transport system, providing supplies for cells, carrying chemical messages, and removing waste so cells can maintain equilibrium. Blood contains cells, fluid, and other substances. It travels through miles and miles of blood vessels to reach every cell in your body.

Active Reading

12 Identify As you read this page, underline the parts of the heart that stop the blood from flowing backward.

The **left atrium** receives oxygen-rich blood from the lungs.

The **right atrium** receives oxygen-poor blood from the body.

The **right ventricle** pumps oxygen-poor blood to the lungs.

The **left ventricle** pumps oxygen-rich blood to the body.

13 Infer Why is it important for your heart to keep oxygen-rich blood separate from oxygen-poor blood?

_____

_____

_____

_____

Blood Vessels

Blood travels throughout your body in tubes called *blood vessels*. The three types of blood vessels are arteries, capillaries, and veins.

An **artery** is a blood vessel that carries blood away from the heart. Arteries have thick walls with a layer of smooth muscle. Each heartbeat pumps blood into your arteries at high pressure, which is your *blood pressure*. This pressure pushes blood through the arteries. Artery walls are strong and stretch to withstand the pressure. Nutrients, oxygen, and other substances must leave the blood to get to your body's cells. Carbon dioxide and other wastes leave body cells and are carried away by blood. A **capillary** is a tiny blood vessel that allows these exchanges between body cells and the blood. The gas exchange can take place because capillary walls are only one cell thick. Capillaries are so narrow that blood cells must pass through them in single file! No cell in the body is more than three or four cells away from a capillary.

Capillaries lead to veins. A **vein** is a blood vessel that carries blood back to the heart. Blood in veins is not under as much pressure as blood in arteries is. Valves in the veins keep the blood from flowing backward. The contraction of skeletal muscles around veins can help blood move in the veins.

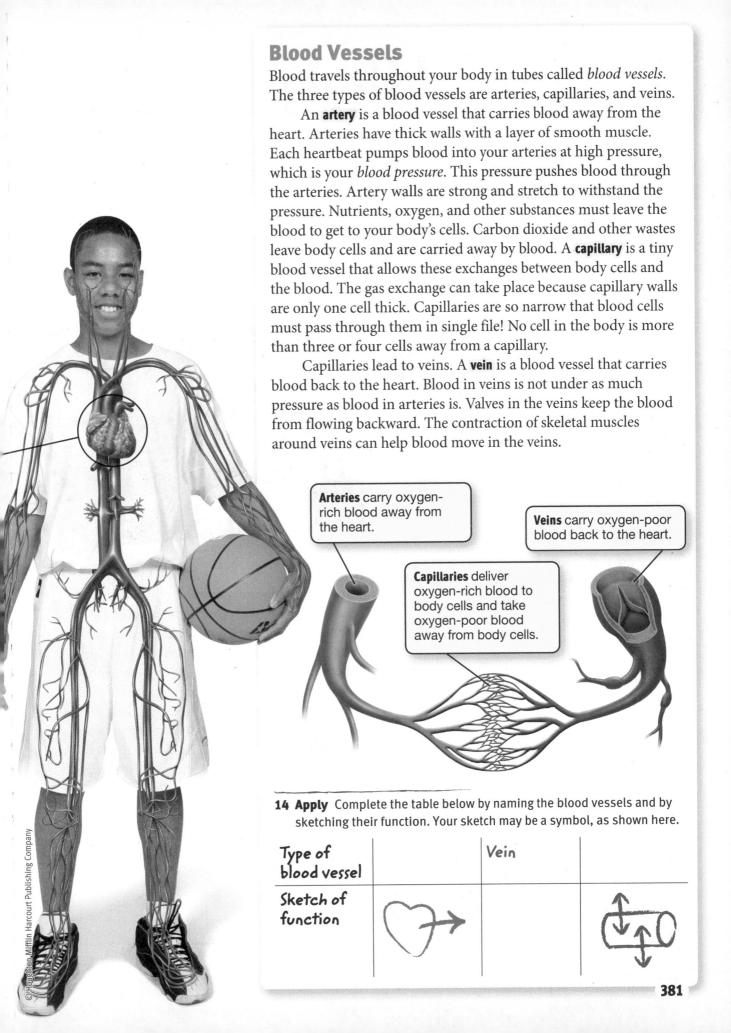

Arteries carry oxygen-rich blood away from the heart.

Capillaries deliver oxygen-rich blood to body cells and take oxygen-poor blood away from body cells.

Veins carry oxygen-poor blood back to the heart.

14 Apply Complete the table below by naming the blood vessels and by sketching their function. Your sketch may be a symbol, as shown here.

Type of blood vessel		Vein	
Sketch of function			

It's in the Blood

What is blood made of?

An adult human body has about 5 liters of blood. Your body probably has a little less than that. Blood is made up of plasma, platelets, and red and white blood cells. Blood is a tissue because it is made of at least two different cell types. If you looked at blood under a microscope, you would see these differently shaped cells and platelets.

The Blood Files

Plasma

The fluid part of the blood is called *plasma*. Plasma is a mixture of water, minerals, nutrients, sugars, proteins, and other substances. This fluid also carries waste. Platelets, white blood cells, and red blood cells are found in plasma.

White blood cell

Red blood cell

Platelet

Platelets

Platelets are tiny pieces of larger cells found in bone marrow. Platelets last for only five to ten days, but they have an important role. When you cut or scrape your skin, you bleed because blood vessels have been cut open. As soon as bleeding starts, platelets begin to clump together in the cut area. They form a plug that helps reduce blood loss. Platelets also release chemicals that react with proteins in plasma. The reaction causes tiny fibers to form. The fibers help create a blood clot.

White Blood Cells

White blood cells help keep you healthy by fighting pathogens such as bacteria and viruses. Some white blood cells squeeze out of blood vessels to search for pathogens. When they find one, they destroy it. Other white blood cells form antibodies. *Antibodies* are chemicals that identify pathogens. White blood cells also keep you healthy by destroying body cells that have died or have been damaged.

Red Blood Cells

Most blood cells are red blood cells. *Red blood cells* are disk-shaped cells that do not have a nucleus. They bring oxygen to every cell in your body. Cells need oxygen to carry out life functions. Each red blood cell has hemoglobin. *Hemoglobin* is an oxygen-carrying protein; it clings to the oxygen molecules you inhale. Red blood cells can then transport oxygen to cells in every part of the body. The disk shape of red blood cells helps them squeeze into capillaries.

15 Predict How would the body be affected if red blood cells had low levels of hemoglobin?

_____

_____

_____

_____

_____

How does blood move through the body?

Blood is pumped from the right side of the heart to the lungs. From the lungs, it returns to the left side of the heart. The blood is then pumped from the left side of the heart to the body. It flows to the tiny capillaries around the body before returning to the right side of the heart. Blood in the arteries that come out of the heart is under great pressure because of the force from the pumping action of the heart. Blood in veins is under much less pressure than arterial blood because veins have larger internal diameters than arteries do. Veins carry larger volumes of blood more slowly.

Blood Moves in Circuits

Blood moves in two loops or circuits around the body. The beating heart moves blood to the lungs and also around the body. The flow of blood between the heart and the lungs is called the *pulmonary circulation*. As blood passes through the lungs, carbon dioxide leaves the blood and oxygen is picked up. The oxygen-rich blood then flows back to the heart, where it is pumped around the rest of the body. The circulation of blood between the heart and the rest of the body is called *systemic circulation*. Oxygen-poor blood returns to the heart from body cells in the systemic circulation.

Active Reading **16 Compare** What is the difference between the pulmonary and systemic circulations?

_____

_____

_____

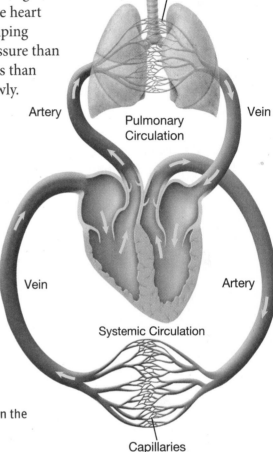

In pulmonary circulation, blood is pumped to the lungs where carbon dioxide leaves the blood and oxygen enters the blood.

Capillaries

Artery

Vein

Pulmonary Circulation

Vein

Artery

Systemic Circulation

Capillaries

In systemic circulation, blood moves around the body.

Visualize It!

17 Apply Put a box around the part of the diagram that shows the pulmonary circulation. Where in the diagram would you find oxygen-poor blood?

_____

_____

_____

_____

How does circulation help maintain body temperature?

The circulation of blood also helps homeostasis. When the brain senses that body temperature is rising, it signals blood vessels in the skin to widen. As the vessels widen, heat from the blood is transferred to the air around the skin. This transfer helps lower body temperature. When the brain senses that body temperature is normal, it signals the blood vessels to return to normal. When the brain senses that the body temperature is getting too low, it signals the blood vessels near the skin to get narrower. This allows the blood to stay close to internal organs to keep them warm.

What are some problems that affect the cardiovascular system?

Cardiovascular disease is the leading cause of death in the United States. Cardiovascular disease can be caused by smoking, poor diet, stress, physical inactivity, or in some cases, heredity. Eating a healthy diet and regular exercise can reduce the risk of developing cardiovascular problems.

Atherosclerosis

A major cause of heart disease is a condition called *atherosclerosis* (ath•uh•roh•skluh•ROH•sis). Atherosclerosis is a hardening of artery walls caused by the buildup of cholesterol and other lipids. The buildup causes the blood vessels to become narrower and less elastic. Blood cannot flow easily through a narrowed artery. When an artery supplying blood to the heart becomes blocked, oxygen cannot reach the heart muscle and the person may have a heart attack.

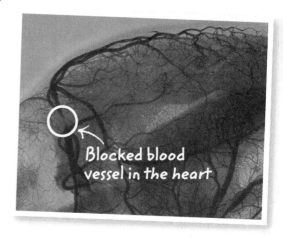

Blocked blood vessel in the heart

Blood pressure checks can help detect illness.

Hypertension

Hypertension is abnormally high blood pressure. Atherosclerosis may be caused in part by hypertension. The higher a person's blood pressure is, the greater their risk of developing cardiovascular problems, such as heart attacks and strokes. Hypertension that is not treated can also cause kidney damage and shorten life expectancy. Regular checkups can help detect problems with blood pressure. Hypertension can be controlled with diet and sometimes with medication.

Heart Attacks and Strokes

A heart attack happens when an artery that supplies blood to the heart becomes blocked and the heart muscle tissue that depends on that blood supply does not get oxygen. Cells and tissues that do not get oxygen get damaged and can die. If enough heart muscle cells are damaged, the heart may stop beating.

A stroke can happen when a blood vessel in the brain becomes blocked or bursts. As a result, that part of the brain receives no oxygen. Without oxygen, brain cells die. Brain damage that occurs during a stroke can affect many parts of the body. People who have had a stroke may experience paralysis or difficulty in speaking.

Think Outside the Book Inquiry

18 Research Doctors often use an electrocardiogram (ECG) reading to see if there is something wrong with how a person's heart is beating. An ECG is a type of graph that "draws" the pumping activity of the heart. How might graphing the heartbeat help a doctor tell if there is a problem?

Take a Deep Breath

What are the functions of the respiratory system?

Your cells need a constant supply of oxygen to stay alive. Your cells must also be able to get rid of the waste product carbon dioxide, which is toxic to them. Breathing takes care of both of these needs. The **respiratory system** is another subsystem of the body, and is the group of organs that takes in oxygen and gets rid of carbon dioxide. *Respiration,* or breathing, is the transport of oxygen from outside the body to cells and tissues, and the transport of carbon dioxide and wastes away from cells and to the environment. Proper respiration is necessary for sustaining life. When the body does not get enough oxygen, or when the body has too much carbon dioxide, it throws off the equilibrium, causing people to become ill.

Active Reading

19 Identify As you read this page, underline the gas that is needed by your body for cellular respiration.

Takes in Oxygen

When a person inhales, air is drawn into the lungs. Oxygen in the air moves into the blood from the lungs. The oxygen-rich blood flowing away from the lungs is carried to all the cells in the body. Oxygen leaves the capillaries and enters the body cells. Inside each cell, oxygen is used for cellular respiration. During cellular respiration, the energy that is stored in food molecules is released. Without oxygen, body cells would not be able to survive.

Releases Carbon Dioxide

When a person exhales, carbon dioxide is released from the body. Carbon dioxide is a waste product of cellular respiration, and the body needs to get rid of it. Carbon dioxide moves from body cells and into capillaries where it is carried in the blood all the way to the lungs. Blood that flows to the lungs contains more carbon dioxide than oxygen. The carbon dioxide moves out of the capillaries and into the lungs, where it is exhaled.

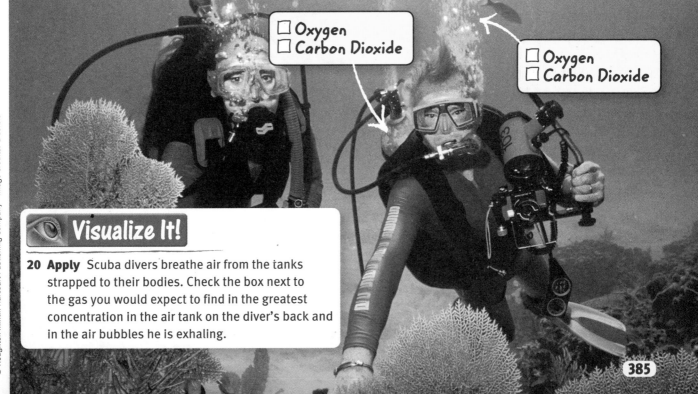

☐ Oxygen
☐ Carbon Dioxide

☐ Oxygen
☐ Carbon Dioxide

Visualize It!

20 Apply Scuba divers breathe air from the tanks strapped to their bodies. Check the box next to the gas you would expect to find in the greatest concentration in the air tank on the diver's back and in the air bubbles he is exhaling.

Breathe Easy

What are the parts of the respiratory system?

Breathing is made possible by your respiratory system. Air enters your respiratory system through your nose or mouth when you breathe in. From there, the air moves through a series of tubes to get to your lungs.

Nose, Pharynx, and Larynx

Air enters your respiratory system through your nose and your mouth. From the nose, air flows into the **pharynx** (FAIR•ingks), or throat. The pharynx branches into two tubes. One tube, the *esophagus*, leads to the stomach. The other tube, called the *larynx,* leads to the lungs. The **larynx** (LAIR•ingks) is the part of the throat that holds the vocal cords. When air passes across the vocal cords, they vibrate, making the voice.

Bronchioles and Alveoli

In the lungs, the bronchioles lead to tiny sacs called **alveoli** (singular, *alveolus*). Alveoli are surrounded by blood vessels. Gases in the air move across the thin walls of the alveoli and blood vessels. As you breathe, air is sucked into and forced out of alveoli. Breathing is carried out by the diaphragm and rib muscles. The *diaphragm* is a dome-shaped muscle below the lungs. As you inhale, the diaphragm contracts and moves down. The volume of the chest increases. As a result, a vacuum is created and air is sucked in. Exhaling reverses this process.

Trachea

The larynx is connected to a large tube called the **trachea** (TRAY•kee•uh), or windpipe. Air flows from the larynx through the trachea to the lungs. The trachea splits into two branches called **bronchi** (singular, *bronchus*). One bronchus connects to each lung. Each bronchus branches into smaller tubes called *bronchioles*.

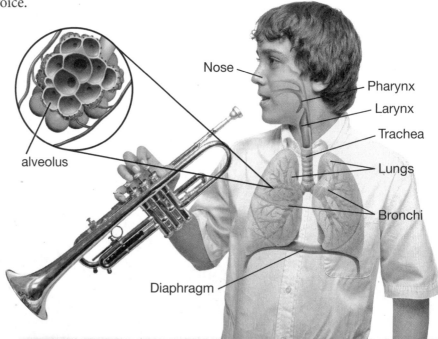

alveolus

Nose
Pharynx
Larynx
Trachea
Lungs
Bronchi
Diaphragm

👁 Visualize It!

21 Apply Draw arrows showing the direction of air flow into the lungs. How would an object blocking a bronchus affect this airflow?

_____

_____

What are some disorders of the respiratory system?

Millions of people suffer from respiratory disorders. These disorders include asthma, pneumonia, emphysema, and lung cancer. Some respiratory problems such as emphysema and lung cancer are strongly linked to cigarette smoke. Other respiratory disorders, such as pneumonia, are caused by pathogens, and some are genetic disorders. Depending on the cause, there are many different ways to treat respiratory diseases.

Active Reading

22 Identify As you read, underline the characteristics of the different respiratory disorders.

Asthma

Asthma is a condition in which the airways are narrowed due to inflammation of the bronchi. During an asthma attack, the muscles in the bronchi tighten and the airways become inflamed. This reduces the amount of air that can get into or out of the lungs. Asthma is treated with medicines that open the bronchioles.

Pneumonia

Pneumonia (noo•MOHN•yuh) is an inflammation of the lungs that is usually caused by bacteria or viruses. Inflamed alveoli may fill with fluid. If the alveoli are filled with too much fluid, the person cannot take in enough oxygen and he or she may suffocate. Pneumonia can be treated with medicines that kill the pathogens.

Emphysema

Emphysema (em•fuh•SEE•muh) occurs when the alveoli have been damaged. As a result, oxygen cannot pass across into the blood as well as it could in a normal alveolus. People who have emphysema have trouble getting the oxygen they need and removing carbon dioxide from the lungs. This condition is often linked to long-term use of tobacco.

Visualize It!

23 Compare How are these two lungs different? How can you tell the diseased lung from the healthy lung?

_____

_____

_____

_____

Think Outside the Book

24 Imagine Pretend you are a lung. The behavior of your body has not been very healthy, and as a result you are sick. Write a plea to your body to help you improve your health. Be sure to explain how the structures and functions of the respiratory system help maintain equilibrium and support life.

Emphysema lung

Healthy lung

Visual Summary

To complete this summary, fill in the blanks with the correct word or phrase. Then use the key below to check your answers. You can use this page to review the main concepts of the lesson.

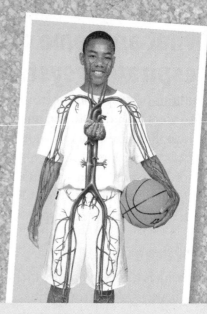

The lymphatic system returns fluid to the blood.

25 The lymph organs found in your throat are called

_____.

Circulatory and Respiratory Systems

The cardiovascular system moves blood throughout the body and carries nutrients and oxygen to body cells.

26 The two gases that the blood carries around the body are

_____ and

_____.

The respiratory system takes oxygen into the body and releases carbon dioxide.

27 Oxygen enters the blood and carbon dioxide leaves the blood in the

_____ of the lungs.

Answers: 25 tonsils; 26 oxygen, carbon dioxide; 27 alveoli

28 Relate Describe how a problem with the respiratory system could directly affect the cardiovascular system.

Lesson Review

Vocabulary

In your own words, define the following terms.

1 Blood

_____

_____

2 Lymph

_____

_____

3 Alveoli

_____

_____

Key Concepts

Fill in the table below.

System	Structures
4 Identify What are the main structures of the lymphatic system?	
5 Identify What are the main structures of the cardiovascular system?	
6 Identify What are the main structures of the respiratory system?	

7 Explain How does blood help maintain homeostasis in the body?

_____

_____

_____

8 Contrast How are arteries and veins different?

_____

_____

_____

9 Relate How might a blockage of the lymph vessels affect the function of the cardiovascular system?

_____

_____

_____

Critical Thinking

Use this image to answer the following questions.

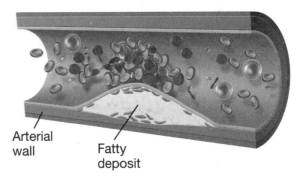

Arterial wall

Fatty deposit

10 Relate To what body system does this structure belong?

_____

11 Predict How might what is happening in this image affect the nervous system?

_____

_____

_____

12 Infer Why is it important that lymph vessels are spread throughout the body?

_____

_____

_____

My Notes

Olufunmilayo Falusi Olopade

MEDICAL DOCTOR

Dr. Olufunmilayo Olopade is the head of the University of Chicago's Cancer Risk Clinic. The MacArthur Foundation awarded her $500,000 for her creative work in breast cancer research.

Born in Nigeria, Dr. Olopade began her career as a medical officer at the Nigerian Navy Hospital in Lagos. She later came to Chicago to do cancer research. She became a professor at the University of Chicago in 1991, and founded the Cancer Risk Clinic shortly after that time.

Dr. Olopade found that tumors in African-American women often come from a different group of cells than they do in Caucasian women. These tumors, therefore, need different treatment. Dr. Olopade designs treatments that address the source of the tumor. More importantly, her treatments try to address the particular risk factors of each patient. These can include diet, heredity, age, and activity. The MacArthur Foundation recognized Dr. Olopade for designing such new and practical treatment plans for patients. Studying cells has provided Dr. Olopade with clues on how to improve the lives of millions of African-American women.

A color-enhanced scanning electron micrograph (SEM) of a breast cancer cell

JOB BOARD

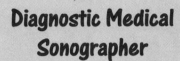

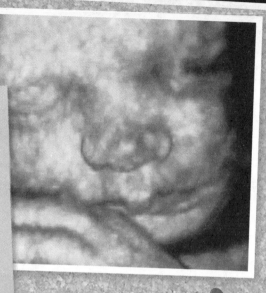

Diagnostic Medical Sonographer

What You'll Do: Operate and take care of the sonogram equipment that uses sound waves to create pictures of inside human bodies that a doctor can interpret.

Where You Might Work: Hospitals, clinics, and private offices that have sonogram equipment.

Education: A two- or four-year undergraduate degree or a special certification program is necessary.

Physical Therapist

What You'll Do: Use exercise, ultrasound, heat, and other treatments when working with patients to help them improve their muscular strength, endurance, and flexibility.

Where You Might Work: Hospitals, clinics, and private physiotherapy offices, as well as some gyms and yoga studios.

Education: A master's degree from an accredited physical therapy program is required.

Prosthetics Technician

What You'll Do: Create, test, fit, maintain, and repair artificial limbs and other prosthetic devices for people who need them.

Where You Might Work: Hospitals with prosthetic divisions and private companies.

Education: Technicians must have an associate, bachelor's, or post-graduate degree in orthotics and prosthetics. Some companies may require additional certification.

Language Arts Connection

Find one report of a new discovery in cancer prevention. Summarize the key points of the discovery in a paragraph. Be sure to include information about what the discovery is, who made it, how the discovery was made, and how it changes what we know about cancer.

The Digestive and Excretory Systems

ESSENTIAL QUESTION

How do your body's digestive and excretory systems work?

By the end of this lesson, you should be able to relate the parts of the digestive and excretory systems to their roles in the human body.

7.LS1.5

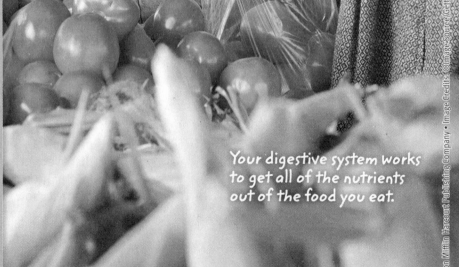

Your digestive system works to get all of the nutrients out of the food you eat.

Lesson Labs

Quick Labs
- Bile Function
- Peristalsis Race
- Mechanical Digestion

S.T.E.M. Lab
- Modeling a Kidney

 Engage Your Brain

1 Predict Fill in the blanks with the words that you think best complete the following sentences.

Inside your _____, food is chewed and broken down by teeth and saliva.

The _____ is a muscle inside your mouth that helps you to swallow food and liquids.

If you eat too much food too quickly, you may get a _____ache.

2 Imagine How is a blender like your stomach?

_____
_____
_____
_____

 Active Reading

3 Synthesize You can often define an unknown word if you see it used in a sentence. Use the sentence below to make an educated guess about the meaning of the word *enzyme*.

Example sentence
Enzymes in the mouth, stomach, and small intestine help in the chemical digestion of food.

enzyme:

_____
_____
_____
_____
_____

Vocabulary Terms

- digestive system
- enzyme
- esophagus
- stomach
- small intestine
- large intestine
- pancreas
- liver
- excretory system
- kidney
- nephron
- urine

4 Apply As you learn the meaning of each vocabulary term in this lesson, create your own definition or sketch to help you remember the meaning of the term.

You are what you eat!

What is the digestive system?

Your cells need a lot of energy for their daily activities. Cells use nutrients, which are substances in food, for energy, growth, maintenance, and repair. The **digestive system**, a subsystem of the body, breaks down the food you eat into nutrients that can be used as building materials and that can provide energy for cells. Having the right nutrients and energy keeps the body in equilibrium, giving us enough energy to stay alive, grow, and be active.

The digestive system interacts with other body systems to obtain and use energy from food. Blood, part of the circulatory system, transports nutrients to other tissues. In order to extract energy from nutrients, cells need oxygen. The respiratory system is responsible for obtaining this oxygen from the environment. The nervous system controls and regulates the functioning of the digestive system.

What are the two types of digestion?

Digestion is the process of breaking down food into a form that can pass from the digestive system into the bloodstream. There are two types of digestion: mechanical and chemical.

The Stomach

The deep pits and grooves in the stomach lining help grind food.

Inquiry

6 Infer The stomach lining is made up of deep muscular grooves. How do you think these structures help the stomach to break down food?

_____

_____

_____

_____

Mechanical Digestion

Mechanical digestion is the breaking, crushing, and mashing of food. Chewing is a type of mechanical digestion. Chewing creates small pieces of food that are easier to swallow and digest than are large pieces. Mechanical digestion increases the surface area of food for the action of chemical digestion.

Chemical Digestion

Chemical digestion is the process in which large molecules of food are broken down into smaller molecules so they can pass into the bloodstream. An **enzyme** (EN•zym) is a chemical the body uses to break down large molecules into smaller molecules. Enzymes act like chemical scissors. They "cut up" large molecules into smaller pieces. Mechanical digestion breaks up food and increases surface area so that enzymes can break nutrients into smaller molecules. Without mechanical digestion, chemical digestion would take days instead of hours!

 **Visualize It!**

7 Categorize Decide whether each of these steps in digestion is an example of mechanical digestion or chemical digestion. Then put a check in the correct box.

In your mouth, teeth grind food.
- ☐ mechanical
- ☐ chemical

Salivary glands release a liquid called saliva, which helps to break food down.
- ☐ mechanical
- ☐ chemical

In the stomach, muscles contract to grind food into a pulpy mixture.
- ☐ mechanical
- ☐ chemical

In the small intestine, most nutrients are broken down by enzymes.
- ☐ mechanical
- ☐ chemical

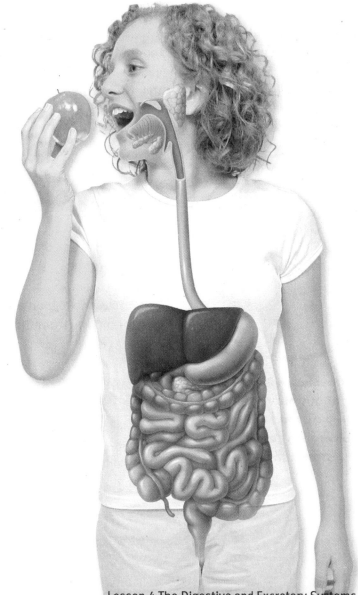

Chew on this

What are the parts of the digestive system?

Has anyone ever reminded you to chew your food? Chewing food is the first part of digestion. After food is chewed and swallowed, pieces of that food move through other organs in the digestive system, where the food is broken down even more.

Active Reading

8 As you read, underline the function of each organ of the digestive system.

The Mouth

Digestion begins in the mouth with both mechanical and chemical digestion. Teeth, with the help of strong jaw muscles, break and crush food.

As you chew, food is moistened by a liquid called *saliva*. Glands in your mouth make saliva. Saliva contains many substances, including an enzyme that begins the chemical digestion of starches in food.

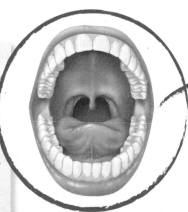

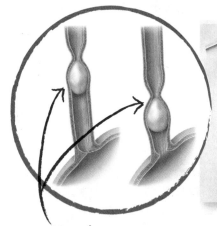

Muscles in the esophagus move this clump of food from your mouth to your stomach.

The Esophagus

Once food has been chewed, it is swallowed. The food moves through the throat, and then into a long tube called the **esophagus** (ih•SAWF•uh•gus). Waves of muscle contractions called *peristalsis* (per•ih•STAWL•sis) move the food into the stomach. The muscles move food along in much the same way as you move toothpaste from the bottom of the tube with your thumbs.

Visualize It!

9 Infer Consider the order of organs in the digestive system and their functions. How do the digestive system processes maintain equilibrium in the body and help support life?

_____

_____

_____

_____

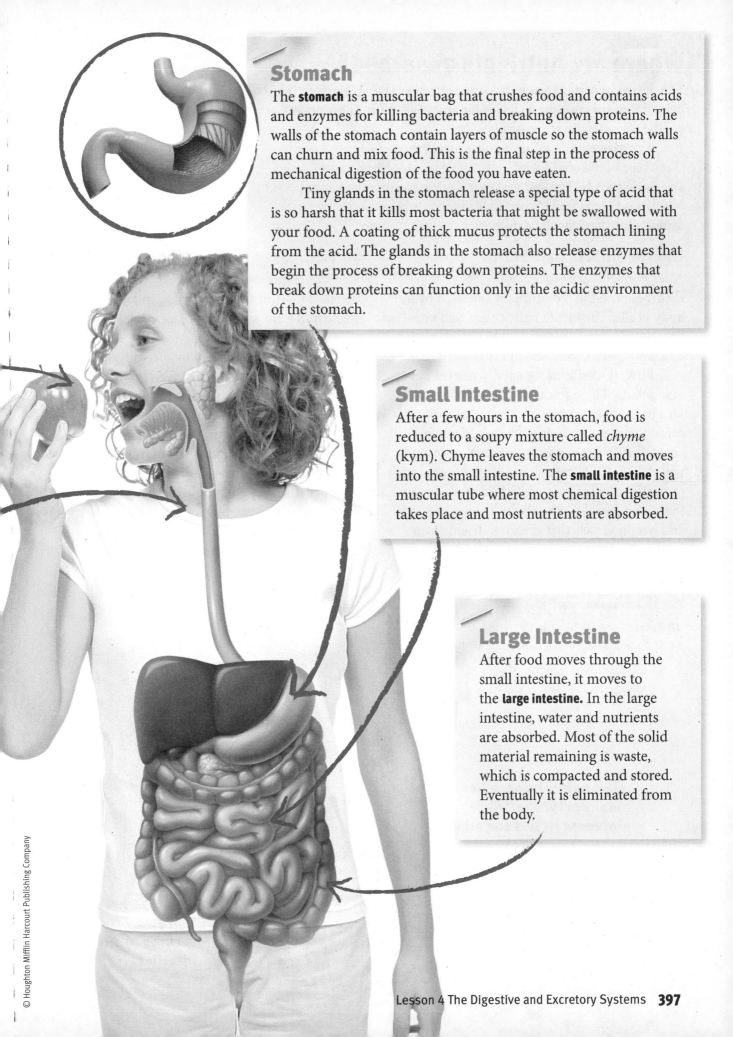

Stomach

The **stomach** is a muscular bag that crushes food and contains acids and enzymes for killing bacteria and breaking down proteins. The walls of the stomach contain layers of muscle so the stomach walls can churn and mix food. This is the final step in the process of mechanical digestion of the food you have eaten.

Tiny glands in the stomach release a special type of acid that is so harsh that it kills most bacteria that might be swallowed with your food. A coating of thick mucus protects the stomach lining from the acid. The glands in the stomach also release enzymes that begin the process of breaking down proteins. The enzymes that break down proteins can function only in the acidic environment of the stomach.

Small Intestine

After a few hours in the stomach, food is reduced to a soupy mixture called *chyme* (kym). Chyme leaves the stomach and moves into the small intestine. The **small intestine** is a muscular tube where most chemical digestion takes place and most nutrients are absorbed.

Large Intestine

After food moves through the small intestine, it moves to the **large intestine.** In the large intestine, water and nutrients are absorbed. Most of the solid material remaining is waste, which is compacted and stored. Eventually it is eliminated from the body.

Where are nutrients absorbed?

The digestion of nutrients in the small intestine takes place with the help of three organs that attach to the small intestine. These organs are the *pancreas*, *liver*, and *gall bladder*.

The **pancreas** (PANG•kree•uhz) makes fluids that break down every type of material found in foods: proteins, carbohydrates, fats, and nucleic acids. The **liver** makes and releases a mixture called *bile* that is then stored in the gall bladder. Bile breaks up large fat droplets into very small fat droplets.

In the Small Intestine

After nutrients are broken down, they are absorbed into the bloodstream and used by the body's cells. The inside wall of the small intestine has three features that allow it to absorb nutrients efficiently: folds, villi, and microvilli.

First, the walls of the small intestine have many folds. These folds increase the surface area inside the intestine wall, creating more room for nutrients to be absorbed. Each fold is covered with tiny fingerlike projections called *villi* (VIL•eye). In turn, the villi are covered with projections called microvilli. Microvilli increase the surface area of the villi. Villi contain blood and lymph vessels that absorb nutrients from food as it passes through the small intestine.

In the Large Intestine

The large intestine removes water from mostly-digested food, absorbs vitamins, and turns food waste into semi-solid waste called feces.

Some parts of food, such as the cell walls of plants, cannot be absorbed by the body. Bacteria live in the large intestine that feed off of this undigested food. The bacteria produce vitamins that are absorbed by the large intestine along with most of the water in the undigested food.

The *rectum* is the last part of the large intestine. The rectum stores feces until it can be expelled. Feces pass to the outside of the body through an opening called the *anus*. It takes about 24 hours for a meal to make the full journey through a person's digestive system.

Visualize It!

10 Relate How is the structure and function of this sponge similar to that of the small intestine?

_____

_____

_____

_____

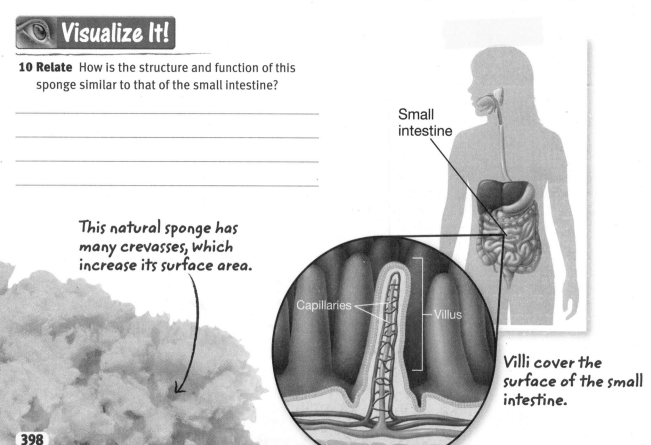

This natural sponge has many crevasses, which increase its surface area.

Small intestine

Capillaries — Villus

Villi cover the surface of the small intestine.

Toxic Waste!

What are the functions of the excretory system?

You have toxic waste in your body! As your cells perform the chemical activities that keep you alive, waste products, such as carbon dioxide and ammonia, are made. These waste products are toxic to cells. If waste builds up in a cell, homeostasis will be disrupted and the cell may die. The **excretory system** eliminates cellular wastes from the body through the lungs, skin, kidneys, and digestive system.

Waste Removal (Excretion)

After you read the text, answer the associated questions below.

To Sweat

Your skin is part of the excretory and the integumentary systems. Waste products, such as excess salts, are released through your skin when you sweat.

11 Identify Sweat releases wastes through your _____.

To Exhale

Your lungs are part of the excretory and respiratory systems. Lungs release water and toxic carbon dioxide when you exhale.

12 List Two waste products that are released when you exhale are _____ and _____.

To Produce Urine and Feces

Kidneys, part of the urinary system, remove all types of cellular waste products from your blood. Your digestive system eliminates feces from your body.

13 Identify The urinary system filters waste out of your _____.

Cleanup crew

What organs are in the urinary system?

The urinary system collects cellular waste and eliminates it from the body in the form of liquid waste. Waste products enter the urinary system through the kidneys.

Kidneys

The **kidney** is one of a pair of organs that remove waste from the blood. Inside each kidney are more than 1 million microscopic structures called **nephrons** (NEF•rahnz). Fluid is filtered from the blood into the nephron through a structure called the *glomerulus* (gloh•MEHR•yuh•luhs). Filtered blood leaves the glomerulus and circulates around the tubes that make up the nephron. These structures return valuable salts and ions to the blood. Tubes in the kidneys collect the wastes from the nephrons. Water and the wastes filtered out of the blood form a liquid known as **urine.**

Ureters

Urine forms in the kidneys. From the kidneys, urine travels through the *ureters*. The ureters are tubes that connect the kidneys to the bladder.

Bladder

The urine is transported from the kidneys to the bladder. The bladder is a saclike organ that stores urine. Voluntary muscles hold the urine until it is ready to be released. At that time, the muscles contract and squeeze urine out of the bladder.

Urethra

Urine exits the bladder through a tube called the *urethra*.

© Houghton Mifflin Harcourt Publishing Company • Image Credits: ©Victoria Smith/HMH

Active Reading

14 Identify As you read, underline the functions of the organs in the urinary system.

— Kidney

— Ureter

— Urinary bladder

— Urethra

Filtering Blood

Nephron

Unfiltered blood enters the kidney and flows into millions of tiny capillaries attached to the nephrons.

Artery

Unfiltered blood

Filtered blood

Vein

As blood flows through the capillaries, wastes are drawn out of the blood and into the nephron.

Ureter

Once the blood has been filtered, it flows back out of the kidney.

Urine is collected from all of the nephrons and then flows out of the kidney through the ureter.

Urine

Visualize It!

15 Identify After blood enters the kidneys, name the two paths the fluid takes.

_____
_____
_____
_____
_____
_____
_____
_____
_____

How does the urinary system maintain homeostasis?

Your cells have to maintain a certain level of water and salt in order to function properly. The excretory system works with the endocrine system to help maintain homeostasis and support life. Chemical messengers called *hormones* signal the kidneys to filter more or less water or salt, depending on the levels of water and salt in the body. For example, when you sweat a lot, the water content of your blood can drop. When this happens, a hormone is released that signals the kidneys to conserve more water and make less urine. When your blood has too much water, less of the hormone is released. As a result, the nephrons conserve less water, and more urine is produced by the kidneys.

Household or environmental toxins that enter the body through the skin, lungs, or mouth eventually end up in the bloodstream. When the kidneys are damaged, many toxins can accumulate in the blood. Infections can also affect the kidneys. Bacterial infections can occur when bacteria around the opening of the urethra travels up to the bladder and possibly the kidneys.

Active Reading

16 Explain How does exercise affect the balance of salt and water in your body?

_____
_____
_____
_____
_____
_____
_____
_____

Visual Summary

To complete this summary, fill in the blanks with the correct word or phrase. Then, use the answer key to check your answers. You can use this page to review the main concepts of the lesson.

The digestive system breaks down the food you eat into nutrients that provide energy and building materials for cells.

17 The two types of digestion that take place in the mouth are _____ and _____.

The excretory system removes waste from the body.

18 The _____ remove waste from the blood.

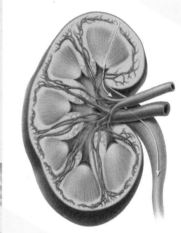

Digestion and Excretion

The digestive and excretory sytems work together to process the food that you eat.

19 To process this salad, food is broken down by the _____ _____ and wastes are removed by the _____.

Answers: 17 mechanical, chemical; 18 kidneys; 19 digestive system, excretory system

20 **Summarize** What types of wastes does the excretory system remove?

Lesson Review

Vocabulary

Fill in the blank with the term that best completes the following sentences.

1 The _____ system helps the body maintain homeostasis by giving it the nutrients it needs to perform different functions.

2 The _____ system eliminates cellular waste through the lungs, skin, and kidneys.

3 The _____ is the name for the hollow muscular organ that stores urine.

Key Concepts

4 Compare What is the difference between mechanical digestion and chemical digestion in the mouth?

_____

_____

_____

_____

5 Describe Starting with the mouth, describe the pathway that food takes through the digestive system.

_____

_____

_____

_____

6 Explain How does the circulatory system interact with the digestive system?

_____

_____

_____

_____

7 Identify Where does urine go after it exits the kidneys?

_____

_____

_____

8 Summarize How do kidneys work with other body systems to maintain equilibrium through homeostasis and support life?

_____

_____

_____

_____

Use the diagram to answer the following question.

9 Apply Identify the organs numbered below.

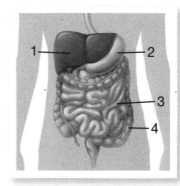

_____

_____

Critical Thinking

10 Relate Why would damaged kidneys affect your health?

_____

_____

_____

11 Infer Suppose a person has a small intestine that has fewer villi than normal. Would the person most likely be overweight or underweight? Explain.

_____

_____

_____

_____

My Notes

The Nervous and Endocrine Systems

ESSENTIAL QUESTION

How do the nervous and endocrine systems work?

By the end of this lesson, you should be able to relate the structures of the nervous and endocrine systems to their functions in the human body.

7.LS1.5

This sky diver can sense his surroundings and feel the rush of excitement with the help of his nervous and endocrine systems.

✋ **Lesson Labs**

Quick Labs
• Negative Feedback
• Measuring Reaction Time

Exploration Lab
• Mapping Sensory Receptors

 Engage Your Brain

1 Predict Check T or F to show whether you think each statement is true or false.

T   F

☐   ☐   The central nervous system allows us to sense the environment.

☐   ☐   The endocrine system functions by sending chemical signals.

☐   ☐   The spinal cord is part of the peripheral nervous system.

☐   ☐   The endocrine system helps regulate our blood sugar after we eat a meal.

2 Describe Think about a situation that makes you feel very nervous or anxious. Describe how this makes you feel inside. What do you think is going on in your body?

_____

_____

_____

_____

_____

_____

 Active Reading

3 Apply You can often understand the meaning of a word if you use it in a sentence. Use the following definition to write your own sentence that has the word *gland*.

Definition
<u>gland</u>: a group of cells that make special chemicals for the body

gland:

_____

_____

_____

_____

_____

Vocabulary Terms

• nervous system   • dendrite
• brain   • endocrine system
• spinal cord   • hormone
• neuron   • gland
• axon

4 Apply As you learn the definition of each vocabulary term in this lesson, create your own definition or sketch to help you remember the meaning of the term.

Brainiac!

What is the function of the nervous system?

The **nervous system**, another major subsystem of the body, is made of the structures that control the actions and reactions of the body in response to stimuli from the environment. Your nervous system has two parts: the central nervous system (CNS) and the peripheral (puh•RIFF•uh•rahl) nervous system (PNS). The nervous system works with all other systems in the body to maintain equilibrium and support life.

The CNS Processes Information

The brain and the spinal cord make up the CNS. The **brain** is the body's central command organ. It constantly receives impulses from all over the body. Your **spinal cord** allows your brain to communicate with the rest of your body. Your nervous system is mostly made up of specialized cells that send and receive electrical signals.

The PNS Connects the CNS to Muscles and Organs

Your PNS connects your CNS to the rest of your body. The PNS has two main parts—the sensory part and the motor part. Many processes that the brain controls happen automatically—you have no control over them. These processes are called *involuntary*. For example, you could not stop your heart from beating even if you tried. However, some of the actions of your brain you can control—these are *voluntary*. Moving your arm is a voluntary action.

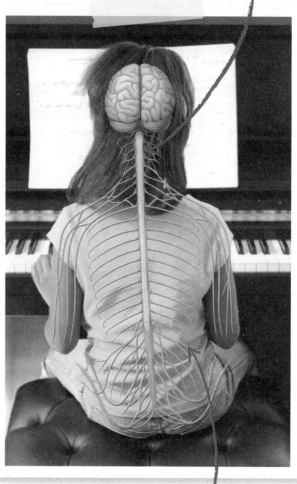

The CNS is shown in yellow.

The PNS is shown in green.

Parts of the CNS

_____

and _____

The CNS and PNS are both made of

Parts of the PNS

_____

and _____

5 Compare Fill in the Venn diagram to compare and contrast the structure of the CNS and the PNS.

What are the parts of the CNS?

The CNS is made up of the brain and the spinal cord.

The Brain

The three main areas of the brain are the cerebrum, the cerebellum, and the brain stem. The largest part of the brain is the cerebrum. The cerebrum is where you think and problem-solve, and where most of your memories are stored. It controls voluntary movements and allows you to sense touch, light, sound, odors, taste, pain, heat, and cold. The second largest part of your brain is the cerebellum. It processes information from your body. This allows the brain to keep track of your body's position and coordinate movements. The brain stem connects your brain to your spinal cord. The medulla is part of the brain stem. It controls involuntary processes, such as blood pressure, body temperature, heart rate, and involuntary breathing.

6 Identify List a function of each part of the brain shown here.

Cerebrum

_____

_____

_____

Cerebellum

_____

_____

_____

Brain stem

_____

_____

The Spinal Cord

The spinal cord is made of bundles of nerves. A *nerve* is a collection of nerve cell extensions bundled together with blood vessels and connective tissue. Nerves are everywhere in your body. The spinal cord is surrounded by protective bones called *vertebrae*.

Special cells in your skin and muscles carry sensory information to the spinal cord. The spinal cord carries these impulses to the brain. The brain interprets these impulses as warmth, pain, or other sensations and sends information back to the spinal cord. Different cells in the spinal cord then send impulses to the rest of the body to create a response.

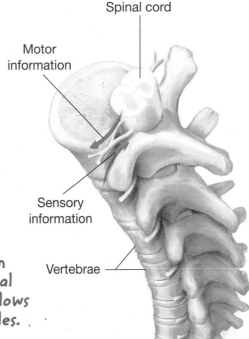

Spinal cord

Motor information

Sensory information

Vertebrae

Sensory information (red) flows in from the environment to the spinal cord. Motor information (blue) flows out from the spinal cord to muscles.

You've Got Nerves!

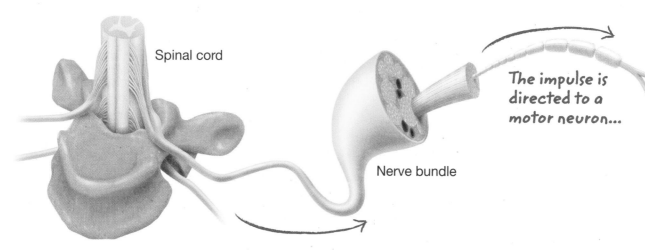

Spinal cord

The impulse is directed to a motor neuron...

Nerve bundle

If you notice that your shoe is untied, your brain interprets this information and sends an impulse down the spinal cord.

How do signals move through the nervous system?

Your nervous system works by receiving information from the environment and translating that information into electrical signals. Those electrical signals are sent from the brain to the rest of the body by special cells called *neurons*. A **neuron** is a cell that moves messages in the form of fast-moving electrical energy. These electrical messages are called *impulses*.

Signals move through the central and peripheral nervous systems with the help of glial (GLEE•uhl) cells. Glial cells do not transmit nerve impulses, but they protect and support neurons. Without glial cells, neurons would not work properly. Your brain has about 100 billion neurons, but there are about 10 to 50 times more glial cells in your brain.

Through Sensory and Motor Neurons

Neurons carry information from the body to the brain, and carry instructions from the brain back to the rest of the body. The two groups of neurons are sensory neurons and motor neurons.

Sensory neurons gather information from in and around your body. They then move this information to the brain. Motor neurons move impulses from the brain and spinal cord to other parts of the body. For example, when you are hot, motor neurons move messages from your brain to your sweat glands to tell the sweat glands to make sweat. Sweating cools your body.

🖉 **Active Reading**

7 Identify As you read, underline the special types of neurons that receive and send messages.

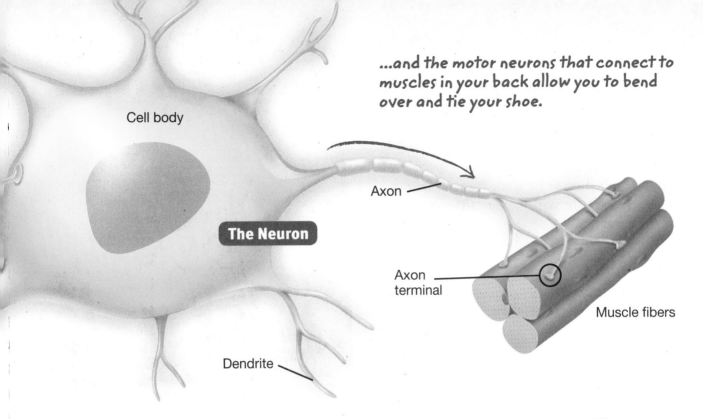

Cell body

...and the motor neurons that connect to muscles in your back allow you to bend over and tie your shoe.

Axon

The Neuron

Axon terminal

Muscle fibers

Dendrite

What are the parts of a neuron?

A neuron is made up of a large region called the *cell body,* a long extension called the *axon*, and short branches called *dendrites*. At the end of the axon is the *axon terminal.*

Like other cells, a neuron's cell body has a nucleus and organelles. But neurons have other structures that allow them to communicate with other cells. A **dendrite** (DEHN•dryt) is a usually short, branched extension of the cell body. A neuron may have one, two, or many dendrites. Neurons with many dendrites can receive impulses from thousands of cells at a time. The cell body gathers information from the dendrites and creates an impulse.

Impulses are carried away from the cell body by extensions of the neuron, called an **axon**. A neuron has only one axon, and they can be very short or quite long. Some long axons extend almost 1 m from your lower back to your toes! Impulses move in one direction along the axon.

At the end of an axon is the axon terminal, where a signal is changed from an electrical signal to a chemical signal. This chemical signal, called a *neurotransmitter,* is released into the gap between the neuron and other cells.

Visualize It!

8 Apply In the boxes below, fill in the appropriate neuron parts, structures, or functions.

NEURON PART	STRUCTURE	FUNCTION
Cell body	region containing nucleus and organelles	
	branches of the cell body	gathers information from other cells
Axon		sends impulse away from cell body
	end of an axon	changes electrical signal to chemical signal

That Makes Sense!

What are the main senses?

The body senses the environment with specialized structures called *sensory organs*. These structures include the eyes, the skin, the ears, the mouth, and the nose.

9 Imagine If you were at this amusement park, what do you think you would see, hear, smell, taste, and feel?

_____

_____

An amusement park is full of sensory information! How do we sense it all?

Sight

Your eye allows you to see the size, shape, motion, and color of objects around you. The front of the eye is covered by a clear membrane called the *cornea*. Light from an object passes through an opening called the *pupil*. Light hits the eye's lens, an oval-shaped piece of clear, curved material. Eye muscles change the shape of the lens to focus light onto the retina. The *retina* (RET•nuh) is a layer of light-sensitive photoreceptor cells that change light into electrical impulses. These cells, called *rods* and *cones*, generate nerve impulses that are sent to the brain.

Rays form an upside-down image on the retina at the back of the eye. This image is translated by the brain.

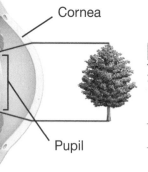

Lens

Cornea

Retina

Pupil

Light enters the eye through the lens. Light rays are bent by the cornea.

Visualize It!

10 Identify What part of the eye focuses light on to the retina?

_____

_____

Touch

You feel a tap on your shoulder. The tap produces impulses in sensory receptors on your shoulder. These impulses travel to your brain. Once the impulses reach your brain, they create an awareness called a *sensation*. In this case, the sensation is that of your shoulder being touched. The skin has different kinds of receptors that detect pressure, temperature, pain, and vibration.

Hearing

Ears pick up sound wave vibrations. These sound waves push air particles, creating a wave of sound energy. The sensory cells of your ears turn sound waves into electrical impulses. These electrical impulses then travel to your brain. Each ear has an outer, a middle, and an inner portion. Sound waves reaching the outer ear are funneled toward the middle ear. There, the waves make the eardrum vibrate. The *eardrum* is a thin membrane separating the outer ear from the middle ear. The vibrating eardrum makes three tiny bones in the middle ear vibrate. The last of these bones vibrates against the *cochlea* (KOH•klee•uh), a fluid-filled organ of the inner ear. Inside the cochlea, the vibrations make waves in the fluid. Sensory receptors called *hair cells* move about in the fluid. Movement of the hair cells causes neurons in the cochlea to send electrical impulses. These impulses travel to the brain via the auditory nerve and are interpreted as sound.

The ears also help you maintain balance. Special fluid-filled canals in the inner ear are filled with hair cells that respond to changes in head orientation. These hair cells then send signals to the brain about the position of the head with respect to gravity.

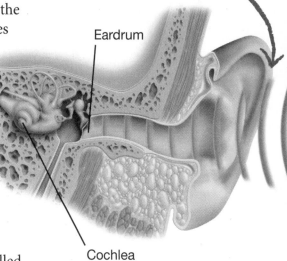

Sound waves enter the ear and cause the eardrum to vibrate. The vibrations are translated by receptors.

Eardrum

Cochlea

Taste

Your tongue is covered with taste buds. These taste buds contain clusters of *taste cells* that respond to signals in dissolved molecules in food. Taste cells react to five basic tastes: sweet, sour, salty, bitter, and savory. Your sense of taste can protect you from eating something that could be harmful.

Smell

The nose is your sense organ for smell. Receptors for smell are located in the upper part of your nasal cavity. Sensory receptors called *olfactory cells* react to chemicals in the air. These molecules dissolve in the moist lining of the nasal cavity and trigger an impulse in the receptors. The nerve impulses are sent to the brain, where they are interpreted as an odor. Your senses of taste and smell work together to allow you to taste a variety of food flavors. Both senses detect chemical cues in the environment.

Olfactory cells

11 Apply If you have a cold that causes congestion in your sinuses, how might that affect your sense of smell?

_____

_____

_____

_____

Molecules in the air enter your nose. There, they bind to receptors in the top of your nasal cavity.

Keep Your Cool!

What is the function of the endocrine system?

Your **endocrine system**, one of the most important subsystems in the body, controls body functions and helps maintain homeostasis by using hormones. These hormones help to regulate the body's equilibrium and help to support a healthy life. A **hormone** is a chemical messenger made in one cell or tissue that causes a change in another cell or tissue in a different part of the body. Hormones are produced by endocrine glands or tissues. A **gland** is a group of cells that make special chemicals for your body. Unlike direct signals of the nervous system, the signals sent by the endocrine system are indirect because they cycle through the whole body.

Active Reading

12 Identify As you read, underline the structure which allows hormones to affect only certain cells.

How do hormones work?

Hormones travel through the bloodstream. They travel from the endocrine gland where they are made and can reach every cell in the body. However, hormones affect only the cells that have specific *receptors*. Each hormone has its own receptor and affects only cells that have that receptor. These cells are called *target cells*. Many cells throughout the body have the same receptors, so hormones are able to perform many functions at the same time in different cells.

Visualize It!

13 Apply Explain the difference between an endocrine cell and a target cell.

_____

_____

When you are surprised, a hormone called adrenaline makes you more alert.

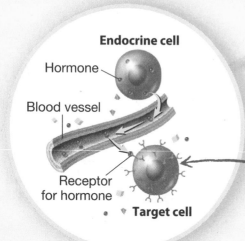

- Endocrine cell
- Hormone
- Blood vessel
- Receptor for hormone
- Target cell

Hormones are released from an endocrine cell and travel through the bloodstream to bind to a receptor on a target cell. Sometimes a target cell is very far away!

What glands make up the endocrine system?

Your body has several endocrine glands or tissues that make up the endocrine system.

- Your pituitary gland is very important because it secretes hormones that affect other glands. It also stimulates growth and sexual development.
- The hypothalamus is a gland in the brain that controls the release of hormones from the pituitary gland.
- The pineal gland, also in the brain, produces hormones essential in the control of sleep, aging, reproduction, and body temperature.
- Hormones from the thyroid control your metabolism.
- The parathyroid gland controls calcium levels in the blood.
- Hormones made in the reproductive organs (ovaries or testes) control reproduction.
- Other endocrine glands include the pancreas and adrenal glands. The pancreas regulates blood sugar levels and the adrenal glands control the body's fight or flight response in dangerous situations.

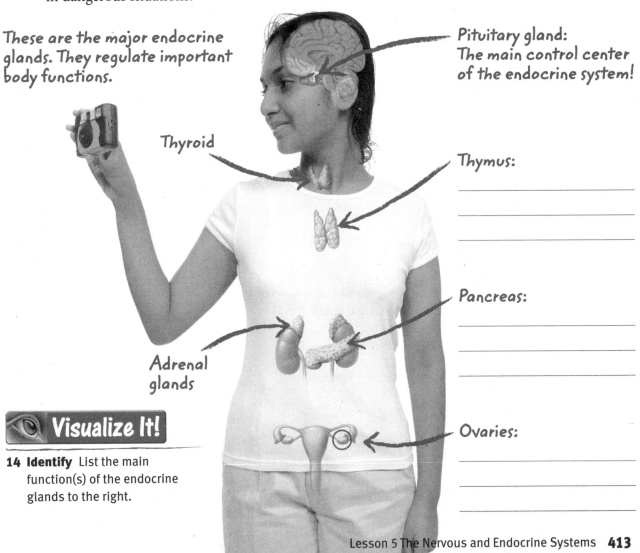

These are the major endocrine glands. They regulate important body functions.

Thyroid

Adrenal glands

Pituitary gland:
The main control center of the endocrine system!

Thymus:
_____
_____
_____

Pancreas:
_____
_____
_____

Ovaries:
_____
_____
_____

Visualize It!

14 Identify List the main function(s) of the endocrine glands to the right.

Feed←Back

How are hormone levels controlled?

The endocrine system keeps the body's internal environment in homeostasis. It does this by increasing or decreasing the amount of hormones in the bloodstream, some of which may have opposite effects on body cells. Such a process is called a feedback mechanism. A *feedback mechanism* is a cycle of events in which information from one step controls or affects a previous step.

By Feedback Mechanisms

There are two types of feedback, positive and negative. In negative feedback, the effects of a hormone in the body cause the release of that hormone to be turned down. For example, when you eat food, your blood sugar levels go up. Insulin is released and blood sugar levels are lowered. Once this happens, the lower blood sugar levels tell the pancreas to stop releasing insulin. In other words, when the proper level of blood sugar is reached, the insulin-releasing cells are turned off.

In positive feedback, the effects of a hormone stimulate the release of more of that hormone. For example, the hormone oxytocin stimulates contractions of the uterus. When a fetus matures in the uterus, both it and the mother produce oxytocin. The oxytocin stimulates contractions, and these contractions stimulate more oxytocin to be released. The contractions expel a baby from the mother's uterus at birth.

Active Reading

15 Compare Describe the difference between negative and positive feedback.

_____

_____

_____

_____

_____

Negative Feedback

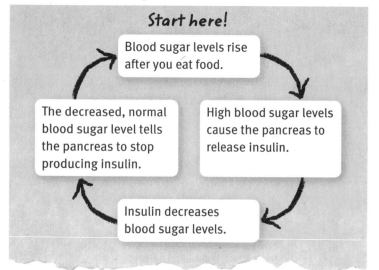

Start here!

Blood sugar levels rise after you eat food.

High blood sugar levels cause the pancreas to release insulin.

Insulin decreases blood sugar levels.

The decreased, normal blood sugar level tells the pancreas to stop producing insulin.

In negative feedback, hormone levels are kept from rising too high.

Positive Feedback

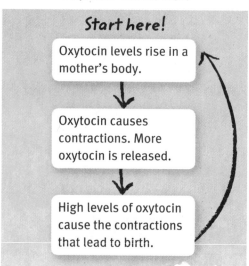

Start here!

Oxytocin levels rise in a mother's body.

Oxytocin causes contractions. More oxytocin is released.

High levels of oxytocin cause the contractions that lead to birth.

In positive feedback, the level of hormones continues to rise.

What are disorders of the endocrine and nervous systems?

The endocrine system and nervous system are both responsible for sending messages around our bodies. If a problem developed with one or more of these systems, other systems of the body would need to adjust to compensate for this loss.

Hormone Imbalances

Disorders of the endocrine system occur when an endocrine gland makes too much or not enough of a hormone. For example, a person whose pancreas does not make enough insulin has a condition called type 1 diabetes. This condition causes an imbalance of the blood sugar. A person who has diabetes may need daily injections of insulin to keep blood sugar levels within safe limits. Some patients receive their insulin automatically from a small pump worn next to the body. New technology allows people with type 1 diabetes to intake insulin using an inhaler.

Think Outside the Book

16 Compare Many systems you use every day send messages, such as e-mail, a thermostat, and TV remote controls. Research how one of these systems sends and receives messages. Make a chart to compare this system to the endocrine system.

17 Describe How does the insulin pump help a person with type 1 diabetes maintain equilibrium, or balance?

_____

_____

_____

_____

_____

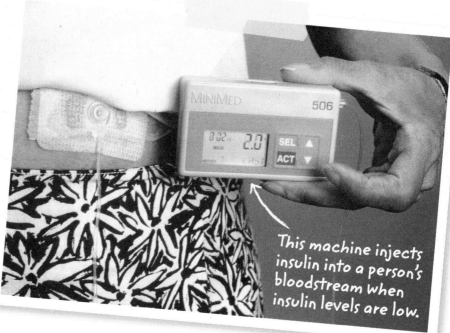

This machine injects insulin into a person's bloodstream when insulin levels are low.

Nerve Damage

Disorders of the nervous system include Parkinson's disease, multiple sclerosis, and spinal cord injury. In Parkinson's disease, the cells that control movement are damaged. Multiple sclerosis affects the brain's ability to send signals to the rest of the body.

A spinal cord injury may block information to and from the brain. For example, impulses coming from the feet and legs may be blocked. People with such an injury cannot sense pain in their legs. The person would also not be able to move his or her legs, because impulses from the brain could not get past the injury site.

Visual Summary

To complete this summary, fill in the blank to answer the question. Then, use the key below to check your answers. You can use this page to review the main concepts of the lesson.

The nervous system gathers information and responds by sending electrical signals.

18 Nerve cells called _____ carry electrical messages called _____.

The endocrine system controls conditions in your body by sending chemical messages.

19 Hormones have specific actions by attaching to _____ on target cells.

Sending Signals

Hormones are controlled by feedback mechanisms.

20 _____ feedback is when higher levels of a hormone turn off the production of that hormone.

Negative Feedback
Start here!

Blood sugar levels rise after you eat food.

High blood sugar causes the pancreas to release insulin.

Insulin decreases blood sugar levels.

The decreased, normal blood sugar level tells the pancreas to stop producing insulin.

21 **Apply** Describe how both your nervous and endocrine systems would be involved if you walked into a surprise party and were truly surprised.

Lesson Review

Vocabulary

Use a term from the section to complete each sentence below.

1 The _____ is made up of the brain and spinal cord.

2 Glands in the _____ send messages to target cells.

3 Use *gland* and *hormone* in the same sentence.

_____

_____

_____

4 Use *hormone* and *feedback mechanism* in the same sentence.

_____

_____

Key Concepts

5 Identify Describe the function of the PNS and the CNS.

_____

_____

_____

6 Apply What are the parts of a neuron?

_____

_____

_____

7 Identify How are the messages of the endocrine system moved around the body?

_____

_____

_____

8 Identify What is the main sense organ for each of the five senses?

_____

_____

_____

Critical Thinking

The images below show how an eye responds to different light levels. Use the image to answer the following question.

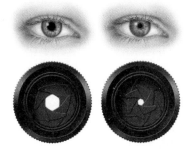

9 Interpret The pupil opens and closes automatically in response to light. What part of your nervous system controls this response?

_____

10 Infer Explain whether this is a voluntary or involuntary action.

_____

_____

_____

_____

11 Predict How would your body be affected if your pituitary gland was not working properly?

_____

_____

_____

_____

My Notes

Lesson 6

The Reproductive System

ESSENTIAL QUESTION

How does your reproductive system work?

By the end of this lesson, you should be able to relate the structure of the reproductive system to its function in the human body.

7.LS1.5

Many pregnant women do exercises, such as yoga or other stretches, to stay healthy as their baby develops.

© Houghton Mifflin Harcourt Publishing Company • Image Credits: (bkgd) ©Blend Images/Alamy

 Engage Your Brain

1 Predict Have you met a woman who was pregnant? Write a short answer describing what type of development you think is going on inside a pregnant woman.

_____

_____

_____

_____

_____

_____

_____

2 Apply Name five things that have changed about you from your fifth to your tenth birthday.

_____

_____

_____

_____

_____

_____

_____

 Active Reading

3 Explain You may be familiar with the eggs that farmers collect from chickens. Females of many species, including humans, produce eggs as part of the reproductive cycle. How do you think a human egg is similar to a chicken egg? How do you think they are different?

_____

_____

_____

_____

_____

_____

Vocabulary Terms

- sperm
- testes
- penis
- egg
- ovary
- uterus

- vagina
- embryo
- placenta
- umbilical cord
- fetus

4 Apply As you learn the definition of each vocabulary term in this lesson, create your own definition or sketch to help you remember the meaning of the term.

Reproduction

What are the main functions of the male reproductive system?

The male reproductive system, a subsystem of the human body, functions to produce sperm and deliver sperm to the female reproductive system. **Sperm** are the male cells that are used for reproduction. Each sperm cell carries 23 chromosomes, half of the chromosomes of other body cells. The male reproductive system also produces hormones.

Hormones are chemical messengers that control many important body functions, such as growth, development, and sex-cell production. The **testes** (singular, *testis*) are the main organs of the male reproductive system. These organs produce *testosterone*, the male sex hormone. Testosterone causes male characteristics to develop, such as facial hair and a deep voice.

The testes also make sperm. After sperm mature, they are stored in the *epididymis* (EH•puh•DIH•duh•miss). They leave the epididymis through a tube called the *vas deferens* and mix with fluids from several glands. This mixture of sperm and fluids is called *semen*. To leave the body, semen passes through the *urethra*, the tube that runs through the penis. The **penis** is the organ that delivers semen into the female reproductive system.

Active Reading

5 Identify As you read, underline the functions of the main hormones in the male and female reproductive systems.

Male Reproductive System

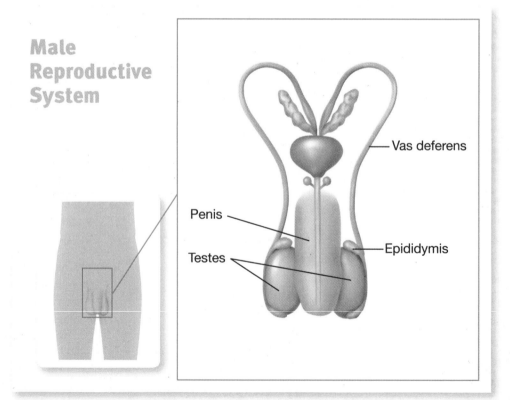

Vas deferens

Penis

Epididymis

Testes

What are the main functions of the female reproductive system?

The female reproductive system, another subsystem of the body, produces hormones and eggs, and provides a place to nourish a developing human. An **egg** is the female sex cell. Like sperm, egg cells have 23 chromosomes, only half the number of other body cells.

The female reproductive system produces the sex hormones *estrogen* and *progesterone*. These hormones control the development of female characteristics, such as breasts and wider hips. They also regulate the development and release of eggs, and they prepare the body for pregnancy.

An **ovary** is the reproductive organ that produces eggs. At sexual maturity, females have hundreds of thousands of immature eggs in their ovaries. Eggs are produced through the process of meiosis. During a female's lifetime, usually about 400 of her eggs will mature and be released from the ovaries.

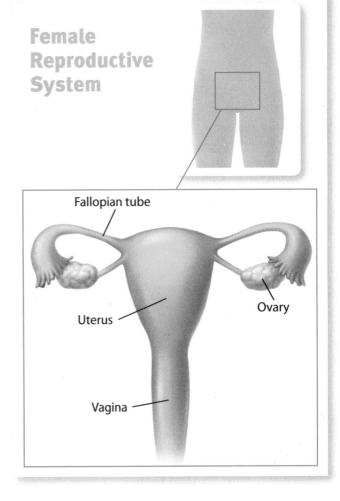

Female Reproductive System

Fallopian tube

Uterus

Ovary

Vagina

---

6 Summarize Fill in the chart below to summarize the structures of the male and female reproductive systems.

Sex	Sex cell	Organ that produces sex cell	Other reproductive organs
Male			
Female			

---

7 Contrast What makes sperm cells and egg cells different from almost all other types of body cells?

_____

_____

_____

Fertile ground

How are eggs released?

Active Reading

8 Summarize As you read, underline the path an egg takes through the female reproductive system.

A woman's reproductive system goes through changes that produce an egg, release the egg, and prepare the body for pregnancy. These changes are called the *menstrual cycle* and usually take about one month. About halfway through the cycle, an egg is released from the ovary. The egg travels through one of the *fallopian tubes,* a pair of tubes that connect each ovary to the uterus. The **uterus** is the organ in which a fertilized egg develops into a baby. When a baby is born, it passes through the **vagina**, the canal between the uterus and the outside of the body.

If an egg is not fertilized, it is shed with the lining of the uterus. The monthly discharge of blood and tissue from the uterus is called *menstruation*. When menstruation ends, the lining of the uterus thickens and the cycle begins again.

9 Number Place a number in the circles to order the steps of the menstrual cycle.

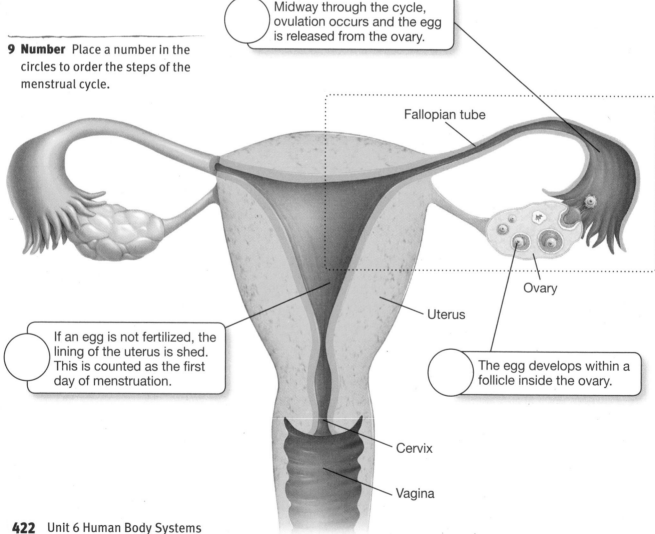

Midway through the cycle, ovulation occurs and the egg is released from the ovary.

Fallopian tube

If an egg is not fertilized, the lining of the uterus is shed. This is counted as the first day of menstruation.

The egg develops within a follicle inside the ovary.

Ovary

Uterus

Cervix

Vagina

422 Unit 6 Human Body Systems

How are eggs fertilized?

When sperm enter the female reproductive system, a few hundred make it through the uterus into a fallopian tube. There, the sperm release enzymes that help dissolve the egg's outer covering.

When a sperm enters an egg, the egg's membrane changes to stop other sperm from entering. During fertilization, the egg and sperm combine to form one cell. Once cell division occurs, the fertilized egg becomes an **embryo**. The genetic material from the father and the mother combine and a unique individual begins to develop. Usually, only one sperm gets through the outer covering of the egg. Sometimes, the fertilized eggs splits, resulting in identical twins; sometimes, two eggs are fertilized by two sperm, resulting in fraternal twins. However, if more than one sperm enters the egg, which is rare, it is called *polyspermy* and usually results in the egg not surviving. After fertilization, the embryo travels from the fallopian tube to the uterus over five to six days, and attaches to the thickened and nutrient-rich lining of the uterus.

Inquiry

10 Infer Sometimes more than one egg is released at a time. What do you think would happen if two eggs were released and both were fertilized? Explain your answer.

_____

_____

_____

_____

_____

11 Summarize Determine what happens if an egg is fertilized and if it is not fertilized, and fill in both of the boxes.

Was the egg fertilized?

yes →

no →

Steps of Fertilization

③ The embryo implants into the lining of the uterus.

② The egg is fertilized in the fallopian tube by a sperm.

① The egg is released from the ovary.

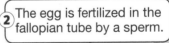

Happy Birthday!

What are the stages of pregnancy?

A normal pregnancy lasts about nine months. These nine months are broken down into three 3-month periods, called *trimesters*.

Active Reading **12 Identify** Underline three things that take place during each trimester.

First Trimester

Soon after implantation, the placenta begins to grow. The **placenta** is a network of blood vessels that provides the embryo with oxygen and nutrients from the mother's blood and carries away waste. The embryo is surrounded by the *amnion*, a sac filled with fluid that protects the embryo. The embryo connects to the placenta by the **umbilical cord**. After week 10, the embryo is called a **fetus**. Many organs such as the heart, liver and brain form. Arms and legs, as well as fingers and toes, also form during this trimester.

Second Trimester

During the second trimester, joints and bones start to form. The fetus's muscles grow stronger. As a result, the fetus can make a fist and begins to move. The fetus triples its size within a month and its brain begins to grow rapidly. Eventually, the fetus can make faces. The fetus starts to make movements the mother can feel. Toward the end of the trimester, the fetus can breathe and swallow.

Third Trimester

During the third trimester, the fetus can respond to light and sound outside the uterus. The brain develops further, and the organs become fully functional. Bones grow and harden, and the lungs completely develop. By week 32, the fetus's eyes can open and close. By the third trimester the fetus can also dream. After 36 weeks, the fetus is almost ready to be born. A full-term pregnancy usually lasts about 40 weeks.

How are babies born?

As birth begins, the mother's uterus starts a series of muscular contractions called *labor*. Usually, these contractions push the fetus through the mother's vagina, and the baby is born. The umbilical cord is tied and cut. All that will remain of the place where the umbilical cord was attached is the navel. Finally, the mother pushes out the placenta, and labor is complete.

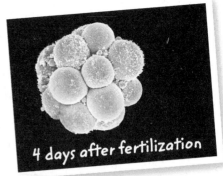

4 days after fertilization

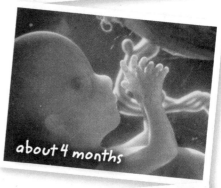

about 4 months

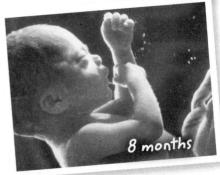

8 months

What changes occur during infancy and childhood?

Development during infancy and childhood includes gaining control of skeletal muscles and learning to speak. Generally, infancy is the stage from birth to age 2. During infancy, babies grow quickly and baby teeth appear. Baby teeth are replaced by permanent teeth. The nervous system develops, and babies become more coordinated and start to walk. Many babies begin to say words by age 1. During this time, the body is growing rapidly. Childhood lasts from age 2 to puberty. Children learn to speak fluently, and their muscles become more coordinated, allowing them to run, jump, and perform other activities.

What changes occur during adolescence and adulthood?

The stage from puberty to adulthood is *adolescence*. During adolescence, a person's reproductive system becomes mature. In most boys, puberty takes place between the ages of 9 and 16. During this time, the young male's body becomes more muscular, his voice becomes deeper, and body and facial hair appear. In most girls, puberty takes place between the ages of 9 and 15. During this time, the amount of fat in the hips and thighs increases, the breasts enlarge, body hair appears, and menstruation begins.

During adulthood, a person reaches physical and emotional maturity. A person is considered a young adult from about age 20 to age 40. Beginning around age 30, changes associated with aging begin. The aging process continues into middle age (between 40 and 65 years old). During this time, hair may turn gray, athletic abilities decline, and skin may wrinkle. A person older than 65 years is considered an older adult. Exercising and eating well-balanced diets help people stay healthy as they grow older.

Do the Math

Everyone grows as they age, but does the amount you grow change as you get older?

Sample Problem

To calculate growth rate, divide the difference in height by the difference in age. For example, the growth rate between the ages of one and five for the girl shown below is:

$$(102 \text{ cm} - 71 \text{ cm}) \div (5 \text{ years} - 1 \text{ year}) = 8 \text{ cm/year}$$

You Try It

13 Calculate Determine the growth rate for the girl between the ages of 14 and 19. Is the amount of growth greater between ages 1 and 5 or between ages 14 and 19?

14 years, 160 cm

19 years, 163 cm

5 years, 102 cm

1 year, 71 cm

Think Outside the Book

14 Research Learning a new language can be easier for young children. This phenomenon is known as a "critical period." Research critical periods for language and write a short report describing what you learned.

Infections

What causes STIs?

Sexually transmitted infections (STIs) are infections that are passed from one person to another during sexual contact. STIs can be caused by viruses, bacteria, or parasites.

Active Reading **15 Identify** As you read, underline the symptoms of each STI listed below.

Viruses

Acquired immunodeficiency syndrome (AIDS) is caused by the human immunodeficiency virus (HIV). This virus infects and destroys immune system cells. As a result, people with AIDS show symptoms of many other illnesses that the immune system of a healthy person usually can fight. Most HIV infections are transmitted through sexual contact.

A much more common, but less deadly, viral STI is genital herpes. Most people with herpes do not have symptoms, but some individuals develop painful sores.

The human papillomavirus (paa•puh•LOH•muh•vy•russ) (HPV) and hepatitis B are two other common viral STIs that are often symptomless. Because some people do not have symptoms, they do not know they are spreading the virus. In the case of hepatitis B, the virus attacks the liver. This can lead to death.

Bacteria and Parasites

A common bacterial STI in the United States is chlamydia. Symptoms include a burning sensation when urinating or a discharge from the vagina or penis. The symptoms for gonorrhea, another bacterial STI, are similar to the symptoms of chlamydia. Both of these infections can be treated with antibiotics. Another STI, syphilis, is caused by the bacterium *Treponema pallidum*. Its symptoms, such as swollen glands, rash and fever, are hard to distinguish from those of other diseases.

Some STIs are caused by parasites. For example, the STI trichomoniasis is caused by the protozoan *Trichomonas vaginalis*. It is the most common curable STI for young women. Symptoms are more common in women and may include a genital discharge and pain during urination. Another parasitic STI is a pubic lice infestation. Pubic lice are tiny insects that feed on blood. The most common symptom of a pubic lice infection is genital itching.

16 Label For each photo below, label the type of infection as a virus, a bacterium, or a parasite.

Chlamydia cell

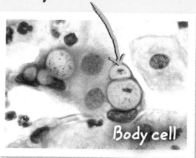

Body cell

Herpes-infected immune cells

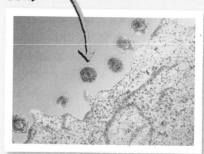

Syphilis cell

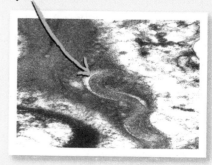

Seeing Double

Multiple births occur when two or more babies are carried during the same pregnancy. In humans, the most common type of multiple births occurs when the mother gives birth to two children, or twins. About 3% of all births in the United States result in twins.

Fraternal Siblings

Fraternal siblings form when two sperm fertilize two or more separate eggs. Fraternal siblings can be the same gender or different genders and are as different genetically as any ordinary siblings.

Identical Twins

Identical twins form when a single sperm fertilizes a single egg. The developing embryo then divides in two. Identical twins are always the same gender and are genetically identical.

Triplets

While twinning is the most common type of multiple birth, other multiples still occur. About 0.1% of all births are triplets.

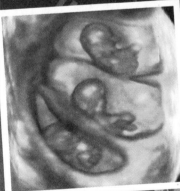

Extend

Inquiry

17 Infer Based on how identical twins form, infer how identical triplets could develop.

18 Research Describe some shared behavioral traits or language between twins and give an example.

19 Create Illustrate how fertilized eggs develop into fraternal triplets. You may choose to make a poster, make a model, or write a short story.

Visual Summary

To complete this summary, circle the correct word. Then, use the key below to check your answers. You can use this page to review the main concepts of the lesson.

The male reproductive system makes hormones and sperm cells.

20 Sperm are produced in the penis / testes.

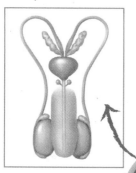

The female reproductive system makes hormones and egg cells, and protects a developing baby if fertilization occurs.

21 Eggs are produced in the ovary / vagina.

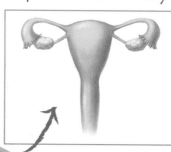

Reproduction and Development

A baby goes through many changes as it develops into an adult.

22 During pregnancy, a growing baby gets oxygen and nourishment from an organ called the embryo / placenta.

Sexually transmitted infections (STIs) are caused by viruses, bacteria, and parasites.

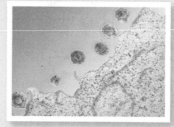

23 STIs are spread through the air / sexual contact.

Answers: 20 testes; 21 ovary; 22 placenta; 23 sexual contact

24 **Applying Concepts** Why does the egg's covering change after a sperm has entered the egg?

Lesson Review

Vocabulary

1 Use *uterus* and *vagina* in the same sentence.

_____

_____

_____

2 Use *sperm* and *egg* in the same sentence.

_____

_____

_____

Key Concepts

3 Compare Compare the functions of the male and female reproductive systems.

_____

_____

_____

_____

_____

4 Summarize Summarize the processes of fertilization and implantation.

_____

_____

_____

_____

5 Identify Explain what causes STIs and how they are transmitted.

_____

_____

_____

_____

_____

6 Explain How does a fetus get nourishment up until the time it is born?

_____

_____

Use the graph to answer the following question.

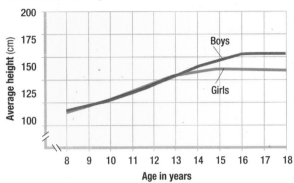

Growth Rates in Boys and Girls

Source: Centers for Disease Control and Prevention

7 Interpret At what age is the difference between the average height of boys and girls greatest? Estimate this difference to the nearest centimeter.

_____

_____

Critical Thinking

8 Predict How might cancer of the testes affect a man's ability to make sperm?

_____

_____

_____

_____

9 Apply Explain the difference beween identical twins and fraternal twins. Include in your answer how they form and their genetic makeup.

_____

_____

_____

_____

_____

_____

My Notes

Engineering and Life Science

ESSENTIAL QUESTION

How is engineering related to life science?

By the end of this lesson, you should be able to describe how organisms can be used in engineering, and how engineering can help organisms.

7.ETS2.1

Studying human movement helps engineers build robots like this one.

Lesson Labs

Quick Labs
• Natural and Artificial Insulation
• Yeast Gas Production

Engage Your Brain

1 Predict Check T or F to show whether you think each sentence below about technology and life science is correct.

T F

☐ ☐ Technology is used to help people with disabilities.

☐ ☐ All bacteria are harmful to humans.

☐ ☐ Animals can be a product of engineering.

☐ ☐ We cannot learn about engineering by observing nature.

☐ ☐ Living things can inspire new technology.

2 Describe Write a caption for this photograph that explains the relationship between this athlete and technology.

_____

_____

_____

_____

_____

Active Reading

3 Synthesize You can often define an unknown word if you know the meaning of its word parts. Use the word parts and sentence below to make an educated guess about the meaning of the word *biomimicry*.

Word part	Meaning
bio-	life
mimic	imitate

Example sentence
Engineers used biomimicry to build robots that move like spiders.

biomimicry:

_____

_____

_____

Vocabulary Terms

• technology • engineering

4 Identify As you read, place a question mark next to any words that you do not understand. When you finish reading the lesson, go back and review the text that you marked. If the information is still confusing, consult a classmate or teacher.

Living Technology

How are organisms used as technology?

Technology is the application of science for practical purposes. When people talk about technology, they are talking about products, processes, and systems. Technology can be a familiar, simple object, like a hammer, or a complex machine, such as a satellite. Did you know that a living organism can also be a type of technology? *Biotechnology* is the use of living things to make products or perform tasks.

To Make Products

 **5 Identify** As you read this page, underline examples of products manufactured with the help of living organisms.

Living organisms help us make many of the products we use. For example, bakers use a microorganism, yeast, to make bread. Gas bubbles produced by the yeast give the bread a fluffy texture when it is baked. Many types of cheese get their unique flavors, odors, and textures from bacteria and fungi that cheese makers add to milk or cream. Other kinds of bacteria produce compounds that people use to make some life-saving medicines, including insulin and many antibiotics.

Visualize It!

6 Label Look at the following photographs. What two ways are microorganisms used in the making of cheese?

_____

_____

_____

_____

Cheese production begins with large vats of milk to which bacteria are added to help the milk gel.

To Perform Tasks

Active Reading **7 Identify** As you read, underline examples of different tasks performed by organisms.

Many living organisms perform very helpful tasks. For example, people use bacteria to treat wastewater and to clean up oil spills. Leeches are used to keep blood from pooling after reattachment of a severed body part, such as a finger. Humans have trained animals to work for them for many centuries. For example, horses pull wagons and carry people from place to place. Dogs guide visually impaired people safely through busy city streets. Dogs have also been trained to search for drugs, bombs, fugitives, and hikers lost in the woods. Trained bottlenose dolphins and sea lions dive to the sea floor to retrieve lost equipment. People have even used pigeons as a form of air mail. Believe it or not, these helpful organisms are also examples of biotechnology.

Once the milk has gelled, microorganisms are added to some cheeses to give them their own unique flavors.

These microscopic bacteria are just one example of living organisms used as technology.

Organisms help make many foods, including the bread and cheese in this sandwich.

Think Outside the Book (Inquiry)

8 Infer Research fermentation. Then, discuss with classmates how people may have first learned to use bacteria and yeast to change foods.

Building on Life

What technology is used to change organisms or make new organisms?

Throughout history, people have changed the traits of organisms to better meet human needs. This can be done by using naturally occurring differences among individuals or by changing an organism's DNA.

Selective Breeding

Compare two herds of cattle and you may observe many different traits. Cattle breeders use a process called *selective breeding* to emphasize traits that occur naturally in their cattle. Animals with desired traits are selected to reproduce and pass on their genes. Some cattle have been bred for meat. Others have been bred to produce milk. Still others are bred to survive in harsh climates. Farmers use selective breeding for plants as well. For example, some types of corn have been bred to have a sweet flavor. Other types are not as sweet and are grown as food for animals.

Active Reading

9 Define What does the word *selective* mean when it is used in the term *selective breeding*?

_____

_____

_____

Visualize It!

10 Compare These photos show three bulls that are very different from each other. Identify one trait for each bull and suggest a reason why that trait was selected.

Scottish Highland

_____

_____

_____

Texas Longhorn

_____

_____

_____

Belgian Blue

_____

_____

_____

_____

These fluorescent fish may someday help find pollution. A gene inserted into their DNA makes them glow brightly but does not make any other change.

Genetic Engineering

Traits can also be changed by modifying the DNA inside a living cell. This technology is known as *genetic engineering* or *genetic modification*. **Engineering** is the application of science and mathematics to solve real-life problems. There are many types of engineers, including chemical and biological engineers that focus on issues related to health. In one type of genetic modification, engineers extract DNA from a donor cell. Chemicals are used to cut the DNA into small fragments. The small fragments are mixed with bacteria. Because bacteria tend to absorb DNA from their environment, some of the bacteria will take up the cut DNA. The bacteria grow and reproduce along with the inserted DNA. At this point, the bacteria will produce the protein that is coded for by the inserted DNA. That protein can be used for medical treatments. The bacteria can also be used to supply DNA for further applications.

© Houghton Mifflin Harcourt Publishing Company • Image Credits: ©Pichi Chuang/Reuters/Corbis

Active Reading

11 Sequence As you read, write the numbers 1 to 5 beside the steps that occur when scientists modify a person's DNA.

The Process of Genetic Modification

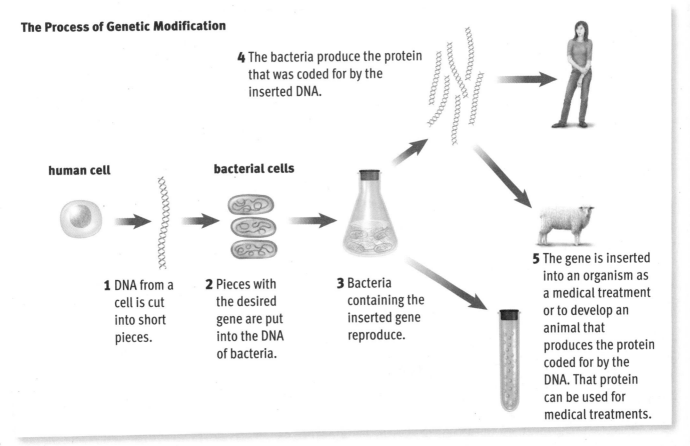

4 The bacteria produce the protein that was coded for by the inserted DNA.

human cell

bacterial cells

1 DNA from a cell is cut into short pieces.

2 Pieces with the desired gene are put into the DNA of bacteria.

3 Bacteria containing the inserted gene reproduce.

5 The gene is inserted into an organism as a medical treatment or to develop an animal that produces the protein coded for by the DNA. That protein can be used for medical treatments.

Lending a Helping Hand

What technology is used to help organisms?

One role of technology in life sciences is helping organisms, usually humans, with everyday tasks. Technology also helps organisms fight life-threatening diseases and conditions.

Assistive and Adaptive Technology

Assistive and adaptive technology plays a very important role in helping people with everyday activities. This technology includes devices such as hearing aids, wheelchairs, and titanium rods used to set broken bones. Other examples include devices that replace damaged or lost limbs, help keep hearts beating with a regular rhythm, and focus blurry vision. Some technology is so common that we seldom notice it. For example, ramps from the street to the sidewalk are a technological solution to make the use of wheelchairs, strollers, or even grocery carts easier. Other devices are less common but essential to the people who use them. For example, replacement knee and hip joints often work so well that they go unnoticed even by the person who uses them.

12 **List** What are four technological devices that assist people or help them adapt to their environments?

_____

_____

_____

_____

Early prosthetics replaced a missing limb, but the device was not really useful. The fingers could not move like those of a real hand.

This prosthetic doesn't look much like a hand, but it allowed a person to do detailed work.

Medicines, Medical Technology, and Biomaterials

Medicines are chemical products that help an organism fight disease or regulate body functions. People have used medicines for thousands of years. Every year, scientists test thousands of chemical compounds to find new medicines. Medical technology has made many diseases easy to control or to cure. Genetic modification has added a new tool for medical research. Using specific genes to make medical compounds may help researchers find ways to design medicines that are perfectly matched to each individual patient. Biomaterials are natural or synthetic (manmade) substances that are designed to work with the human body for some medical purpose. Examples of biomaterials are synthetic skin or prosthetic limbs. Although biomaterials are designed to help, there are some that can cause problems. For instance, an implanted organ can be rejected by the person's body.

Visualize It!

13 Describe What kinds of changes have allowed modern prosthetic arms to function better than those made many years ago?

_____

_____

_____

_____

Think Outside the Book

14 Research Find a biomaterial that may cause a medical problem. Identify the problem; then come up with a solution. Your solution should include criteria (requirements), constraints (limitations), and scientific principles.

Modern prosthetics combine artificial joints, for better functionality, with a more realistic appearance.

The newest prosthetics have electrodes that connect to nerves on a person's body. These devices are controlled by the user's brain.

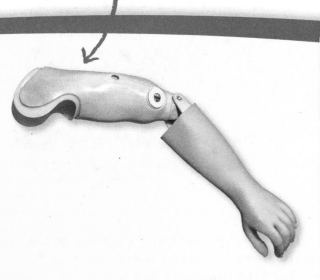

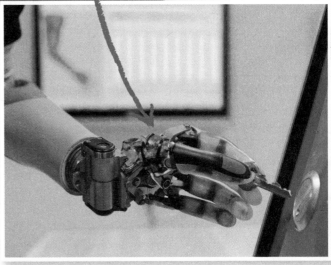

It's Natural

How can new technology be inspired by nature?

No matter what you want to do with a machine or process, there is a good chance that there is an organism that does it naturally. Do you need an aircraft that can hover and fly backwards? The hummingbird does that. How about a machine that can dig a tunnel? Moles are experts at making tunnels. Engineers often get their inspiration from nature when they want to improve a design. *Biomimicry* is the imitation of living organisms to create technological products.

By Copying Materials Made by Organisms

Just as nature has a form for just about any function, one can also find a material for just about any purpose. For example, researchers are constantly looking for ways to make a strong, yet lightweight, fiber. One of the strongest known materials is spider silk. Scientists study spider webs to find out what spider silk is made of. If researchers could synthesize natural spider silk, it would be the perfect material to manufacture strong, lightweight ropes. When barnacles attach themselves to the side of a ship, they are almost impossible to remove. Even after years of soaking in salt water and being bashed by waves, barnacles remain firmly attached to a ship. Researchers are investigating ways to make glue with the same properties as the barnacle's adhesive.

The silk made by spiders is one of the strongest materials known.

Detail of shark skin

Detail of swimsuit fabric

When swimsuit designers wanted to make a surface that moves smoothly through the water, they modeled a fabric after the skin of the fast-swimming shark.

15 Infer Why would scientists choose shark skin as a model for a swimsuit designed for competitive swimmers?

_____

_____

_____

_____

By Copying the Structure of Organisms

Engineers often use designs that mimic the shapes that are found in nature. For example, the shape of whale flippers allows whales to move water efficiently. Engineers copied this shape to build more efficient blades for wind turbines. Engineers were also inspired by nature when designing the Japanese bullet train. This train travels more than 270 km/h (168 mi/h). But when the train emerged from a tunnel, the compressed air waves created a boom that disturbed nearby residents. In order to design a quieter train, designers studied the shape of the kingfisher's beak, which cuts through water without producing waves.

 **Visualize It!**

16 Model The photos below show how engineers copied the shape of the kingfisher beak to design the front of a fast-moving train. Look at the photo of the frog below. Use the space provided to sketch a technology that could be based on the characteristics of a frog.

Visual Summary

To complete this summary, fill in the blanks with the correct word or phrase. Then, use the key below to check your answers. You can use this page to review the main concepts of the lesson.

Engineering and Life Science

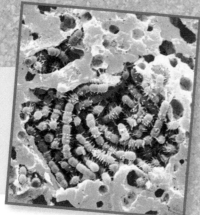

Organisms may be used to make products or perform tasks.

17 Using living things to perform tasks or make products is called

_____.

Technology can be applied to develop new or changed organisms.

18 _____

is a process in which segments of DNA are inserted into cells in order to change the organism.

Technology helps organisms with life processes. Technology can be inspired by living things.

19 Wheelchairs, eyeglasses, and artificial limbs are all examples of adaptive or assistive

_____.

Answers: 17 biotechnology; 18 genetic modification or Genetic engineering; 19 technology

20 Relate How is the selective breeding process related to genetic engineering of organisms?

Lesson Review

Vocabulary

1 _____ uses natural differences in organisms to develop traits over many generations.

2 _____ introduces changes to the DNA of organisms to develop traits within a single generation.

3 _____ is the imitation of living organisms to create technological products for humans.

Key Concepts

4 List What are two ways in which living organisms can be used as part of technological applications?

_____

_____

_____

5 Explain What are some advantages to farmers of using selective breeding of crops?

_____

_____

_____

6 Compare What is a benefit of genetic engineering compared to selective breeding?

_____

_____

_____

7 List What are four examples of technologies used to help improve people's lives?

_____

_____

_____

_____

_____

Critical Thinking

Use this diagram to answer the following question.

8 Explain Describe the process of genetic modification shown in the diagram above.

_____

_____

_____

_____

9 Explain Choose a biomaterial and explain how it uses life sciences and engineering.

_____

_____

_____

_____

10 Predict How would a community be affected if technology such as wheelchairs and hearing aids were not available?

_____

_____

_____

My Notes

S.T.E.M. Engineering & Technology

Engineering Design Process

Skills

Identify a need

✓ Conduct research

✓ Brainstorm solutions

✓ Select a solution

✓ Design a prototype

Build a prototype

Test and evaluate

Redesign to improve

✓ Communicate results

Objectives

- Identify the criteria for an effective prosthesis.
- Describe the constraints of prosthetic devices.
- Explain the scientific principles that limit the functionality of a prosthetic device.
- Design a technological solution to a problem.

Prosthetic Devices

Some of the earliest biomaterials were prosthetic (prahs•THEH•tik) devices. A prosthesis (prahs•THEE•sis) is biomaterial that replaces a body part either lost due to disease or injury, or not present at birth. The oldest known prosthetic device was made between 950 and 710 BCE, and was found in Egypt. It was not an arm or a leg; it was just a big toe. The big toe was important to Egyptians because they needed their big toes to wear traditional Egyptian sandals.

Since that time, prostheses have come a long way due to advances in technology, materials, and design. For example, advances in engineering have allowed heavy wooden prosthetics to be replaced by limbs made from much lighter biomaterials, such as titanium and aluminum.

There are currently prosthetic devices for legs, arms, hands, joints, and teeth that allow people to carry out their physical functions. There are even prosthetic eyes that fill the eye socket to look like a real eye, but do not allow the wearer to see out of it.

1 Identify What are some reasons a person might need a prosthetic device?

_____

_____

_____

_____

_____

In 1846, Benjamin Franklin Palmer was issued a patent for his design of an artificial leg. Palmer pioneered the idea of putting springs and movement into the prosthesis to give the appearance of natural movement.

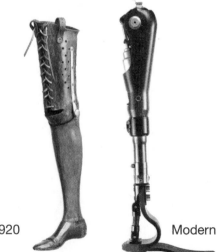

c. 1920   Modern

Criteria and Constraints

Before designing prostheses, scientists and engineers often identify the criteria and constraints. *Criteria* are the requirements that must be met. For example, one of the criteria for designing a prosthetic knee would be fashioning a joint that allows the replacement to bend. *Constraints* are restrictions or limitations. Common constraints in the biomedical field include resources, size, time, money, and functionality. For instance, a constraint for developing a prosthetic knee is that the prosthesis needs to be small enough to fit inside the leg.

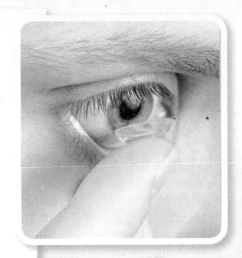

Scientific Principles

If you believed everything you saw in the movies, then bionic men and women are just around the corner. While it is fun to imagine what is possible with biomaterials, scientists must base their research and design on *scientific principles*. Scientists deal with facts and follow a strict process to ensure the accuracy and validity of their work.

Much of the work that goes on in the field of biomaterials is research. Laboratories all over the world are constantly seeking new materials and methods that can be used to design biomaterials. Machines such as 3D printers could custom-print prosthetic devices for a fraction of the cost of traditionally manufactured devices. However, the medical-grade materials necessary to make this sort of printer work do not yet exist. Therefore, this technology remains a concept.

Contact lenses are biomaterials made possible by synthetic hydrogels that allow the contact lens to float on the tear film layer on the surface of the cornea.

2016

Soviet scientist Vladimir Demikhov performed the first heart transplant surgery in 1937. In that year, he transplanted a heart into a dog. The first human to receive an artificial heart, Barney Clark, survived 112 days after receiving his Jarvik-7 heart in December 1982.

2 Describe Name a biomaterial from a movie you recently watched, or a book you recently read, and describe its function.

_____

_____

_____

 **You Try It!** ⟶

Now it is your turn to design a prosthetic device to replace a missing body part.

 **You Try It!**

Now it's your turn to develop a prosthetic device.

(1) Conduct Research

Develop a new type of prosthetic limb that is lighter in weight and has smart technology features built in. Do some research to help you answer these questions: What are the criteria for your design? What must the prosthesis be able to do? How will you test to make sure the prosthesis meets the criteria? Then identify the constraints of your design.

Criteria	Test

Constraints:

_____

_____

_____

(2) Brainstorm Solutions

In the space below, sketch a few draft designs of your prosthesis. Think about the features you need to include in order to meet the criteria.

③ Select a Solution

Reflect on each of your designs. Then pick the design that you believe best meets the criteria. Which design did you pick, and why?

_____

_____

_____

④ Design a Prototype

In the space below, make a detailed drawing of your prototype prosthesis. Label the features of your prototype.

⑤ Communicate Results

Summarize your design. Describe how your prototype meets the criteria and identify the constraints for the prosthesis. What kinds of smart technology features does the prosthesis contain? How will that be helpful to the person wearing the device?

_____

_____

_____

_____

_____

Unit 6 Big Idea

The human body is made up of systems that carry out unique functions and work together to maintain equilibrium and support life.

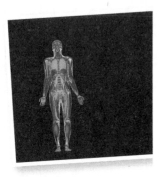

Lesson 1

ESSENTIAL QUESTION
How do the body systems work together to maintain homeostasis?

Describe the functions of the human body systems, including how they work together to maintain homeostasis.

Lesson 2

ESSENTIAL QUESTION
How do your skeletal and muscular systems work?

Explain how the skeletal and muscular (musculoskeletal) systems work together to allow movement of the body.

Lesson 3

ESSENTIAL QUESTION
How do the circulatory and respiratory systems work?

Relate the structures of the circulatory and respiratory systems to their functions in the human body.

Lesson 4

ESSENTIAL QUESTION
How do your body's digestive and excretory systems work?

Relate the parts of the digestive and excretory systems to their roles in the human body.

Lesson 5

ESSENTIAL QUESTION
How do the nervous and endocrine systems work?

Relate the structures of the nervous and endocrine systems to their functions in the human body.

Lesson 6

ESSENTIAL QUESTION
How does your reproductive system work?

Relate the structure of the reproductive system to its function in the human body.

Lesson 7

ESSENTIAL QUESTION
How is engineering related to life science?

Describe how organisms can be used in engineering, and how engineering can help organisms.

Think Outside the Book

2 Synthesize Choose one of these activities to help synthesize what you have learned in this unit.

☐ Using what you learned in lessons 1–6, choose a human body system and create a poster presentation to explain its structures and functions.

☐ Using what you learned in lessons 2, 3, 4, and 5, write a short story that explains which body systems are involved when a person eats an apple.

Connect ESSENTIAL QUESTIONS
Lessons 5 and 6

1 Explain How does the endocrine system regulate the function of the reproductive system in males and females?

_____

_____

_____

Name _____

Vocabulary

Fill in each blank with the term that best completes the following sentences.

1 _____ is the maintenance of a stable environment inside the body.

2 The _____ are the specialized tubes in the kidneys in which waste is collected from the blood.

3 A place where two or more bones are connected is called a(n) _____.

4 The _____ is the body system that controls growth, metabolism, and regulates reproduction through hormones.

5 The _____ is the female reproductive organ that produces egg cells.

Key Concepts

Read each question below, and circle the best answer.

6 Which of these statements correctly describes a key difference between aerobic activity and anaerobic activity?

A Aerobic activity is intense and of short duration, while anaerobic activity involves moderate effort over a long period of time.

B Muscles do not use oxygen during aerobic activity, but they do during anaerobic activity.

C Aerobic activity increases muscle endurance, while anaerobic activity increases muscle strength.

D Lifting weights is an aerobic activity, while jogging is an anaerobic activity.

7 Which body system is made up of the tissues and organs responsible for collecting fluid that leaks from the blood and returning it to the blood?

A excretory system

C endocrine system

B cardiovascular system

D lymphatic system

8 The diagram below shows the main parts of the respiratory system.

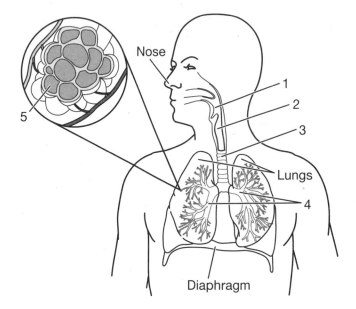

Which of these correctly names the parts of the respiratory system numbered 1 through 5 in the diagram above?

A 1. larynx, 2. pharynx, 3. trachea, 4. bronchi, 5. alveoli

B 1. pharynx, 2. larynx, 3. trachea, 4. bronchi, 5. alveoli

C 1. pharynx, 2. larynx, 3. bronchi, 4. trachea, 5. alveoli

D 1. larynx, 2. trachea, 3. pharynx, 4. alveoli, 5. bronchi

9 Which of these correctly maps the circulation of blood from the heart through the blood vessels and back to the heart?

A heart → arteries → capillaries → veins → heart

B heart → veins→ capillaries → arteries → heart

C heart → capillaries → arteries → veins → capillaries → heart

D heart → arteries → capillaries → veins → capillaries → heart

10 Which sentence best describes the esophagus?

A It produces bile that helps the digestive system break down fats.

B It is a muscular tube that moves food from the throat to the stomach.

C It releases enzymes into the small intestine that aid in chemical digestion.

D It is a muscular bag that churns food and produces acid and enzymes for chemical digestion.

11 Look at the diagram of DNA.

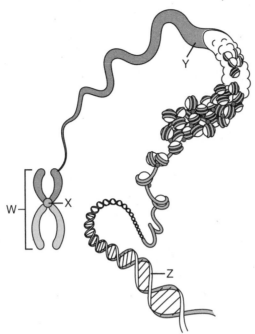

The spot labeled Z shows a place where a genetic engineer could use "chemical scissors" to cut the DNA. Why might a genetic engineer want to cut DNA?

A to create a new organism through selective breeding

B to study and learn more about what makes up DNA

C to insert a gene from a bacterium that will make a protein for use as a medical treatment

D to create a large model of DNA

12 Which statement is correct about the role of the kidney in maintaining equilibrium in the body?

A The kidney helps to keep smooth muscle contracting efficiently.

B The kidney filters wastes, such as sodium, from the blood.

C The kidney stores bile, which breaks down fats in the intestine.

D The kidney works with the endocrine system to help the body react to stimuli that occur outside the body.

13 Which gland of the endocrine system would you suspect has a problem if someone has an abnormal level of sugar in the blood?

A pineal gland   **C** pancreas

B parathyroid   **D** pituitary gland

14 Which picture shows a nerve cell?

A
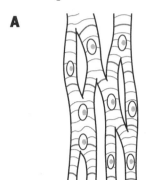

C

B
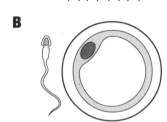

D
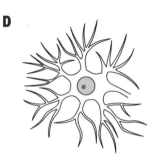

15 Which development occurs in the third trimester of pregnancy?

A The eyes of the fetus first open and blink.

B The embryo becomes a fetus.

C The embryo moves from the fallopian tube to the uterus.

D Contractions in the uterus move the fetus from the uterus through the vaginal canal.

16 Which of these is a function of the testes?

A to produce egg cells

B to produce a hormone that causes facial hair to grow

C to produce a hormone that causes growth of wider hips

D to deliver semen into the female reproductive system

17 Iona made a list of four advances in technology that were inspired by living things. She listed one item in error. Which item should not be on Iona's list?

A cardboard boxes for shipping goods

B wings on airplanes

C a drug for treating diabetes by controlling blood sugar

D flippers scuba divers wear on their feet to help them swim

Critical Thinking

Answer the following questions in the space provided.

18 The diagram below shows some of the muscles and bones of the arm.

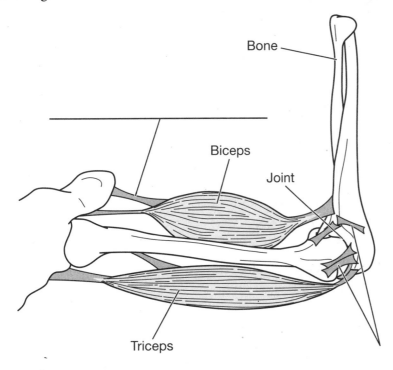

Bone

Biceps

Joint

Triceps

Fill in the blank lines in the diagram above to label the two types of connective tissue shown; then describe the function of each below.

_____

_____

_____

19 Explain the difference between pulmonary circulation and systemic circulation.

_____

_____

_____

_____

_____

_____

_____

20 The diagram below shows the two main parts of the human nervous system.

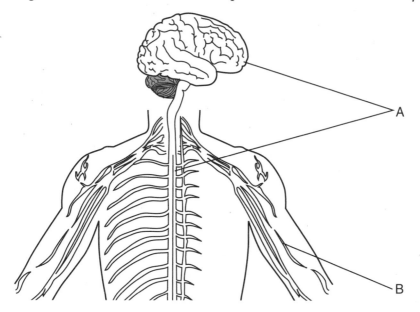

Write the names for the two parts of the nervous system labeled A and B.
Then describe the main functions of each part.

A Name: _____

Function: _____

B Name: _____

Function: _____

Connect **ESSENTIAL QUESTIONS**
Lessons 1, 2, 3, and 5

Answer the following question in the space provided.

21 When you burn yourself after touching something hot, you pull your hand away
quickly. Use what you learned in lessons 1, 2, 3, and 5 to describe how your skeletal,
muscular, circulatory, endocrine, and nervous systems work together to make you
react and to start healing your burn.

_____

_____

_____

_____

_____

_____

_____

_____

Earth's Atmosphere

Big Idea

Earth's atmosphere is a mixture of gases that interacts with solar energy.

7.ESS3.1, 7.ESS3.2

Earth's atmosphere is divided into different layers. These clouds have formed in the troposphere, the lowest layer of the atmosphere where most weather occurs.

Wind is the movement of air caused by differences in air pressure.

What do you think?

Like other parts of the Earth system, energy is transferred through Earth's atmosphere. What are the three processes by which energy is transferred through the atmosphere?

Unit 7
Earth's Atmosphere

CITIZEN SCIENCE
Clearing the Air

In some areas, there are many vehicles on the roads every day. Some of the gases from vehicle exhausts react with sunlight to form ozone. There are days when the concentration of ozone is so high that it becomes a health hazard. Those days are especially difficult for people who have problems breathing. What can you do to reduce gas emissions?

① Think About It

A How do you get to school every day?

_____

_____

_____

B How many of the students in your class come to school by car?

_____

Gas emissions are high during rush-hour traffic.

② Ask A Question

How can you reduce the number of vehicles students use to get to school one day each month?

With your teacher and classmates, brainstorm different ways in which you can reduce the number of vehicles students use to get to school.

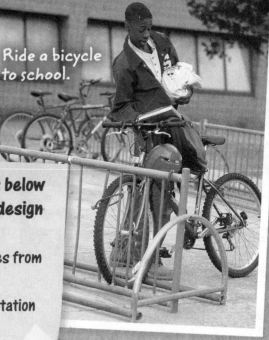

Ride a bicycle to school.

Check off the points below as you use them to design your plan.

☐ how far a student lives from school

☐ the kinds of transportation students may have available to them

③ Make A Plan

A Write down different ways that you can reduce the number of vehicles that bring students to school.

_____

_____

_____

_____

_____

_____

_____

B Create a short presentation for your principal that outlines how the whole school could become involved in your vehicle-reduction plan. Write down the points of your presentation in the space below.

_____

_____

_____

_____

_____

_____

_____

_____

_____

C In the space below, design a sign-up sheet that your classmates will use to choose how they will come to school on the designated day.

Take It Home

Give your presentation to an adult. Then, have the adult brainstorm ways to reduce their daily gas emissions. See *ScienceSaurus*® **for more information about conservation of energy.**

The Atmosphere

ESSENTIAL QUESTION

What is the atmosphere?

By the end of this lesson, you should be able to describe the composition and structure of the atmosphere and explain how the atmosphere protects life and insulates Earth.

7.ESS3.1

The atmosphere is a very thin layer compared to the whole Earth. However, it is essential for life on our planet.

Lesson Labs

Quick Labs
- Modeling Air Pressure
- Modeling Air Pressure Changes with Altitude

Field Lab
- Measuring Oxygen in the Air

Engage Your Brain

1 Predict Check T or F to show whether you think each statement is true or false.

T	F	
☐	☐	Oxygen is in the air we breathe.
☐	☐	Pressure is not a property of air.
☐	☐	The air around you is part of the atmosphere.
☐	☐	As you climb up a mountain, the temperature usually gets warmer.

2 Explain Does the air in this balloon have mass? Why or why not?

_____

_____

_____

_____

_____

Active Reading

3 Synthesize Many English words have their roots in other languages. Use the ancient Greek words below to make an educated guess about the meanings of the words *atmosphere* and *mesosphere*.

Greek word	Meaning
atmos	vapor
mesos	middle
sphaira	ball

Vocabulary Terms

- atmosphere
- air pressure
- thermosphere
- mesosphere
- stratosphere
- troposphere
- ozone layer
- greenhouse effect

4 Apply As you learn the definition of each vocabulary term in this lesson, create your own definition or sketch to help you remember the meaning of the term.

atmosphere:

_____

_____

mesosphere:

_____

_____

Up and Away!

What is Earth's atmosphere?

The mixture of gases that surrounds Earth is the **atmosphere** (AT•muh•sfeer). This mixture is most often referred to as air. The atmosphere has many important functions. It protects you from the sun's damaging rays and also helps to maintain the right temperature range for life on Earth. For example, the temperature range on Earth allows us to have an abundant amount of liquid water. Many of the components of the atmosphere are essential for life, such as the oxygen you breathe.

A Mixture of Gases and Small Particles

The atmosphere is made mostly of nitrogen gas (78%) and oxygen gas (21%). The remaining 1% is other gases. The atmosphere also contains small particles such as dust, volcanic ash, sea salt, and smoke. There are even small pieces of skin, bacteria, and pollen floating in the atmosphere! All of these gases and particles have the potential to cause atmospheric change, depending on how much of them are present.

Water is also found in the atmosphere. Liquid water, as water droplets, and solid water, as snow and ice crystals, are found in clouds. But most water in the atmosphere exists as an invisible gas called *water vapor*. Under certain conditions, water vapor can change into solid or liquid water. Then, snow or rain might fall from the sky.

Visualize It!

5 Graph Draw a bar graph, with percentages, for the gases found in the atmosphere. Be sure to label your x-axis with the names of the gases, and your y-axis with numbers for the percentages.

Nitrogen is the most abundant gas in the atmosphere.

Oxygen is the second most abundant gas in the atmosphere.

The remaining gas in the atmosphere is made up of argon, carbon dioxide, water vapor, and other gases.

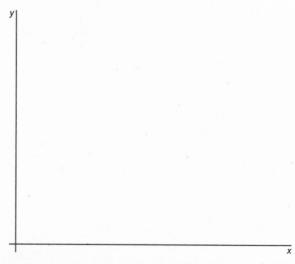

Composition of the Atmosphere

Percentages are by volume.

How do pressure and temperature change in the atmosphere?

 **Active Reading**

6 Identify As you read, underline what happens to temperature and to pressure as altitude increases.

The atmosphere is held around Earth by gravity. Gravity pulls gas molecules in the atmosphere toward Earth's surface, causing air pressure. **Air pressure** is the measure of the force with which air molecules push on an area of a surface. At sea level, air pressure is over 1 lb for every square centimeter of your body. That is like carrying a 1-liter bottle of water on the tip of your finger!

However, air pressure is not the same throughout the atmosphere. Although there are many gas molecules that surround you on Earth, there are fewer and fewer gas molecules in the air as you move away from Earth's surface. So, as altitude increases, air pressure decreases.

As altitude increases, air temperature also changes. These changes are mainly due to the way solar energy is absorbed in the atmosphere. Some parts of the atmosphere are warmer because they contain a high percentage of gases that absorb solar energy. Other parts of the atmosphere contain less of these gases and are cooler.

Inquiry

7 Explain Why does a mountain climber need an oxygen supply at very high altitudes, even though the air still contains 21% oxygen?

_____

_____

_____

At high altitudes such as the top of Mount Everest, air pressure and temperature are lower than they are at sea level.

Look Way

What are the layers of the atmosphere?

Earth's atmosphere is divided into four layers, based on temperature and other properties. As shown at the right, these layers are the troposphere (TROH•puh•sfir), stratosphere (STRAT•uh•sfir), mesosphere (MEZ•uh•sfir), and thermosphere (THER•muh•sfir). Although these names sound complicated, they give you clues about the layers' features. *Tropo-* means "turning" or "change," and the troposphere is the layer where gases turn and mix. *Strato-* means "layer," and the stratosphere is where gases are layered and do not mix very much. *Meso-* means "middle," and the mesosphere is the middle layer. Finally, *thermo-* means "heat," and the thermosphere is the layer where temperatures are highest.

Think Outside the Book

8 **Describe** Research the part of the thermosphere called the ionosphere. Describe what the aurora borealis is.

The aurora borealis occurs in the thermosphere.

Thermosphere

The **thermosphere** is the uppermost layer of the atmosphere. The temperature increases as altitude increases because gases in the thermosphere absorb high-energy solar radiation. Temperatures in the thermosphere can be 1,500 °C or higher. However, the thermosphere feels cold. The density of particles in the thermosphere is very low. Too few gas particles collide with your body to transfer heat energy to your skin.

Mesosphere

The **mesosphere** is between the thermosphere and stratosphere. In this layer, the temperature decreases as altitude increases. Temperatures can be as low as −120 °C at the top of the mesosphere. Meteoroids begin to burn up in the mesosphere.

Stratosphere

The **stratosphere** is between the mesosphere and troposphere. In this layer, temperatures generally increase as altitude increases. Ozone in the stratosphere absorbs ultraviolet radiation from the sun, which warms the air. An ozone molecule is made of three atoms of oxygen. Gases in the stratosphere are layered and do not mix very much.

Troposphere

The **troposphere** is the lowest layer of the atmosphere. Although temperatures near Earth's surface vary greatly, generally, temperature decreases as altitude increases. This layer contains almost 80% of the atmosphere's total mass, making it the densest layer. Almost all of Earth's carbon dioxide, water vapor, clouds, air pollution, weather, and life forms are in the troposphere.

In the graph, the green line shows pressure change with altitude.
The red line shows temperature change with altitude.

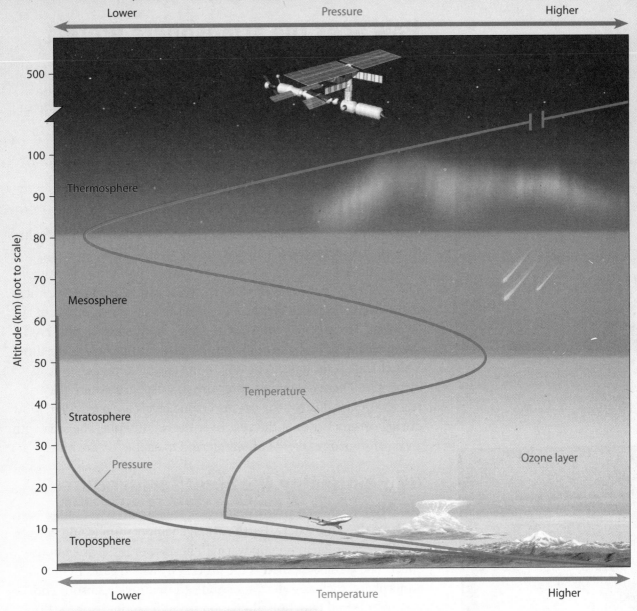

The layers of the atmosphere are defined by changes in temperature.

9 Analyze Discuss the potential for atmospheric change. Using the graph and descriptions provided, indicate if air pressure and temperature increase or decrease with increased altitude in each layer of the atmosphere. One answer has been provided for you.

Layer	Air pressure	Temperature
Thermosphere	decreases	
Mesosphere		
Stratosphere		
Troposphere		

How does the atmosphere protect life on Earth?

The atmosphere surrounds and protects Earth. The atmosphere provides the air we breathe. It also protects Earth from harmful solar radiation and from space debris that enters the Earth's system. In addition, the atmosphere controls the temperature on Earth.

By Absorbing or Reflecting Harmful Radiation

Earth's atmosphere reflects or absorbs most of the radiation from the sun. The **ozone layer** is an area in the stratosphere, 15 km to 40 km above Earth's surface, where ozone is highly concentrated. The ozone layer absorbs most of the solar radiation. The thickness of the ozone layer can change between seasons and at different locations. However, as shown at the left, scientists have observed a steady decrease in the overall volume of the ozone layer over time. This change is thought to be due to the use of certain chemicals by people. These chemicals enter the stratosphere, where they react with and destroy the ozone. Ozone levels are particularly low during certain times of the year over the South Pole. The area with a very thin ozone layer is often referred to as the "ozone hole."

By Maintaining the Right Temperature Range

Without the atmosphere, Earth's average temperature would be very low. How does Earth remain warm? The answer is the greenhouse effect. The **greenhouse effect** is the process by which gases in the atmosphere, such as water vapor and carbon dioxide, absorb and give off infrared radiation. Radiation from the sun warms Earth's surface, and Earth's surface gives off infrared radiation. Greenhouse gases in the atmosphere absorb some of this infrared radiation and then reradiate it. Some of this energy is absorbed again by Earth's surface, while some energy goes out into space. Because greenhouse gases keep energy in the Earth's system longer, Earth's average surface temperature is kept at around 15 °C (59 °F). In time, all the energy ends up back in outer space.

Active Reading **11 List** Name two examples of greenhouse gases.

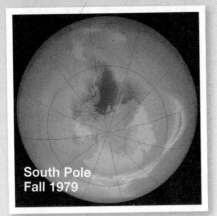

South Pole
Fall 1979

Less ozone — More ozone

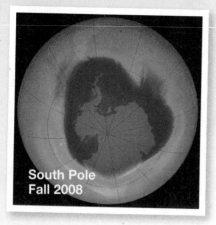

South Pole
Fall 2008

10 Compare How did the ozone layer over the South Pole change between 1979 and 2008?

© Houghton Mifflin Harcourt Publishing Company • Image Credits: (tl) ©NASA; (bl) ©NASA

the Sun ...

The Greenhouse Effect

Greenhouse gas molecules absorb and emit infrared radiation.

Atmosphere without Greenhouse Gases

Without greenhouse gases in Earth's atmosphere, radiation from Earth's surface is lost directly to space.
Average Temperature: -18 °C

Atmosphere with Greenhouse Gases

With greenhouse gases in Earth's atmosphere, radiation from Earth's surface is lost to space more slowly, which makes Earth's surface warmer.
Average Temperature: 15 °C

▬ sunlight ▬ infrared radiation

The atmosphere is much thinner than shown here.

Visualize It!

12 Illustrate Draw your own version of how greenhouse gases keep Earth warm.

Visual Summary

To complete this summary, fill in the blanks with the correct word or phrase. Then, use the key below to check your answers. You can use this page to review the main concepts of the lesson.

Both air pressure and temperature change within the atmosphere.

13 As altitude increases, air pressure

_____ .

The atmosphere protects Earth from harmful radiation and helps to maintain a temperature range that supports life.

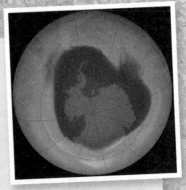

14 Earth is protected from harmful solar radiation by the

_____ .

The Atmosphere

The atmosphere is divided into four layers, according to temperature and other properties.

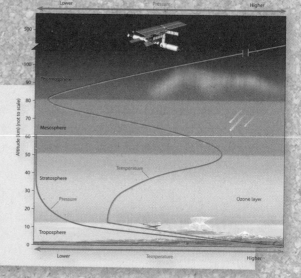

15 The four layers of the atmosphere are the

_____ ,

_____ ,

_____ , and

_____ .

Answers: 13 decreases; 14 ozone layer; 15 troposphere, stratosphere, mesosphere, thermosphere

16 Hypothesize What do you think Earth's surface would be like if Earth did not have an atmosphere?

Lesson Review

Vocabulary

Fill in the blanks with the terms that best complete the following sentences.

1 The _____ is a mixture of gases that surrounds Earth.

2 The measure of the force with which air molecules push on a surface is called _____ .

3 The _____ is the process by which gases in the atmosphere absorb and reradiate heat.

Key Concepts

4 List Name three gases in the atmosphere.

_____

_____

5 Identify What layer of the atmosphere contains the ozone layer?

_____

_____

6 Identify What layer of the atmosphere contains almost 80% of the atmosphere's total mass?

_____

7 Describe How and why does air pressure change with altitude in the atmosphere?

_____

_____

_____

8 Explain What is the name of the uppermost layer of the atmosphere? Why does it feel cold there, even though the temperature can be very high?

_____

_____

_____

_____

Critical Thinking

9 Hypothesize What would happen to life on Earth if the ozone layer was not present?

_____

_____

10 Criticize A friend says that temperature increases as altitude increases because you're moving closer to the sun. Is this true? Explain.

_____

_____

11 Predict Why would increased levels of greenhouse gases contribute to higher temperatures on Earth?

_____

_____

_____

Use this graph to answer the following questions.

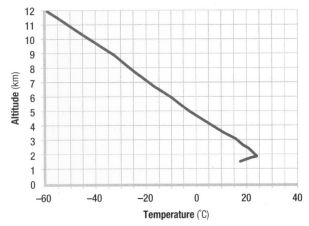

Changes in Temperature with Altitude

Source: National Weather Service. Data taken at Riverton, Wyoming, 2001

12 Analyze The top of Mount Everest is at about 8,850 m. What would the approximate air temperature be at that altitude? _____

13 Analyze What is the total temperature change between 3 km and 7 km above Earth's surface? _____

My Notes

Human Impact on the Atmosphere

ESSENTIAL QUESTION

How do humans impact Earth's atmosphere?

By the end of this lesson, you should be able to identify the impact that humans have had on Earth's atmosphere.

7.ESS3.1, 7.ESS3.2

Human activities that involve burning fuels, such as driving vehicles and keeping buildings cool, can cause air pollution.

Engage Your Brain

1 Identify Check T or F to show whether you think each statement is true or false.

T F

☐ ☐ Human activities can cause air pollution.

☐ ☐ Air pollution cannot affect you if you stay indoors.

☐ ☐ Air pollution does not affect places outside of cities.

☐ ☐ Air pollution can cause lung diseases.

2 Analyze The photo above shows the same city as the photo on the left, but on a different day. How are these photos different?

_____

_____

_____

_____

Active Reading

3 Apply Use context clues to write your own definitions for the words *contamination* and *quality*.

Example sentence
You can help prevent food <u>contamination</u> by washing your hands after touching raw meat.

contamination:

_____

_____

_____

Example sentence
The good sound <u>quality</u> coming from the stereo speakers indicated they were expensive.

quality:

_____

_____

_____

Vocabulary Terms

- air pollution
- smog
- particulate
- acid precipitation
- ozone
- air quality

4 Apply As you learn the definition of each vocabulary term in this lesson, create your own definition or sketch to help you remember the meaning of the term.

AIR
What Is It Good For?

Why is the atmosphere important?

If you were lost in a desert, you could survive a few days without food and water. But you wouldn't last more than a few minutes without air. Air is an important natural resource. The air you breathe forms part of Earth's atmosphere. The *atmosphere* is a mixture of gases that surrounds Earth. Most organisms on Earth have adapted to the natural balance of gases found in the atmosphere.

It Provides Gases That Organisms Need to Survive

Oxygen is one of the gases that make up Earth's atmosphere. It is used by most living cells to get energy from food. Every breath you take brings oxygen into your body. The atmosphere also contains carbon dioxide. Plants need carbon dioxide to make their own food through *photosynthesis* (foh•toh•SYN•thuh•sys).

It Absorbs Harmful Radiation

High-energy radiation from space would harm life on Earth if it were not blocked by the atmosphere. Fast-moving particles, called *cosmic rays,* enter the atmosphere every second. These particles collide with oxygen, nitrogen, and other gas molecules and are slowed down. A part of the atmosphere called the *stratosphere* contains ozone gas. The ozone layer absorbs most of the high-energy radiation from the sun, called *ultraviolet* (UV) *radiation,* that reaches Earth.

It Keeps Earth Warm

Without the atmosphere, temperatures on Earth would not be stable. It would be too cold for life to exist. The *greenhouse effect* is the way by which certain gases in the atmosphere, such as water vapor and carbon dioxide, absorb and reradiate thermal energy. This slows the loss of energy from Earth into space. The atmosphere acts like a warm blanket that insulates the surface of Earth, preventing the sun's energy from being lost. For this reason, carbon dioxide and water vapor are called *greenhouse gases.*

A Sunlight (radiant energy) passes through the windows of the car.

B Energy as heat is trapped inside by the windows.

C The temperature inside the car increases.

Visualize It!

5 Synthesize How is a car with closed windows a good analogy of the atmosphere's greenhouse effect?

_____

_____

_____

_____

Active Reading **6 Explain** How is Earth's atmosphere similar to a warm blanket?

_____

_____

What is air pollution?

The contamination of the atmosphere by pollutants from human and natural sources is called **air pollution**. Air pollution is something that leads to the potential for atmospheric change. Natural sources of air pollution include volcanic eruptions, wildfires, and dust storms. In cities and suburbs, most air pollution comes from the burning of fossil fuels, such as oil, gasoline, and coal. Oil refineries, chemical manufacturing plants, dry-cleaning businesses, and auto repair shops are just some potential sources of air pollution. Scientists classify air pollutants as either gases or particulates.

Active Reading

7 Identify As you read, underline sources of air pollution.

Visualize It!

8 Analyze Which one of these images could be both a natural and a human source of air pollution? Give reasons for your answer and discuss the potential for atmospheric change caused by pollution.

_____

_____

_____

_____

Factory emissions

Vehicle exhaust

Forest fires and wildfires

Gases

Gas pollutants include carbon monoxide, sulfur dioxide, nitrogen oxide, and ground-level ozone. Some of these gases occur naturally in the atmosphere. These gases are considered pollutants only when they are likely to cause harm. For example, ozone is important in the stratosphere, but at ground level it is harmful to breathe. Carbon monoxide, sulfur dioxide, and nitrogen dioxide are released from burning fossil fuels in vehicles, factories, and homes. They are a major source of air pollution.

Particulates

Particle pollutants can be easier to see than gas pollutants. A **particulate** (per•TIK•yuh•lit) is a tiny particle of solid that is suspended in air or water. Smoke contains ash, which is a particulate. The wind can pick up particulates such as dust, ash, pollen, and tiny bits of salt from the ocean and blow them far from their source. Ash, dust, and pollen are common forms of air pollution. Vehicle exhaust also contains particulates. The particulates in vehicle exhaust are a major cause of air pollution in cities.

It Stinks!

What pollutants can form from vehicle exhaust?

In urban areas, vehicle exhaust is a common source of air pollution. Gases, such as carbon monoxide, and particulates, such as soot and ash, are in exhaust fumes. Vehicle exhaust may also react with other substances in the air. When this happens, new pollutants can form. Ground-level ozone and smog are two types of pollutants that form from vehicle exhaust.

Active Reading

9 Identify As you read, underline how ground-level ozone and smog can form.

Ground-Level Ozone

Ozone in the ozone layer is necessary for life, but ground-level ozone is harmful. It is produced when sunlight reacts with vehicle exhaust and oxygen in the air. You may have heard of "Ozone Action Days" in your community. When such a warning is given, people should limit outdoor activities because ozone can damage their lungs.

Smog

Smog is another type of pollutant formed from vehicle exhaust. **Smog** forms when ground-level ozone and vehicle exhaust react in the presence of sunlight. Smog is a problem in large cities because there are more vehicles on the roads. It can cause lung damage and irritate the eyes and nose. In some cities, there can be enough smog to make a brownish haze over the city.

Visualize It!

Some compounds in smoke and exhaust are harmful by themselves. And some compounds in smoke and exhaust can react in the atmosphere to form other pollutants, such as smog and acid precipitation.

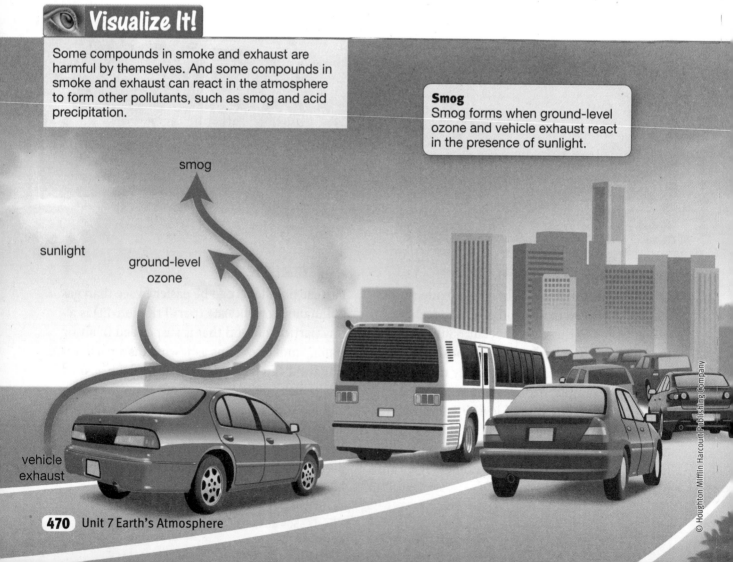

Smog
Smog forms when ground-level ozone and vehicle exhaust react in the presence of sunlight.

smog

sunlight

ground-level ozone

vehicle exhaust

How does pollution from human activities produce acid precipitation?

10 Identify As you read, underline how acid precipitation forms.

Precipitation (prih•sip•ih•TAY•shuhn) such as rain, sleet, or snow that contains acids from air pollution is called **acid precipitation**. Burning fossil fuels releases sulfur dioxide and nitrogen oxides into the air. When these gases mix with water in the atmosphere, they form sulfuric acid and nitric acid. Precipitation is naturally slightly acidic. When carbon dioxide in the air and water mix, they form carbonic acid. Carbonic acid is a weak acid. Sulfuric acid and nitric acid are strong acids. They can make precipitation so acidic that it is harmful to the environment.

What are some effects of acid precipitation?

Acid precipitation can cause soil and water to become more acidic than normal. Plants have adapted over long periods of time to the natural acidity of the soils in which they live. When soil acidity rises, some nutrients that plants need are dissolved. These nutrients get washed away by rainwater. Bacteria and fungi that live in the soil are also harmed by acidic conditions.

Acid precipitation may increase the acidity of lakes or streams. It also releases toxic metals from soils. The increased acidity and high levels of metals in water can sicken or kill aquatic organisms. This can disrupt habitats and result in decreased biodiversity in an ecosystem. Acid precipitation can also erode the stonework on buildings and statues.

blowing winds

Smoke and fumes from factories and vehicles contain sulfur dioxide and nitrogen oxide gases, which can be blown long distances by winds.

11 Analyze Explain how pollution from one location can affect the environment far away from the source of the pollution.

_____

_____

_____

_____

Acid Precipitation
These gases dissolve in water vapor, and form sulfuric acids and nitric acids, which fall to Earth as acid precipitation.

How's the AIR?

What are measures of air quality?

Measuring how clean or polluted the air is tells us about **air quality**. Pollutants reduce air quality. Two major threats to air quality are vehicle exhausts and industrial pollutants. The air quality in cities can be poor. As more people move into cities, the cities get bigger. This leads to increased amounts of human-made pollution. Poor air circulation, such as a lack of wind, allows air pollution to stay in one area where it can build up. As pollution increases, air quality decreases.

Air Quality Index

The Air Quality Index (AQI) is a number used to describe the air quality of a location such as a city. The higher the AQI number, the more people are likely to have health problems that are linked to air pollution. Air quality is measured and given a value based on the level of pollution detected. The AQI values are divided into ranges. Each range is given a color code and a description. The Environmental Protection Agency (EPA) has AQIs for the pollutants that pose the greatest risk to public health, including ozone and particulates. The EPA can then issue advisories to avoid exposure to pollution that may harm health.

Indoor Air Pollution

The air inside a building can become more polluted than the air outside. This is because buildings are insulated to prevent outside air from entering the building. Some sources of indoor air pollution include chlorine and ammonia from household cleaners and formaldehyde from furniture. Harmful chemicals can be released from some paints and glues. Radon is a radioactive gas released when uranium decays. Radon can seep into buildings through gaps in their foundations. It can build up inside well-insulated buildings. *Ventilation*, or the mixing of indoor and outside air, can reduce indoor air pollution. Another way to reduce indoor air pollution is to limit the use of items that create the pollution.

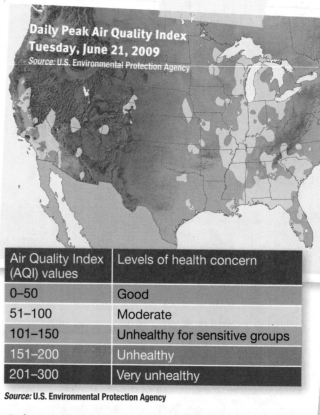

Air Quality Index (AQI) values	Levels of health concern
0–50	Good
51–100	Moderate
101–150	Unhealthy for sensitive groups
151–200	Unhealthy
201–300	Very unhealthy

Source: U.S. Environmental Protection Agency

Color codes based on the Air Quality Index show the air quality in different areas.

Visualize It!

12 Recommend If you were a weather reporter using this map, what would you recommend for people living in areas that are colored orange?

_____

_____

_____

_____

_____

Visualize It!

13 Apply If this was your house, how might you decrease the sources of indoor air pollution?

_____

_____

Nitrogen oxides from unvented gas stove, wood stove, or kerosene heater

Chlorine and ammonia from household cleaners

Chemicals from dry cleaning

Fungi and bacteria from dirty heating and air conditioning ducts

Chemicals from paint strippers and thinners

Gasoline from car and lawn mower

Carbon monoxide from car left running

Formaldehyde from furniture, carpeting, particleboard, and foam insulation

How can air quality affect health?

Daily exposure to small amounts of air pollution can cause serious health problems. Children, elderly people, and people with asthma, allergies, lung problems, and heart problems are especially vulnerable to the effects of air pollution. The short-term effects of air pollution include coughing, headaches, and wheezing. Long-term effects, such as lung cancer and emphysema, are dangerous because they can cause death.

Think Outside the Book Inquiry

14 Evaluate Think about the community in which you live. What different things in your community and the surrounding areas might affect the air quality where you live?

Air Pollution and Your Health

Short-term effects	Long-term effects
coughing	asthma
headaches	emphysema
difficulty breathing	allergies
burning/itchy eyes	lung cancer
	chronic bronchitis

15 Identify Imagine you are walking next to a busy road where there are a lot of exhaust fumes. Circle the effects listed in the table that you are most likely to have while walking.

Things Are CHANGING

How are humans changing Earth's climate?

The burning of fossil fuels releases greenhouse gases, such as carbon dioxide, into the atmosphere. The atmosphere today contains about 43% more carbon dioxide than it did in the mid-1700s, and that level continues to increase. Average global temperatures have also risen in recent decades.

Many people are concerned about how the greenhouse gases from human activities add to the observed trend of increasing global temperatures. Earth's atmosphere and other systems work together in complex ways, so it is hard to know exactly how much the extra greenhouse gases change the temperature. Climate scientists make computer models to understand the effects of climate change. Models predict that average global temperatures are likely to rise another 4.5 °C (8.0 °F) by the year 2100.

16 Graph Make a graph that shows how the continued use of fossil fuels at the same rate as today will affect the amount of carbon dioxide in the atmosphere in 1000, 2000, and 3000 years from now. Be sure to label both the *x*- and *y*- axes on your graph. Explain what might happen to our climate based on the data.

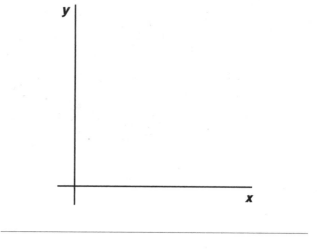

_____

_____

_____

What are some predicted effects of climate change?

Active Reading **17 Identify** As you read, underline some effects of an increasing average global temperature.

Scientists have already noticed many changes linked to warmer temperatures. For example, some glaciers and the Arctic sea ice are melting at the fastest rates ever recorded. A warmer Earth will lead to changes in rainfall patterns, rising sea levels, and possibly more severe storms. These changes will have many negative impacts for life on Earth. Other predicted effects include drought in some regions and increased precipitation in others. Farming practices and the availability of food is also expected to be impacted by increased global temperatures. Such changes will likely have political and economic effects on the world, especially in developing countries.

Melted water pours from an iceberg that broke away from the Jakobshavn Glacier in West Greenland.

How is the ozone layer affected by air pollution?

In the 1980s, scientists reported an alarming discovery about Earth's protective ozone layer. Over the polar regions, the ozone layer was thinning. Chemicals called *chlorofluorocarbons* (klor•oh•flur•oh•kar•buhns) (CFCs) were causing ozone to break down into oxygen, which does not block harmful UV rays. The thinning of the ozone layer allows more UV radiation to reach Earth's surface. UV radiation is dangerous to organisms, including humans, as it causes sunburn, damages DNA (which can lead to cancer), and causes eye damage.

CFCs once had many industrial uses, such as coolants in refrigerators and air-conditioning units. CFC use has now been banned, but CFC molecules can stay in the atmosphere for about 100 years. So, CFCs released from a spray can 30 years ago are still harming the ozone layer today. However, recent studies show that breakdown of the ozone layer has slowed.

The dark blue area on this map shows the size of the ozone hole over the South Pole.

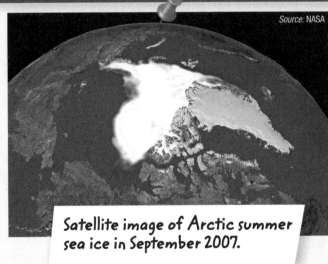

18 Infer How might these penguins near the South Pole be affected by the ozone hole?

_____

_____

_____

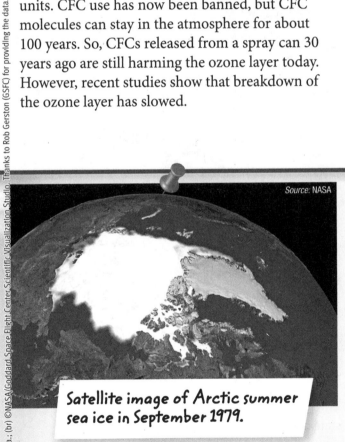

Source: NASA

Satellite image of Arctic summer sea ice in September 1979.

Source: NASA

Satellite image of Arctic summer sea ice in September 2007.

Inquiry

19 Relate What effect might melting sea ice have for people who live in coastal areas?

_____

_____

Visual Summary

To complete this summary, fill in the blanks with the correct word or phrase. Then use the key below to check your answers. You can use this page to review the main concepts of the lesson.

Human activities are a major cause of air pollution.

20 Two types of air pollutants are gases and _____ .

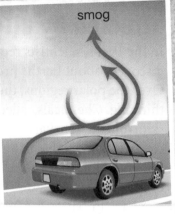

Car exhaust is a major source of air pollution in cities.

21 _____ is formed when exhausts and ozone react in the presence of sunlight.

Human Impact on the Atmosphere

Air quality and levels of pollution can be measured.

Air Quality Index (AQI) values	Levels of health concern
0–50	Good
51–100	Moderate
101–150	Unhealthy for sensitive groups
151–200	Unhealthy
201–300	Very unhealthy

22 As pollution increases, _____ decreases.

Climate change may lead to dramatic changes in global weather patterns.

23 The melting of polar ice is one effect of _____ .

Answers: 20 particulates; 21 smog; 22 air quality; 23 global warming/climate change

24 **Apply** Explain in your own words what the following statement means: Each of your breaths, every tree that is planted, and every vehicle on the road affects the composition of the atmosphere.

© NASA/Goddard Space Flight Center Scientific Visualization Studio. Thanks to Rob Gerston (GSFC) for providing the data.

Lesson Review

Vocabulary

Draw a line to connect the following terms to their definitions.

1 air pollution

2 air quality

3 particulate

4 smog

A tiny particle of solid that is suspended in air or water

B the contamination of the atmosphere by the introduction of pollutants from human and natural sources

C pollutant that forms when ozone and vehicle exhaust react with sunlight

D a measure of how clean or polluted the air is

Key Concepts

5 Identify List three effects that an increase in urbanization can have on air quality.

_____

_____

_____

6 Relate How are ground-level ozone and smog related?

_____

_____

_____

7 Explain How can human health be affected by changes in air quality?

_____

_____

_____

Critical Thinking

Use this graph to answer the following questions.

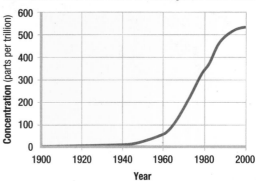

Concentration of a CFC in the Atmosphere Over Time

8 Analyze At what time in the graph did CFCs begin building up in the atmosphere?

_____

_____

9 Synthesize Since the late 1970s, the use of CFCs has been reduced, with a total ban in 2010. But CFCs can stay in the atmosphere for up to 100 years. In the space below, draw a graph showing the concentration of CFCs in the atmosphere over the next 100 years.

10 Apply Do you think it is important that humans control the amount of human-made pollution? Explain your reasoning.

_____

_____

_____

_____

_____

My Notes

Engineering Design Process

Skills
Identify a need
Conduct research
✓ Brainstorm solutions
✓ Select a solution
Design a prototype
✓ Build a prototype
✓ Test and evaluate
✓ Redesign to improve
✓ Communicate results

Objectives
• Explain how a need for clean energy has driven a technological solution.
• Describe two examples of wind-powered generators.
• Design a technological solution to a problem.
• Test and modify a prototype to achieve the desired result.

Building a Wind Turbine

During the Industrial Revolution, machines began to replace human and animal power for doing work. From agriculture and manufacturing to transportation, machines made work faster and easier. However, these machines needed fuel. Fossil fuels, such as coal, oil, and gasoline, powered the Industrial Revolution and are still used today. But burning fossil fuels produces waste products that harm the environment. In addition, fossil fuels will eventually run out. As a result, we need to better understand alternative, renewable sources of energy.

Brainstorming Solutions

There are many sources of energy besides fossil fuels. One of the most abundant renewable sources is wind. A wind turbine is a device that uses energy from the wind to turn an axle. The turning axle can be attached to other equipment to do jobs such as pumping water, cutting lumber, or generating electricity. To generate electricity, the axle spins magnets around a coiled wire. This causes electrons to flow in the wire. Flowing electrons produce an electric current. Electric current is used to power homes and businesses or electrical energy can be stored in a battery.

1 Brainstorm What are other possible sources of renewable energy that could be used to power a generator?

_____

_____

_____

_____

_____

_____

_____

HAWTs must be pointed into the wind to work. A motor turns the turbine to keep it facing the wind. HAWT blades are angled so that wind strikes the front of the blades, and then pushes the blades as it flows over them. Because wind flows over the blades fairly evenly, there is little vibration. So HAWTs are relatively quiet, and the turbines last a long time.

Wind direction

Blade moves counterclockwise

The Modern Design

There are two general types of modern wind turbines. A horizontal-axis wind turbine (HAWT) has a main axle that is horizontal, and a generator at the top of a tall tower. A vertical-axis wind turbine (VAWT) has a main axle that is vertical, and a generator at ground level. The blades are often white or light gray, to blend with the clouds. Blades can be more than 40 meters (130 ft) long, supported by towers more than 90 meters (300 ft) tall. The blade tips can travel more than 320 kilometers (200 mi) per hour!

2 Infer What problems may have been encountered as prototypes for modern wind turbines were tested?

_____

_____

_____

VAWTs do not need to be pointed into the wind to work. The blades are made so that one blade is pushed by the wind while the other returns against the wind. But because each blade moves against the wind for part of its rotation, VAWTs are less efficient than HAWTs. They also tend to vibrate more and, as a result, make more noise.

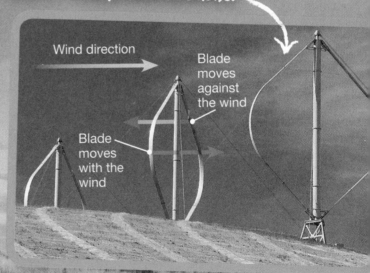

Wind direction

Blade moves against the wind

Blade moves with the wind

👋 You Try It!

Now it's your turn to design a wind turbine that will generate electricity and light a small bulb.

 # You Try It!

Now it's your turn to design an efficient wind turbine that will generate enough electricity to light a small bulb.

Materials

✓ assorted wind turbine parts

✓ fan

✓ gears

✓ small bulb

✓ small motor

✓ socket

① Brainstorm solutions

Brainstorm ideas for a wind turbine that will turn an axle on a small motor. The blades must turn fast enough so that the motor generates enough electricity to light a small bulb. Fill in the table below with as many ideas as you can for each part of your wind turbine. Circle each idea you decide to try.

Type of axis	Shape of turbine	Attaching axis to motor	Control speed

② Select a solution

From the table above, choose the features for the turbine you will build. In the space below, draw a model of your wind turbine idea. Include all the parts and show how they will be connected.

(3) Build a prototype

Now build your wind turbine. As you built your turbine, were there some parts of your design that could not be assembled as you had predicted? What parts did you have to revise as you were building the prototype?

_____

_____

_____

_____

(4) Test and evaluate

Point a fan at your wind turbine and see what happens. Did the bulb light? If not, what parts of your turbine could you revise?

_____

_____

_____

_____

(5) Redesign to improve

Choose one part to revise. Modify your design and then test again. Repeat this process until your turbine lights up the light bulb.

_____

_____

_____

_____

(6) Communicate results

Which part of the turbine seemed to have the greatest effect on the brightness of the light bulb?

_____

_____

_____

_____

_____

Climate Change

ESSENTIAL QUESTION

What are the causes and effects of climate change?

By the end of this lesson, you should be able to describe climate change and the causes and effects of climate change.

7.ESS3.2

Temperatures are rising in the Arctic. Warmer temperatures cause the ice sheets to freeze later and melt sooner. With less time on the ice to hunt for seals, polar bears are struggling to survive.

Engage Your Brain

1 Predict Check T or F to show whether you think each statement is true or false.

T F

☐ ☐ There have been periods on Earth when the climate was colder than the climate is today.

☐ ☐ The ocean does not play a role in climate.

☐ ☐ Earth's climate is currently warming.

☐ ☐ Humans are contributing to changes in climate.

2 Describe Write your own caption relating this photo to climate change.

_____

_____

_____

Active Reading

3 Apply Many scientific terms, such as *greenhouse effect,* also have everyday meanings. Use context clues to write your own definition for the words *greenhouse* and *effect*.

Example sentence
The <u>greenhouse</u> is filled with tropical plants that are found in Central America.

greenhouse:

_____

_____

_____

Example sentence
What are some of the <u>effects</u> of staying up too late?

effect:

_____

_____

_____

Vocabulary Terms

- climate
- ice age
- greenhouse effect
- global warming

4 Identify As you read, create a reference card for each vocabulary term. On one side of the card, write the term and its meaning. On the other side, draw an image that illustrates or makes a connection to the term. These cards can be used as bookmarks in the text so that you can refer to them while studying.

The Temps are a–**Changin'**

What are some natural causes of climate change?

The weather conditions in an area over a long period of time are called **climate**. Natural events have changed Earth's climate many times during our planet's history. Natural changes in climate can be long-term or short-term.

Movement of Tectonic Plates

Tectonic plate motion has contributed to long-term climate change over billions of years. And Earth's plates are still moving!

The present continents once fit together as a single landmass called *Pangaea* (pan•JEE•uh). Pangaea began to break up about 200 million years ago. By 20 million years ago, the continents had moved close to their current positions. Some continents grew warmer as they moved closer to the equator. Other continents, such as Antarctica, moved to colder and higher latitudes.

The eruption of Mount Pinatubo sent ash and gases as high as 34 km into the atmosphere.

Visualize It!

5 Infer Today, Antarctica is the coldest desert on Earth. But fossils of trees and dinosaurs have been found on this harsh continent. Explain how life could thrive on ancient Antarctica.

_____

_____

_____

_____

EURASIA

NORTH AMERICA

Tethys Sea

SOUTH AMERICA

AFRICA

INDIA

AUSTRALIA

ANTARCTICA

Antarctica was part of the supercontinent Pangaea about 250 million years ago. Antarctica is located at the South Pole today.

EURASIA

NORTH AMERICA

AFRICA

PACIFIC OCEAN

SOUTH AMERICA

ATLANTIC OCEAN

INDIAN OCEAN

AUSTRALIA

ANTARCTICA

If you look closely at the current shapes of the continents, you can see how they once fit together to form Pangaea.

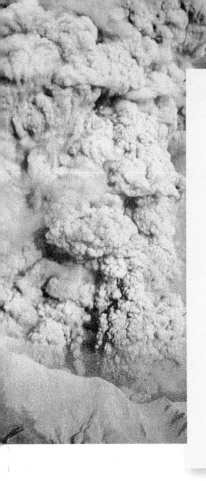

Climate Change After Mount Pinatubo Eruption

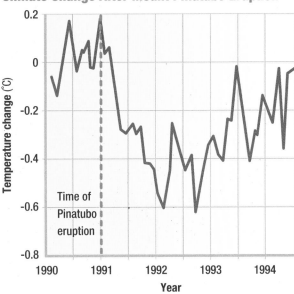

Source: Goddard Institute for Space Studies, NASA, 1997

This graph shows the *change* in average global temperature, not the actual temperature.

Particulates in the Atmosphere

Short-term changes in climate can be due to natural events that send *particulates* into the atmosphere. Particulates are tiny, solid particles that are suspended in air or water. They absorb some of the sun's energy and reflect some of the sun's energy back into space. This process temporarily lowers temperatures on Earth.

Where do particulates come from? Asteroid impacts throw large amounts of dust into the atmosphere. Dust from the asteroid that struck near Mexico around 65 million years ago would have blocked the sun's rays. This reduction in sunlight may have limited photosynthesis in plants. The loss of plant life may have caused the food chain to collapse and led to dinosaur extinction.

Volcanic eruptions also release enormous clouds of ash and gases into the atmosphere. Particulates from large eruptions can circle Earth. The average global surface temperature fell by about 0.5 °C for several years after the 1991 eruption of Mount Pinatubo in the Philippines. Twenty million tons of sulfur dioxide and 5 km³, which is about 1.8 billion tons, of ash were blasted into the atmosphere. The sulfur-rich gases combined with water to form an Earth-cooling haze.

Active Reading **7 Describe** Give one example of a long-term and one example of a short-term change in climate caused by natural factors.

_____

_____

Visualize It!

6 Analyze What happened to global temperatures after the eruption of Mount Pinatubo? How long did this effect last?

_____

_____

_____

What are some causes of repeating patterns of climate change?

From day to day, or even year to year, the weather can change quite a lot. Some of these changes are relatively unpredictable, but others are due to predictable patterns or cycles. These patterns are the result of changes in the way energy is distributed around Earth.

Sun Cycles

Most of Earth's energy comes from the sun, and the output from the sun is very slightly higher during times of higher sunspot activity. Sunspots are dark areas on the sun that appear and disappear. Sunspot activity tends to increase and decrease in a cycle that lasts approximately 11 years. The effect of this sunspot cycle on global temperatures is not dramatic. But studies show a possible link between the sunspot cycle and global rain patterns.

El Niño and La Niña

Changes in ocean temperature also affect climate. During El Niño years, ocean temperatures are higher than usual in the tropical Pacific Ocean. The warmer water causes changes in global weather patterns. Some areas are cooler and wetter than normal. Other areas are warmer and dryer than normal.

The opposite effect occurs during La Niña years. Ocean temperatures are cooler than normal in the equatorial eastern Pacific Ocean. El Niño and La Niña conditions usually alternate, and both can lead to conditions such as droughts and flooding.

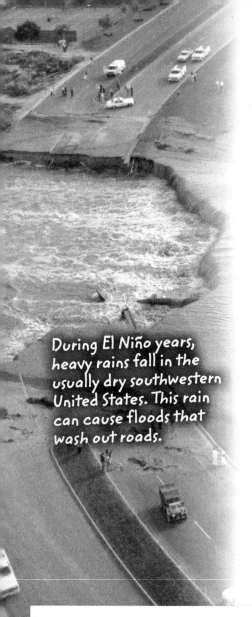

During El Niño years, heavy rains fall in the usually dry southwestern United States. This rain can cause floods that wash out roads.

 **Do the Math**

8 Calculate About what percentage of years are El Niño years, with warmer than average ocean temperatures? About what percentage are La Niña years? About what percentage are neither El Niño or La Niña years?

_____

_____

Cycles of El Niño and La Niña

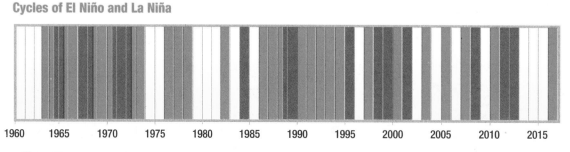

1960   1965   1970   1975   1980   1985   1990   1995   2000   2005   2010   2015

■ La Niña years
■ El Niño years

Source: NOAA Center for Weather and Climate Prediction 2016

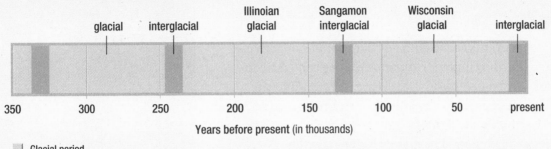

Visualize It!

During the last 2 million years, continental ice sheets have expanded far beyond the polar regions. There have been multiple advances of ice sheets (glacial periods) and retreats of ice sheets (interglacial periods). The timeline shows recent glacial and interglacial periods.

Cycles of the Recent Ice Age

glacial   interglacial   Illinoian glacial   Sangamon interglacial   Wisconsin glacial   interglacial

350   300   250   200   150   100   50   present

Years before present (in thousands)

□ Glacial period
■ Interglacial period

Source: NOAA Paleoclimatology, 2007

Much of North America was covered with thick ice sheets during the last glacial period. This glacial period ended 10,000 to 14,000 years ago.

PACIFIC OCEAN

NORTH AMERICA

ATLANTIC OCEAN

□ Land covered by ice
— Ice Age shoreline
— Present-day shoreline
— Present-day border

Ice Ages

The geological record shows that at different times Earth's climate has been both cooler *and* warmer than it is today. Earth's history contains multiple extremely cold periods when thick sheets of ice covered much of the continents. These periods are called *ice ages*. An **ice age** is a long period of cooling, during which ice sheets spread beyond the polar regions. The exact cause of ice ages is not fully understood. Some hypotheses propose that ice ages include changes in Earth's orbit, shifts in the balance of incoming and outgoing solar radiation, and changes in heat exchange rates between the equator and the poles.

Geologic evidence indicates that ice ages occur over widely spaced intervals of time—approximately every 200 million years. Each ice age lasts for millions of years. The most recent ice age began about 2 million years ago, with its peak about 20,000 years ago. Large ice sheets still cover Greenland and Antarctica.

9 Infer Locate your home state on the map. Then, describe the climate your state likely experienced during the last glacial period.

_____

_____

_____

Active Reading **10 List** What are some possible causes of ice ages?

_____

© Houghton Mifflin Harcourt Publishing Company

How do humans affect climate change?

Although natural events cause climate change, human activities may also affect Earth's climate. Human activities can cause the planet to warm when greenhouse gases are released into the atmosphere. Certain gases in the atmosphere, known as *greenhouse gases*, warm Earth's surface and the lower atmosphere by a process called the *greenhouse effect*. The **greenhouse effect** is the process by which gases in the atmosphere absorb and radiate energy as heat back to Earth. Greenhouse gases include carbon dioxide (CO_2), water vapor, methane, and nitrous oxide. Without greenhouse gases, energy would escape into space, and Earth would be colder. Two ways that humans release greenhouse gases into the atmosphere are by burning fossil fuels and by deforestation.

Active Reading **11 List** What are four greenhouse gases?

Smokestacks from a coal-burning power plant release water vapor and carbon dioxide into the atmosphere. Water vapor and carbon dioxide are greenhouse gases.

By Burning Fossil Fuels

There is now evidence to support the idea that humans are causing a rise in global CO_2 levels. Burning fossil fuels, such as gasoline and coal, adds greenhouse gases to the atmosphere. Since the 1950s, scientists have measured increasing levels of CO_2 and other greenhouse gases in the atmosphere. During this same period, the average global surface temperature has also been rising.

Correlation is when two sets of data show patterns that can be related. Both CO_2 level and average global surface temperature have been increasing over the same period of time, as shown by the graphs on the following page. There is a correlation between CO_2 levels in Earth's atmosphere and rising temperature. However, even though the two trends can be correlated, this does not show causation, or that one causes the other. In order to show causation, an explanation for how one change causes another has to be accepted. The explanation lies in the greenhouse effect. CO_2 is a greenhouse gas. An increase in greenhouse gases will warm Earth's surface and lower atmosphere. As greenhouse gas levels in the atmosphere have been rising, Earth's surface temperatures have been increasing with temperatures in Earth's lower atmosphere. This shows that it is likely that rising CO_2 levels are causing global warming.

By Deforestation

Some processes, such as burning fossil fuels, add CO_2 and other carbon-based gases to the atmosphere. Processes that emit carbon into the atmosphere are called *carbon sources*. Processes such as the growth of plants and trees remove carbon from the atmosphere. Processes that remove carbon from the atmosphere are called *carbon sinks*. Deforestation is the mass removal of trees for farming, timber, and land development. The loss of trees represents the loss of an important carbon sink. Deforestation often includes the burning of trees, which is another source of carbon dioxide. Deforestation affects the amount of carbon in the atmosphere by converting a carbon sink into a carbon source.

Scientists think that the deforestation of rain forests plays a large role in greenhouse gas emissions. Tropical deforestation is thought to release 1.5 billion tons of carbon each year.

Deforestation is one of the leading sources of greenhouse gases.

Visualize It!

12 Apply Based on the trend shown in the graph, how do you expect CO_2 levels to change over the next 20 years?

_____

_____

13 Explain Describe the changes in average global temperature during the years represented by the CO_2 graph.

_____

_____

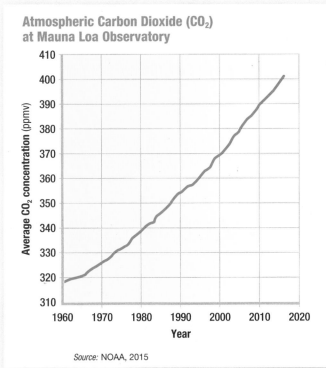

Source: NOAA, 2015

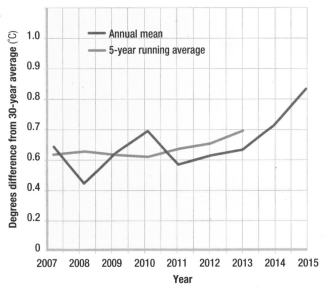

Source: Goddard Institute for Space Studies, NASA, 2016

14 Synthesize Based on the data shown in the graphs, make a prediction about what Earth's temperature and carbon dioxide concentrations will be in 2030. Support your position with evidence.

_____

_____

_____

_____

What are some predicted effects of climate change?

Data show that the world's climate has been warming in recent years. **Global warming** is a gradual increase in average global temperature. Global warming affects global weather patterns, global sea level, and life on Earth.

Effects on the Atmosphere

Studies show that the average global surface temperature has increased by 0.8–0.9 degrees C since 1880. Even small changes in temperature can greatly affect weather and precipitation. Scientists predict that warming will generate more severe weather. Predictions suggest that storms will be more powerful and occur more frequently. It has also been predicted that as much as half of Earth's surface may be affected by drought.

Effects on the Hydrosphere and Cryosphere

Much of the ice on Earth occurs in glaciers in mountains, Arctic sea ice, and ice sheets that cover Greenland and Antarctica. As temperatures increase, some of this ice will melt. The Arctic Report Card 2016 reported record-setting hot temperatures in the Arctic, which resulted in record ice melt.

When ice on land melts, global sea level rises because water flows into the ocean. Global sea level rose by 10 to 20 cm during the 1900s. Scientists project that sea level may rise 60 cm by 2100. Higher sea level is expected to increase flooding in coastal areas, some of which are highly populated. Some cities that could be affected are New York (U.S.), Shanghai (China), and Mumbai (India).

15 Infer How do melting ice caps and glaciers affect sea level?

_____

_____

_____

Mount Kilimanjaro has lost much of its glacier in recent years due to rising temperatures.

Mount Kilimanjaro
February 1993

Mount Kilimanjaro
February 2000

A warmer climate may force some species northward, including sugar maples.

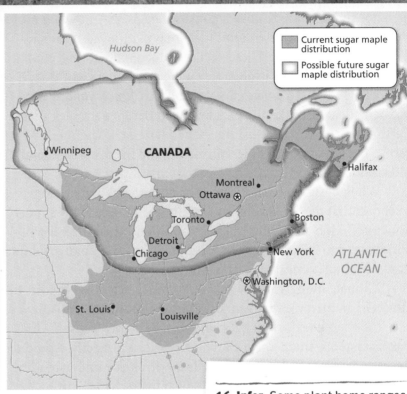

Current sugar maple distribution

Possible future sugar maple distribution

Hudson Bay

CANADA

Winnipeg

Halifax

Montreal
Ottawa ⊗

Toronto

Boston

Detroit
Chicago

New York

ATLANTIC OCEAN

⊗ Washington, D.C.

St. Louis

Louisville

Effects on the Biosphere

Active Reading **17 Summarize** Underline some of the effects of predicted climate change on the biosphere.

Scientists predict that global warming will change ecosystems. These changes may threaten the survival of many plant and animal species. Some species may move to cooler areas or even go extinct. Some butterflies, foxes, and alpine plants have already moved north to cooler climates. In Antarctica, emperor penguin populations could be reduced by as much as 95 percent by the end of this century if sea ice loss continues at its current rate. On the other hand, some species, such as pine beetles, starfish, and trumpeter swans, may benefit from expanded habitats in a warmer world.

Changes in temperature and precipitation will affect crops and livestock. If Earth warms more than a few degrees Celsius, many of the world's farms could suffer. Higher temperatures, reduced rainfall, and severe flooding can reduce crop production. Changes in weather will especially affect developing countries with large rural areas, such as countries in South Asia. A less severe warming would actually help agriculture in some regions by lengthening the growing season.

Warmer temperatures could increase the number of heat-related deaths and deaths from certain diseases, such as malaria. However, deaths associated with extreme cold could decrease.

16 Infer Some plant home ranges are shifting northward due to regional warming. What might happen to plant populations that are unable to spread northward?

_____

_____

_____

_____

How are climate predictions made?

Instruments have been placed in the atmosphere, in the oceans, on land, and in space to collect climate data. NASA now has more than a dozen spacecraft in orbit that are providing continuous data on Earth's climate. These data are added to historical climate data that are made available to researchers at centers worldwide. The data are used to create climate models. *Climate models* use mathematical formulas to describe how different variables affect Earth's climate. Today, there are about a dozen climate models that can be used to simulate different parts of the Earth's system and the interactions that take place between them.

When designing a model to predict future climate change, scientists first model Earth's current climate system. If the model does a good job describing current conditions, then the variables are changed to reflect future conditions. Scientists usually run the model multiple times using different variables.

Climate models are the means by which scientists predict the effects of an increase in greenhouse gases on future global climate. These models use the best data available about the ways in which Earth's systems interact. No climate model can perfectly reproduce the system that is being modeled. However, as our understanding of Earth's systems improves, models of climate change are becoming more accurate.

Visualize It!

18 Predict As Earth is warming, the oceans are rising. This is due to both melting ice and the expansion of water as it warms. Predict what the change in sea level will be by the year 2020 if the current trend continues. You may draw on the graph to extend the current trend.

_____

_____

Sea level has been rising steadily since the late 1800s. By the year 2000, global average sea level had risen 50 mm above mean sea level, represented as 0 on the graph.

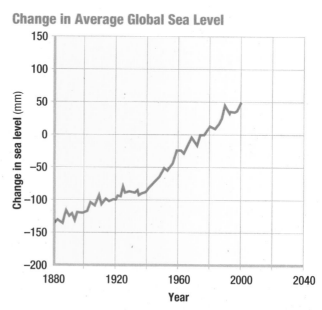

Change in Average Global Sea Level

Source: National Climatic Data Center, NOAA, 2007

Think Clean and Green

How can humans address the causes of climate change?

People can take action to reduce climate change and its effects. Countries are working together to reduce their impact on Earth's climate. Communities and individuals are also doing their part to reduce greenhouse gas emissions.

Reduce Greenhouse Gas Emissions

The Paris Agreement, an international environmental agreement to limit the increase in global temperatures, was adopted in 2015, and went into effect November 4, 2016. The goal of the Paris Agreement is to help prevent the most devastating effects of climate change by limiting the increase in global temperatures to 2 °C. One of the greatest challenges is that the agreement is voluntary, and that even if every country achieves its promised goals, the increase in temperature would be closer to 2.7 °C. Another challenge to this agreement is that there is no telling for how long each country will agree to participate in these climate efforts.

Individuals can reduce their impact on climate by conserving energy, increasing energy efficiency, and reducing the use of fossil fuels. Greenhouse gas emissions can be reduced by driving less and by switching to nonpolluting energy sources. Simple energy conservation solutions include turning off lights and replacing light bulbs. Recycling and reusing products also reduce energy use.

For most materials, recycling uses less energy than making products from scratch. That means fewer greenhouse gases are emitted.

Do the Math — You Try It

19 Calculate How much energy is saved by using recycled aluminum to make new aluminum cans instead of making aluminum cans from raw materials?

_____

_____

_____

20 Calculate By what percentage does recycling aluminum reduce energy use?

_____

_____

_____

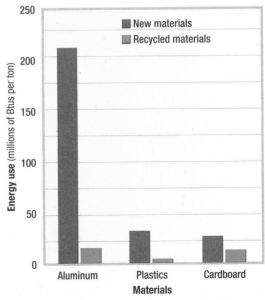

Energy Use for New vs. Recycled Materials

Source: U.S. EPA Solid Waste Management and Greenhouse Gases, 200?

- Reduce use of automobiles.
- Use new, cleaner technologies.
- Plant a tree.

Reduce the Rate of Deforestation

Deforestation contributes up to 20% of greenhouse gases globally. Planting trees and supporting reforestation programs are ways that carbon sources can be balanced by carbon sinks. Another solution is to educate people about the importance of the carbon that is stored in forests for stabilizing climate. In 2008, the United Nations began a program called REDD, or *Reducing Emissions from Deforestation and Forest Degradation*. REDD offers incentives to developing countries to reduce deforestation. The program also teaches conservation methods, which include forestry management.

Use New Technologies

Energy-efficient practices for homes, businesses, industry, and transportation reduce greenhouse gas emissions. These practices not only reduce the amount of greenhouse gases in the atmosphere, they also save money.

Clean-energy technologies are being researched and used in different parts of the world. New biofuels, solar power, wind power, and water power reduce the need to burn fossil fuels. In the United States, water power is the leading source of renewable energy, and the use of wind power is increasing rapidly. However, many new technologies are currently more expensive than fossil fuels.

21 Summarize Use the table to summarize ways in which sources of greenhouse gases in the atmosphere can be reduced.

Sources of greenhouse gases	Ways to reduce greenhouse gases
cars	Walk or use bikes more often.

Think Outside the Book Inquiry

22 Evaluate Make a scientific argument as to why the use of wind power, solar power, and water power will benefit the climate. Draw a bar graph showing how much energy will be saved with the use of each versus the use of typical greenhouse gas emitters. Be sure to label your *x*– and *y*–axes. Explain your argument.

What are some economic and political issues related to climate change?

Active Reading **23 Identify** Underline some of the economic and political issues that are related to climate change.

Climate change affects the entire Earth, no matter where greenhouse gases are produced. This makes climate change a global issue. The scientific concerns that climate change poses are not the only issues that have to be taken into account. There are economic and political issues involving climate change that are equally important.

Climate change is an economic issue. The cost of climate change includes the costs of crop failure, storm damage, and human disease. However, developing countries may not be able to afford technologies needed to reduce human impact on climate.

Climate change is also a political issue. Political action can lead to regulations that reduce greenhouse gas emissions. However, these laws may be challenged by groups who disagree with the need for change or disagree about what needs to change. No matter what choices are made to handle the challenges of climate change, it will take groups of people working together to make a difference.

Think Outside the Book **Inquiry**

24 Apply Research a recent extreme weather event from anywhere in the world. How might this event be related to climate change? Present your findings to the class as a news report or poster.

Climate change may make unusual weather the new norm. Rome, Italy, was brought to a standstill by unusually cold and snowy weather in 2010.

In 2016, wildfires in the forest around Gatlinburg, Tennessee, burned over 700 buildings in the historic town. The worst drought in 10 years fueled the wildfires.

25 Predict What are the possible economic and social consequences of unusually warm weather in a cold climate or unusually cool weather in a warm climate?

_____

_____

_____

How can science contribute?

There is a lot of research and attention focused on the causes of climate change. Scientists work hard to develop solutions to address the effects of climate change. Some solutions are even out of this world!

Global Warming

One idea that scientists are working on is that of constructing a giant space umbrella to deflect, or bounce, light from the sun before it reaches the Earth's atmosphere. Scientists use computer models to study the effects of deflecting heat away from Earth's surface with such solar shields. They estimate that by diverting just 2 to 4 percent of the sun's light, Earth could go back to its preindustrial climate.

Ocean fertilization is a type of climate engineering that reduces global warming. Fertilizing the Earth's oceans with iron increases the growth of phytoplankton. Phytoplankton are one of the producers in the oceans' food chain. They convert light energy to chemical energy through photosynthesis. This process captures the greenhouse gas CO_2. When the phytoplankton die, the CO_2 they have captured settles to the bottom of the ocean—far from the atmosphere.

Rising Sea Levels

Satellite imaging technology shows that rising sea levels threaten coastal communities. New research shows that as many as 13 million people live in areas along the U.S. coast that may be under water by 2100. To help lessen the effects of rising sea levels, some communities are restoring wetlands, marshes, and other natural features that help absorb energy from storm surges and protect the coastline.

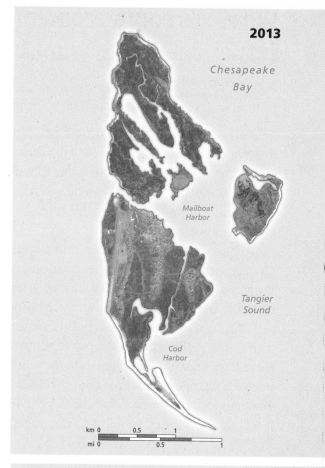

Visualize It!

26 Apply Tangier Island, Virginia, on the right, is one-third of the size it was in the 1850s. Based on the projections shown in the photographs, what recommendations would you make to the people living on Tangier Island?

_____

_____

_____

_____

Saving Species from Climate Change

Humans are not the only species affected by climate change. Animals and plants are impacted by rising temperatures and the loss of habitat due to climate change. In Tennessee, the Junaluska salamander and the pygmy salamander are found only in high elevation, cool, humid habitats, which are at risk due to climate change.

In some cases, to save species threatened by the effects of climate change, a decision is made to move them. For example, in 1995, the U.S. Fish and Wildlife Service moved 31 gray wolves from Canada to Yellowstone National Park in Montana, Wyoming, and Idaho. In just 20 years, the population rose to over 1,700 wolves in almost 300 packs.

But managed relocation is controversial. Some scientists worry that moving species from one place to another may spread disease. It could even threaten the survival of plants and animals native to the new location. However, without such steps, many species will be threatened with extinction.

The Junaluska salamander is at risk of extinction due in part to climate change.

27 Summarize Use the table to summarize ways in which science helps address the effects of climate change.

Climate change effect	Science contributions to address the effect
Global Warming	
Rising Sea Levels	
Species Endangerment	

Visual Summary

To complete this summary, fill in the blanks with the missing word or phrase. Then, use the key below to check your answers. You can use this page to review the main concepts of the lesson.

Natural factors have changed Earth's climate many times during Earth's history.

28 _____ have moved across Earth's surface over time and once formed a supercontinent called Pangaea.

Global warming affects many of Earth's systems.

30 If average global surface temperature continues to rise, then severe storms may become more _____ .

Climate Change

Greenhouse gases have a warming effect on the surface of Earth.

29 Scientists think that there is a connection between rising levels of _____ and rising _____ .

There are steps that people can take to reduce their impact on climate change.

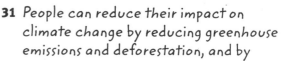

31 People can reduce their impact on climate change by reducing greenhouse emissions and deforestation, and by _____ .

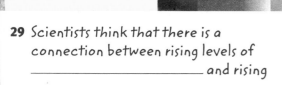

Sample answers: 28 Tectonic plates; 29 CO$_2$ (carbon dioxide); global temperatures; 30 frequent; 31 using new technologies

32 **Synthesize** How can burning fossil fuels cause global warming?

Lesson Review

Vocabulary

Fill in the blank with the term that best completes the following sentences.

1 _____ is a gradual increase in average global surface temperature.

2 A long period of climate cooling during which ice sheets spread beyond the polar regions is called a(n) _____.

3 The warming of Earth's surface and lower atmosphere that occurs when greenhouse gases absorb and reradiate energy is called the _____.

Key Concepts

4 Identify What are some natural events that have caused changes in Earth's climate?

_____

_____

_____

_____

5 Identify What are some predicted effects of climate change linked to global warming?

_____

_____

_____

_____

_____

6 Summarize List ways in which humans can reduce the rate of climate change.

_____

_____

_____

_____

_____

_____

Critical Thinking

Use the graph to answer the following questions.

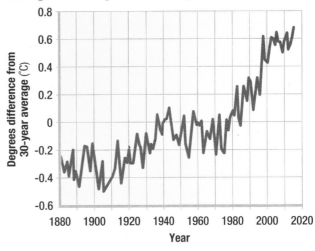

Change in Average Global Temperature

Source: Goddard Institute for Space Studies, NASA, 2015

7 Analyze Describe the trend shown in this graph. Why is it helpful to have many decades of data to make a graph such as this?

_____

_____

_____

_____

8 Infer What might cause the average global surface temperature to rise and fall from year to year?

_____

_____

_____

_____

_____

9 Infer Why might some countries be more reluctant than others to take steps to reduce levels of greenhouse gases?

_____

_____

_____

_____

_____

My Notes

J. Marshall Shepherd

METEOROLOGIST AND CLIMATOLOGIST

J. Marshall Shepherd

Dr. Marshall Shepherd, who works at the University of Georgia, has been interested in weather since he made his own weather-collecting instruments for a school science project. Although the instruments he uses today, like computers and satellites, are much larger and much more powerful than the ones he made in school, they give him some of the same information.

In his work, Dr. Shepherd tries to understand weather events, such as hurricanes and thunderstorms, and relate them to current weather and climate change. He once led a team that used space-based radar to measure rainfall over urban areas. The measurements confirmed that the areas downwind of major cities experience more rainfall in summer than other areas in the same region. He explained that the excess heat retained by buildings and roads changes the way the air circulates, and this causes rain clouds to form.

While the most familiar field of meteorology is weather forecasting, research meteorology is also used in air pollution control, weather control, agricultural planning, climate change studies, and even criminal and civil investigations.

Social Studies Connection

An almanac is a type of calendar that contains various types of information, including weather forecasts and astronomical data, for every day of the year. Many people used almanacs before meteorologists started to forecast the weather. Use an almanac from the library or the Internet to find out what the weather was on the day that you were born.

JOB BOARD

Atmospheric Scientist

What You'll Do: Collect and analyze data on Earth's air pressure, humidity, and winds to make short-range and long-range weather forecasts. Work around the clock during weather emergencies like hurricanes and tornadoes.

Where You Might Work: Weather data collecting stations, radio and television stations, or private consulting firms.

Education: A bachelor's degree in meteorology, or in a closely related field with courses in meteorology, is required. A master's degree is necessary for some jobs.

Airplane Pilot

What You'll Do: Fly airplanes containing passengers or cargo, or for crop dusting, search and rescue, or fire-fighting. Before flights, check the plane's control equipment and weather conditions. Plan a safe route. Pilots communicate with air traffic control during flight to ensure a safe flight and fill out paperwork after the flight.

Where You Might Work: Flying planes for airlines, the military, radio and tv stations, freight companies, flight schools, farms, national parks, or other businesses that use airplanes.

Education: Most pilots will complete a four-year college degree before entering a pilot program. Before pilots become certified and take to the skies, they need a pilot license and many hours of flight time and training.

Snow Plow Operator

What You'll Do: In areas that receive snowfall, prepare the roads by spreading a mixture of sand and salt on the roads when snow is forecast. After a snowfall, drive snow plows to clear snow from roads and walkways.

Where You Might Work: For public organizations or private companies in cities and towns that receive snowfall.

Education: In most states, there is no special license needed, other than a driver's license.

Unit 7 [Big Idea] Earth's atmosphere is a mixture of gases that interacts with solar energy.

Lesson 1
ESSENTIAL QUESTION
What is the atmosphere?

Describe the composition and structure of the atmosphere and explain how the atmosphere protects life and insulates Earth.

Lesson 2
ESSENTIAL QUESTION
How do humans impact Earth's atmosphere?

Identify the impact that humans have had on Earth's atmosphere.

Lesson 3
ESSENTIAL QUESTION
What are the causes and effects of climate change?

Describe climate change and the causes and effects of climate change.

Think Outside the Book

2 Synthesize Choose one of these activities to help synthesize what you have learned in this unit.

☐ Using what you learned in lessons 1, 2, and 3, write a fable that explains how human activities can pollute air resources and create climate change. Provide a moral for your story that explains why people should try to prevent pollution.

☐ Using what you learned in lessons 1 and 3, explain in a short essay how weather predictions might change if additional greenhouse gases in Earth's atmosphere caused Earth to warm by several degrees C.

Connect ESSENTIAL QUESTIONS
Lessons 2 and 3

1 Synthesize Explain how human activity affects the atmosphere in ways that cause and counteract climate change.

_____

_____

Unit 7 Review

Name _____

Vocabulary

Fill in each blank with the term that best completes the following sentences.

1 _____ is the measure of the force with which air molecules push on an area of the surface.

2 The process by which certain gases in the atmosphere, such as water vapor and carbon dioxide, absorb and reradiate infrared radiation is called the

_____.

3 _____ forms when the gases from vehicle exhaust react with sunlight.

4 _____ is the characteristic weather conditions in an area over a long period of time.

5 A long period of climate cooling during which ice sheets spread beyond the polar regions is called a(n) _____.

Key Concepts

Read each question below, and circle the best answer.

6 Smog usually forms from ground-level ozone and what other human-made pollutant?

A acid precipitation

C vehicle exhaust

B volcanic gases

D smoke from cigarettes

7 Which is a source of indoor air pollution?

A greenhouse gases

B steam from a hot shower

C chemicals from certain cleaning products

D radiation from sunlight entering windows

8 The graph below shows how the amount of carbon dioxide (CO_2) in our atmosphere has changed since 1960.

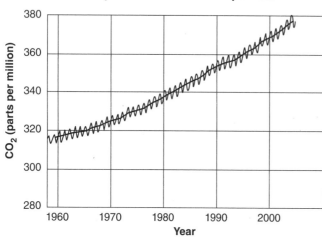

Amount of Atmospheric Carbon Dioxide per Year

Based on the information given in the graph, which of these phenomena has likely increased since 1960?

A land erosion

B coastal erosion

C ozone depletion

D greenhouse effect

9 In which layer of the atmosphere can almost all of Earth's air pollution be found?

A the thermosphere   **C** the stratosphere

B the mesosphere   **D** the troposphere

10 How did the eruption of Mount Pinatubo in 1991 affect the atmosphere?

A It caused the loss of plant life in Mexico.

B It caused five years of La Niña.

C It caused flooding around the planet.

D It caused an Earth-cooling haze.

11 An increase in greenhouse gases does what to Earth's surface and atmosphere?

  A warms both Earth's surface and lower atmosphere

  B warms both Earth's surface and upper atmosphere

  C cools both Earth's surface and lower atmosphere

  D cools both Earth's surface and upper atmosphere

12 Which gas mostly makes up Earth's atmosphere?

 A oxygen

 B water vapor

 C nitrogen

 D carbon dioxide

13 Which of these is not a currently predicted effect of global climate change?

  A rising sea levels

  B increased precipitation everywhere on the globe

  C reduction in Arctic sea ice

  D more severe storms

Critical Thinking

Answer the following questions in the space provided.

14 Suppose you were a superhero who could fly up through the atmosphere. You would feel the temperature and air pressure change around you as you flew higher. Describe your flight in a paragraph. In your answer, name the four main atmosphere layers. Tell how the temperature and air pressure change as you pass through each layer.

_____

_____

_____

_____

15 Can the atmosphere be considered a natural resource? Explain.

_____

_____

_____

Give two examples of how the atmosphere is important to life on Earth.

_____

_____

_____

Connect ESSENTIAL QUESTIONS
Lessons 1, 2, and 3

Answer the following question in the space provided.

16 Describe various ways we can make sure Earth's atmosphere does not get destroyed by human activities or climate change in the future.

_____

_____

_____

_____

_____

_____

⟨Technology⟩
and ⟨Coding⟩

This breathtaking image of Earth was taken from the International Space Station, an international laboratory orbiting Earth. The operation of the International Space Station is controlled by 52 computers and millions of lines of computer code. Its many high-tech features include solar panels that power the laboratory and a human-like robotic astronaut.

This is Robonaut 2, a robot designed to do routine maintenance at the International Space Station.

Data Driven

What is computer science?

If you like computer technology and learning about how computers work, computer science might be for you. *Computer science* is the study of computer technology and how data is processed, stored, and accessed by computers. Computer science is an important part of many other areas, including science, math, engineering, robotics, medicine, game design, and 3D animation.

Computer technology is often described in terms of *hardware*, which are the physical components, and *software,* which are the programs or instructions that a computer runs. Computer scientists must understand how hardware and software work together. Computer scientists may develop new kinds of useful computer software. Or they may work with engineers to improve existing computer hardware.

The first electronic computer, the computer ENIAC (Electronic Numerical Integrator And Computer), was developed at the University of Pennsylvania in 1946.

The integrated circuit (IC), first developed in the 1950s, was instrumental in the development of small computer components.

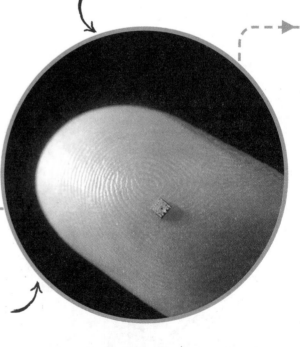

The development of the IC made it possible to reduce the overall size of computers and their components and to increase their processing speed.

How has computer technology changed over time?

Modern, digital computer technology is less than 100 years old. Yet in that short amount of time, it has advanced rapidly. The earliest digital computers could perform only a limited number of tasks and were the size of an entire room. Over the decades, engineers continued to develop smaller, faster, and more powerful computers. Today's computers can process hundreds of millions of instructions per second!

Computer scientists and engineers think about what people want or need from computer technology. The most advanced hardware is not useful if people do not know how to use it. So computer scientists and engineers work to create software that is reliable, useful, and easy to use. Today's tablet computers, cell phones, and video game consoles can be used without any special training.

Advances in digital computer technology have helped make computers cheaper and easier to operate, which has allowed many more people to work and play with them.

1 Compare Are modern computers simpler or more complex than early computers? Explain.

_____

_____

_____

Computer Logic

What do computer scientists do?

Many people enjoy developing computer technology for fun. Learning how to create mobile phone games or Internet-enabled gadgets can be rewarding hobbies. For some people, that hobby may one day become a career in computer science. Working in computer science is a bit like solving a puzzle. Applying knowledge of how computers work to solve real-world problems requires collaboration, creativity, and logical, step-by-step thinking.

They collaborate across many disciplines

Computers are valuable tools in math and science because they can perform complex calculations very quickly. Computers are useful to many other fields, too. For example, animators use computer technology to create realistic lighting effects in 3D animated films. Mechanics use computers to diagnose problems in car systems. For every field that relies on special software or computer technology, there is an opportunity for computer scientists and engineers to collaborate and develop solutions for those computing needs. Computer scientists must be able to define and understand the problems presented to them and to communicate and work with experts in other fields to develop the solutions.

This is a kayak folded up.

Computational origami is a computer program used to model the ways in which different materials, including paper, can be folded. It combines computer science and the art of paper folding to create new technologies, such as this kayak.

Tracking software helps biologists study animal behavior.

satellite →

satellite data receiving center

satellite data processing center

transmitter

They help solve real-world problems

Some computer scientists carry out theoretical research. Others apply computer science concepts to develop software. Theoretical computer science and practical software development help solve real-world problems. For example, biologists need ways to safely and accurately track endangered animals. Computer science theories on artificial intelligence and pattern recognition have been applied to advanced animal-tracking technologies, such as satellite transmitters and aerial cameras. New kinds of image processing software now allow biologists to analyze the collected data in different ways.

They use logical, step-by-step thinking

Computers perform tasks given to them, and they do this very well. But in order to get the results they expect, computer scientists and programmers must write very accurate instructions. Computer science and programming requires logical thinking, deductive reasoning, and a good understanding of cause-and-effect relationships. When designing software, computer scientists must consider every possible user action and how the computer should respond to each action.

2 Explain How is computer science helping this scientist do her research?

_____

_____

_____

_____

Transmitters can be attached to animals to help track their movements.

Up to <Code>

How is computer software created?

Imagine that you are using a computer at the library to learn more about the history of electronic music. You use the library's database application to start searching for Internet resources. You also do a search to look for audio recordings. Finally, you open a word processor to take notes on the computer. Perhaps without realizing it, you've used many different pieces of software. Have you ever wondered how computer software is created?

Computer software is designed to address a need

Computer software can help us to learn more about our world. It can be useful to business. Or it can simply entertain us. Whatever its purpose, computer software should fulfill some human want or need. The first steps in creating software are precisely defining the need or want being addressed and planning how the software will work.

Computer software source code is written in a programming language

The instructions that tell a computer how to run video games, word processors, and other kinds of software are not written in a human language. They are written in a special programming language, or *code*. Javascript, C++, and Python are examples of programming languages. Programming languages—like human languages—must follow certain rules in order to be understood by the computer. A series of instructions written in a programming language is called *source code*.

Identifying what need a computer program addresses is one of the first development steps.

Source code is revised

Sometimes, programmers make mistakes in their code. Many programming environments have a feature that alerts the programmer to certain errors, such as spelling mistakes in commands, missing portions of code, or logical errors in the sequence of instructions. However, many mistakes go undetected, too. Some errors may cause the program to function incorrectly or not at all. When this happens, the programmer must identify the error, correct it, and test the software again.

Computer software is user tested, and revised

Once the software is created, it must be tested thoroughly to make sure it does not fail or behave in unexpected ways. It must also be tested to ensure that it meets users' needs. The creators of a piece of software might observe how people use it. Or they might ask users to provide feedback on certain features and test the software again.

3 Identify This source code contains an error. Infer where the error is located. What does this code "tell" the computer to do? Write your answers below.

_____

_____

_____

_____

```
13
14   # Scores are not tied, so check
15   # which player wins the round
16 ▾ if player1_score > player2_score:
17       print ("Player 1 wins!")
18 ▾ else:
19       prnt ("Player 2 wins!")
20
────────────────────────────────────────

! Syntax error, line 19
```

Test running a program is important for finding and fixing errors in the code.

Play it Safe

How should I work with computers?

It is easy to lose track of time when you're sitting in front of a computer or game console. It's also easy to forget that things you say or do online can be seen and shared by many different people. Here are some tips for using computers safely and responsibly.

✓ **Maintain good posture**

Time can pass by quickly when you are working on a computer or another device. Balance computer time with other activities, including plenty of physical activity. When you are sitting at a computer, sit upright with your shoulders relaxed. Your eyes should be level with the top of the monitor and your feet should be flat on the ground.

✓ **Observe electrical safety**

Building your own electronics projects can be fun, but it's important to have an understanding of circuits and electrical safety first. Otherwise, you could damage your components or hurt yourself. The potential for an electrical shock is real when you open up a computer, work with frayed cords or, use ungrounded plugs or attempt to replace parts without understanding how to do so safely. Ask an adult for help before starting any projects. Also, avoid using a connected computer during thunderstorms.

head and neck in a straight, neutral position

shoulders are relaxed

wrists are straight

feet are flat on the ground

Good posture will help you avoid the aches and injuries related to sitting in front of a computer for a long time.

✓ Handle and maintain computers properly

Be cautious when handling and transporting electronic devices. Dropping them or spilling liquids on them could cause serious damage. Keep computers away from dirt, dust, liquids, and moisture. Never use wet cleaning products unless they are specifically designed for use on electronics. Microfiber cloths can be used to clear smudges from device screens. Spilled liquids can cause circuits to short out and hardware to corrode. If a liquid spills on a device, unplug it and switch it off immediately, remove the battery and wipe up as much of the liquid inside the device as possible. Don't switch the device back on until it is completely dry.

✓ Do not post private information online

Talk to your family about rules for Internet use. Do not use the Internet to share private information such as photographs, your phone number, or your address. Do not respond to requests for personal details from people you do not know.

✓ Treat yourself and others with respect

It is important to treat others with respect when on the Internet. Don't send or post messages online that you wouldn't say to someone in person. Unfortunately, not everyone acts respectfully while online. Some people may say hurtful things to you or send you unwanted messages. Do not reply to unwanted messages. Alert a trusted adult to any forms of contact, such as messages or photos, that make you feel uncomfortable.

4 Apply Fill in the chart below with a suitable response to each scenario.

SCENARIO	YOUR RESPONSE
You receive a text message from an online store asking for your home address.	
You've been lying down in front of a laptop, and you notice that your neck is feeling a little sore.	
You need to take a laptop computer with you on your walk to school.	
You want to try assembling a robotics kit with a friend.	
Someone posts unfriendly comments directed at you.	

Career in Computing: Game Programmer

What do video game programmers do?

Creating your own universe with its own set of rules is fun. Just ask a programmer who works on video games!

What skills are needed in game programming?

A programmer should know how to write code, but there are other important skills a programmer needs as well. An understanding of physics and math is important for calculating how objects move and interact in a game. Game programmers usually work on a team with other people, such as artists, designers, writers, and musicians. They must be able to communicate effectively, and ideally, the programmer should understand the other team members' roles.

How can I get started with game development?

You don't need a big budget or years of experience to try it out. There are books, videos, and websites that can help you get started. When you're first experimenting with game development, start small. Try making a very simple game like Tic-Tac-Toe. Once you've mastered that, you can try something more complex.

---

5 Brainstorm Why would working on a team be important to the game development process?

_____

_____

_____

Resources

Glossary

			Pronunciation Key					
Sound	**Symbol**	**Example**	**Respelling**	**Sound**	**Symbol**	**Example**	**Respelling**
ă	a	pat	PAT	ŏ	ah	bottle	BAHT'l
ā	ay	pay	PAY	ō	oh	toe	TOH
âr	air	care	KAIR	ô	aw	caught	KAWT
ä	ah	father	FAH•ther	ôr	ohr	roar	ROHR
är	ar	argue	AR•gyoo	oi	oy	noisy	NOYZ•ee
ch	ch	chase	CHAYS	o͝o	u	book	BUK
ĕ	e	pet	PET	o͞o	oo	boot	BOOT
ĕ (at end of a syllable)	eh	settee lessee	seh•TEE leh•SEE	ou	ow	pound	POWND
ĕr	ehr	merry	MEHR•ee	s	s	center	SEN•ter
ē	ee	beach	BEECH	sh	sh	cache	CASH
g	g	gas	GAS	ŭ	uh	flood	FLUHD
ĭ	i	pit	PIT	ûr	er	bird	BERD
ĭ (at end of a syllable)	ih	guitar	gih•TAR	z	z	xylophone	ZY•luh•fohn
ī	y eye (only for a complete syllable)	pie island	PY EYE•luhnd	z	z	bags	BAGZ
				zh	zh	decision	dih•SIZH•uhn
				ə	uh	around broken focus	uh•ROWND BROH•kuhn FOH•kuhs
îr	ir	hear	HIR	ər	er	winner	WIN•er
j	j	germ	JERM	th	th	thin they	THIN THAY
k	k	kick	KIK				
ng	ng	thing	THING	w	w	one	WUHN
ngk	ngk	bank	BANGK	wh	hw	whether	HWETH•er

A

acid precipitation (AS·id prih·sip·ih·TAY·shuhn) rain, sleet, or snow that contains a high concentration of acids (471)
  precipitación ácida lluvia, aguanieve o nieve que contiene una alta concentración de ácidos

active transport (AK·tiv TRANS·pohrt) the movement of substances across the cell membrane that requires the cell to use energy (207)
  transporte activo el movimiento de sustancias a través de la membrana celular que requiere que la célula gaste energía

adaptation (ad·ap·TAY·shuhn) a characteristic that improves an individual's ability to survive and reproduce in a particular environment (294)
  adaptación una característica que mejora la capacidad de un individuo para sobrevivir y reproducirse en un determinado ambiente

air pollution (AIR puh·LOO·shuhn) the contamination of the atmosphere by the introduction of pollutants from human and natural sources (469)
  contaminación del aire la contaminación de la atmósfera debido a la introducción de contaminantes provenientes de fuentes humanas y naturales

air pressure (AIR PRESH·er) the measure of the force with which air molecules push on a surface (459)
  presión del aire la medida de la fuerza con la que las moléculas del aire empujan contra una superficie

air quality (AIR KWAHL·ih·tee) a measure of the pollutants in the air that is used to express how clean or polluted the air is (472)
  calidad de aire una medida de los contaminantes presentes en el aire que se usa para expresar el nivel de pureza o contaminación del aire

allele (uh·LEEL) one of the alternative forms of a gene that governs a characteristic, such as hair color (306)
  alelo una de las formas alternativas de un gen que rige un carácter, como por ejemplo, el color del cabello

alveolus (al·VEE·uh·luhs) tiny, thin-walled, capillary-rich sac in the lungs where the exchange of oxygen and carbon dioxide takes place; also called air sac (386)
  alveolo saco diminuto ubicado en los pulmones, de paredes delgadas y rico en capilares, en donde ocurre el intercambio de oxígeno y dióxido de carbono

Animalia (an·uh·MEY·lee·uh) a kingdom made up of complex, multicellular organisms that lack cell walls, can usually move around, and quickly respond to their environment (183)
  Animalia un reino formado por organismos pluricelulares complejos que no tienen pared celular, normalmente son capaces de moverse y reaccionan rápidamente a su ambiente

Archaea (ar·KEE·uh) a domain made up of prokaryotes, most of which are known to live in extreme environments, that are distinguished from other prokaryotes by differences in their genetics and in the makeup of their cell wall (182)
  Archaea un dominio compuesto por procariotes, la mayoría de los cuales viven en ambientes extremos que se distinguen de otros procariotes por su genética y por la composición de su pared celular

Archaebacteria (ahr·kee·bak·TEER·ee·uh) a kingdom in the domain Archaea that consists of unicellular organisms that survive in extreme and harsh environments (182)
  Archaeabacteria un reino del dominio Archaea que comprende organismos unicelulares que pueden sobrevivir en ambientes extremos en los que rigen condiciones severas

artery (AR·tuh·ree) a blood vessel that carries blood away from the heart to the body's organs (381)
  arteria un vaso sanguíneo que transporta sangre del corazón a los órganos del cuerpo

asexual reproduction (ay·SEHK·shoo·uhl ree·pruh·DUHK·shuhn) reproduction that does not involve the union of sex cells and in which one parent produces offspring that are genetically identical to the parent (284)
  reproducción asexual reproducción que no involucra la unión de células sexuales, en la que un solo progenitor produce descendencia que es genéticamente igual al progenitor

atmosphere (AT·muh·sfir) a mixture of gases that surrounds a planet, moon, or other celestial body (458)
  atmósfera una mezcla de gases que rodea un planeta, una luna u otros cuerpos celestes

atom (AT·uhm) the smallest unit of an element that maintains the properties of that element (52, 101, 156)
  átomo la unidad más pequeña de un elemento que conserva las propiedades de ese elemento

atomic number (uh·TAHM·ik NUM·ber) the number of protons in the nucleus of an atom; the atomic number is the same for all atoms of an element (106)
  número atómico el número de protones en el núcleo de un átomo; el número atómico es el mismo para todos los átomos de un elemento

average atomic mass (AV·er·ij uh·TAHM·ik MAS) the weighted average of the masses of all naturally occurring isotopes of an element (116)
  masa atómica promedio el promedio ponderado de las masas de todos los isótopos de un elemento que se encuentran en la naturaleza

axon (AK·sahn) an elongated extension of a neuron that carries impulses away from the cell body (409)
  axón una extensión alargada de una neurona que transporta impulsos hacia fuera del cuerpo de la célula

B

Bacteria (bak·TIR·ee·uh) a domain made up of prokaryotes that usually have a cell wall and that usually reproduce by cell division (182)

Bacteria un dominio compuesto por procariotes que por lo general tienen pared celular y se reproducen por división celular

behavioral adaptation (bih·HEYV·yer·al ad·ap·TAY·shuhn) a change that allows an organism to survive by altering the way it acts (296)

adaptación conductual un cambio que altera la conducta de un organismo y le permite a este sobrevivir

blood (BLUHD) the fluid that carries gases, nutrients, and wastes through the body and that is made up of platelets, white blood cells, red blood cells, and plasma (376)

sangre el líquido que lleva gases, nutrientes y desechos por el cuerpo y que está formado por plaquetas, glóbulos blancos, glóbulos rojos y plasma

boiling (BOYL·ing) the change of state from a liquid to a gas that occurs at a specific temperature (80)

ebullición el cambio de estado de líquido a gaseoso que ocurre a una temperatura específica

brain (BRAYN) the organ that is the main control center of the nervous system (406)

encéfalo el órgano que es el centro principal de control del sistema nervioso

bronchus (BRAHNG·kuhs) one of the two main branches of the trachea that lead directly to the lungs—plural, bronchi (386)

bronquio una de las dos ramificaciones principales de la tráquea que conducen directamente a los pulmones

C

capillary (KAP·uh·lehr·ee) a tiny blood vessel that allows an exchange between blood and cells in tissue (381)

capilar diminuto vaso sanguíneo que permite el intercambio entre la sangre y las células de los tejidos

carbohydrate (kar·boh·HY·drayt) a class of molecules that includes sugars, starches, and fiber; contains carbon, hydrogen, and oxygen (159)

carbohidrato una clase de moléculas entre las que se incluyen azúcares, almidones y fibra; contiene carbono, hidrógeno y oxígeno

carbon cycle (KAR·buhn SY·kuhl) the movement of carbon from the nonliving environment into living things and back (246)

ciclo del carbono el movimiento del carbono del ambiente sin vida a los seres vivos y de los seres vivos al ambiente

cardiovascular system (kahr·dee·oh·VAS·kyuh·ler SIS·tuhm) a collection of organs that transport blood throughout the body; the organs in this system include the heart, the arteries, and the veins (376)

aparato cardiovascular un conjunto de órganos que transportan la sangre a través del cuerpo; los órganos de este sistema incluyen al corazón, las arterias y las venas

cell (SEL) in biology, the smallest unit that can perform all life processes; cells are covered by a membrane and contain DNA and cytoplasm (146)

célula en biología, la unidad más pequeña que puede realizar todos los procesos vitales; las células están cubiertas por una membrana y tienen ADN y citoplasma

cell cycle (SEL SY·kuhl) the life cycle of a cell (264)

ciclo celular el ciclo de vida de una célula

cell membrane (SEL MEM·brayn) a phospholipid layer that covers a cell's surface and acts as a barrier between the inside of a cell and the cell's environment (150)

membrana celular una capa de fosfolípidos que cubre la superficie de la célula y funciona como una barrera entre el interior de la célula y el ambiente de la célula

cell wall (SEL WAWL) a rigid structure that surrounds the cell membrane in plants, fungi, and some bacteria, and provides support to the cell (170)

pared celular una estructura rígida que rodea la membrana celular en las plantas, los hongos y algunas bacterias, y le brinda soporte a la célula

cellular respiration (SEL·yuh·luhr res·puh·RAY·shuhn) the process by which cells use oxygen to produce energy from food (204, 232)

respiración celular el proceso por medio del cual las células utilizan oxígeno para producir energía a partir de los alimentos

chemical change (KEM·ih·kuhl CHAYNJ) a change that occurs when one or more substances change into entirely new substances with different properties (38)

cambio químico un cambio que ocurre cuando una o más sustancias se transforman en sustancias totalmente nuevas con propiedades diferentes

chemical equation (KEM·ih·kuhl ih·KWAY·zhuhn) a representation of a chemical reaction that uses symbols to show the relationship between the reactants and the products (125)

ecuación química una representación de una reacción química que usa símbolos para mostrar la relación entre los reactivos y los productos

chemical formula (KEM·ih·kuhl FOHR·myuh·luh) a combination of chemical symbols and numbers to represent a substance (125)

fórmula química una combinación de símbolos químicos y números que se usan para representar una sustancia

chemical property (KEM·ih·kuhl PRAHP·uhr·tee) a property of matter that describes a substance's ability to participate in chemical reactions (26)

propiedad química una propiedad de la materia que describe la capacidad de una sustancia de participar en reacciones químicas

chemical reaction (KEM·ih·kuhl re·AK·shuhn) the process in which atoms are rearranged and chemical bonds are broken and formed to produce a chemical change of a substance (124)

reacción química el proceso por el cual los átomos cambian su disposición y se rompen y forman enlaces químicos de manera que se produce un cambio químico en una sustancia

chemical symbol (KEM·ih·kuhl SIM·buhl) a one-, two-, or three-letter abbreviation of the name of an element (116)

símbolo químico una abreviatura de una, dos o tres letras del nombre de un elemento

chlorophyll (KLOHR·uh·fil) a green pigment that captures light energy for photosynthesis (231)

clorofila un pigmento verde que capta la energía luminosa para la fotosíntesis

chloroplast (KLOHR·oh·plast) an organelle found in plant and algae cells where photosynthesis occurs (171)

cloroplasto un organelo que se encuentra en las células vegetales y en las células de las algas, en el cual se lleva a cabo la fotosíntesis

chromosome (KROH·muh·sohm) in a eukaryotic cell, one of the structures in the nucleus that are made up of DNA and protein; in a prokaryotic cell, the main ring of DNA (263)

cromosoma en una célula eucariótica, una de las estructuras del núcleo que está hecha de ADN y proteína; en una célula procariótica, el anillo principal de ADN

climate (KLY·mit) the weather conditions in an area over a long period of time (484)

clima las condiciones del tiempo en un área durante un largo período de tiempo

codominance (koh·DAHM·uh·nuhns) a condition in which two alleles are expressed such that the phenotype of a heterozygous individual is a combination of the phenotypes of the two homozygous parents (311)

codominancia una condición en la que dos alelos están expresados de modo que el fenotipo de un individuo heterocigoto es una combinación de los fenotipos de los dos padres homocigotos

compound (KAHM·pownd) a substance made up of atoms of two or more different elements joined by chemical bonds (53)

compuesto una sustancia formada por átomos de dos o más elementos diferentes unidos por enlaces químicos

condensation (kahn·den·SAY·shuhn) the change of state from a gas to a liquid (81)

condensación el cambio de estado de gas a líquido

cytokinesis (sy·toh·kuh·NEE·sis) the division of the cytoplasm of a cell (265)

citocinesis la división del citoplasma de una célula

cytoplasm (sy·tuh·PLAZ·uhm) the region of the cell within the membrane that includes the fluid, the cytoskeleton, and all of the organelles except the nucleus (150)

citoplasma la región de la célula dentro de la membrana, que incluye el líquido, el citoesqueleto y los organelos, pero no el núcleo

cytoskeleton (sy·toh·SKEL·ih·tn) the cytoplasmic network of protein filaments that plays an essential role in cell movement, shape, and division (167)

citoesqueleto la red citoplásmica de filamentos de proteínas que juega un papel esencial en el movimiento, forma y división de la célula

dendrite (DEHN·dryt) branchlike extension of a neuron that receives impulses from neighboring neurons (409)

dendrita la extensión ramificada de una neurona que recibe impulsos de las neuronas vecinas

density (DEN·sih·tee) the ratio of the mass of a substance to the volume of the substance (13)

densidad la relación entre la masa de una sustancia y su volumen

deposition (dep·uh·ZISH·uhn) the change of state from a gas directly to a solid (83)

sublimación inversa cambio de estado por el cual un gas se convierte directamente en un sólido

diffusion (dih·FYOO·zhuhn) the movement of particles from regions of higher concentrations to regions of lower concentrations (206)

difusión el movimiento de partículas de regiones de mayor concentración a regiones de menor concentración

digestive system (dy·JES·tiv SIS·tuhm) the organs that break down food so that it can be used by the body (394)

aparato digestivo los órganos que descomponen la comida de modo que el cuerpo la pueda usar

DNA (dee·en·AY) deoxyribonucleic acid, a molecule that is present in all living cells and that contains the information that determines the traits that a living thing inherits and needs to live (263, 328)

ADN ácido desoxirribonucleico, una molécula que está presente en todas las células vivas y que contiene la información que determina los caracteres que un ser vivo hereda y necesita para vivir

dominant (DAHM·uh·nuhnt) in genetics, describes an allele that is fully expressed whenever the allele is present in an individual (307)

dominante en la genética, término que describe a un alelo que se expresa por completo siempre que el alelo está presente en un individuo

ecosystem (EE·koh·sis·tuhm) a specific community of organisms and their physical environment (241)

ecosistema una comunidad específica de organismos y su ambiente físico

egg (EG) a sex cell produced by a female (421)

óvulo una célula sexual producida por una hembra

electron (ee·LEK·trahn) a subatomic particle that has a negative charge (102)

electrón una partícula subatómica que tiene carga negativa

electron cloud (ee·LEK·trahn KLOWD) a region around the nucleus of an atom where electrons are likely to be found (103)

nube de electrones una región que rodea al núcleo de un átomo en la cual es probable encontrar a los electrones

element (EL·uh·muhnt) a substance that cannot be separated or broken down into simpler substances by chemical means (53)

elemento una sustancia que no se puede separar o descomponer en sustancias más simples por medio de métodos químicos

embryo (EM·bree·oh) in humans, a developing individual from first division after fertilization through the 10th week of pregnancy (423)

embrión en los seres humanos, un individuo en desarrollo desde la primera división después de la fecundación hasta el final de la décima semana de embarazo

endocrine system (EN·duh·krin SIS·tuhm) a collection of glands and groups of cells that secrete hormones that regulate growth, development, and homeostasis; includes the pituitary, thyroid, parathyroid, and adrenal glands, the hypothalamus, the pineal body, and the gonads (412)

sistema endocrino un conjunto de glándulas y grupos de células que secretan hormonas, las cuales regulan el crecimiento, el desarrollo y la homeostasis; incluye las glándulas pituitaria, tiroides, paratiroides y suprarrenal, el hipotálamo, el cuerpo pineal y las gónadas

endocytosis (en·doh·sy·TOH·sis) the process by which a cell membrane surrounds a particle and encloses the particle in a vesicle to bring the particle into the cell (208)

endocitosis el proceso por medio del cual la membrana celular rodea una partícula y la encierra en una vesícula para llevarla al interior de la célula

endoplasmic reticulum (ehn·doh·PLAZ·mik ri·TIK·yuh·luhm) a system of membranes that is found in a cell's cytoplasm and that assists in the production, processing, and transport of proteins and in the production of lipids (169)

retículo endoplásmico un sistema de membranas que se encuentra en el citoplasma de la célula y que tiene una función en la producción, procesamiento y transporte de proteínas y en la producción de lípidos

endothermic reaction (en·doh·THER·mik ree·AK·shuhn) a chemical reaction that requires energy input, usually as heat (128)

reacción endotérmica una reacción química que requiere la entrada de energía, generalmente en forma de calor

energy (EN·er·jee) the ability to do work (240)

energía la capacidad de realizar un trabajo

energy pyramid (EN·er·jee PIR·uh·mid) a triangular diagram that shows an ecosystem's loss of energy, which results as energy passes through the ecosystem's food chain; each row in the pyramid represents a trophic (feeding) level in an ecosystem, and the area of a row represents the energy stored in that trophic level (242)

pirámide de energía un diagrama con forma de triángulo que muestra la pérdida de energía que ocurre en un ecosistema a medida que la energía pasa a través de la cadena alimenticia del ecosistema; cada hilera de la pirámide representa un nivel trófico (de alimentación) en el ecosistema, y el área de la hilera representa la energía almacenada en ese nivel trófico

engineering (en·juh·NIR·ing) the application of science and mathematics to solve real-life problems (435)

ingeniería la aplicación de las ciencias y las matemáticas para resolver problemas de la vida diaria

enzyme (EN·zym) a type of protein that speeds up metabolic reactions in plants and animals without being permanently changed or destroyed (395)

enzima un tipo de proteína que acelera las reacciones metabólicas en plantas y animales, sin ser modificada permanentemente ni ser destruida

esophagus (ih·SAHF·uh·guhs) a long, straight tube that connects the pharynx to the stomach (396)

esófago un conducto largo y recto que conecta la faringe con el estómago

Eubacteria (yoo·bak·TEER·ee·uh) a kingdom in the domain Bacteria that consists of unicellular organisms with cell walls, but lacks a nucleus and organelles (182)
Eubacteria un reino del dominio Bacteria que comprende organismos unicelulares cuyas células tienen pared celular, pero carecen de núcleo u organelos

Eukarya (yoo·KAIR·ee·uh) in a modern taxonomic system, a domain made up of all eukaryotes; this domain aligns with the traditional kingdoms Protista, Fungi, Plantae, and Animalia (182)
Eukarya en un sistema taxonómico moderno, un dominio compuesto por todos los eucariotes; este dominio coincide con los reinos tradicionales Protista, Fungi, Plantae y Animalia

eukaryote (yoo·KAIR·ee·oht) an organism made up of cells that have a nucleus enclosed by a membrane; eukaryotes include protists, animals, plants, and fungi but not archaea or bacteria (151)
eucariote un organismo cuyas células tienen un núcleo contenido en una membrana; entre los eucariotes se encuentran protistas, animales, plantas y hongos, pero no arqueas ni bacterias

evaporation (ee·vap·uh·RAY·shuhn) the change of state from a liquid to a gas that usually occurs at the surface of a liquid over a wide range of temperatures (80)
evaporación el cambio de estado de líquido a gaseoso que ocurre generalmente en la superficie de un líquido en un amplio rango de temperaturas

evolution (ev·uh·LOO·shuhn) the process in which inherited characteristics within a population change over generations such that new species sometimes arise (295)
evolución el proceso por medio del cual las características heredadas dentro de una población cambian con el transcurso de las generaciones de manera tal que a veces surgen nuevas especies

exaptation (egs·AP·tay·zhuhn) an adaptation resulting from natural selection for a particular purpose (297)
exaptación una adaptación que ocurre a partir de la selección natural y sirve a un propósito específico

excretory system (EK·skrih·tohr·ee SIS·tuhm) the system that collects and excretes nitrogenous wastes and excess water from the body in the form of urine (399)
aparato excretor el sistema que recolecta y elimina del cuerpo los desperdicios nitrogenados y el exceso de agua en forma de orina

exocytosis (ek·soh·sy·TOH·sis) the process in which a cell releases a particle by enclosing the particle in a vesicle that then moves to the cell surface and fuses with the cell membrane to be released (208)
exocitosis el proceso por medio del cual una célula libera una partícula encerrándola en una vesícula que luego se traslada a la superficie de la célula y se fusiona con la membrana celular para de allí liberarla

exothermic reaction (ek·soh·THER·mik ree·AK·shuhn) a chemical reaction in which energy is released to the surroundings, usually as heat (128)
reacción exotérmica una reacción química en la que se libera energía en el ambiente, generalmente en forma de calor

fertilization (fer·tl·ih·ZAY·shuhn) the union of a male and female gamete to form a zygote (286)
fecundación la unión de un gameto masculino y femenino para formar un cigoto

fetus (FEE·tuhs) a developing human from the end of the 10th week of pregnancy until birth (424)
feto un ser humano en desarrollo desde el final de la décima semana del embarazo hasta el nacimiento

freezing (FREEZ·ing) the change of state from a liquid to a solid (78)
congelación el cambio de estado de líquido a sólido

function (FUNGK·shuhn) the special, normal, or proper activity of an organ or part (194)
función la actividad especial, normal o adecuada de un órgano o parte

Fungi (FUHN·jy) a kingdom made up of nongreen, eukaryotic organisms that have no means of movement, reproduce by using spores, and get food by breaking down substances in their surroundings and absorbing the nutrients (183)
Fungi un reino formado por organismos eucarióticos no verdes que no tienen capacidad de movimiento, se reproducen por esporas y obtienen alimento al descomponer sustancias de su entorno y absorber los nutrientes

gas (GAS) a form of matter that does not have a definite volume or shape (67)
gas un estado de la materia que no tiene volumen ni forma definidos

gene (JEEN) one set of instructions for an inherited trait (306)
gene un conjunto de instrucciones para un carácter heredado

genotype (JEEN·uh·typ) the entire genetic makeup of an organism; also the combination of genes for one or more specific traits (307)
genotipo la constitución genética completa de un organismo; también, la combinación de genes para uno o más caracteres específicos

gland (GLAND) a group of cells that make chemicals for use elsewhere in the body (412)

   glándula un grupo de células que elaboran sustancias químicas para su utilización en otra parte del cuerpo

global warming (GLOH·buhl WOHR·ming) a gradual increase in average global temperature (490)

   calentamiento global un aumento gradual de la temperatura global promedio

Golgi complex (GOHL·jee KAHM·plekz) a cell organelle that helps make and package materials to be transported out of the cell (169)

   aparato de Golgi un organelo celular que ayuda a hacer y a empacar los materiales que serán transportados al exterior de la célula

greenhouse effect (GREEN·hows ih·FEKT) the warming of the surface and lower atmosphere of Earth that occurs when water vapor, carbon dioxide, and other gases absorb and reradiate thermal energy (462, 488)

   efecto invernadero el calentamiento de la superficie y de la parte más baja de la atmósfera, el cual se produce cuando el vapor de agua, el dióxido de carbono y otros gases absorben y vuelven a irradiar la energía térmica

group (GROOP) a vertical column of elements in the periodic table; elements in a group share chemical properties (118)

   grupo una columna vertical de elementos de la tabla periódica; los elementos de un grupo comparten propiedades químicas

heredity (huh·RED·ih·tee) the passing of genetic material from parent to offspring (304)

   herencia la transmisión de material genético de padres a hijos

heterogeneous (het·uhr·uh·JEE·nee·uhs) describes something that does not have a uniform structure or composition throughout (60)

   heterogéneo término que describe algo que no tiene una estructura o composición totalmente uniforme

homeostasis (hoh·mee·oh·STAY·sis) the maintenance of a constant internal state in a changing environment (202, 356)

   homeostasis la capacidad de mantener un estado interno constante en un ambiente en cambio

homogeneous (hoh·muh·JEE·nee·uhs) describes something that has a uniform structure or composition throughout (60)

   homogéneo término que describe a algo que tiene una estructura o composición global uniforme

homologous chromosomes (hoh·MAHL·uh·guhs KROH·muh·sohmz) chromosomes that have the same sequence of genes and the same structure (272)

   cromosomas homólogos cromosomas con la misma secuencia de genes y la misma estructura

hormone (HOHR·mohn) a substance that is made in one cell or tissue and that causes a change in another cell or tissue in a different part of the body (412)

   hormona una sustancia que es producida en una célula o un tejido, la cual causa un cambio en otra célula u otro tejido ubicado en una parte diferente del cuerpo

ice age (EYES AYJ) a long period of climatic cooling during which the continents are glaciated repeatedly (487)

   edad de hielo un largo período de enfriamiento del clima, durante el cual los continentes se ven repetidamente sometidos a la glaciación

incomplete dominance (in·kuhm·PLEET DAHM·uh·nuhns) a condition in which two alleles are expressed such that the phenotype of a heterozygous individual is an intermediate of the phenotypes of the two homozygous parents (310)

   dominancia incompleta una condición en la que dos alelos se expresan de modo que el fenotipo de un individuo heterocigoto es intermedio entre los fenotipos de sus dos padres homocigotos

interphase (IN·ter·fayz) the period of the cell cycle during which activities such as cell growth and DNA replication occur without visible signs of cell division (264)

   interfase el período del ciclo celular durante el cual las actividades como el crecimiento celular y la replicación del ADN se producen sin signos visibles de división celular

joint (JOYNT) a place where two or more bones meet (366)

   articulación un lugar donde se unen dos o más huesos

kidney (KID·nee) one of the organs that filter water and wastes from the blood, excrete products as urine, and regulate the concentration of certain substances in the blood (400)

   riñón uno de los órganos que filtran el agua y los desechos de la sangre, excretan productos como orina y regulan la concentración de ciertas sustancias en la sangre

kingdom (KING·duhm) the second highest taxonomic rank for classifying organisms (183)

reino el segundo nivel del sistema taxonómico usado para clasificar organismos

L

large intestine (LAHRJ in·TES·tin) the broader and shorter portion of the intestine, where water is removed from the mostly digested food to turn the waste into semisolid feces, or stool (397)

intestino grueso la porción más ancha y más corta del intestino, donde el agua se elimina de la mayoría de los alimentos digeridos para convertir los desechos en heces semisólidas o excremento

larynx (LAIR·ingks) the part of the respiratory system between the pharynx and the trachea; has walls of cartilage and muscle and contains the vocal cords (386)

laringe la parte del aparato respiratorio que se encuentra entre la faringe y la tráquea; tiene paredes de cartílago y músculo y contiene las cuerdas vocales

law of conservation of energy (LAW UHV kahn·suhr·VAY·shuhn UHV EN·er·jee) the law that states that energy cannot be created or destroyed but can be changed from one form to another (129, 241)

ley de la conservación de la energía la ley que establece que la energía ni se crea ni se destruye, sólo se transforma de una forma a otra

law of conservation of mass (LAW UHV kahn·suhr·VAY·shuhn UHV MAS) the law that states that mass cannot be created or destroyed in ordinary chemical and physical changes (42, 126, 241)

ley de la conservación de la masa la ley que establece que la masa no se crea ni se destruye por cambios químicos o físicos comunes

ligament (LIG·uh·muhnt) a type of tissue that holds together the bones in a joint (364)

ligamento un tipo de tejido que mantiene unidos los huesos en una articulación

lipid (LIP·id) a fat molecule or a molecule that has similar properties; examples include oils, waxes, and steroids (158)

lípido una molécula de grasa o una molécula que tiene propiedades similares; algunos ejemplos son los aceites, las ceras y los esteroides

liquid (LIK·wid) the state of matter that has a definite volume but not a definite shape (67)

líquido el estado de la materia que tiene un volumen definido, pero no una forma definida

liver (LIV·er) the largest organ in the body; it makes bile, stores and filters blood, and stores excess sugars as glycogen (398)

hígado el órgano más grande del cuerpo; produce bilis, almacena y filtra la sangre, y almacena el exceso de azúcares en forma de glucógeno

lymph (LIMF) the clear, watery fluid that leaks from blood vessels and contains white blood cells; circulates in the lymphatic system; returned to bloodstream through lymph vessels (376)

linfa el fluido claro y acuoso que se filtra de los vasos sanguíneos y contiene glóbulos blancos; circula por el sistema linfático; regresa al torrente sanguíneo a través de los vasos linfáticos

lymph node (LIMF NOHD) small, bean-shaped masses of tissue that remove pathogens and dead cells from the lymph; concentrated in the armpits, neck, and groin; high concentration of white blood cells found in lymph nodes (378)

nodo linfático masas de tejido pequeñas y con forma de frijol que eliminan los patógenos y las células muertas de la linfa; están concentrados en las axilas, el cuello y la ingle; los nodos linfáticos presentan una alta concentración de glóbulos blancos

lymphatic system (lim·FAT·ik SIS·tuhm) a network of organs and tissues that collect the fluid that leaks from blood and returns it to blood vessels; includes lymph nodes, lymph vessels, and lymph; the place where certain white blood cells mature (376)

sistema linfático una red de órganos y tejidos que recolectan el fluido que se filtra de la sangre y lo regresan a los vasos sanguíneos; incluye los nodos linfáticos, los vasos linfáticos y la linfa; el lugar donde maduran ciertos glóbulos blancos

lysosome (LY·suh·sohm) an animal cell organelle that contains digestive enzymes (172)

lisosoma un organelo de las células animales que contiene enzimas digestivas

M

mass (MAS) a measure of the amount of matter in an object (7)

masa una medida de la cantidad de materia que tiene un objeto

mass number (MAS NUM·ber) the sum of the numbers of protons and neutrons in the nucleus of an atom (107)

número de masa la suma de los números de protones y neutrones que hay en el núcleo de un átomo

matter (MAT·er) anything that has mass and takes up space (6, 240)

materia cualquier cosa que tiene masa y ocupa un lugar en el espacio

meiosis (my·OH·sis) a process in cell division during which the number of chromosomes decreases to half the original number by two divisions of the nucleus, which results in the production of sex cells (gametes or spores) (273)

meiosis un proceso de división celular durante el cual el número de cromosomas disminuye a la mitad del número original por medio de dos divisiones del núcleo, lo cual resulta en la producción de células sexuales (gametos o esporas)

melting (MELT·ing) the change of state from a solid to a liquid (79)

fusión el cambio de estado de sólido a líquido

mesosphere (MEZ·uh·sfir) the layer of the atmosphere between the stratosphere and the thermosphere and in which temperature decreases as altitude increases (460)

mesosfera la capa de la atmósfera que se encuentra entre la estratosfera y la termosfera, en la cual la temperatura disminuye al aumentar la altitud

metal (MET·l) an element on the left side of the periodic table that is shiny and that conducts heat and electricity well (117)

metal un elemento que se encuentra en la parte izquierda de la tabla periódica y que es brillante y conduce bien el calor y la electricidad

metalloid (MET·l·oyd) an element that has properties of both metals and nonmetals (117)

metaloide un elemento que tiene propiedades tanto de metal como de no metal

mitochondrion (my·toh·KAHN·dree·uhn) in eukaryotic cells, the organelle that is the site of cellular respiration, which releases energy for use by the cell (168)

mitocondria en las células eucarióticas, el organelo donde se lleva a cabo la respiración celular, la cual libera energía para que utilice la célula

mitosis (my·TOH·sis) in eukaryotic cells, a process of cell division that forms two new nuclei, each of which has the same number of chromosomes (205, 265)

mitosis en las células eucarióticas, un proceso de división celular que forma dos núcleos nuevos, cada uno de los cuales posee el mismo número de cromosomas

mixture (MIKS·cher) a combination of two or more substances that are not chemically combined (53)

mezcla una combinación de dos o más sustancias que no están combinadas químicamente

molecule (MAHL·ih·kyool) a group of atoms that are held together by chemical forces; a molecule is the smallest unit of a compound that keeps all the properties of that compound (157)

molécula un grupo de átomos unidos por fuerzas químicas; una molécula es la unidad más pequeña de un compuesto que conserva todas las propiedades de ese compuesto

muscular system (MUS·kyuh·ler SIS·tuhm) the organ system whose primary function is movement and flexibility (368)

sistema muscular el sistema de órganos cuya función principal es permitir el movimiento y la flexibilidad

mutation (myoo·TAY·shuhn) a change in the nucleotide-base sequence of a gene or DNA molecule (294, 333)

mutación un cambio en la secuencia de la base de nucleótidos de un gen o de una molécula de ADN

N

natural selection (NACH·uhr·uhl sih·LEK·shuhn) the process by which individuals that are better adapted to their environment survive and reproduce more successfully than less-well-adapted individuals do (295)

selección natural el proceso por medio del cual los individuos que están mejor adaptados a su ambiente sobreviven y se reproducen con más éxito que los individuos menos adaptados

nephron (NEF·rahn) the unit in the kidney that filters blood (400)

nefrona la unidad del riñón que filtra la sangre

nervous system (NER·vuhs SIS·tuhm) the structures that control the actions and reactions of the body in response to stimuli from the environment; it is formed by billions of specialized nerve cells, called neurons (406)

sistema nervioso las estructuras que controlan las acciones y reacciones del cuerpo en respuesta a los estímulos del ambiente; está formado por miles de millones de células nerviosas especializadas, llamadas neuronas

neuron (NUR·ahn) a nerve cell that is specialized to receive and conduct electrical impulses (408)

neurona una célula nerviosa que está especializada en recibir y transmitir impulsos eléctricos

neutron (NOO·trahn) a subatomic particle that has no charge and that is located in the nucleus of an atom (103)

neutrón una partícula subatómica que no tiene carga y que está ubicada en el núcleo de un átomo

nitrogen cycle (NY·truh·juhn SY·kuhl) the cycling of nitrogen between organisms, soil, water, and the atmosphere (245)

ciclo del nitrógeno el ciclado del nitrógeno entre los organismos, el suelo, el agua y la atmósfera

nonmetal (nahn·MET·l) an element on the right side of the periodic table that conducts heat and electricity poorly (117)

no metal un elemento que se encuentra en la parte derecha de la tabla periódica y que es mal conductor del calor y la electricidad

nucleic acid (noo·KLAY·ik AS·id) a molecule made up of subunits called nucleotides that carries information in cells (159)

ácido nucleico una molécula formada por subunidades llamadas nucleótidos y que transporta información en la célula

nucleotide (NOO·klee·oh·tyd) in a nucleic-acid chain, a subunit that consists of a sugar, a phosphate, and a nitrogenous base (331)
   nucleótido en una cadena de ácidos nucleicos, una subunidad formada por un azúcar, un fosfato y una base nitrogenada

nucleus (NOO·klee·uhs) in physical science, an atom's central region, which is made up of protons and neutrons (103); in a eukaryotic cell, a membrane-bound organelle that contains the cell's DNA and that has a role in processes such as growth, metabolism, and reproduction (150)
   núcleo en ciencias físicas, la región central de un átomo, la cual está constituida por protones y neutrones; en una célula eucariótica, un organelo cubierto por una membrana, el cual contiene el ADN de la célula y participa en procesos tales como el crecimiento, el metabolismo y la reproducción

organ (OHR·guhn) a collection of tissues that carry out a specialized function of the body (192)
   órgano un conjunto de tejidos que desempeñan una función especializada en el cuerpo

organ system (OHR·guhn SIS·tuhm) a group of organs that work together to perform body functions (193)
   aparato (o sistema) de órganos un grupo de órganos que trabajan en conjunto para desempeñar funciones corporales

organelle (ohr·guhn·EL) one of the small bodies in a cell's cytoplasm that are specialized to perform a specific function (150)
   organelo uno de los cuerpos pequeños del citoplasma de una célula que están especializados para llevar a cabo una función específica

organism (OHR·guh·niz·uhm) a living thing; anything that can carry out life processes independently (146, 190)
   organismo un ser vivo; cualquier cosa que pueda llevar a cabo procesos vitales independientemente

osmosis (ahz·MOH·sis) the diffusion of water through a semipermeable membrane (206)
   ósmosis la difusión del agua a través de una membrana semipermeable

ovary (OH·vuh·ree) in the female reproductive system of animals, an organ that produces eggs (421)
   ovario en el aparato reproductor femenino de los animales, un órgano que produce óvulos

ozone (OH·zohn) a gas molecule that is made up of three oxygen atoms (470)
   ozono una molécula de gas que está formada por tres átomos de oxígeno

ozone layer (OH·zohn LAY·er) the layer of the atmosphere at an altitude of 15 to 40 km in which ozone absorbs ultraviolet solar radiation (462)
   capa de ozono la capa de la atmósfera ubicada a una altitud de 15 a 40 km, en la cual el ozono absorbe la radiación solar ultravioleta

pancreas (PANG·kree·uhs) the organ that lies behind the stomach and that makes digestive enzymes and hormones that regulate sugar levels (398)
   páncreas el órgano que se encuentra detrás del estómago y que produce las enzimas digestivas y las hormonas que regulan los niveles de azúcar

particulate (per·TIK·yuh·lit) a tiny particle of solid that is suspended in air or water (469)
   material particulado una pequeña partícula de material sólido que se encuentra suspendida en el aire o el agua

passive transport (PAS·iv TRANS·pohrt) the movement of substances across a cell membrane without the use of energy by the cell (206)
   transporte pasivo el movimiento de sustancias a través de una membrana celular sin que la célula tenga que usar energía

pedigree (PED·ih·gree) a diagram that shows the occurrence of a genetic trait in several generations of a family (322)
   pedigrí un diagrama que muestra la incidencia de un carácter genético en varias generaciones de una familia

penis (PEE·nis) the male organ that transfers sperm to a female and that carries urine out of the body (420)
   pene el órgano masculino que transfiere espermatozoides a una hembra y que lleva la orina hacia el exterior del cuerpo

period (PIR·ee·uhd) in chemistry, a horizontal row of elements in the periodic table (119)
   período en química, una hilera horizontal de elementos en la tabla periódica

periodic table (pir·ee·AHD·ik TAY·buhl) an arrangement of the elements in order of their atomic numbers such that elements with similar properties fall in the same column, or group (113)
   tabla periódica un arreglo de los elementos ordenados en función de su número atómico, de modo que los elementos que tienen propiedades similares se encuentran en la misma columna, o grupo

pharynx (FAIR·ingks) the part of the respiratory system that extends from the mouth to the larynx (386)
   faringe la parte del aparato respiratorio que va de la boca a la laringe

phenotype (FEEN·uh·typ) an organism's appearance or other detectable characteristic (307)
   fenotipo la apariencia de un organismo u otra característica perceptible

phospholipid (fahs·foh·LIP·id) a lipid that contains phosphorus and that is a structural component in cell membranes (160)

fosfolípido un lípido que contiene fósforo y que es un componente estructural de la membrana celular

photosynthesis (foh·toh·SIN·thih·sis) the process by which plants, algae, and some bacteria use sunlight, carbon dioxide, and water to make food (204, 230)

fotosíntesis el proceso por medio del cual las plantas, las algas y algunas bacterias utilizan la luz solar, el dióxido de carbono y el agua para producir alimento

physical change (FIZ·ih·kuhl CHAYNJ) a change of matter from one form to another without a change in chemical properties (36)

cambio físico un cambio de materia de una forma a otra sin que ocurra un cambio en sus propiedades químicas

physical property (FIZ·ih·kuhl PRAHP·er·tee) a characteristic of a substance that does not involve a chemical change, such as density, color, or hardness (22)

propiedad física una característica de una sustancia que no implica un cambio químico, tal como la densidad, el color o la dureza

placenta (pluh·SEN·tuh) the partly fetal and partly maternal organ by which materials are exchanged between a fetus and the mother (424)

placenta el órgano parcialmente fetal y parcialmente materno por medio del cual se intercambian materiales entre el feto y la madre

Plantae (PLAN·tee) a kingdom made up of complex, multicellular organisms that are usually green, have cell walls made of cellulose, cannot move around, and use the sun's energy to make sugar by photosynthesis (183)

Plantae un reino formado por organismos pluricelulares complejos que normalmente son verdes, tienen una pared celular de celulosa, no tienen capacidad de movimiento y utilizan la energía del Sol para producir azúcar mediante la fotosíntesis

pneumonia (noo·MOHN·yuh) an inflammation of the lungs that is usually caused by bacteria or viruses (367)

probability (prahb·uh·BIL·ih·tee) the likelihood that a possible future event will occur in any given instance of the event (320)

probabilidad la probabilidad de que ocurra un posible suceso futuro en cualquier caso dado del suceso

product (PRAHD·uhkt) a substance that forms in a chemical reaction (125)

producto una sustancia que se forma en una reacción química

prokaryote (proh·KAIR·ee·oht) a single-celled organism that does not have a nucleus or membrane-bound organelles; examples are archaea and bacteria (151)

procariote un organismo unicelular que no tiene núcleo ni organelos cubiertos por una membrana, por ejemplo, las arqueas y las bacterias

protein (PROH·teen) a molecule that is made up of amino acids and that is needed to build and repair body structures and to regulate processes in the body (158)

proteína una molécula formada por aminoácidos que es necesaria para construir y reparar estructuras corporales y para regular procesos del cuerpo

Protista (proh·TIS·tuh) a kingdom of mostly one-celled eukaryotic organisms that are different from plants, animals, archaea, bacteria, and fungi; it contains protozoans and algae (183)

Protista un reino compuesto principalmente por organismos eucarióticos unicelulares que son diferentes de las plantas, los animales, las arqueas, las bacterias y los hongos; comprende los protozoarios y las algas

proton (PROH·tahn) a subatomic particle that has a positive charge and that is located in the nucleus of an atom; the number of protons in the nucleus is the atomic number, which determines the identity of an element (103)

protón una partícula subatómica que tiene una carga positiva y que está ubicada en el núcleo de un átomo; el número de protones que hay en el núcleo es el número atómico, y éste determina la identidad del elemento

Punnett square (PUH·nuht SKWAIR) a graphic used to predict the results of a genetic cross (318)

cuadro de Punnett una gráfica que se usa para predecir los resultados de una cruza genética

pure substance (PYOOR SUHB·stuhns) a sample of matter, either a single element or a single compound, that has definite chemical and physical properties (54)

sustancia pura una muestra de materia, ya sea un solo elemento o un solo compuesto, que tiene propiedades químicas y físicas definidas

R

ratio (RAY·shee·oh) a comparison of two numbers using division (320)

razón comparación de dos números mediante la división

reactant (ree·AK·tuhnt) a substance that participates in a chemical reaction (125)

reactivo una sustancia que participa en una reacción química

recessive (ree·SES·iv) describes an allele that will be masked unless the organism is homozygous for the trait (307)

recesivo término que describe un alelo que no se expresa a menos que el organismo sea homocigoto para el carácter

replication (rep·lih·KAY·shuhn) the duplication of a DNA molecule (332)

replicación la duplicación de una molécula de ADN

© Houghton Mifflin Harcourt Publishing Company

respiratory system (RES·per·uh·tohr·ee SIS·tuhm) a collection of organs whose primary function is to take in oxygen and expel carbon dioxide; the organs of this system include the lungs, the throat, and the passageways that lead to the lungs (385)

aparato respiratorio un conjunto de órganos cuya función principal es tomar oxígeno y expulsar dióxido de carbono; los órganos de este aparato incluyen a los pulmones, la garganta y las vías que llevan a los pulmones

ribosome (RY·buh·sohm) a cell organelle composed of RNA and protein; the site of protein synthesis (168, 335)

ribosoma un organelo celular compuesto de ARN y proteína; el sitio donde ocurre la síntesis de proteínas

RNA (ar·en·AY) ribonucleic acid, a molecule that is present in all living cells and that plays a role in protein production (334)

ARN ácido ribonucleico, una molécula que está presente en todas las células vivas y que juega un papel en la producción de proteínas

S

sexual reproduction (SEHK·shoo·uhl ree·pruh·DUHK·shuhn) reproduction in which the sex cells from two parents unite to produce offspring that share traits from both parents (286)

reproducción sexual reproducción en la que se unen las células sexuales de los dos progenitores para producir descendencia que comparte caracteres de ambos progenitores

skeletal system (SKEL·ih·tl SIS·tuhm) the organ system whose primary function is to support and protect the body and to allow the body to move (362)

sistema esquelético el sistema de órganos cuya función principal es sostener y proteger el cuerpo y permitir que se mueva

small intestine (SMAWL in·TES·tin) the organ between the stomach and the large intestine where most of the breakdown of food happens and most of the nutrients from food are absorbed (397)

intestino delgado el órgano que se encuentra entre el estómago y el intestino grueso en el cual se produce la mayor parte de la descomposición de los alimentos y se absorben la mayoría de los nutrientes

smog (SMAHG) air pollution that forms when ozone and vehicle exhaust react with sunlight (470)

esmog contaminación del aire que se produce cuando el ozono y algunas sustancias químicas como los gases de los escapes de los vehículos reaccionan con la luz solar

solid (SAHL·id) the state of matter in which the volume and shape of a substance are fixed (66)

sólido el estado de la materia en el cual el volumen y la forma de una sustancia están fijos

sperm (SPERM) the male sex cell (420)

espermatozoide la célula sexual masculina

spinal cord (SPY·nuhl KOHRD) a column of nerve tissue running from the base of the brain through the vertebral column (406)

médula espinal una columna de tejido nervioso que se origina en la base del cerebro y corre a lo largo de la columna vertebral

stomach (STUHM·uhk) the saclike, digestive organ that is between the esophagus and the small intestine and that breaks down food by the action of muscles, enzymes, and acids (397)

estómago el órgano digestivo con forma de bolsa, ubicado entre el esófago y el intestino delgado, que descompone la comida por la acción de músculos, enzimas y ácidos

stratosphere (STRAT·uh·sfir) the layer of the atmosphere that is above the troposphere and in which temperature increases as altitude increases (460)

estratosfera la capa de la atmósfera que se encuentra encima de la troposfera y en la que la temperatura aumenta al aumentar la altitud

structural adaptation (STRUHK·cher·uh·l ad·ap·TAY·shuhn) a change in some physical part of an organism that allows it to survive (296)

adaptación estructural un cambio sufrido por un organismo en alguna de sus partes y que le permite a este sobrevivir

structure (STRUHK·cher) the arrangement of parts in an organism (194)

estructura el orden y distribución de las partes de un organismo

sublimation (suhb·luh·MAY·shuhn) the change of state from a solid directly to a gas (82)

sublimación cambio de estado por el cual un sólido se convierte directamente en un gas

T

technology (tek·NAHL·uh·jee) the application of science for practical purposes; the use of tools, machines, materials, and processes to meet human needs (432)

tecnología la aplicación de la ciencia con fines prácticos; el uso de herramientas, máquinas, materiales y procesos para satisfacer las necesidades de los seres humanos

tendon (TEN·duhn) a tough connective tissue that attaches a muscle to a bone or to another body part (369)

tendón un tejido conectivo duro que une un músculo con un hueso o con otra parte del cuerpo

testes (TES·teez) the primary male reproductive organs, which produce sperm cells and testosterone (singular, testis) (420)

testículos los principales órganos reproductores masculinos, los cuales producen espermatozoides y testosterona

thermosphere (THER·muh·sfir) the uppermost layer of the atmosphere, in which temperature increases as altitude increases (460)

termosfera la capa más alta de la atmósfera, en la cual la temperatura aumenta a medida que la altitud aumenta

tissue (TISH·oo) a group of similar cells that perform a common function (191)

tejido un grupo de células similares que llevan a cabo una función común

trachea (TRAY·kee·uh) thin-walled tube that extends from the larynx to the bronchi; carries air to the lungs; also called windpipe (386)

tráquea el conducto de paredes delgadas que va de la laringe a los bronquios; lleva el aire a los pulmones

troposphere (TROH·puh·sfir) the lowest layer of the atmosphere, in which temperature decreases at a constant rate as altitude increases (460)

troposfera la capa inferior de la atmósfera, en la que la temperatura disminuye a una tasa constante a medida que la altitud aumenta

umbilical cord (uhm·BIL·ih·kuhl KOHRD) the ropelike structure through which blood vessels pass and by which a developing mammal is connected to the placenta (424)

cordón umbilical la estructura con forma de cuerda a través de la cual pasan vasos sanguíneos y por medio de la cual un mamífero en desarrollo está unido a la placenta

urine (YUR·in) the liquid excreted by the kidneys, stored in the bladder, and passed through the urethra to the outside of the body (400)

orina el líquido que excretan los riñones, se almacena en la vejiga y pasa a través de la uretra hacia el exterior del cuerpo

uterus (YOO·ter·uhs) in female placental mammals, the hollow, muscular organ in which an embryo embeds itself and develops into a fetus (422)

útero en los mamíferos placentarios hembras, el órgano hueco y muscular en el que el embrión se incrusta y se desarrolla hasta convertirse en feto

vacuole (VAK·yoo·ohl) a fluid-filled vesicle found in the cytoplasm of plant cells or protozoans (170)

vacuola una vesícula llena de líquido que se encuentra en el citoplasma de las células vegetales o de los protozoarios

vagina (vuh·JY·nuh) the female reproductive organ that connects the outside of the body to the uterus (422)

vagina el órgano reproductivo femenino que conecta la parte exterior del cuerpo con el útero

variation (vair·ee·AY·shuhn) the occurrence of hereditary or nonhereditary differences between different individuals of a population (294)

variabilidad la incidencia de diferencias hereditarias o no hereditarias entre distintos individuos de una población

vein (VAYN) in biology, a vessel that carries blood to the heart (381)

vena en biología, un vaso que lleva sangre al corazón

vestigial adaptation (ve·STIJ·ee·uhl ad·ap·TAY·shuhn) adaptations that no longer serve their original purpose but might still be present in the organisms (297)

adaptación vestigial una adaptación que ya no cumple su propósito original, pero continúa presente en el organismo

volume (VAHL·yoom) the amount of space that an object takes up, or occupies (9)

volumen la cantidad de espacio que ocupa un objeto

water cycle (WAW·ter SY·kuhl) the continuous movement of water between the atmosphere, the land, the oceans, and living things (244)

ciclo del agua el movimiento continuo del agua entre la atmósfera, la tierra, los océanos y los seres vivos

weight (WAYT) a measure of the gravitational force exerted on an object; its value can change with the location of the object in the universe (7)

peso una medida de la fuerza gravitacional ejercida sobre un objeto; su valor puede cambiar en función de la ubicación del objeto en el universo

Index

Page numbers for definitions are printed in **boldface** type.
Page numbers for illustrations, maps, and charts are printed in *italics*.

history of, 102–103
ATP (adenosine triphosphate), 232–233
atrium, 380, *380*
aurora borealis, *460*
average atomic mass, **116**
axial skeleton, 364
axon, 409, *409*
axon terminal, 409, *409*

bacteria
  biotechnology and, 432–433, *433*
  genetic engineering and, 435
  nitrogen fixation and, 245
Bacteria (domain), **182**
bacterial cells, *146,* 285
  photosynthesis and, 204
bacterial infection, 185
baking soda
  chemical change and, 43, 124
  chemical properties of, 27, *27*
  pH of, 57
balance, 411
balance (tool), 8, *8*
balance, in cells, 203. *See also* homeostasis.
ball-and-socket joint, *366*
barnacle, 438
base, nucleotide, 331, *331,* 334
basic compound, 57
bee orchid, *298*
behavioral adaptation, **296**
beryllium, *104*
Big Idea, 1, 88, 95, 136, 141, 216, 223, 252, 257, 340, 347, 446, 453
bile, 398
binary fission, 285, *285*
biochemical, 57
biomaterial, 437, 442–443, *442–443*
biomimicry, 438–439
biosphere, effect of global warming on, 491
biotechnology, 432–433
biotic factor, 241
birth, 424
bismuth, *112*
bladder, 400, *400*
blood, 203, **376,** 380–383. *See also* cardiovascular system.
  artery, *377,* **381,** *381,* 383–384
  capillary, 377, *377,* **381,** *381*
  circulation, 383, *383*
  composition of, 382, *382*
  filtration and kidneys, 400–401, *401*
  homeostasis and, 376, 380, 383
  plasma, 382
  platelets, 382, *382*
  vein, **381,** *381*
  vessel, 355, 381, 384, *384*
blood cell, 363, *363*
  red, 382, *382*

white, 377–379, 382, *382*
blood pressure, 381, 384
blood sugar, 414–415
blood type, 311
blood vessel, 203, 355, 381, 384, *384*
  artery, *377,* **381,** *381,* 383–384
  capillary, 377, *377,* **381,** *381*
  smooth muscle and, 368
  vein, **381,** *381*
body coverings and parts, **299,** *299*
body system, 352–357
  communication and, 355, 356
  homeostasis and, 356–357
  interdependence of, 355, 377, 394
  overview of, 352–353
  shared organs, 355
  structure and function, 354
Bohr, Niels, 103
boiling, **80**
  change of state and, 70, 80
boiling point, as physical property of matter, 25, *25*
bone, 362–367. *See also* skeletal system.
  compact, 362, 364, *365*
  connective tissue and, 364
  fractures and sprains, 367, *367*
  growth plate, 365
  joints and, 366, *366*
  ligaments and, 364, *365*
  lymphatic system and, 378
  minerals and, 364
  spongy, 364, *365*
bone marrow, 363–364, *365,* 378, *378*
brain, 352, 355, **406–407,** *407*
  stroke and, 384
brain stem, 407, *407*
breast cancer, 390, *390–391*
breathing, 386. *See also* respiratory system.
breeding, 304–305, 434. *See also* heredity.
bromine, *112*
bronchiole, 386
bronchus, **386**
bubonic plague, 379
budding, 285, *285*
bullet train, 439, *439*
butterfly wing cell, 149

C (cytosine), 328, 331, 334
cactus, 183, *183*
calcium, 364, 367
calorie, 213
camouflage, **298,** *299*
cancer, 390, *390*
Canis familiaris, 181, *181*
capillary, 377, *377,* **381,** *381*
carbohydrate, 57, **159**
carbon
  in atmosphere, 246, 468–474
  as energy source, 240

cycle, 243, **246,** *246–247,* 251, *251*
  carbon dioxide, 468
carbon cycle, 243, **246,** *246–247,* 251, *251*
carbon dioxide, 82, 468, 488–489
  cellular respiration and, 204, 233
  photosynthesis and, 230, 231
  respiration and, 385
carbon sink, 489
carbon source, 489
carbonic acid, 471
cardiac muscle, 368–369, *369*
cardiovascular system, 203, *352,* 355, *376,* **376–377,** 380–384, *381*
  blood, **376,** 380–383
  blood circulation, 383, *383*
  blood vessels, 381
  diseases of, 384
  heart, 380, *380*
carnivore, in energy cycle, 242
carrier, disease, 322
cartilage, 364–366, *365*
catalyst, 130, *130*
cell, **146–**151, *150, 161, 166,* 354
  animal, 172, *205*
  bacteria, *146*
  bone marrow and, 363, *363*
  characteristics of, 146–151
  communication, 355
  cycle, 205, **264–267**
  cytoplasm, 150, *150,* 167, *167*
  cytoskeleton, **167**
  diploid, 272
  division, 205, *205,* 262–267, *265,* 285
  DNA, 150
  energy and, 204, 228
  eukaryotic, **151,** *151,* 166–167
  glial, 408
  growth and repair, 262
  haploid, 273
  homeostasis, **202–**203, 209
  human skin, *146*
  membrane, **150,** *150,* 160, 167, *167,* 206–207
  muscle, 368–369, *368–369*
  nerve, 354, *354*
  nucleus, **150,** 167, *167*
  organelle, **150,** *150*
  organization, 190
  parts of, 150, *150,* 167–173
  plant, *146,* 170–171, *170–171, 205, 229*
  prokaryotic, **151,** *151,* 166
  reproduction and, 190, 262
  rod and cone, 410
  size, 147
  skin, 354, *354*
  specialized, 180
  sperm, 354, *354*
  structure and function, 166, **194,** 354
  surface area-to-volume ratio, 147
  taste, 411
  theory, 148–149
  transport of materials, 206–208

codominance (trait), **311**
coefficient, in chemical equation, 126, 134, *134*, 135
co-extinction, **297**
collagen, 364
colloid, 60
color, as indication of chemical change, 41, 124
colorblindness, 322
combustion, 247
compact bone, 362, 364, *365*
complementary base, nucleotide, 331–332
complete dominance, 307
complex carbohydrate, 159
complex organisms, 180, 183–185
compound, **53**, 157
    classification, 52–53, 57
    as pure substance, **54**
compound, organic, 57
    carbohydrate, 57
    lipid, 57
    nucleic acid, 57
    protein, 57
    role in human body, 57
compound molecule, 54
computer model
    climate change, 474
    rising sea level, 496
concentration, effect on reaction rate, 130, *130*
condensation, **81**
connective tissue, 191
conservation of energy
    change of state and, 77
    law of, 129
conservation of mass
    change of state and, 85
    law of, **42**, **126**
constraint (of a design), **443**
consumer, 229, 251, *251*
    energy source for, 240
    energy transfer and, 240–242
    matter transfer and, 243, 245
contact lens, 443, *443*
contrail, 81, *81*
copper, 55, *112*
corn, selective breeding of, 434
cornea, 410, *410*
cosmic ray, 468
countermass, 8
cow, selective breeding of, 434, *434*
Crick, Francis, 329, *329*
criterion (of a design), **443**
cryosphere, effects of global warming on, 490
cubic centimeter (cm³), 10, 12
cycling of matter, 230, 232, 235, 241
cystic fibrosis, 322
    pedigree, *322*
cytokinesis, **265**, *265*
    meiosis and, 274–275, *274–275*
    mitosis and, 265, *265*, *267*
cytoplasm, 150, *150*, 167, *167*
cytosine (C), 328, 331, 334
cytoskeleton, 167

D

Daily Value (DV) nutrition guidelines, 213
Dalton, John, 102
dandelion, *284*
Darwin, Charles, 295, *295*
daughter cell, 262, 264–265, 267, 273
decomposer, 183, 184–185, 229, 251, *251*
    in ecosystem cycle, 243, 245
decomposition, 247
deforestation, 489
    reducing, 494
deletion (DNA mutation), 333, *333*
Democritus, 100
dendrite, **409**, *409*
density, **13**
    measuring, 14
    as physical property of matter, 24, *24*
deoxyribonucleic acid, 263. *See also* **DNA.**
dependent variable, 338
deposition, **83**
dermis, *354*
design, 442–443
development, child, 425
diabetes, 357, 415
diagnostic medical sonographer, 391
diaphragm, 386
diatom, *190*
didinium, *203*
diffusion, **206**
digestion, 353, 394–395
digestive system, 193, *193*, 196, 197, *197*, 353, **394**–398, *395*
    absorption of nutrients, 398
    chemical and mechanical digestion, 395
    esophagus and, 386, 396, *396*
    large intestine and, *397*, 397–398
    mouth and, 396, *396*
    nervous system and, 394
    respiratory system and, 394
    small intestine and, *397*, 397–398
    smooth muscle and, 368
    stomach and, 394, 397, *397*
diploid cell, *176*, *272*, *273*, *276*
diseased lung, *387*
displacement, 12
division, cellular, 205, *205*, 262–267, 285
    cell cycle and, 264–267
    genetic material and, 263
    for growth and repair, 262
    for reproduction, 262
DNA (deoxyribonucleic acid), 150, 159, *159*, 167, 259, **263**, *263*, 328–335, *330–331*, 435, *435*
    in cell cycle, 205, 263, 264
    in cell nucleus, 167
    discovery of, 328–329
    double helix, 330, *330–331*
    genes and, 306
    as a genetic code, 328, 331
    mutation, 284, **333**, *333*
    nucleotide, 159, **331**, *331*
    in prokaryotes, 151, *151*
    replication, **332**, *332*
    ribosomes and, 168, 335
    RNA and, 334–335
    technology, 280
    transcription, 334, *334*
    translation, 335, *335*
    x-ray image, *329*
Do the Math!, 10–12, 14–15, 31, 126–127, 147, 320–321, 425, 486, 493
dog, domestic, 181
domain, 181, *181*, **182**–183
domestic dog, 181, *181*
dominant, **307**
    allele, 307
    trait, 305
double helix, 330, *330–331*
Down syndrome, 277
dry ice, 82, *82*
duckweed cell, *166*
ductile, metal, 117
dust, 469
DV (Daily Value) nutrition guidelines, 213

E

E. coli, 182, *182*
ear, 411, *411*
eardrum, 411, *411*
ECG (electrocardiogram), 384
ecosystem, **241**
    abiotic factor, 241
    biotic factor, 241
    carbon cycle in, 246–247, *246–247*
    effect of global warming on, 491
    energy in, 241–242
    matter in, 243
    nitrogen cycle in, 245, *245*
    water cycle in, 244, *244*
egg, **421**–423, 427
egg cell, *270*, 273, *273*, 275, 286, *286*
El Niño, 486, *486*
electric charge
    of parts of atoms, 104–105
    theory of, 102–103
electrical conductivity
    as physical property of matter, 24, *24*
electrocardiogram (ECG), 384
electron, **102**
    as part of atom, 105
    valence, 118
electron cloud, **103**
    as part of atom, 105
electron microscope, 143
element, **53**, 112, 156
    classification of, 52–53, 56
    in periodic table, 113–119, *114–115*
    as pure substance, **54**
elemental molecule, 54

embryo, **423**–424, *424*
emphysema, 387
endangered species, 497
    maintaining genetic diversity in, 323
endocrine system, *353*, 355, *412*,
    412–415
    disorders of, 415
    glands of, 413, *413*
    homeostasis and, 401, 414
endocytosis, 207, **208**, *208*
endoplasmic reticulum (ER), **169**, *169*
    ribosomes and, 168
endoskeleton, 362
endothermic reaction, **128**
endurance exercise, 371
energy, 41, **240**
    change of, 41, 76
    change of state and, 76
    chemical reaction and, 128–129
    conservation of, 77, 129
    conversion and transfer of, 240–242
    cycling of energy, 230, 232, 235, 241
    enzyme and, 131, *131*
    in ecosystem, 241–242
    law of conservation of, 241
    particle motion and, 67, 70
    sun as source of, 240, 242
    from water and wind, 478–479
energy, for cell, 204
    cellular respiration, **204**, **232**–235
    chemical, 229, 231
    from food, 229, 232
    need for, 228
    photosynthesis, **204**, 230–231,
        230–231
    sources of, 229
energy pyramid, **242**, *242*
energy resource, sun as, 240, 242
Engage Your Brain, 5, 21, 35, 51, 65,
    75, 99, 111, 123, 145, 155, 165,
    179, 189, 201, 227, 239, 261, 271,
    283, 293, 303, 317, 327, 351, 361,
    375, 393, 405, 419, 431, 457, 467,
    483
engineering, **435**. *See also* technology.
    genetic, 435
Engineering and Technology. *See also*
    S.T.E.M. (Science, Technology,
    Engineering, and Mathematics).
    Analyzing Nutrients, 212–215
    Building an Insulated Cooler, 46–49
    Building a Wind Turbine, 478–481
    Prosthetic Devices, 442–445
environmental impact on traits, 309
environmental issue. *See also*
    pollution.
    acid precipitation, **471**, *471*
    air quality, 469–475
    climate change, 474–475, 488–495
    deforestation, 489
    energy from wind, 479–480
    fossil fuels, 469
    greenhouse effect, *463*, 493
    ozone layer, **462**, *462*, 475
Environmental Protection Agency

(EPA), 472
enzyme, 131, 158, 170, 172, **395**,
    396–397
EPA (Environmental Protection
    Agency), 472
epidermis, *354*
epididymis, 420, *420*
epithelial tissue, 191
equation,
    balancing, 134–135, *134–135*
    chemical, 134–135
equilibrium, 352, 356, 363, 368, 376,
    394, 406, 412
ER (endoplasmic reticulum), **169**, *169*
    ribosomes and, 168
esophagus, 193, 386, **396**, *396*
Essential Question, 4, 20, 34, 50, 64,
    74, 98, 110, 122, 144, 154, 164,
    178, 188, 200, 226, 238, 260, 270,
    282, 292, 302, 316, 326, 350, 360,
    374, 392, 404, 418, 430, 456, 466,
    482
estrogen, 421
Eubacteria, 182
euglena, *166*
Eukarya, 182–183
eukaryote, **151**, *151*, 166, 183–185
    budding, 285, *285*
    cell division, 205, *205*, 260
    cellular respiration, 232
    ribosomes and, 168
eukaryotic cell, *151*, 166–173
    membrane-bound organelle,
        168–172
    nucleus, 167, *167*
    support and protection, 167
evaporation, **80**, 244
    change of state and, 80
Everest, Mount, *459*
evolution, **295**
exaptation, **297**
excretion, 353, 399. *See also* excretory
    system.
excretory system, 196, 197, *197*, 353,
    399–401
    functions of, 399
    homeostasis and, 401
    urinary system and, 399–401
exercise, 371
    aerobic, 371
    anaerobic, 371
exocytosis, 207, **208**, *208*
exothermic reaction, **128**
extensor, **369**, *369*
extinction, 497
    co-extinction, **497**
extreme environment, 182
eye, 410, *410*

F

fallopian tube, 421, 422, *422*
family, 181, *181*
family (element), **118**

farming, climate change and, 474
feces, 398–399
feedback mechanism, 414
female reproductive system, *352*,
    421–424, *421–423*
    egg, **421**–423, 427
    fertilization and, 423, *423*, 427
    functions of, 421
    menstrual cycle and, 422, *422*
    multiple births and, 427
    ovary, *421*–422, **421**–423
    pregnancy and, 424
    uterus, *421*, **422**, *422*, 423
    vagina, *421*, **422**
fermentation, 235
fertilization, 190, 273, **286**, *286*,
    423, *423*, 427. *See also* heredity;
    meiosis; sexual reproduction.
fetus, **424**, *424*
fiber (food), 57, 159. *See also*
    carbohydrate.
fiber analysis, 29
filariasis, 379
fire
    as source of pollution, 469, *469*
first generation, 305, *305*
fixed joint, 366
flagella, 151
flammability, 27, *27*
Fleming, Alexander, 185
Flemming, Walther, 259
flexibility, 371
flexor, **369**, *369*
flow of energy, 230, 232, 235, 242
food, 229
    analyzing nutrients in, 212–213
    for consumers, decomposers, and
        producers, 229
    for energy, 229, 232
    as energy source, 240
food digestion
    enzyme and, 131
    organic compound and, 57
food label, 213
forensic science, 29
formula
    chemical, 125
    for density, 14
    for volume, 10
fossil fuel, 474, 488, 489
    pollution and, 469
fracture, bone, 367, *367*
fragmentation, 287
Franklin, Rosalind, 329, *329*
fraternal twins, 427
freezing, 78
    change of state and, 70, 78, *78*
freezing point, 78
frog, biomimicry of, 439, *439*
fruit fly, *259*
function, **194**–195, *195*
    of cells, 166
    in organisms, 194
    of tissues and organs, 194, *195*
Fungi, 183